W9-AUV-367

REDS AT THE BLACKBOARD

Reds at the Blackboard

COMMUNISM, CIVIL RIGHTS, AND THE
NEW YORK CITY TEACHERS UNION

Clarence Taylor

COLUMBIA UNIVERSITY PRESS New York

Columbia University Press
Publishers Since 1893
New York Chichester, West Sussex
Copyright © 2011 Columbia University Press
All rights reserved

Library of Congress Cataloging-in-Publication Data
Taylor, Clarence.
Reds at the blackboard : communism, civil rights, and the New York City Teachers
Union / Clarence Taylor
p.   cm.
Includes bibliographical references and index.
ISBN 978–0–231–15268–6 (cloth) : alk. paper) — ISBN 978–0–231–52648–7 (e-book)
1. Teachers' Union of the City of New York—History—20th century 2. Teachers'
unions—New York (State) — New York — History — 20th century. 3. Teachers—New York
(State) — New York— History — 20th century. 4. Teachers — Political activity — New
York (State) — New York — History — 20th century. 5. Communism and education —
New York (State) — New York — History — 20th century. 6. Civil rights — New York
(State) — New York— History — 20th century. I. Title.
LB2844.53.U62N78   2011
331.88'1137110097471—dc22
2010033069

Casebound editions of Columbia University Press books are
printed on permanent and durable acid-free paper.
Printed in the United States of America

c 10 9 8 7 6 5 4 3 2 1

References to Internet Web sites (URLs) were accurate at the time of writing.
Neither the author nor Columbia University Press is responsible for Web sites
that may have expired or changed since the book was prepared.

for

Marsha

CONTENTS

ACKNOWLEDGMENTS

I am indebted to a number of people who helped me throughout the years I have worked on this book. I wish to thank Jill Hannum, Myrna Chase, and Gail Leggio for their careful reading and editing of the entire manuscript and their very helpful recommendations. I am grateful to Alan Snitlow for reading chapters of the manuscript, for sharing Lucille Spence's FBI file and Virginia L. Snitlow's essay, "Why I Teach Negro Girls," and for recommending Jill Hannum. I am indebted to Jonathan Birnbaum for his carefully reading of chapter 4. His recommendations for that chapter helped sharpen my major argument in *Reds at the Blackboard*.

No one has been more supportive of this project than Anne Filardo. Anne encouraged me every step of the way, suggesting people I should interview, allowing me to look at materials on the Teachers Union, and giving me helpful suggestions for shaping the manuscript. Although she passed away before the book was published, I am happy she did read a rough draft of the complete work.

I believe there is no one who has studied the files on the Teachers Union more than Lori Styler and Lisa Harbarkan. I wish to thank both Lisa and Lori for the numerous conversations we had on the Teachers Union, for their willingness to share materials on TU members, and for their suggestions on the several chapters of the manuscript. I also owe a debt to Henry Foner, who has been quite generous with his time and materials on the Rapp-Coudert Committee. Paul Becker was very helpful in providing vital information on the waning days of the Teachers Union.

I am thankful for Carol Smith's friendship and for arranging an interview with Annette Rubinstein in 2005. The staff at the Tamiment Library and Robert F. Wagner Archives at NYU, especially Peter Filardo, Donna Davey,

Gail Malmgreen, and Gail Gottfried, were quite diligent in locating material on the Teachers Union with expediency. They were also very encouraging, spending time with me to learn about the project. I wish to thank the staff at Catherwood Library Kheel Center, Cornell University's School of Industrial Relations, for their help in locating, and making what seems like countless numbers of copies of the files of, the Teachers Union. The staff of the Walter Reuther Library Manuscripts at Wayne State University was quite generous in allowing me to explore the minutes of the American Federation of Teachers and sending me copies of those minutes in a timely fashion. The staff of the State Library of New York in Albany was also helpful in providing me with the Rapp-Coudert Files. I owe a special debt to David Ment and the archivists in the special collections section of the Library of Teachers College, Columbia University. David and his staff helped me locate the numerous files on the hearings on suspended teachers and other Board of Education records needed for this book.

I am thankful to my friend Douglas R. Egerton for his support. Doug, one of the best historians of the nineteenth century and probably the leading scholar on slave rebellions, claims to know little about the twentieth century. However, my conversations over the years with him about my project prove to me that Doug is quite familiar with cold war history, and I wish to thank him for his recommendations. I am appreciative of the work of Joshua Freeman, Jerald Podair, Martha Biondi, Johanna Fernandez, Barbara Ransby, Daniel Perlstein, Brian Purnell, Jeanne Theoharis, Komazi Woodard, Peter Eisenstadt, Thomas Sugrue, and Wendell Pritchett for their scholarship because it gave me a clearer understanding of the northern freedom struggle.

I owe many thanks to my editor, Philip Leventhal, and to Susan Pensak, senior manuscript editor, at Columbia University Press for their painstaking work in helping to shape the manuscript into a book. Lastly, I wish to thank Marsha for her help with this project. I am convinced she has heard more about the history of the TU and content and organization of *Reds at the Blackboard* than she really wished to know. Nevertheless, she never complained about my enthusiasm for this project. It is her love and patience that helped me finish *Reds at the Blackboard*.

REDS AT THE BLACKBOARD

INTRODUCTION

The history of the New York City Teachers Union is, in large part, a story of the American left. Some of the most tumultuous battles of the left, including the fight between the Communist Party and Jay Lovestone's Communist Party Opposition, the Communists' struggle against anti-Communist forces from the 1930s to the McCarthy period of the 1950s, and the battle for civil rights involved the New York City Teachers Union. *Reds at the Blackboard* examines the struggle to define teacher unionism in the early and middle part of the twentieth century. Once the Communist Rank and File caucus gained control of the Teachers Union in 1935, the union adopted a brand of unionism whose objectives did not limit its activities to the traditional goals of service unionism—increasing salaries and improving working conditions for teachers. Its type of social unionism embraced the struggle for racial equality, child welfare, the advancement of the trade union movement, academic freedom, and better relationships with parents and communities. But the union's association with the Communist Party was problematic.

The New York City Teachers Union was organized in 1916 by a group of teachers who believed that the interest of teachers could be best served by acting collectively. The same year it was organized the Teachers Union received a charter from the American Federation of Teachers, becoming AFT Local 5 and the first teachers union in New York City. The two most important early leaders of Local 5 were Henry Linville and Abraham Lefkowitz. Linville was a biology teacher who received his Ph.D. from Harvard University in 1897. He was chair of the Biology Department at Dewitt Clinton High School, Manhattan, from 1897 to 1908 and chair of the Biology Department at Jamaica High School, Long Island, from 1908 to 1921. Linville was a socialist who supported the steel strike of 1919 (conducted by the

Amalgamated Association of Iron, Steel and Tin Workers in an attempt to organize the steel industry), the American Civil Liberties Union, and, like many other socialists, he opposed U.S. involvement in World War I. For nineteen years, from 1916 to 1935, Linville led the Teachers Union. Born in Revish, Hungary in 1884, Abraham Lefkowitz immigrated to the United States in 1885. He received his doctoral degree in education in 1914 from New York University. Lefkowitz served as the TU's legislative representative and vice president until 1935. Linville and Lefkowitz's major objective was to win recognition of teachers as professionals. As professionals, the two TU leaders insisted, teachers should be awarded decent salaries and treated by administrators with respect. Under Linville and Lefkowitz the TU fought against loyalty oaths and for academic freedom. Although Linville and Lefkowitz had the support of the vast majority of TU members, by the early 1920s a group of left-leaning teachers opposed their leadership. The opposition, made up of members of the Communist Party and the Communist Opposition Party, called for organizing the unemployed and private school teachers, pushed for the union to defend classroom teachers against school administrators, and advocated a more confrontational approach toward the Board of Education.

Studies on the Teachers Union usually fall into two categories, anti-Communist and revisionist. Adopting a cold war paradigm, the anti-Communists argue that the union was nothing more than a front for the American Communist Party carrying out the program of Moscow. The loyalty of the TU, according to this camp, was with the Communist Party and not with the teachers it served. In fact, its aim was to undermine an independent course for the American labor movement and assure the dominance of the Communist Party over the movement.[1] The revisionists, for the most part, have highlighted the accomplishments of the TU, including its effort in the fight for social equality. However, revisionists pay little or no attention to the union's Communist affiliation. Instead, they have written on the Board of Education's campaign to purge union members from the system but have not addressed any other impact of Party affiliation.[2]

The evidence is clear that members of the TU, especially those in the Communist Party, supported Communist Party policies. But does the evidence show that the TU was a tool of the Communist Party, unconcerned with the interest of teachers, or did the union act independently of the Party? *Reds at the Blackboard* addresses this and other important questions raised by the union's detractors and supporters. I argue that the anti-Communists' attack and the revisionists' defense are too simplistic. This book does not shy away from the connection that the Teachers Union had with the Communist Party. In fact, that relationship was an important part of the union's history. Communist members of the union openly embraced the programs and policies of the Party, including the campaign to save the Loyalist government of Spain, defense of the Soviet Union, and building a popular front. However, this book argues that, while adopting the Communist Party's policies, these teachers did not abandon the interests of TU members. They equated Communists with militant fighters for the rights of teachers, workers, and nationally oppressed groups, in particular African Americans.

The Teachers Union advocated what labor scholars today call social movement unionism, making strong alliances with unions, black and Latino parents, civil rights and civil organizations, and political parties in order to gain greater resources for the schools and communities in which they worked. In particular, the union fought diligently to end racial discrimination, poverty, and other barriers to success for children.[3] To be sure, they worked to increase teachers' salaries and improve working conditions. However, they went beyond professional unionism and advocated a unionism that would help transform the larger society. Their uncritical support for the Soviet Union and the American Communist Party was a detriment to them and their objectives. Nevertheless, the Party's analysis of racism and class exploitation, and its professed objective of working to build a society where these social impediments no longer existed attracted these teachers and explain why they saw the Communist Party as an important tool in building a just society. Leaders of the Teachers Union contended that higher wages and better working conditions did not take priority over social justice. Building strong ties with parents to improve schools and communities benefited teachers as well as children.

The subject of race and teacher unionism has received a great deal of scholarly attention. A number of scholars writing on race and teacher unionism in northern urban communities have addressed the question why teachers and parents, two groups that seemed to be natural allies, can become locked in bitter conflict.[4] According to biographer Richard Kahlenberg, Albert Shanker, head of the United Federation of Teaches, and later president of the American Federation of Teachers, embraced "integration, nonviolence and colorblindness." However, the "[Martin Luther] King/[Bayard] Rustin/Shanker mode came up against a new radical call for 'Black Power.'" According to Kahlenberg, black power activists rejected school integration, seeing it as a means to maintain white supremacy. Kahlenberg contends that the first major battle for black power did not take place in the South but at Intermediate School 201 in Harlem where "some black activists" called for community control of the school. Kahlenberg argues that "race-based" solutions rather than Shanker's advocacy of color blindness were the cause of the school crisis of the late 1960s.[5] Historian Vincent Cannato also blames black militants for the school crisis in the late 1960s: "The issue of community control was driven, in large part, by radicals within the black community. Frustration with the slow pace of school integration led to a growing militancy. But there was a dark side to this: increasing violence and hostility directed at the mostly white teachers and principals. Black militancy was a strong influence on education reform in New York during the 1960s."[6] Citing a number of examples, Cannato argues that "black militants in Brooklyn engaged in low-level terrorism against white principals and teachers in schools in Brownsville and Bedford-Stuyvesant."[7]

While these works have shed some light on the conflict between teacher unions and race in the 1960s and 1970s, they have focused on the United Federation of Teachers and have ignored the earlier history of the Teachers Union and its attempt to build strong parent-teacher relations. Although the relationship between the TU's main rival, the Teachers Guild, and segments of the black community was bitter, the New York Teachers Union was successful in building ties with black and Latino communities.

Reds at the Blackboard notes that before 1960 service unionism was not the only model, nor was its eventual dominance inevitable. The failure of the TU's brand of unionism was more than just a matter of teachers having made a choice. This book details the long battle that the Teachers Union waged against anti-Communist forces, including state and federal agencies, civic organizations, labor, and the New York City Board of Education. In large part, the campaign against the TU was responsible for its eventual demise and for the failure of a teachers' brand of social unionism.

Reds at the Blackboard is divided into three parts. Part 1 examines the early history of the Teachers Union, including the battles between Communists and social democratic leadership, the Communist takeover of the TU, the impact of the TU's affiliation with the Communist Party, and how the union remained dedicated to its struggle against racism and bigotry. Chapter 1 examines the rise of left caucuses and their battle with the union's social democratic leadership. The chapter looks at the ideological divide between the Communists caucuses and the union leadership, Linville and Lefkowitz's unsuccessful attempt to remove the Communists from the union, the 1935 schism, and the formation of the Teachers Guild.

After the 1935 walkout of Linville, Lefkowitz, and seven hundred members of the Teachers Union, the Communists gained control of the union. Chapter 2 addresses the claim by TU opponents and some scholars that the main objective of the Communist-controlled union was not to protect the interest of teachers but to carry out the dictates of the Soviet Union. It also takes on the defenders of the TU who ignore the Communist Party's influence. There is ample evidence proving that the union supported Communist Party policies, and its position on certain issues was indistinguishable from the Party's. However, I argue that the TU did not ignore teachers' interests. The Communist leadership of the union fought for higher wages, better working conditions, and academic freedom. While supportive of Moscow, the TU also worked to improve working conditions for teachers. While opponents and others criticized the TU for its unyielding support for the Communist Party, the union itself made no distinction between its loyalty to the Party and its drive to improve working conditions for teachers. The TU blurred the line between its work on behalf of teachers and pushing Communist Party policies.

Chapter 3 turns to a crucial period in the Teachers Union history, the revocation of its charter. The argument that the union was Communist-operated led to the union being thrown out of the AFT. The anti-Communist forces were also successful in winning an AFT charter for the social democrats who had created a rival union, the Teachers Guild. This was the first major victory for the anti-TU forces in their attempt to destroy the union.

A number of scholars and writers have argued that the Communist Party abandoned its fight for racial equality once the Soviet Union was attacked by Nazi Germany. They contend that the major objective of Party members was to protect the Soviet Union against Nazism and fascism. Therefore, racial equality had to take a back seat. However, I argue in chapter 4 that the Communist-controlled Teachers Union did not abandon the fight for racial equality. Instead, the TU placed the fight against racial, ethnic, and religious bigotry in the context of the war. According to the union, opposing racism was an essential component of the war effort because racism destroyed national unity. The TU did not abandon the fight for racial equality during the war; it equated this fight with patriotism. To be sure, the TU embraced the politics of the popular front, attempting to create a broad coalition in the fight against Nazism and fascism. The TU contended that fighting racism was an essential objective for the success of the popular front.

The protracted campaign against the TU weakened the union and was, in large part, the reason for its eventual demise. Part 2 looks at the long campaign against the Teachers Union. It began soon after the 1935 walkout with the American Federation of Teachers' investigation. By the late 1940s the drive against the union became broader, involving national, state, and local governmental agencies, labor, fraternal, civil rights, and religious organizations.

The New York City Board of Education had joined the coalition to wipe out the TU, helping to make New York City a major battleground in the cold war struggle. The board and anti-Communist forces targeted the Teachers Union, claiming it was part of an international conspiracy. The board used a variety of strategies including interrogation, firing teachers, forcing them to resign or retire, banning the union from operating in schools, and using undercover police agents and informers. Chapter 5 turns to the early victims of the purge and the role played in the anti-TU campaign by the Taft-Hartley Sub-Committee on Education and Labor, a bi-partisan body of the United States Congress investigating Communist influence in labor unions and other institutions. In May 1950 Superintendent of Schools William Jansen suspended eight teachers, all members of the Teachers Union. Chapter 6 focuses on the suspension and Board of Education hearings of the eight and how board officials used these hearings to develop a mechanism to eliminate Communist teachers from the school system.

The Teachers Union's greatest crisis came in 1950 when Board of Education member George Timone proposed a resolution banning the TU from operating in the schools. Chapter 7 examines the battle over the Timone Resolution. I argue that the resolution was not simply a confrontation between the Board of Education and the Teachers Union. The battle over Timone demonstrated the division in the city created by the cold war. The supporters of the resolution included not only board officials but also those at the grassroots level, such as Catholic lay organizations and fraternal and civic groups. Supporters argued that the TU was part of a worldwide conspiracy and stood in opposition to those who contended that teachers had a right to select a union of their choice. Numerous groups including civic, religious, and labor organizations as well as individuals also lined up to denounce the resolution, arguing that it was undemocratic and would take away the union's ability to operate as a representative of teachers in grievances and contract talks, denying it the right to hold meetings in the schools, and thus ending its long history as a legitimate trade union. The fight over Timone became a major contest in the city, eventually determining which type of teacher unionism would be able to legitimately operate in the schools.

One of the crucial issues in the campaign against the TU was anti-Semitism. The suspension of the eight teachers in May 1950 unleashed several anti-Semitic verbal attacks, sometimes equating Jews with Communism. According to TU officials and some of their supporters, these opponents targeted the union because of their hatred of Jews. But the TU did not only blame those who used racist attacks. They contended that the board used a double standard, attempting to fire Jewish teachers while ignoring the antics of anti-Semitic and racist teachers. Although there is no evidence that board members were motivated by anti-Semitism, some of those involved in the campaign did target union members because they were Jewish. In fact, some opponents took part in a letter-writing campaign that attacked the teachers because they were Jews. But the issue of anti-Semitism was complex. Some of the union's adversaries accused the TU of playing the anti-Semitism card by using it to cover up its Communist affiliation. Chapter 8 looks at the uses of anti-Semitism in the campaign and how this issue was used by defenders and opponents of the TU.

I conclude part 2 with a close examination of the employment by the Board of Education of undercover police agents, informers, and cooperating witnesses. No work on the Teachers Union has paid attention to the elaborate spy network used by those carrying out the campaign to rid the school system of Communists. I have uncovered Board of Education records, detailing the use of the New York City Police Department's infamous Red Squad and other police agencies by Superintendent of Schools William Jansen and Assistant Corporation Counsel Saul Moskoff. The use of police and personnel to spy on teachers was a violation of academic freedom and freedom of speech, and it helped create a police state atmosphere.

The TU lost its right to represent teachers before the Board of Education, thanks to the Timone Resolution and the board's ongoing investigation, which led to the union's loss of thousands of members. Despite the horrible conditions, the Teachers Union did not immediately disband. Chapter 10 details TU campaigns to eliminate racist and bigoted textbooks from classrooms, hire more black teachers, and promote black history month. The TU remade itself into a leading voice in the New York City civil rights movement by challenging the Board of Education's discriminatory polices.

The vast majority of TU members were women. Yet few works have examined the role women played in shaping the union. *Reds at the Blackboard* looks at women's leadership and how they helped foster union ties with parents, labor, political figures, and civil rights and civic groups. Women's efforts were responsible for the social unionism of the TU.

This history of the New York City Teachers Union explores how one union helped create a unique type of unionism that was in the forefront of the struggle for civil rights and academic freedom, attempting to empower teachers as well as black and Latino communities to confront those in power. It created a model of parent and teacher relations that has never been duplicated. It also fought militantly to improve working conditions for teachers at the same time that it championed broader social concerns. *Reds at the Blackboard* examines an important chapter in American history by examining the fight to determine which brand of teacher unionism would triumph.

ONE

1 / THE WAR WITHIN
Battling for the Soul of the Union

Communist control of the Teachers Union had its origins in the battles of the American left, especially the early schism between the American Communist Party and those associated with the American Communist Opposition (ACO) in 1929. The conflict between Jay Lovestone, the leader of the ACO, and the American Communist Party would lead to the formation of the two major caucuses in the Teachers Union: the Rank and File, affiliated with the Communist Party, and the Progressive Group, made up of followers of Lovestone and the ACO. Just as important, the battle that began in the 1920s between the Communists and the union leadership, then made up of social democrats, would result in a split in 1935 and the formation of a rival union. The central objective of the factions was to determine which direction teacher unionism would take in New York City.

Although the Rank and File in the TU advocated policies of the Communist Party and the Progressive Group promoted policies of the ACO, the caucuses were more than just conduits for spreading party doctrine. Issues such as working conditions, wages, union democracy, and the fate of the unemployed were at the forefront of these two caucuses' agenda. Those opposing the union leadership advocated building a strong union by organizing a large segment of the teaching body of the city. This included substitutes, the unemployed, private school teachers, and, later, teachers hired under the New Deal's Work Projects Administration. The leadership, or what was called the administration, on the other hand, advocated professionalism and cooperation between employees and management, stressing ways to improve the craft of teaching. The leadership also wanted to limit membership in the union to full-time teachers, arguing that such teachers had more at stake in the profession than substitutes and the unemployed. Part-time teachers and the unemployed, the administration contended, took away from the professional identity of teachers.

At the root of the confrontation in the Teachers Union was the attempt by Communist teachers to forge a unionism that was inclusive of all categories of teachers, no matter their status in the profession. Modeling themselves after industrial unionists, the Communists wanted the TU to fight for higher salaries, health care, pensions, and better working conditions. But these items were not going to come by emphasizing professionalism. Rather, improvements for teachers would take place when greater pressure was placed on management to act. The Communists identified with industrial workers, arguing that the relationship between management and worker was adversarial. The advocates of a more militant unionism ridiculed those who pushed for white-collar unionism, which supported higher salaries, benefits, and improved working conditions; they wanted professional integrity and autonomy. But, instead of stressing an adversarial relationship with management, advocates of professional unionism argued for a more collaborative relationship with management. This divide within the teachers union would lead to a major crisis by the middle 1930s.

THE CAUCUSES

When the league was granted a charter in 1916 by the American Federation of Teachers, it became Local 5 of the AFT. Communist influence in Local 5 dates to 1923, when a number of its members established the Research Study Group. Headed by the union's membership secretary, Benjamin Mandel, the Research Study Group advocated affiliation with the Educational Workers International, a group created by the Red International of Labor Unions in 1923, a labor group affiliated with the Comintern. The Comintern was organized at the Third International in 1919 as a body to promote world revolution on the Russian Communist model. The Educational Workers International argued that teachers were not professionals but members of an exploited class who had the support of other exploited workers. It called on all teachers to join the struggle against capitalism and capitalist exploitation.[1] This argument led to a confrontation, with the majority of Local 5 members rejecting affiliation with the Communist organization. The number of Communists in the union, prior to 1929, remained small.

Testifying in January 1941 before New York's Joint Legislative Committee to Investigate the Educational System of the State of New York, popularly known as the Rapp-Coudert Committee, Mandel, who had been expelled from the Communist Party and became a "research worker" for the Special House Committee on Un-American Activities in 1939, listed among the few Communists in Local 5 Ben Davidson, Bertram Wolfe, Jacob Lind, Rae Ragozin, Jack Hardy (Dale Zysman), Sarah Golden, Clara Reiber, Abraham Zitron, and Isidore Begun.[2]

Despite their small numbers, the Teachers Union members affiliated with the Communist Party formed a caucus challenging the administration. As early as 1925, TU executive board members complained about Communists on the board using disruptive tactics and interfering with the work of the union and the "American Labor Movement." TU leaders objected to Communists issuing resolutions criticizing other labor organizations that were supportive of the union and publicly attacking the leadership.[3] In 1935 Henry Linville testified before a special AFT committee that factionalism in the TU had been a concern for over a decade. On May 16, 1925, a group of "loyal" union members issued a letter that, according to Linville, accused a few executive board members of forming a group, using "disruptive and vituperative tactics to hinder the work" of the TU. The Communist opposition demanded "contributions to Communist and outlaw locals and acceptance of resolutions sent from the Workers [Communist] Party headquarters." The opposition also condemned the American Federation of Labor (AFL) and the Central Trade and Labor Council, and supported a vote on the "lack of confidence" in the union leadership.[4] But, because the Communist numbers were small, they posed little threat to the leadership. In fact, TU members, regardless of political affiliation, were assured freedom of speech and academic freedom as long as the leadership's power was not threatened. But all this would change by the early 1930s.

By 1931 the major opposition group had split into two main factions, the Rank and File and the Progressive Group. The split in the left was attributed to the schism in the American Communist Party. Jay Lovestone, who had become head of the American Communist Party in 1928, opposed the International determining the policy of the American Communist Party. Specifically, Lovestone rejected the view that the Comintern should decide the best tactics for achieving socialism; instead, each country's labor movement should make its own decisions. Allowing workers to work out the methods used to transform their country into a socialist state would plant the seed for democracy by involving the working class at an early stage. This view became known as the doctrine of "exceptionalism."[5] Lovestone was a follower of Nikolai Bukharin, who had become president of the Comintern in 1926 and argued for a more conservative economic path for the Soviet Union, which meant introducing market capitalism into certain sections of the Soviet economy. Lovestone's main opponent in the American Communist Party was William Z. Foster, who followed Moscow's line that Communist parties must submit to the will of the Comintern. The conflict between Lovestone and Foster was heard before the Comintern in 1929. Stalin, who by then had consolidated his power and removed Bukharin from leadership, later having him arrested and killed, demanded that Lovestone give up his fight with Foster. When Lovestone refused, he was expelled from the party.[6] Lovestone, joined by Bertram Wolfe, who also had been expelled from the Communist party because of his defense of the theory of exceptionalism, Benjamin Mandel, and Ben Davidson, established the Communist Party (Opposition). Wolfe and Davidson, who were both New York City teachers, also broke away from the Communist-dominated opposition in the TU and created the Progressive Group.[7]

Despite the formation of the Progressive Group, the Communist-dominated Rank and File became the largest and strongest caucus in the Teachers Union. As early as 1932, the Communist Party noted that it had attracted new converts among New York City teachers, although it had fallen short of its recruitment goal. The leadership of the Rank and File included dedicated radical labor activists, such as Isidore Begun, considered to be the leader of the Rank and File and the most outspoken critic of the leadership of Henry Linville and Abraham Lefkowitz.[8] Begun began serving on the TU executive board in September 1932, becoming the first Rank and File member in a union leadership position. Although he claimed that he did not join the Communist Party until the mid 1930s, some in the union declared that he was openly a Communist before 1934. By 1935 he was on the payroll of the New York State Committee of the Communist Party. Attracted to left ideology at an early age, he graduated from City College in 1924 and began working on his doctorate, completing his course work in 1927. Months after graduating, he became a teacher and joined the union.[9]

Questioned by the Rapp-Coudert Committee in October 1941, Begun asserted that Communists supported anyone working to build a strong union, including the Rank and File, who struggled to "broaden out the union, not to keep it a little bunch of people that thought themselves intellectual aristocrats, I mean, school teachers and all that kind of stuff, but really wanted a union to include the profession, which is what a union is [suppose] to be, and that would mean people of every kind and shape." Although Begun evaded answering questions about Communist affiliations, the industrial program of the Rank and File was essentially the same as that of the Communist Party, which included organizing the unemployed.[10]

Begun claimed that the major bone of contention between the Rank and File and the administration regarded how to build the union, "how to broaden it out, how to strengthen it. And that is where the differences ran." He denied that the Rank and File had political designs. Its major concern was to organize teachers into a trade union. Teachers were too divided, with "76 teacher organizations" functioning in the city. When asked if he knew teachers who were party members, Begun mentioned only Morris Schappees, an open Communist who had joined the Department of English at City College in 1928, was fired in 1936 for his political affiliation, and would serve thirteen months in prison for not cooperating with the Rapp-Coudert Committee. Begun maintained that the union did not ask people's political affiliations and was organizing teachers to participate in the class struggle. When specifically asked about the political affiliation of Williana Burroughs, Alice Citron, Ben Davidson, Bella Dodd, and other TU members who were also members of the Communist Party, Begun simply denied knowing. The leader of the Rank and File caucus was not the only person who was not forthcoming with the Rapp-Coudert Committee. Others, including historians Philip and Jack Foner and Richard Hofstadter, denied their membership or denied having knowledge of the membership of others. Their strategy was political. They knew that having knowledge of their affiliation with the Party would only be used to persecute them.[11]

Another important leader of the Rank and File was Alice Citron, a graduate of Hunter College (1928) who began teaching at P.S. 84 in Harlem in 1931. Conditions in the Harlem community and at P.S. 84 helped motivate Citron to become an activist. Although she had experienced poverty as a child, she was unprepared for the dire conditions in Harlem, including abandoned buildings and hungry children. P.S. 84 was housed in an old and neglected building. Like other schools in predominantly black and Hispanic areas, it was understaffed and overcrowded. As a new teacher, Citron had over forty students in her class, and her assigned classroom had a broken blackboard. Citron was determined to improve conditions. By the mid 1930s she had helped form the TU's Harlem Committee, which led the drive to remove racist textbooks from the public schools and convince the Board of Education to recognize Negro History Week, and called for the construction of new schools in the area to relieve overcrowding.[12]

Citron, like her common-law husband, Isidore Begun, was a member of the American Communist Party. However, while Begun did not hide his political affiliation, Citron was not open about her membership in the Party. Nevertheless, Benjamin Mandel, acting as an "expert witness" for the House Committee on Un-American Activities (HUAC), claimed that he knew Citron from Communist Party meetings.[13]

Celia Lewis (who would later marry and become Celia Lewis Zitron) was another important leader of the Rank and File. Born in Slutsk, Russia in 1899, she came to the United States with her family in 1907 and became a naturalized citizen in 1914. Zitron, a high school teacher of Latin who became a member of the TU executive board and head of its Academic Freedom Committee, was identified as a member of the Communist Party by Louis Budnez. Budnez, a former Communist Party member who became an "expert witness" for HUAC after he joined the Catholic Church and renounced Communism, contended that Zitron was a member of the Communist Party in the early 1930s.[14] Other early key members of the Rank and File included Abraham Feingold, Williana Burroughs, Matthew Besdine, Clara Rieber, Max Diamond, Israel Wallach, Meyer Case, and Abraham Zitron.

Although the left factions in the TU were often at odds, the major battle in the Teachers Union was between the Rank and File and the leadership. The leadership emphasized professionalism, collaboration with management, and legislation as ways of improving the working conditions for teachers. The more left-leaning teachers, critical of the leadership, advocated a more militant program. They did not view teachers as professionals but as members of the industrial working class whose major objective was to take part in the struggle against capital. The Board of Education was not seen as a neutral body but as pro-capital, taking part in the exploitation of workers.

The divide between the opposition and the leadership was partly generational. Linville, who became Local 5's first president, and Lefkowitz, who remained a close associate of Linville, had been with the union since its founding in 1916 and had become entrenched as union leaders. They resented any challenge to their authority, especially from those who were much younger and who had far less experience. The younger opposition wanted the union to take stronger action against what they saw as deteriorating working conditions.[15]

The issue of organizing substitutes reflected the divide between the Rank and File caucus's industrial union organizing approach and the professionalism advocated by the leadership. The left wing of the union endorsed organizing substitute teachers, many of whom had regular appointments but lost their positions or were victims of the decision of the board not to issue regular licenses due to budget considerations. Broadening the definition of a teacher by including those who were not regularly licensed would, the Rank and File believed, protect the most vulnerable and exploited workers in the school system. Advocates argued that a major function of the union was to expand the rights of all teachers. One important way of protecting these teachers, the opposition insisted, was for the Board of Education to grant substitutes regular licenses.

Linville and many others in the union leadership were dead set against granting union rights to substitutes, part-time workers who would be given the opportunity to hold office and decide policy. Linville relied heavily on older teachers for support, teachers who had regular licenses and shared his view on professionalism. He also feared that giving substitute teachers the vote would increase the power of the Rank and File. Undoubtedly, the substitutes were loyal to the left and, if allowed, would vote it into power. Besides opposing full union rights for substitutes, Linville also strengthened his control over the union by a number of measures: limiting the number of general membership meetings in a year, which denied the opposition groups a platform to voice their grievances, ending recall of executive board members, allowing the executive board the power to fill vacant board positions, and limiting discussion at membership meetings.[16]

THIRD PERIOD POLITICS

The Rank and File came of age during the Communist Party's third period, 1928–1934, which represented an attempt to inject life into the movement after the Party's second period retreat from revolution, highlighted by Lenin's New Economic Policy (NEP) from 1924 to 1928. Under the NEP, in order to bolster a sluggish economy private ownership was reintroduced (on a temporary basis) to segments of the Soviet Union, including the farming sector. The third period allowed Communists to take off the gloves and reject alliances with social democrats, whom they labeled social fascists. The language of third period revolution was evident at the Sixth Comintern Congress held in July 1928: "When the revolutionary tide is rising, when the ruling classes and the disorganized and the masses [are] in a state of revolutionary ferment, when the middle strata are inclined to turn toward the proletariat and the masses display their readiness for battle . . . it is the task of proletarian party to lead the masses to a frontal assault on the bourgeois state." There were several ways of achieving these objectives, including "organizing mass action" and carrying out general strikes. According to the Congress, an "essential preliminary to actions of this kind is the organization of the broad masses in militant bodies which by their very form must embrace and set in motion the largest number of working people." It was assumed that capitalism was in a crisis and that "social fascists" would bond with fascist states to overthrow the Soviet Union, the true representative of the working class.[17]

To encourage working-class unity, delegates at a Party convention in August 1929 voted to create the Trade Union Unity League (TUUL). The TUUL was the American Communist Party's response to the Sixth World Congress's order that Communist parties create revolutionary unions to compete against the conservative AFL, which had failed to address what the Party deemed to be the revolutionary crisis.[18]

Adhering to third period politics, the Rank and File leaders embraced an industrial model for the Teachers Union, rejecting the professional model advocated by the leadership. Clinging to a policy of noncompromise with social democrats, Rank and File leaders argued that the union leadership was far too passive when confronting the Board of Education. Rank and File members who were affiliated with the American Communist Party saw organizing workers, conducting mass demonstrations, and taking other militant actions as the best way of improving conditions for teachers. The Rank and File's uncompromising position was illustrated by its response to the issue of payless furloughs. In an attempt to address the city's fiscal crisis during the Depression, Mayor LaGuardia endorsed the 1933 Bankers Agreement, acquiescing to a negotiated agreement hammered out by banking interests that changed some of the city's fiscal practices. Banks agreed to refund $130 million in revenue bonds, to establish a revolving fund to assist the city during the crisis, and to buy millions of dollars of serial notes to help pay for unemployment and home relief programs. The city, in return, agreed to several concessions, including dropping new taxes on stocks, savings banks, and life insurance companies, thus giving up millions of dollars in city revenue. In 1934 LaGuardia also signed a bill that created payless furloughs for city workers, an average 4 percent annual pay cut.[19]

In January 1934 Abraham Lefkowitz negotiated with Mayor LaGuardia at City Hall over the payless furlough, while members of the TU waited outside. Taking an "uncompromising" stand against the furlough, Rank and File leaders spoke out against the meeting. "The union leadership," Rank and File leaders told the crowd, "did not prepare the teachers to meet the present attacks." Speakers representing the radical caucus lambasted Lefkowitz and Linville for claiming that LaGuardia's plan was "like a bolt from the clear sky" and for demonstrating an "unwillingness or inability" to fight the cuts. According to the Rank and File, Lefkowitz had caved in by expressing sympathy for the mayor and urging union members to leave and allow the "left wingers" to stand alone.[20]

By attacking the leadership, the Rank and File hoped to portray itself as more militant than the leadership. True to the third period politics of refusing to compromise with capitalists or social democrats, the Rank and File declared that the administration was engaged in class collaboration. Isidore Begun mounted the steps of City Hall while the administration of the union was negotiating with the mayor and announced that the union should oppose the furlough plan. He attacked Lefkowitz for stating that he would meet the mayor halfway if the telephone, gas, and electric companies would lower their rates. Under no circumstances should teachers be willing to meet bankers and other financiers "halfway" by reducing their salaries. Instead, the caucus demanded a repudiation of the bankers' four-year agreement because it meant "pay-less-paydays."[21] Bugun's actions indicated that third period politics did not just mean subordination to the dictates of Moscow. His uncompromising position demonstrated a fierce defense of working-class people. He was trying to stop what amounted to a pay cut for teachers.

In one attempt to bolster its own image while tarnishing the union's leadership, the Rank and File issued a leaflet charging that the administration had "shown distrust and contempt for the mass of classroom teachers in the schools" and had not taken advantage of opportunities to make the union an agency for real change. Instead, Linville and Lefkowitz were more concerned with holding on to power by creating a "dictatorship of the Executive Board." This rhetoric proved appealing, especially at a time when many teachers were joining the ranks of the unemployed. The Rank and File's militant tone was paying off. TU election results indicated that more members of the militant caucus were winning positions on the executive board. By 1934, Rank and File members Meyer Case, Williana Burroughs, and Matthew Besdine had won seats on the board, joining Benjamin Davidson of the Progressive Group, who was elected in 1932.[22] More important, the Rank and File's emphasis on organizing teachers had paid off. For example, the January 4, 1930, executive board minutes, reflect that twenty-three people had applied for membership. A month later there were fifty names. In early April 1932 the executive board reported that seventy-six people applied, and on February 2, 1933, ninety-one teachers were reported as wanting to join. In February 1934 ninety-five teachers submitted applications.[23]

In its critique of the leadership the Rank and File explained that the job of a labor union was to "activize and organize every co-worker, unionized or not, with the view of achieving mutual protection and betterment of working" and improving living standards. The administration was blamed for fostering an attitude of indifference and accused of showing distrust of and even "contempt" for the ordinary classroom teacher by stepping on the rights of members. The membership had been "unconstitutionally deprived of power," as reflected in the fact that it spent membership and delegate assembly meetings focusing on legislative reports and making no important decisions. Moreover, the leadership was dictatorial and worked hard to crush the will of the ordinary member.[24] Calling on the union to initiate and "lead mass actions, mass delegations, mass meetings" in defense of teachers, the Rank and File maintained that members should be an "agent for stimulating the classroom teachers and parents in each school into active participation in the defense of the school." Every member should become an organizer of teachers, parents, and students. The union should lower dues, making it affordable for the unemployed and those at the lower end of the pay scale, and conduct a "mass defense" of all teachers victimized because they organized teachers and parents. The union, the Rank and File claimed, must become democratic. A united front of all classroom teachers would defend the interests of children as well as teachers. Replacing the leadership of the union because it failed to "lead a mass struggle" was crucial to this agenda.[25]

The best example of the Rank and File's mass organizing strategy was its Classroom Teacher Group (CTG), the formation of which prompted accusations by the Rank and File's opponents that they were obeying the dictates of the International's call for dual unionism—i.e., a union operating within an existing union. The CTG organized chapters in various public schools to address the needs of teachers, thus distinguishing itself from the administration, which seemed remote from the everyday classroom. Although they were not present in every school in the system, these groups, of course, alarmed the leadership. Members of the opposition were taking on school administrators in order to fight for classroom teachers and were winning teachers' loyalty. Bella Dodd, who became legislative representative of the TU in the mid 1930s and would later become an informer for HUAC, contended that the Classroom Teachers Group (she called it the Classroom Teachers Association), allegedly a grass-roots movement, was recruiting teachers for "mass action" and was "carefully organized on the basis of the class struggle philosophy." She claimed that the CTG was a disciplined organization, secretly associated with William Foster's Trade Union Unity League and having two objectives: to convert a considerable number of teachers to a revolutionary approach to problems and to recruit for the Communist Party as many members as possible. Some CTG teachers were also members of Teachers Union Local 5 and, therein, they formed an organized minority opposition to the prevailing noncommunist leadership.[26]

According to Dodd, the Classroom Teacher Groups, "like all Red unions of the early thirties," emphasized "bread and butter problems acute at the time," such as unemployment among teachers and the high number of substitute teachers working for low wages. The CTG helped the Communists gain support in part because it used a variety of methods, including sending delegations to the Board of Education and leveling public attacks against city officials and the leadership of the Teachers Union. Identifying "Celia Lewis, Clara Richer [perhaps she meant Clara Rieber], and Max Diamond" as the leaders of the "Red minority" within the TU, Dodd suggested that the Communist tactic of organizing unemployed teachers could result in them gaining control of the TU.[27]

The CTG also disturbed TU members who identified with the Communist Party Opposition and worried about dual unionism, a position rejected by those who were loyal to Jay Lovestone. In his testimony before the Rapp-Coudert Committee, Ben Davidson claimed that the CTG was used to criticize the "teachers union movement at public meetings. I think the group is responsible for that policy." Although he had no evidence and admitted he had never attended a meeting of the CTG or knew of its size, Davidson maintained that members of the Rank and File "tended to praise, to endorse the work of the classroom teacher group" and "held it up as an example of good work." He continued: "I drew my conclusions that they believed that policy and in so far as they had influence they were pushing that policy." Despite his criticism, Davidson more than hinted that the CTG was tackling the concerns of classroom teachers, many of them teachers dissatisfied with the TU leadership's unwillingness to address their problems. The CTG seemed to be the only organization addressing those grievances.[28]

The Rank and File followed other Communist Party positions. The Party during the third period was pushing an antiwar agenda. The Comintern introduced the theory of "social fascism," arguing that capitalist powers, in times of economic crisis, were willing to make alliances with fascists and Nazis in order to save capitalism. "Social fascists" were no different from fascists and Nazis. Indeed, Communists should prevent all preparations for war in capitalist nations by, for example, portraying social democrats as enemies of Communism. In fact, Stalin declared during the third period that fascism and social democracy were "twin brothers." In 1933 the American Communist Party helped organize the American League Against War and Fascism, which targeted religious and labor groups in defense of the "masses" against fascism and Nazism.[29]

The TU's Rank and File caucus also pushed the antiwar objective. At the February 3, 1934, executive board meeting, Rank and Filers introduced a motion that the union petition FDR, urging him not to spend $475 million on armaments. Instead the president should use the money to deal with the education crisis and provide funds to assure the continuation of the projects under the New Deal Civil Works Administration, which created work for millions of workers. Another motion, approved at the same meeting, put the union on record opposing a bill to make Armistice Day a school holiday because a day off would interrupt the work for "peace propaganda" in the schools.[30] In its program for immediate action in the schools, the Rank and

File called for establishing an antiwar committee as well as sending a delegate to an antiwar event sponsored by the Seventh Congress of the Communist International, scheduled for September 28–30, 1934 in Chicago. In its efforts to undermine "social fascism," the TU claimed that its agenda—which fought salary cuts, the attack on tenure, and the firing of militant teachers—was the best. Moreover, reducing the U.S. military budget would provide funds for education. The Rank and File even linked military spending to repression of teachers: "In line with the greater expenditures on armaments, loyalty oaths have been demanded of teachers, and prospective teachers are to be eliminated if they have subversive and 'un-American' attitudes."[31]

THE ADMINISTRATION FIGHTS BACK

As early as 1932 the administration of Local 5 attempted to put a halt to the opposition. The fact that more teachers than ever before in the union's history were union members, especially those who were unemployed, demonstrated the success of the Rank and File action and posed a serious threat to leadership control. In reaction to Isidore Begun's public complaint that union money was being used to bribe state legislators, Abraham Lefkowitz demanded an investigation. Tension between the opposition and the administration was high. In June of that year, Lefkowitz introduced a resolution before the executive board calling for a host of charges to be brought against the Communist members of the TU.[32]

In September the executive board appointed a Special Committee to prepare charges against opposition members who had been disruptive at TU meetings, essentially leading members of the Rank and File and Progressive Group, including all their candidates in the 1932 union election of officers. Apparently, the leadership had second thoughts about ousting the entire opposition. The list of expulsions would be too long; if the leadership attempted to kick out so many on the left, it might create a crisis in the union. Instead, the Special Committee was enlarged after October 7 to include all officers of the executive board. This body was given the task of preparing charges against teachers who disrupted union meetings. In addition, it had to prepare a report to the general membership.[33]

The October 27, 1932, Special Report of the Joint Committee claimed that it was not attempting to bring legal charges against any member of

the union. In fact, before issuing its report, the committee tried to recon-
cile the differences between the leadership and the two main factions.[34]
But, despite its claim, the committee accused Rank and File members of
carrying on "propaganda in union meetings," attempting to tie the TU to
"extreme political radicalism," trying to get the union to endorse aspects
of their left program, and attacking the leadership and accusing it of being
"undemocratic." Despite concessions to the left, there was no peace within
the TU: "Apparently left-wing groups are unwilling to accept a practicable
basis of harmony."

Charges were specifically brought against five Rank and File members—
Joseph Leboit, Clara Rieber, Alice Citron, Abraham Zitron, Isidore Begun—
and one Progressive Group member, Bertram Wolfe. Leboit was charged
with sabotage against the TU and the AFT because in June, Ruth Hardy,
membership chairperson and a supporter of Linville claimed, Leboit was at
a meeting in Newark "attacking the N.Y. Union and attempting to discredit
it to the Newark teachers." Rieber was accused of distributing Rank and File
circulars at TU meetings without permission from the leadership. The committee also claimed that Rieber "failed to give proper regard to courtesies"
to guest speakers, handing out circulars while they were speaking. The circulars contained untrue accusations: that the executive board proposed to
eliminate members' participation, that only six members of the executive
board possessed the power to overrule a majority of the board and that the
union did not rally to protest the Board of Education's attempt to cut teachers salaries. In addition, Rieber was charged with sabotage, using disruptive
tactics, and antagonizing members and nonmembers "by bitter and ungov-
erned speech, and for destroying spirit of friendly cooperation."

Like Rieber, Citron was accused of making false charges against the TU,
distributing Rank and File literature at union meetings, "making insolent
and ill-mannered attacks on those responsible for the conduct of the meetings and activities," and attacking the work of the Joint Committee on
Teacher Unemployment. Apparently, Citron had organized a competing
committee on unemployment called the Unemployed Teachers Association
and became its secretary, despite the fact that she was a regular appointed
teacher. According to the committee's report, Abraham Zitron was so disruptive that even the Rank and File had to discipline him at meetings and
so uncooperative that members of his school had become bitter toward the
union. He was also charged with promoting the dual union movement. The

Special Joint Committee report branded Progressive Group member Bertram Wolfe the "recognized intellectual leader of the left-wing movement of the Teachers Union," first starting to serve on the TU's executive board in early 1930, and accused him of supporting attacks on the leadership. The committee claimed that Wolfe circulated harmful statements denouncing the administration for its "reactionary revision of the Constitution," threatened the existence of the TU, refused to obey the time rule when debating at meetings, and created disorder.

The most extensive charges, including that of advocating dual unionism, were brought against Isidore Begun. Begun, who helped found the Rank and File caucus, was implicated for "having guilty knowledge of the existence of the dual union and the publication of its anonymous periodical" and charged with circulating false statements to hinder and discredit the work of the union. The committee singled out Begun's responsibility for printing the anonymous dual-union *Education Worker*, whose January, March, and July 1932 issues contained slurs and bogus charges against union officers and members of the executive board. One serious allegation was that Lefkowitz was accused of stating at an executive board meeting that money collected from the membership was used to "grease the palms" of legislators. Many of the charges against the six followed a familiar formula—"insolent and offensive behavior" at meetings, sabotaging the work of the TU by accusing the administration of reactionary and undemocratic acts. In reaction to the charges, the union elected a grievance committee that included John Dewey, who served as chair, and Charles Hendley. While its job was ostensibly to recommend a means of handling the union's problem with the left, in reality, the leadership hoped it would come up with a way to purge the caucuses.[35]

The Joint Committee's report concluded that it had not found a solution to "securing cooperation" with members of the left-wing groups. Therefore, it was leaving the matter in the hands of the members. A Grievance Committee was created to hear the complaints against the left-wing caucus members. The committee decided not to appoint any person as a "prosecuting counsel." Instead, the purpose was to gain an understanding of the wider state of affairs within the TU as well as to hear evidence against the six teachers.[36]

Despite its claims of impartiality, the Grievance Committee blamed the factional problem in the TU on the Rank and File and the Progressive Group. The left portrayed the administration, according to the committee, as a clique concerned with holding on to power. The committee contended that the two left groups also distrusted one another: the Rank and File accused the Progressive Group of being a "pseudo-opposition," in reality an "ally of the Administration"; the Progressive Group accused the Rank and File of trying to split the union. Despite their differences and animosity toward one another, both groups were working to undermine the leadership of the TU. As proof that they were hostile factions, the Grievance Committee pointed out that each group had its own executive board, or members who could attend executive sessions, secretary and other officers. With the existence of two permanent organized factions and growing antagonism toward the administration, the union's effectiveness was being hindered. According to the Grievance Committee, the factionalism was so grave that, if not addressed, it threatened the very existence of the union.[37]

The Grievance Committee had no evidence that most members of the Rank and File and the Progressive Group were Communists. "Moreover, the testimony is far from showing that it is the conscious intention of the bulk of those affiliated with these opposition groups to use the Union as a tool of any particular economic political creed." Still, the committee maintained that the leaders of both factions were clearly connected to the Communists. The political views of union members became problematic only when groups tried to use the union as an instrument to carry out the policies of outside organizations. It was no accident that the Rank and File and Progressive Group advocated the same programs as Communist factions in other unions or that the Teachers Union's Rank and File and Progressive Group criticized one another in ways similar to how the Communist Party and Communist Opposition criticized one another. The opposition groups, the committee asserted, were using the union as an instrument in the war to overthrow capitalism.

The Grievance Committee offered two important recommendations: the creation of a delegates' assembly, made up of elected representatives from each school, to replace the cumbersome membership meetings and a chairperson with the power to suspend from a meeting any person culpable of disruptive "improper conduct at a meeting." Moreover, a person or group making false charges against any member or other group in the TU or using disruptive tactics at meetings or demonstrating insubordination to a chairperson could be suspended, after receiving a hearing from the executive board, for up to six months.[38]

MINORITY RESPONSE

In response to the charges and attempts to expel their executive board members, the Rank and File and the Progressive Group issued an Executive Board Minority Report. The executive board refused to allow them to present their report at the October 27 meeting, even though Ben Davidson, a member of the opposition, had served notice at the board's June and September meetings that he was going to file such a report; no member of the board had challenged the group's right to do so. The authors of the minority report, Florence Gitlin, Ben Davidson, David M. Wittes, and Isidore Begun, protested the refusal as a violation of regular parliamentary procedure. Eventually, the minority report was issued to the Grievance Committee and general membership.[39] The minority report accused the administration of being undemocratic because, in the fall of 1931, it had proposed changing the union's constitution to allow only one-third of the membership to confirm expulsions recommended by the executive board. Fortunately, the 250 members in attendance defeated the motion. The administration, determined to rid the union of dissenters, proposed revising the constitution to allow expulsion to be based on a vote by a majority of executive board members. The membership could not hear the opposition's point of view. The minority group even accused the administration of trying to take decision-making powers out of the hands of the membership.[40]

While the administration claimed it did not care about a person's political affiliation, the opposition countered that affiliation was at the heart of the conflict: "Leading members of the administration have indulged in open Red-baiting, well knowing that the accusation of Communism in the New York City school system means almost certain loss of jobs." To back up its assertion, the signers of the report pointed out that, at a meeting of the Joint Salary Committee, Lefkowitz said that certain teachers were Communists and that they would be expelled from the TU. He even complained about Begun's behavior toward the superintendent. Begun was eventually called before the superintendent. Linville, Lefkowitz, and the vice president of the union, Mrs. Lindlof, testified against the leader of the Rank and File. The leadership's actions placed the union in a position of working with management against a union member instead of defending his rights. The minority group accused Lindlof of intimidating the opposition by "threatening to expose" them. The minority group claimed that the administration asserted that Begun was not only hurting the members of the TU but was jeopardizing the "purpose and life of the union." Linville and Lefkowitz's turning to management to sabotage the opposition was symptomatic of the collaborative model for labor and management that they advocated.[41]

The charge that the Rank and File and the Progressive Group were trying to gain control of the union was also bogus, according to the executive board's left members. The minority groups claimed they were merely trying to present suggestions and constructive criticism to shape policy. The left was indeed trying to influence membership, but denials about trying to take over the union were more debatable. Labeling union leaders class collaborators was designed to discredit them. The two left groups also refuted the charges of disruptive tactics, accusing Lefkowitz and Lindville of walking out of a union meeting, in December of 1931, to protest granting substitute teachers the right to vote at union meetings. Lefkowitz's describing the Progressive Group as part of the lunatic fringe, "Redbaiting," attempting to prevent meetings by raising the quorum, and numerous other actions all indicated that the administration itself was using disruptive tactics.

While Linville and Lefkowitz wanted to expel the six opposition members, under the union's constitution expulsions required a two-thirds vote of the membership, which was difficult to attain. In the first vote, on the expulsion of Begun, 451 were in favor and 316 were opposed, short of the two-thirds needed. Seeing that it was probably impossible to win a two-thirds vote on the other five, Lefkowitz proposed a motion to drop the other cases, which was approved. Although a majority had voted in favor of disciplining Begun, the opposition had clearly gained enough support to make it a formidable force in the union. Although the administration's proposal for the creation of a delegates assembly was passed by the membership, the larger objective of purging the left failed, a major disappointment for Linville, Lefkowitz, and members of the administration.[42]

SCHISM

The animosity between the leadership and the left did not dissipate. In 1934 Begun and Williana Burroughs were dismissed from their teaching positions by the Board of Education on the grounds of conduct unbecoming a teacher. They had accused the board of unfairly disciplining Rank and File member Isidore Blumberg for taking part in a Rank and File–led teachers demonstration to protest the school agency's refusal to provide adequate salaries for teachers.[43] This kind of persecution enhanced the stature of the Rank and File. In the union election, Begun ran for president, and, although Linville won handily, Begun received a quarter of the vote, confirming the Rank and File as the major caucus in the union. Fearing the growing strength of the left, the leadership suspended Begun from the union in January 1934 for urging union members at a City Hall rally to join the Rank and File. Burroughs was suspended when she charged the administration with contributing to the board's decision to dismiss her and Begun.[44]

In September 1934 William Green, president of the American Federation of Labor, entered into the fray, writing a letter to the AFT leadership demanding the expulsion of Communists in the New York City chapter. However, members of the administration and delegates assembly objected strongly to the interference. Linville and Lefkowitz attempted to pass a compromise resolution at the January 1935 meeting of the delegates assembly calling for the expulsion of members, not for their political affiliation but for advocating dual unionism. However, the delegates defeated the Linville-Lefkowitz proposal and instead passed a resolution opposing "any discrimination against or disciplinary action against any worker because of his political opinions or activity." The resolution opposed Green's "red-baiting letter" which was counter to "Union democracy."[45]

In 1935 the Rank and File received over four hundred votes in the union election. Although Linville had won the presidency, the writing was on the wall. The momentum was on the side of the Rank and File, and the administration could not stop the growing support for the left-leaning caucus. Unable to expel the left, Linville and Lefkowitz tried another strategy. They turned to the AFT, requesting an investigation of factionalism within Local 5. Lefkowitz wanted to have the charter of the TU revoked and to organize a new local that could receive recognition from the national organization.

Lefkowitz, Linville, and other members of the administration accused the left of "antagonistic and destructive activities," including publishing material that attacked and discredited the administration in the eyes of non-teachers and accusing the Rank and File of being affiliated with "outside political groups" wanting to capture the union. It once again called on the AFT to appoint an investigating committee to come to New York and "make recommendations." The vote of the executive board was fourteen to nine in favor of the resolution. The executive board did not bother taking its resolution to the delegate assembly or to a membership meeting. Instead, it sent its request directly to the AFT. The national union appointed a committee of three, including the president and the secretary-treasurer of the AFT, to examine the nature of the factionalism in Local 5.[46]

Wasting little time, the Rank and File joined with the Progressive Group and other "independent forces in the Union" to form the United Committee to Save the Union (UCSU). One flyer distributed at a mass rally on June 7 warned that investigations by the AFT could actually lead to the revocation of Local 5's charter or to splits and expulsions. Speakers at the protest meeting included Charles Hendley, leader of a small socialist faction of the TU, who had first opposed the factionalism of the Rank and File but now said he was appalled by the administration's tactics and lack of democratic procedures. He was joined by Isidore Begun, Louis Fein, and Ben Davidson.[47] The UCSU called on members to "resist any abridgment" of the union constitution. The larger issues involved were members' right to formulate union policies ensuring the TU would not be expelled from the AFT.[48]

The UCSU protest was to no avail. The AFT went ahead with its investigation, holding a hearing on June 7, 1935. Raymond F. Lowery, president of the AFT, described the goal of the meeting as not to go after any individual or group but to help bring about harmony: "I would ask that everyone here this morning, irrespective of personal feelings, [or] preconceived ideas or constructions placed upon publicity granted to this interview this morning, would cast all of that into the background and get together in the spirit of cooperation upon which the American Federation of Teachers is founded."[49]

Presenting the case for the administration, Linville used the occasion to portray the opposition factions as irresponsible and unscrupulous and accused them of publicly taking credit for the work of the union leadership.

"They followed the policy of crediting their own leaders with the work of their Union Leaders"; even though they were a minority they monopolized debate and "consume[d] more time than [the] majority." One of the most damning of the opposition's charges was that the leadership "has shown distrust and contempt for the mass of the classroom teachers." Linville wondered how the leadership could persuade teachers to join the union when such an accusation had been made: "It is in my opinion the most outrageous sabotaging statement that has ever emanated from the Progressive group. When such misstatements are made, how can . . . typical teachers . . . be expected to join the Teachers' Union if its leaders having nothing but contempt?"[50]

Linville dragged up the old charge that the Rank and File and the Progressive Group were Communists using Communist tactics such as "mass action" as a "panacea" for the working class. But, when the leadership of the union sought to use mass action, it was condemned by the Progressives. "The Union is damned if it does and if it doesn't." Linville listed several "Communist controlled" organizations that the left had tried to force the Union to affiliate with: the Committee on Unemployment Insurance, outlawed by the AFL; the Classroom Teachers Group, organized by the Rank and File; the Unemployed Teachers Association, a "Rank and File Communist group"; the Teachers Committee to Protect Salaries; the League Against War and Fascism; the International Labor Defense; and the Teachers League for Academic Freedom.[51] According to Linville, the left tried to divert attention away from its Communist nature and make the administration "impotent" by consistently accusing the leadership of red-baiting. Linville also charged the left with being hypocritical: "At a meeting of [the] Delegate Assembly on January 3, Progressive and Rank and File united to attack President Green [and] like leaders of [the] Union as 'red baiter[s]' but do not so refer to Communist Party which freely uses expulsion upon all dissidents. How sincere is the Rank and File cry for democracy? Democracy for whom?"

Although Linville's testimony was a stinging indictment of the left, the AFT handed the leaders of the TU a decisive defeat when, at the AFT's 1935 convention, it voted 100 to 79 against revoking the charter of Local 5. Not willing to submit to democratic procedures, the Local 5 delegation walked out of the convention and was joined by seven other delegations, including Chicago Women Local 3 and New Bedford, Massachusetts.[52]

In their assessment of the crisis, two anonymous delegates, writing for the *Cleveland Teacher*, remarked that Lefkowitz and Linville, who had dominated Local 5 for sixteen years, were clearly losing control of the union. Lefkowitz and Linville were fearful of the steady increase in minority opposition because it meant that they would no longer be in charge. The delegates were right. With 750 teachers voting in the last TU election, the left received 42 percent. The call for an investigation, according to the anonymous delegates, was sparked by the fact that the administration had learned by May that support for the opposition had increased. The Executive Council received a report from the Investigation Committee and decided that instead of revoking the charter of Local 5 compromise was the best solution, a position rejected by the administration, which threatened to resign.[53]

The two Cleveland delegates saw the administration walkout as undemocratic, revealing an "unwillingness to follow the majority rule." The AFT had nothing to fear, despite the administration's claim of a Communist takeover: "The work in New York will unquestionably go forward with better results and more sureness than it has before. These minority groups have pledged themselves to see to it that this is done. We haven't gone 'Red.'"[54] As the article in the *Cleveland Teacher* suggests, the war within Local 5 had become a national fight. The walkout, the very close vote by AFT delegates, and the tone of the article demonstrated a serious rift within the national teachers union movement.

The UCSU appealed to the members of the administration who had submitted their resignations to reconsider: "The United Committee to Save the Union, in keeping with the policy of conciliation and compromise which it has presented in concrete proposals several times this summer, urges them to give serious thought to this grave step. It trusts they would withdraw their resignations in the interest of the whole union." The executive board designated George Davis, secretary-treasurer of the AFT, and Charles Hendley, vice president of the AFT, as a Liaison Committee. A meeting was scheduled for September 30 or a later date; if the administration went ahead with its September 30 resignation, the scheduled meeting would be used to nominate people to replace the officers as well as members of the executive board who had resigned.

The UCSU argued that the union should gear up for a battle against the foes of free public education who were proposing furloughs, suspensions of salary increments, assaults on pension rights. Setting a militant course, the committee called for a united front of organized labor and the public at the upcoming city budgetary hearings. Teachers would have to "put aside differences, personal grievances and personal attachments which may obstruct our united fight against the common enemy of public education."

After the administration failed to get the support of the American Federation of Teachers, Linville, Lefkowitz, Selma Borchardt, who was the legislative representative and vice president of the AFT, and seven hundred members resigned from Local 5 and formed the Teachers Guild.[55] By the time of the split, Local 5 was in the hands of its left flank, a group that would help shape teacher unionism for the next decade.

2 / COMMUNIST FRONT?

The TU During the Popular Front Era

After the 1935 walkout of the social democrats from the TU, the union turned to new leaders, a number of whom were members of the Communist Party of the United States of America (CPUSA). These included Bella Dodd who became the union's legislative representative, Celia Zitron who became chair of the Academic Freedom Committee, Alice Citron who was active in the union's Harlem Committee, Mildred Flacks who was a founding member of the Bedford-Stuyvesant-Williamsburg School Council, and David Flacks, an editor of the TU's newspaper. It should be noted, however, that Charles Hendley, a member of the Socialist Party, was elected president of the Union in 1935, and Lucille Spence, a founder of the Harlem Committee, and Layle Lane, elected recording secretary, never joined the Communist Party.

Critics of the New York City Teachers Union pointed to its willingness to adopt the Communist Party's domestic and foreign policies, arguing that the union's major objective was not to serve the interests of teachers but the dictates of the Party and the Soviet Union. Historian Philip Taft, for example, wrote in 1973 that, when the Rank and File group gained control of Local 5, "the local was to remain under Communist domination throughout its existence." The new leaders of the TU "hurriedly tied the Teachers Union to such well-known Communist fronts as the League Against War and Fascism, the International Labor Defense, the Youth Congress, and others as they made their debuts." Taft continued: "Unlike some leaders of the Communist-dominated unions in the CIO [The Congress of Industrial Organizations, created in 1938 to organize industrial workers] who initially followed the Party line but shifted their stance when they recognized that they could not function effectively within their unions while simultaneously demonstrating their devotion to the interests of the Party, the leaders of the Teachers Union remained faithful to the end. Those who led the Teachers Union were totally committed to the Party, and went along with it through numerous shifts in policy."[1]

Although sympathetic to the TU, in his history of the union Sidney Gould wrote that the "major cause of the union's decline . . . appeared to be a blind adherence by some of its leaders to a leftist political orientation that proved unattractive in the long run to teachers in New York City."[2] Historian William Eaton contended: "To say that the concern for the activities of Local No. 5 was an anti-Communist crusade would be inaccurate. For the term Communist was too general of a concept. Specifically the concern was for individuals who had joined the Communist party, who espoused the Moscow line via Joseph Stalin, and who were interested in subverting the teachers' union toward realizations of their own personal power to the detriment of the general membership."[3]

On the other hand, the TU's defenders downplayed the union's adoption of the Communists' views on domestic and foreign affairs, or at least they avoided critical analysis of the union's willingness to follow Moscow's line. In defense of the union, Celia Lewis Zitron claimed:

> The Nazi-Soviet nonaggression pact of 1939 intensified hostility to the Soviet Union. . . . Anticommunism, which had been used all through the depression to attack the organizations of the unemployed, the social legislation of the New Deal, and the organizing drives and strikes of the CIO, reached new heights. The Dies (House Un-American Activities) Committee increased its activities. In 1940 in New York City the Coudert Committee's attempt to destroy the Teachers Union and its investigation of alleged subversives in the schools and colleges rivaled, in its grim ugliness, the Lusk investigations of the post–World War I period.

Zitron never gave a hint that blind allegiance to the Soviet's dictates created the impression that the TU lacked independence. In her very insightful piece on the TU's efforts to promote diversity in New York schools from 1935 to 1950, Lauri Johnson never points out that union members had anything to do with the Communist Party.[4]

Neither its harsh detractors nor its uncritical supporters paint an accurate picture of the TU. There is no doubt that the union embraced many of the same policies as the Communist Party; this gave the impression that it was a front organization. To ignore or discount the significance of the TU's intimacy with the Communist Party distorts the union's own historical record. However, it would also be a mistake to conclude that there was justification for the revocation of its charter. The anti-Communist forces' zeal to expel Local 5 from the union's ranks represented a threat to democracy. The claim that the TU's cozy relationship with the Communist Party undermined the interests of teachers lacks merit. Anti-Communist forces ignored fair and impartial procedures in the cause of purging a group it found politically repugnant from the union ranks. Communist associations did not automatically make the union ineffective in fighting to improve education and working conditions for its members. The TU followed the Communist Party's line but, as we shall see in this chapter, it did not compromise its ability to fight for teachers. At the same time that it embraced international and domestic issues adopted by the Communist Party, the TU struggled to improve the working conditions of teachers, increase salaries, reduce class size, and protect academic freedom while operating within the framework of democratic unionism.

THE COMMUNIST PARTY OF THE UNITED STATES AND THE POPULAR FRONT

During the 1930s there was an explosion in union membership nationwide. Labor leaders and activists were successful in organizing millions of workers, largely as a result of section 7a of the National Recovery Act, signed by President Franklin Delano Roosevelt (FDR) in 1935, giving employees the right to organize and bargain collectively. Labor organizers in the steel, textile, rubber, and other industries led strikes to win union recognition and higher wages. Thus the militant labor activism of industry workers led to tremendous growth in unions. But the AFL affiliates and independent unions, not the unions affiliated with the Communist Party's TUUL, were attracting the workers. The United Mine Workers membership jumped from 150,000 in 1933 to 400,000 by 1935, as it successfully organized locals in Kentucky and Alabama. The Amalgamated Clothing workers, headed by socialist Sidney Hillman, gained 50,000 additional members during the same period, and from 1933 to 1935 the International Ladies

Garment Workers Union gained 160,000.[5] Significantly, a strike wave that erupted in 1934 was not conducted by unions affiliated with the Communist Party but by unions such as the AFL's United Textile Workers and other reformist unions.[6]

Despite the militant rhetoric of the Communist Party during the third period, the TUUL, organized in 1929, had little influence over labor. In fact, the AFL's successful organizing drive in several industries convinced many TUUL members to jump ship. The Communist influx, however, also affected the AFL-led unions, increasing the number of members opposed to the traditional AFL's craft and business unionism. Instead, these members dedicated themselves to an organizing approach focused on creating an industrial union that was operated by the rank and file.

The dual unionism advocated during the third period was designed to create revolutionary alternatives to the AFL. At the Communist Party's Eighth Annual Convention in Cleveland, Ohio, General Secretary Earl Browder announced that the Party was giving up dual unionism, in part because most newly organized workers had joined AFL unions. By early 1934 the thinking was that the only way to reach broad numbers of working-class men and women was to infiltrate the ranks of the "reformist" unions, and the CPUSA's executive committee, which was officially called the politburo, was directing Communists to begin working in the AFL unions. Historian Fraser Ottanelli notes that, even before the politburo's directive, the Party started moving its members from Communist-run unions, such as the National Miners Union, the Auto Workers Union, and the Steel and Metal Workers Industrial Union, to the AFL's United Mine Workers Union, United Auto Workers, and Amalgamated Association of Iron, Steel, and Tin Workers.[7]

The Communist Party continued, however, to push a third period analysis in the sphere of politics. The Party publicly opposed the New Deal, claiming that it benefited big business and not the working class, and it argued that FDR and the Democratic Party were not viable alternatives to fascism but merely instruments of the "bourgeoisie" working to divert the "proletariat masses" from seeking a real class solution. In fact, the Party characterized the United States and the Western political establishment as "social fascists."[8] Despite this stance, in 1934 the Party, in practice if not officially, began to move away from third period doctrine and attempted to form a united front with the Socialist Party, the

Farmers Workers Party of Minnesota, and Wisconsin's Progressive Party. The united front called for an ad hoc alliance with progressives and left-of-center groups, with the common objective of forming an antifascist coalition. What caused the Communists to abandon third period politics? The growing danger of Nazism and fascism—Hitler's rapid rearmament of Germany, his threatening moves toward Czechoslovakia, and his arming the fascists in Spain to overthrow an ally of Russia—convinced Communists that Nazi Germany was a far greater menace to socialism than the democratic nations.[9]

By the summer of 1935, the World Congress of the Communist International had officially reversed its third period doctrine and pushed the popular front notion to help build an antifascist alliance. It called for coalitions with social democrats, "reformist trade unions," and other non-communist groups that were antifascist and once were declared enemies of Communism and the working class to confront the growing danger of the regimes of Hitler, Mussolini, and imperial Japan. Coalitions with former enemies did not mean that Communists should stop criticizing the "right-wing" social democrats and trade unions for class collaboration with the "bourgeoisie." On the contrary, Communist parties should continue pointing out the dangers of these right-wing social fascists while cultivating a political relationship with the left-leaning trade unionists and social democrats.[10]

Following Moscow's lead, the CPUSA took steps to form an antifascist popular front, reaching out to socialists, labor and social democrats. During the early phase of the New Deal, the party attacked FDR for his support of big business. FDR's aim during what historians have called the first New Deal was to restore capitalism. However, by 1935, the focus had shifted from saving capitalism to social justice. The second New Deal ushered in programs that reshaped the role of government. The Wagner Act reasserted labor's right to bargain collectively and the Social Security Act created a social contract between labor, business, and the government. Social Security, along with other New Deal programs helped transform the United States into a welfare state that assured the working class a safety net. Moreover, the federal Work Projects Administration (WPA) employed three million people annually, including painters, sculptors, writers, and other artists, and it promoted the building of schools, parks, playgrounds, and bridges, facts that could not be ignored by the Communist Party.

The leadership of the CPUSA realized that if FDR lost the 1936 election, the gains made by workers would be greatly jeopardized. In 1935 some policies under the administration's National Recovery Administration and Agricultural Adjustment Act had been ruled unconstitutional by the Supreme Court, and many other New Deal programs that benefited working people were coming under attack by conservative Republicans and others on the right. Furthermore, American Communists' concerns about fascism and Nazism made it imperative to assure the safety of the world's only Communist regime; the best way of doing this was to form alliances with social democrats. FDR's decision to establish diplomatic relations with the Soviet Union delighted the CPUSA. The Party began to make distinctions between Republicans and Democrats, even referring to the Republican presidential candidate, Governor Alfred M. Landon of Kansas, as a crypto fascist. It stopped leveling attacks at FDR and the New Deal. Although Browder convinced Moscow that the Party should run its own presidential candidate in the 1936 election, the candidate would only attack the Republican and not FDR. The Party indirectly worked for Roosevelt's reelection. Clearly, by 1936, the CPUSA had given up the third period and was pushing the popular front in the arena of labor and politics.[11] The Party moved away from third period militancy and sectarianism and toward common ground with the working class, intellectuals, and "bourgeois" democrats. Browder, for example, declared at a conference of artists and intellectuals that the Party's efforts to build an antifascist front included the literati and artists, who were also threatened by fascism. This type of rhetoric was an important step in the united front campaign.[12]

THE TU AND POPULAR FRONT POLITICS

The Teachers Union embraced popular front politics. As early as December 1934, the Rank and File caucus endorsed the Communist Party's decision to create an antifascist alliance. Contending that, because of the "present world danger of war and fascism, trade unions should join in a large and vigorous united front movement to combat these forces," the left caucus declared a twofold struggle as a fight against fascism and a fight against war. These two goals were not necessarily compatible. The fight against fascism meant forging a collective of Communist, socialist, and social democratic forces to combat the growing threats of Nazi Germany and Fascist Italy. The antiwar aspect of the campaign indicated a fear—on the part of some on the left, including those in the Communist Party—that the United States would join forces with fascist nations against the Soviet Union. An antifascist campaign would thus guard against the United States joining in a war against the Communist nation. The Rank and File pushed the union to affiliate with the American League Against War and Fascism, an organization formed by the left-leaning Congress Against War, which held a meeting of over twenty-six hundred delegates in November 1933. The league consisted of left of center forces, including trade unionists, pacifists, socialists, and the Communist Party. Because the organization had been labeled a Communist Party front, it was important that the American League Against War and Fascism be seen as a broad liberal organization representing "many points of view." The Rank and File attempted to convince the executive board to send delegates from the union to the league's national convention.[13]

Resolutions introduced at executive board meetings indicated the Rank and File's persistence in pushing the Communist Party's objective of forming an antifascist and antiwar coalition. On the eve of the schism in the TU, the union's Anti-War Committee introduced a motion calling for a drive to raise money for labor's antifascist chest, based on a "voluntary tax of one dollar." In fact, the United Committee to Save the Union used the issue of a split to advocate the fight against fascism: "No union member must take a step which may lead to civil war within our ranks and in the organized labor Movement," the United Committee asserted. "Our best defense against reaction and fascism," the committee claimed, was "organized labor."[14]

Soon after the schism, the new leadership of the TU listed a number of issues it would fight for, including "labor and social problems." Consistent with the Rank and File's effort to push the Soviet's international and national policies, the new TU leadership called for the union to "intensify its anti-war and anti-fascist activities," including making the Anti-War Committee "one of the most important union activities." The union should support the labor chest against fascism and work to create a "broad united movement against the war and fascism based on the American Federation of Labor in cooperation with all other liberal and progressive forces in the community." The TU's statement was in step with the American Communist Party and Comintern directives to create a united antifascist front and support the formation of a labor party "based on the economic, political and fraternal organizations of workers and farmers."[15]

By 1935 the Teachers Union had publicly endorsed a united front against Nazism and fascism, arguing that its position was in line with the broader range of antifascist forces. Born during World War I, the TU faced repression and persecution because of nationalist sentiments, and Local 5 claimed its members were aware of the drift toward war. Nonetheless, they were also cognizant of the "many other manifestations of the recrudescence of barbarism known as [N]azism and fascism." Local 5 was willing to defy the "forces of reaction," was a "partisan on the side of democracy and freedom; and will go down, if necessary, battling this current horror." Still the local, as part of a larger mainstream coalition, endorsed the position of the AFL on the issues of war and fascism. AFL President William Green declared that labor would oppose the United States entrance into the war. But the AFL was also in opposition to the "tyranny of fascism."

A motion requesting the American Labor Party "do all in its power to realize an election campaign independent of the major capitalist parties" was adopted at the June 25, 1937, executive board meeting. But the board also called on the ALP to "nominate" a person who would attract the "broadest possible progressive vote," reflecting the push for broad coalition politics. In January 1938 eleven members of the executive board issued a petition calling for affiliation with the American League for Peace and Democracy (formerly the American League Against War and Fascism). Among the eleven were Celia Lewis, Bella Dodd, and Julius Metz, all members of the Communist Party. That same month, the Anti-War and Anti-Fascist Committee voted to select a delegate to the American League for Peace and Democracy's February 5 conference. The union, which voted overwhelmingly at its January 8 meeting for affiliation with the American League for Peace and Democracy, went on record supporting a "collective against Fascist aggressors."[16]

Some union members even attacked the TU leadership because of its transparent support of the Soviet Union's foreign policy. In its campaign literature, the opposition objected to the "pro-war collective security program of the Majority Group, which means reliance on imperialist Great Britain, France, and the United States to preserve peace and curb fascism."

It accused those nations of "arming to the hilt . . . to wage war in defense of their imperialistic interests."[17]

Besides pushing collective security, the TU also embraced the Soviet's position on the civil war in Spain. In 1936 the Spanish military, led by General Francisco Franco, attempted to overthrow the left-leaning government. Nazi Germany and Fascist Italy supported Franco, while the Soviet Union came to the aid of the Spanish government. Close to three thousand Americans, many of them members of the Communist Party, joined the Abraham Lincoln Brigade to fight alongside Spanish citizens to save the government. The TU called on the AFT to support lifting the U.S. embargo on Spain during the Spanish Civil War (in order to assure that the Loyalist government would receive aid) and to take steps to establish a children's hospital in the war-torn country. In October 1938 the TU voted to send a letter to Secretary of Labor Frances Perkins and other officials supporting the admittance to the United States of Abraham Lincoln Brigade members who were not citizens. The TU's executive board authorized its president, Charles Hendley, to send a letter to union members asking them for funds and "all possible aid to Loyalist Spain." When pointing to its accomplishments in 1938, the union specifically noted its antifascist work, including aiding Spain's loyalist government by raising $1,200 for the children of that country, contributing clothes, and fighting to end the embargo.[18]

Clearly, the union was greatly influenced by the American Communist Party, with a focus on broad political alliances that mirrored that Communist Party's fight for unity within the labor movement. The major reason for Communist influence was that Communists held important leadership positions in the union. Of the twenty-seven board members listed in the May 21, 1937, executive board minutes, at least eleven could be identified as Party members. By December 18, 1937, fifteen of the twenty-four members on the board were in the Party, including Isidore Begun, Meyer Case, Bella Dodd, Celia Lewis, Dale Zysman, Abraham Lederman, Julius Metz, and Clara Rieber. The December 1937 minutes also noted that Dale Zysman had become chairman of the executive board, thus placing a Communist in a key position in the union. Communists also led important union committees: Celia Lewis chaired Academic Freedom, Abraham Feingold the Anti-War and Anti-Fascist Committee, Irving Adler Educational Policies, Julius Metz Legal Aid and Grievance, Meyer Case Membership, and Carl Fenichel was editor of weekly *New York Teacher News*.

REPRESENTING TEACHERS' INTERESTS

Despite the substantial evidence of the New York City Teachers Union's strong allegiance to the American Communist Party during the popular front period, it would be a mistake to conclude that the union sacrificed the interests of its members and teachers as a consequence. While pushing the political policies of the Communist Party during the popular front period, it also worked diligently on behalf of teachers. In particular, the TU labored in the fields of teacher professionalism, union democracy, academic freedom, and improving working conditions.

In an attempt to build a broad-based teachers union, the executive board of the TU voted overwhelmingly, fourteen to seven, to change the name of its weekly paper from the *Union Teacher* to *New York Teacher News* sometime after the schism. Reaching beyond those who were "union conscious," the TU wanted to represent all teachers. The paper's old title limited readership to the small segment of teachers already committed to unionism or what Communists identified as "class consciousness." The new title sent the message that the paper was not limited to union members but related to all those in the profession. The focus on unity fostered the popular front line and signaled a movement away from sectarianism.[19] The name change indicated the TU would work for all teachers.

To court broad support, the TU placed greater emphasis on professional concerns and did not limit itself to bread-and-butter issues. The new leadership announced a fresh focus on "educational policy." Professor Goodwin Watson, a leading psychologist at Teachers College, would head the union's Educational Policies Committee, promoting the "art of good teaching." The union declared that an "organization like ours cannot confine itself to a narrow line of economic activity only. Teachers, like other humans, do not live by bread alone." To keep the "creative impulse" alive in teachers, the Educational Policies Committee proposed a number of courses for teachers to enhance their knowledge.[20]

The Teachers Union claimed success in its effort to help teachers try to implement activity programs in their schools. Its first educational forum, "The School in Contemporary Society," disclosed a "strong popular demand for the study of the fundamentals of education," and it would become an annual event. However, the union's version of professionalism differed from the middle-class version held by Linville and the previous administration.

The TU tied teachers to the larger working class by offering courses in working-class history and culture for those who wanted to "participate in the educational movement within the trade unions." A course on trade unionism, created in 1937, covered several topics, including labor from the middle ages through the Industrial Revolution, the growth of British unionism, trade unionism in the United States, labor during the Depression, and contemporary conflicts in the labor movement. A member of the college union, an "expert in the field" such as historians Philip or Jack Foner, "guided" the course. The union urged the Board of Education to offer it as one of its alertness courses, required for teachers as criteria for salary credit. The committee also recommended a series of forums for "non-union teachers" offering topics such as organized labor and education and "why professionals should organize." Eleanor Roosevelt and John L. Lewis were suggested as speakers for the forums. Other courses included modern dance and folk dance, included because of their "recreational and professional value."[21]

The TU's annual educational conference was another important way to promote professionalism. First organized in 1938, the conference attracted up to two thousand teachers and featured panels of experts on a variety of topics, such as ways to improve learning for children in the inner city and the teacher's role as a faculty and union member. According to Celia Zitron, the "forums" [conferences] "added to the knowledge and understanding of the participants and opened vistas for further study and discussions. But it is probable that their greatest contribution was in bringing teachers out of the isolation of their schools and classrooms and into the company of hundreds of concerned colleagues." An annual Teacher Union award was presented at the conference for an "outstanding contribution to education" by an individual.[22]

WORKING CONDITIONS

The Teachers Union fought aggressively to improve working conditions. "The original and prime function of a union is to secure improvement in the conditions under which its members work," the TU declared, vowing to "continue its militant program of action to this end." In its program for the school year 1936–1937, the union demanded that the state legislature pass a bill that would adjust salaries to the 1932 schedule, increase the pay

Figure 2.1 TU membership meeting, September 12, 1947. United Federation of Teachers, part 1, folder 518.

of junior clerks to $2,300, increase pay for substitute teachers, increase pay for evening-session substitutes to match that of day-session substitutes, and provide summer pay for substitutes. Teachers who missed school because of illness or jury duty should not have their pay deducted, and if deductions had been made, they should be refunded retroactively. Laboratory assistants should be designated laboratory assistant teachers. At the August 1938 AFT convention, the union planned to introduce a resolution getting the national to "reaffirm its stand in support of tenure, adequate salaries, sick leave with pay [and] sound pensions." It also called for an AFT study on working conditions for teachers in various places and publication of the findings of such a study. The TU also proposed sabbatical leaves for "professional and cultural improvement, rest [and] recuperation from illness," supported by regular pay increments. The board should not use substitutes and "other low paid" teachers as a way of avoiding appointing teachers with a regular license.[23]

Addressing crucial issues related to teachers' academic freedom and discrimination, the executive board called for the repeal of the Ives Loyalty

Oath, "procedural rights to all teachers at all hearings," the elimination of oath requirements for graduation, the abolition of the section of the education law which made it possible to discriminate "against Negro children," and support for an anti–sex discrimination bill. The union also supported the extension of tenure to upstate and evening-school teachers. Assuring the rights of the Work Projects Administration teachers was another important issue. Many teachers thrown out of work by the Depression were hired under the WPA but remained in a vulnerable position, unable to receive tenure and easily laid off.[24] Accepting WPA Teachers Local 453's call for a work stoppage to protest the firing of WPA teachers, the executive board decided to permit the distribution of literature at its membership meeting and passed a resolution requesting that the Board of Examiners and the Board of Education accept WPA workers' teaching experience as criteria for a regular teaching license.[25]

Classroom overcrowding was another major concern. In her legislative report at the May 21, 1937, executive board meeting, Bella Dodd described the union's five-year plan, which included holding a public conference on overcrowding and presenting a school budget brief to the Board of Education suggesting ways to reduce class size. Dodd's report proposed a salary increase for substitute teachers, the hiring of thirty-seven hundred new teachers, increasing health services in the schools, providing schools with soap and towels, building additional libraries, vocational and recreational facilities, and offering summer schools, child guidance, and evening schools. In 1937 the executive board called "the problem of overcrowding the leading issue before all who are concerned for the advancement of public education." At the start of the previous school year, there were "17,815 classes in the elementary schools of New York City. Only 455 of them contained fewer than twenty-five pupils, a number held as a maximum limit in private schools." One-third of elementary classes, according to the union, had over forty students.[26]

In a November 1938 report to the executive board, Dodd noted that the legislative agenda of the union would emphasize overcrowding, relief, and health and recreation centers. Eventually the maximum should be thirty students in regular classes, twenty-five in "underprivileged areas," and twenty in special classes, with the Lower East Side, East Harlem, and Lower West Side included in underprivileged areas. A "mass delegation" should go to the mayor's and, if necessary, the governor's office to press the union's case.[27] "Overcrowding Week" would kick off a postcard and letter-writing campaign. The union called for the state to launch a study on class size and planned to lobby state assemblymen and senators on the issue of over-crowding. Eliminating overcrowding would benefit not only teachers but students as well, obtaining "for children of the masses the opportunities that are possible in small classes." This objective required a "long-range pro-gram of action." Organized labor and parent associations needed to become involved in the fight to reduce class size.[28]

The TU also addressed pension reform, calling for direct election of teacher members to the Teachers' Retirement Board. Under a special catego-ry labeled "social legislation," the executive board advocated a referendum appropriating $10 million for the relief of needy children, extension of So-cial Security legislation for private school teachers, reducing class size to thirty-five, and $300 million of federal aid to education. To educate mem-bers about their pensions, speakers would discuss ways of investing funds, the soundness of funding, disability retirement, and the right to receive more than half pay after retiring. The TU prepared a "Pension Primer" de-scribing the pension law in layman's terms and calling for state protection of the pension system.[29]

The union suffered defeat, however, on a number of bills in the state legislature, including the Brenner Bill, which would have reduced class size, and the Monoco Bill, which would have ended sex discrimination in ex-aminations and appointment of teachers. While criticizing the reactionary legislative leadership for the defeat of pro-labor legislation, the TU took credit for the successful passage of other bills: the Feld-Andrews Bill, re-pealing section 921 of the state education by-laws, which allowed racially segregated schools; the Livingston-Breitrart Bill, granting procedural rights for probationary and regular licensed teachers; and the Austin Bill, allow-ing boards of education throughout the state to establish nursery schools.[30]

UNION DEMOCRACY

According to historian Philip Taft, after the social democrats walked out of the TU, the Communist faction gained control of the union and "Local 5 faithfully followed every change in the party line." Although Taft acknowl-edged that the TU "remained a labor organization" with an agenda that included higher wages for teachers and improving working conditions, he did not describe the union's activities on behalf of its members. Instead, he focused on the union's ouster from the Joint Committee of Teachers Organizations (JCTO) for behaving in an irresponsible manner. According to Taft, the union was offered several opportunities to substantiate its charges that the JCTO had launched a "whispering campaign" against it, but "failed to provide any proof." Taft also noted that the TU was expelled from the New York City Central Trades and Labor Council, the AFT, and later the Congress of Industrial Organizations (CIO) for following the Communist line, and that it was banned from the school system in 1950 because of its Communist connections. What Taft did not discuss was how the union labored on behalf of teachers. The reader is left with the impression that the union's paramount purpose was not to address the interest of teachers but to fulfill its undying allegiance to the Communist Party.[31]

Taft ignored a basic question: could a union be dominated by Communists and still be democratic and represent the interest of its members? In a close examination of the role Communists played in industrial unions in the 1930s and 1940s, sociologists Judith Stepan-Norris and Maurice Zeitlin contended that "red" unions and unions in which Communists were a significant part of the leadership were democratic. They protected the civil liberties and political rights of their members and assured that there would be fair elections and broad representation in decision-making bodies.[32] Stepan-Norris and Zeitlin maintained that the existence of organized labor was "evidence of the freedom to oppose the existing regime and to struggle for political power, to join and participate actively in organized political associations." The record of the TU during the popular front period confirms Stepan-Norris and Zeitlin's argument. Although Communists were prominent in the union, there was an opposition that openly challenged leadership policies and positions and publicly voiced its opinions with impunity.[33]

After the schism, the main opposition was made up of those who followed Jay Lovestone and called themselves the United Progressives. The leadership and this faction agreed that the union should be a left-leaning organization, but they differed on issues of trade union democracy, membership, and political affiliation. The United Progressives contended that the general membership should have the power to make decisions, while the leadership asserted that the delegate assembly should have more decision-making power.

Those opposed to the new leadership in the TU expressed their differences with it, but, soon after the split, they attempted to provide a unified front. On September 2, 1935, eighteen members of the TU, including Ben Davidson, who belonged to the United Progressives group, and independent Charles Hendley, called for a meeting to put together a progressive agenda for the union. The Program Committee formulated a plan to be discussed at its October 2 meeting at the Prince George Hotel, which called for uniting teachers, adopting democratic procedures, and relying on teachers' "organized power." Recognizing the TU and the AFT as collective bargaining agencies, the committee discouraged teachers from joining any organization independent of these two unions, with the exception of professional groups.[34]

The committee dedicated itself to democratic procedures, specifically noting that the breakaway Teachers Guild, as a dual union and a threat to labor, should be resisted. TU members should make no public criticism of the union, and nonappointed and substitute teachers should be allowed to join Local 5 at reduced membership dues but with full rights. All teachers should be allowed to join, regardless of their "political or economic views or affiliations." The Program Committee was attempting to assure the opposition that it would be able to operate freely. The AFT should also accept into its ranks all categories of teachers, including those working in private schools and WPA teachers. Trade union democracy relied on the membership as the final authority in decision making. Therefore, at least one membership meeting per term was recommended, which would allow members to decide on the policies of the union. Also recommended was a minimum of two forums a year to present vital current problems facing labor and particularly teachers. Special business meetings would be called by the executive board when necessary. The delegate assembly would continue to act as the policy decision-making body between membership meetings. Emphasizing a core principle of trade union democracy, the committee asserted, "The union shall recognize the right of organized expression of minority opinion to exist and to have representation on standing union committees." The committee favored calling a special membership meeting to clarify parts of the union constitution and to help make revisions. The union's job was to defend the interests of teachers, relying on the support and cooperation of labor, parents, and progressive elements in the communities that it served.[35]

The union, according to the committee's progressive program, should be consulted regarding all changes of the Board of Education bylaws; there should be no hindrance or interference by supervisors when union members tried to distribute union material in schools. The committee also recommended that the union take action on several items: restoring the salary schedule, working to repeal the Board of Examiners' loyalty quiz (which the board initiated in the mid 1930s to weed out subversives), defending academic freedom and tenure, and fighting for immediate and unconditional "re-instatement of 89 WPA teachers, opposing an attempt by Board of Superintendents to force these teachers to sign 'yellow dog' agreements" promising not to join a union. It also called for an appropriate educational budget for full education, evening and summer schools, limiting class size to thirty-five, liberalization of sabbaticals, no collection of money from teachers in schools, filling all positions with regular licensed teachers, increasing clerical staff to relieve teachers of paperwork, and relieving teachers of nonteaching duties.[36]

With the exception of forbidding union members to publicly criticize the union, the Program Committee's recommendations were democratic, laying out a plan for governance of the union by its membership, protecting the rights of those holding minority opinions, and attempting to organize and protect the most vulnerable in the school system.

Another indication that the TU protected the democratic rights of its members was the free expression of different opinions. After the 1935 walkout, the union elected as its new president Charles Hendley, then a socialist who was independent of the Rank and File and the United Progressives. The new leadership put out a call for nominations of officers and members of the Eexecutive board and tried to be transparent, sharing its programs with members. All former members of the delegate assembly, except for those who resigned, were to be notified of that body's meetings. The general membership was open to all but those who resigned. The executive board recognized as a delegate anyone "who comes with a signed statement testifying to his/her election as a delegate by members of the school." To assure that schools had proper representation, they were to be notified that they must elect a representative to the delegate assembly.[37]

Despite the attempt to present a unified union, the factions openly criticized one another during the popular front years. In the 1936 TU election campaign, for instance, the United Progressives, who challenged the Rank and File by running candidates for president, the executive council, and other leadership positions, emphasized their differences with their rivals. The group's campaign statement argued for caucuses within Local 5 and insisted that the right to voice differences of opinion was a fundamental principle of trade union democracy.[38] Distinguishing themselves from their opponents, they argued that supervisors should not be allowed into the collective bargaining agency; as employers, they were considered to be adversaries of teachers. Granting experience credit to substitute teachers for placement on the eligibility list was another bone of contention. Only some substitutes received experience credit; providing a privilege to some and not others. The United Progressives opposed any attempt to join small "isolated locals" that were trying to organize a labor party, because these groups were not affiliated with organized labor. The most divisive issue involved cooperation with the newly formed Teachers Guild. The Rank and File introduced a resolution in the delegate assembly calling for cooperation with the guild. The United Progressives and its independents opposed cooperating with the guild because it had tried to undermine the TU's prestige in Albany. United Progressives also accused the guild of attempting to portray itself as part of the organized labor movement and being involved in a "concerted attack on the AFT and Local 5."[39]

Despite the United Progressives' opposition, the delegate assembly passed a resolution introduced by the Rank and File supporting cooperation with the guild. Infuriated, the United Progressives publicly claimed that the membership had not been involved in the vote, accusing its opponents of undemocratic procedures. The United Progressives argued that the guild's major objective was to destroy the TU. Cooperation with the guild would only isolate the TU from the rest of the labor movement because the guild was supporting dual unionism. The United Progressives instead called for negotiations with the guild in an effort to bring its members back into the TU and the AFT. If the guild was willing to stop attacking the TU, a conference to discuss unification should be called. The United Progressives also wanted to publicize the guild's rejection of the proposal for negotiation made by Jerome Davis, president of the American Federation of Teachers.

The fight over the guild highlighted the differences within the union after the split. However, the United Progressives openly criticized opponents on a number of other issues as well, including with which organizations the union should affiliate, how it should best perform the "day to day work

of the union," and how much democracy existed in the union. They criticized the Rank and File's insistence that the union affiliate with the League
Against War and Fascism and the National Negro Congress because those
organizations were not "rooted in the labor movement but have actually
been rejected by it." The United Progressives proposed that union committees be limited in size, in contrast the Rank and File believed committeees
should be open to any member who wished to join. The United Progressives
called for the creation of an "inner-union publication for the presentation
to the members of all important issues before the Union, with a discussion
by the various tendencies of their particular viewpoints on such issues."[40]

In a cooperative and democratic spirit, the new leadership called for a
conference to work out disagreements. In April 1936 representatives of the
Rank and File, the United Progressives, and independents reached agreement on key differences: committees should be limited and, regardless of
caucus affiliation, members should be encouraged to participate; the president would appoint committees subject to the approval of the executive
board; members of the Teachers Guild were to be welcomed back into the
TU. However, the Rank and File accepted the United Progressives' argument
to condemn the "Guild as a dual organization," agreeing to resist the guild's
effort to "undermine our prestige at Albany and ingratiate itself with certain sections of the labor movement." Although the TU would not invite
the guild to cooperate on issues, it would not "refuse to participate" with it
in a joint conference on teacher concerns. All sides agreed that, when there
were differences in the executive board or delegate assembly on "an important matter of policy, a statement discussing the particular issue involved
will go out together with the announcement of the meeting at which the
issue is to be discussed." This policy typified the attempt to avoid factionalism and satisfy the United Progressives' call for an intra-union publication
discussing the differences between the caucuses. When it came to affiliation, the caucuses agreed that their major energy should be devoted to defending the interests of teachers. The labor movement was the best entity
to "rally all progressive and liberal forces for an effective defense against
war and fascism," and the TU should work with organized labor to build
upon a broad base against those dangers.[41]

The agreement among the Rank and File, United Progressives, and independents left gray areas. For instance, who would decide if an issue was
important enough to require issuing statements of disagreement between

the two caucuses? The United Progressives objected to the Rank and File's insistence on affiliating with organizations that were not part of the labor movement. However, the agreement mentioned nothing specifically about the League Against War and Fascism or the National Negro Congress. But the agreement did demonstrate an effort on the part of the new leadership to settle differences through negotiation and cooperation.

Another sign of union democracy was the effort by the leadership to get the membership involved in union activities. The rapid growth in membership soon after the 1935 split, recognized by both the Rank and File and United Progressives, was attributed to the union representing the interests of teachers. After the split, the leadership tried to increase membership participation in the operation of the union. President Hendley sent a letter to members in September 1936 urging those who were "writers, editors, business managers, accountants, statisticians, experts in research, speakers, diplomats, executives, economists, dramatists and those talented in other lines" to serve on the numerous committees. But the plea was not just for those with special talents. The union president called on "hard workers who have the will, the endurance, [and] the patience to undertake hard jobs. . . . We need many honest Jimmy Higginses." Also calling on those who taught in private schools and colleges to volunteer for committee work, Hendley was asking members not just for service but to become active in the most crucial work of the union, not to volunteer just on committees addressing professional concerns (academic freedom, educational policies, legal and grievances, legislative, and finance) but also on the antiwar and antifascist, Harlem, social, and unemployment committees that would help make the TU a social movement. Hendley's plea, "We need your point of view," altered the relationship between the leadership and members by reminding them that they were decision makers working from the ground up. The union leadership was stressing a form of participatory democracy.[42]

Once the Communist leadership gained control of the TU, there were signs indicating that union elections were less than democratic. At its June 4, 1937, executive board meeting, the Election Committee reported that 5,525 ballots had been sent out and 3,411 had been returned. Running for president, Charles Hendley received 3,333 votes, while Bella Dodd and two other opponents received one vote each. Layle Lane got 3,282 votes in her bid to be recording secretary, defeating Begun and Spence, who each received one vote.[43] The Rank and File, which by 1938 was calling itself the

Majority Slate, claimed that 77 percent of the membership voted for its candidates for the executive board in the 1937 election, crediting this success to addressing overcrowding, pensions, teacher grievances, democratization of the schools, rating equal opportunities in Harlem, better conditions in private schools, and other issues vital to its members.[44]

Regarding those cases when non-Communists defeated Communists for key union positions, Bella Dodd, who would later testify before a number of investigative bodies, contended that one strategy of the Communist Party was to place non-Communists in positions of power to give the impression that the union was not a front. However, Dodd did not offer any proof for this assertion, and she painted the non-Communists as dupes who were manipulated by Party members. Layle Lane, a socialist who never joined the Communist Party, was a close ally of Brotherhood of Sleeping Car Porters organizer A. Philip Randolph, who distrusted Communists. Although Lane would later leave the TU, criticizing it for being under Communist control, apparently she did not hold that belief at the time of the breakup. In fact, she became a member of the executive board and recording secretary for the organization. Hendley joined the Communist Party after he left the TU, but while he served as the union's president he identified himself as a socialist. Both Communists and non-Communists were elected to leading positions in the union during the popular front years. Although Dodd offered no proof for the allegation that Communists deliberately voted to place certain non-Communists in office, it seems highly unlikely that a figure as popular as she was would receive only a single vote in a union election. Thus, full democratic expression in union elections after the Communists gained power is, at best, questionable. Nevertheless, the independence of Hendley and Lane is not in question.

Although election results were questionable, public criticism by opponents of the Communist leadership was not stifled. According to Stepan-Norris and Zeitlin, one indication of union democracy is the ability to express opposing views. This was indeed the case in the Teachers Union. The United Progressives circulated numerous letters to union members criticizing the majority group on a host of positions. In December 1937, for instance, a "Progressive Group Bulletin" accused the Rank and File, referred to as the administration, of giving up the fight on the Ives Loyalty Oath, citing a resolution in the delegate assembly requesting that the state's constitutional convention approve a proposal that would not require teachers to take any oath not "required of other citizens." The proposal, the United Progressives maintained, "conceals our fundamental opposition to all loyalty oaths and invites a measure requiring such oaths from all citizens." Introducing such a proposal to the constitutional convention, which would be "under the overwhelming control of ultra-conservative Republicans and Democrats with Liberty Leaguers in the saddle," would only give that body an opportunity to pass a "provision for loyalty oaths for all citizens." The United Progressives argued that the Rank and File's tactic was a sign that the administration was "in line with" those reactionary forces pushing loyalty oaths. Rank and File support for an "imperialist war" suggested that "it is therefore willing and ready to advocate and support any proposal which lays the ground work for the support of loyalty oaths for all citizens, including teachers."[45]

In its December 1937 bulletin the United Progressives also publicly criticized the union leadership for recommending that its labor history course become one of the Board of Education's alertness courses. Before the schism, the union had opposed these courses on the grounds that the only criteria for salary credit "should be satisfactory service." Rejecting the Rank and File's argument that it was attempting to address the problem of alertness courses realistically by offering courses that were "good," the Progressives saw only an "unprincipled position." One could not oppose these courses and at the same time sponsor one. The fact that two hundred teachers had attended the union's activity program and one thousand attended the union's educational conference was proof that there was no need to coerce teachers to take courses for salary credit. The December 1937 bulletin also criticized the leadership's position on the rating system of teachers. Although the union's official policy opposed a rating system, the leadership, according to the Progressives, publicly supported the "reactionary program" of the High School Teachers Association calling for a modified rating system. The opposition demanded that the TU work with other teacher organizations to eliminate the rating system.[46]

In January 1938 the United Progressives issued a stinging attack on the leadership, accusing it of "anti-democratic practices." The opposition was angered by a series of events. The executive board had defeated Florence Gitlin's motion not to allow a public stand by union members on any question once discussion on the question had begun in the delegate assembly. Again, the administration had attempted to circumvent policy changes to be discussed by the delegate assembly by passing an amendment that would make exceptions if "emergencies" occurred. The Independent Group, another organized opposition group that came into existence in 1935, also issued a bulletin in January 1938 criticizing the majority for its position on the eligibility bill then before the state legislature. The bill would make hundreds of teachers who received a substitute license through noncompetitive means eligible for jobs, thus undermining the merit system, which the Independent Group supported. Opposing affiliation with the American Labor Party, which it labeled an "appendage of Tammany Hall," and the American League for Peace and Democracy, the Independent Group specifically criticized leadership for its support of the latter because the League supported FDR's call for an increase in the arms budget. That increase was a "dire threat to our school system," especially on the eve a "new depression," and teachers should support building schools, not battleships: "We must help to rally the forces of labor now against the war-makers and their publicity agents in our midst."[47]

In his book *The Communists and the Schools* historian Robert Iversen does not deny that the TU did its best to represent teachers. However, he attributes the leadership's delay at turning the union into a "party instrument" to the fact that it would have "been too obvious and would have provided public confirmation of all of Linville's worst warnings." According to Iversen, the takeover was a "united-front victory, which meant that the party's allies, the Socialists and the Lovestoneites, insisted upon their share of the spoils." If the Rank and File caucus had ignored the other factions, it would have "broken up the victorious coalition and would have possibly meant the lost of control." Iversen insists that the Communists had to find a way to ease out their partners because they were being watched by the newly formed Teachers Guild and AFL President William Green, who wanted to revoke the union's charter.[48] Iversen is working from the assumption that the TU should be judged not on its program and action on behalf of members but simply on its affiliation with the Communist Party. The question remains: can one be a member of the Party and work on behalf of union members?

THE TU AND ESPIONAGE

Two of the leading scholars on the American Communist Party are John Earl Haynes, a manuscript historian for twentieth-century American history at the Library of Congress, and Harvey Klehr, the Samuel Candler Dobbs Professor of Politics at Emory University. They have written several books together that focus on American Communism.[49]

Haynes and Klehr have defended what they call the "traditionalist view," arguing that the CPUSA was "profoundly antidemocratic" in both theory and practice and its members were subordinate to a "hostile foreign power." They accuse early revisionists, whose books first appeared in the 1970s, of taking a "benign view of Communism." and Communists. Haynes and Klehr also claim that a second wave of revisionists portrayed Communists as "heroic fighters for social justice in the nation's history." They go as far as to charge revisionist scholars with not confronting the evidence of newly released Soviet archives that prove the American party was a tool of Moscow. The later wave of revisionists "tied their research to their own radical sympathies, openly acknowledging that it was driven in part by a desire to validate their political needs."[50]

Haynes and Klehr also accuse revisionists of constructing a narrative of the "lost cause." They argue that revisionists contend that the popular front era was a period in which black and white workers were united under the banner of the left-led and often Communist-dominated "CIO unions to transform not merely American race relations but its economic system as well by implementation of an egalitarian welfare state." However, the "window of opportunity" missed when the working class was put on the defensive, the result of an attack by employers and a campaign by anticommunists that helped to marginalize black Communists, helped demolish the popular front.[51] Labeling the cold war, civil rights thesis as nothing more than a myth, Haynes and Klehr charge revisionists with putting politics before scholarship and being researchers who were more ideological than careful.

Haynes and Klehr's greatest contribution to the scholarship on the American Communist Party has been their work connecting the Party to Soviet espionage. They were the first American scholars to look at the newly released documents at Moscow archives and have been meticulous in uncovering the role American Communists played in clandestine activities. In *The Secret World of American Communism* the two, along with Fridrikh Igorevich Firsov, former head of the Department of Publications of Documents of the Communist Movement at the Russian Center for the Preservation and Study of Documents of Recent History, claim to have examined more than one thousand documents at the Russian Center for the Preservation and Study of Documents of Recent History. They selected over ninety of them that reportedly deal with secret actions in the United States by American Communists. These documents reveal Comintern funding of the CPUSA, U.S. Party members distributing Soviet materials in America, and proof of Julius Rosenberg's role in passing classified information on the atomic bomb to the Soviets. They also confirm the testimony of Whittaker Chambers, Elizabeth Bently, and other former members of the Party who identified Americans accused of spying for the Soviet Union. The authors of *The Secret World of American Communism* argue that the Communist Party was not an indigenous left movement fighting for racial equality, the rights of labor, and social justice. Top figures in the Party such as Earl Browder and Eugene Dennis, both Party leaders, were involved in espionage; but Haynes, Klehr, and Firsov reveal that members of the Communist Party's rank and file were also involved in espionage. Williana Burroughs, one of the few African American school teachers in the system in the 1930s, was an active member of the Communist-led Rank and File caucus of the TU. She joined the party in 1926 and in 1928 became a delegate to the Comintern Congress in Moscow. The Party assigned her the task of helping to organize women, but she did not publicly announce her Party membership until she lost her job as a teacher in the early 1930s. In 1937 she moved to Moscow and began working for Soviet radio.[52]

At least three people affiliated with the New York City school system, Pauline Baskind, Anna Vogel Colloms, and Frances Silverman, were accused of clandestine activity. In *Venona: Decoding Soviet Espionage in America*, Haynes and Klehr refer to Baskind as a "part-time New York City's choolteacher who provided a mail drop for the American end of the KGB's anti-Trotsky operation in Mexico."[53] They also list Colloms, who was in the Communist Party and a teacher at Washington Irving High School, as a member of a subversive secret group that was operating for Soviet intelligence. She was a courier for the Soviet Union to Mexico as part of the plan to free Trotsky's murderer.[54] According to the *New York Times* in December 1950, Baskind, Colloms, and Silverman, who also taught in the New York City Public schools, attempted in the early 1940s to free from prison the person who assassinated Leon Trotsky. However, according to the *New York Times*, United States Intelligence stopped the "Soviet Conspiracy."[55]

Although there is no doubt that the activities of Burroughs, Baskind, Silverman, and Colloms were undertaken on behalf of the Soviet Union, there is no evidence that the Teachers Union was a conduit of Soviet espionage. As noted in Chapter 1, Burroughs was a member of the Communist Party and a member of the TU's Rank and File caucus. However, her work for Soviet radio and as editor of the Soviet Union's English propaganda broadcasts did not begin until after she left the union. There is no connection between Burroughs's work as a broadcaster and the Teachers Union. In fact, Haynes and Klehr present no information on or analysis of her radio broadcasts.[56] Was she advocating the overthrow of the United States? It would seem that the United States had no such information, given that she was not arrested when she returned to the United States.

Although Haynes and Klehr list Pauline Baskind as a part-time New York City schoolteacher, she was employed as a substitute teacher by the board from 1936 to 1941 and was a full-time teacher from 1947 to 1949. When asked by HUAC if she "voluntarily participated in any conspiracy involving the receipt of mail from one source and its subsequent transmission to another source," she declined to answer the question on the ground of self-incrimination. Francis Silverman also testified before HUAC and refused to answer when asked if she were a member of the Party or had been involved in the plot. However, neither Baskind nor Silverman was employed by the board between 1942 and 1943 when they were accused of acting as mail drops.[57]

Anna Vogel Colloms's case is more complicated because she was employed as a teacher during the time (1942 and 1943) the government intelligence agency asserted that she was acting as a mail drop for the plot to free Trotsky's assassin. Like Baskind and Silverman, Colloms's name was on the TU's 1940 membership list. However, there is no evidence that the Teachers Union was involved in this plot or in any clandestine activity. None of the three was an officer of the union. They were never on its executive board or headed any committees of the union. There is no evidence that they influenced policy or positions on the issues or had ties to those in leadership. At its height, the TU had over six thousand members, and it would be ludicrous to blame the union for the actions of a very few members.

Historian Ellen Schrecker notes that although there were one hundred members of the Communist Party involved in spying in the United States for the Soviet Union, the Party was also engaged in many other activities. Espionage was just a part of the story, but it is the only one that interests Haynes and Klehr. They dismiss newer approaches to understanding the

Party, the organizations associated with the Party, or Party members. As Schrecker notes, it is important to understand why people were drawn to Party work.[58] It is equally important to understand why they were attracted to the Teachers Union. Scholars should attempt to explore the seeming contradictions in historic figures. In the case of the TU, the evidence is clear that many in leadership were in the Communist Party and used the union to push Party policies. However, it is also true that many members of the TU, including Party members, saw the union as a crucial vehicle to improve the lives of teachers, children, and communities.

The Communist leanings of the Rank and File led to the 1935 schism and undermined the Teachers Union, which not only lost 700 members but also some of the most dedicated union activists. Yet, despite the breakup, during the popular front years the TU was rapidly gaining members. In January 1937 the executive board reported that 93 applications had been accepted for membership, in May 80, in June 43. On October 14, 1938, the executive board accepted 80 people; a month later 115 applications were approved; in January 1939 65 teachers were accepted. The union leadership contended that it had increased the membership of Local 5 from 1,485 in 1935 to 6,229 by April 1938, but there is no evidence to support the assertion. Moreover, the union did not provide any information on how many people were leaving. Still, the union's 1940 membership book listed the names of 6,034 teachers, making it the largest teachers union in the city and proving that the union's work was attracting teachers. It had clearly bounced back from the 1935 schism. While the union pushed a political agenda akin to the Communist Party, it did not sacrifice the objective of improving working conditions for its members.[59]

3 / THE FIGHT OVER REVOCATION

The mid 1930s through early 1940s was a very difficult period for the New York City Teachers Union. Factionalism had ripped the union apart. To make matters worse, both the American Federation of Labor and, later, the American Federation of Teachers accused the union of being in the hands of Communists and the AFT took action to revoke the TU's charter. The TU worked diligently to defend itself against accusations that it was nothing more than a Communist front. Nevertheless, by adopting the same policies and positions on domestic and international issues as the American Communist Party, the Local 5 leadership made it extremely difficult for any neutral observer, let alone opponent, to believe that it was independent. By 1941, Local 5 had had its AFT charter revoked.

Local 5 leaders had pushed a united front campaign against fascism since 1935, but in the late summer of 1939, it changed direction. The Soviet Union shocked Communists and non-Communists throughout the world by signing a mutual nonaggression pact with Nazi Germany. The *New York Times* reported that Germany's foreign minister, Joachim von Ribbentrop, would fly to Moscow on August 23 to conclude negotiations.[1] While there was some truth to the Soviet Union's claim that it was trying to build a "buffer zone" to avoid invasion, Stalin's argument that he was stalling for time in order to prepare the nation for an eventual war against Germany did not hold up. He was more concerned about empire building than war preparation. Soon after signing the nonaggression pact, the Soviet Union annexed eastern Poland, Estonia, and Latvia, and attacked Finland; its new partner, Germany, took western Poland and Lithuania, launching World War II.[2] Stunned people worldwide wondered how a nation claiming to represent the downtrodden and leading a campaign against fascism and capitalist exploitation could sign a treaty with Hitler's regime. Further shocking its supporters, Moscow sent a communiqué on September 12, 1939, to the U.S. Party making its position clear: Communists were to give up the popular front and go back to blaming imperialist England and France for the world crisis.[3]

Following the lead of the Communist Party, the leadership of Local 5 changed its policies. Instead of emphasizing collective security against fascism, the union turned to anti-imperialist rhetoric, distancing itself from the American League for Peace and Democracy. Opponents of the move responded by charging that the Communist-dominated union was more concerned about the Soviet Union's survival than about the working conditions of teachers.

Before 1940 the TU enjoyed support from its parent organization, the AFT. Although the AFT investigated Local 5 in 1935, it refused to revoke its charter or recognize the guild, even risking disciplinary action from William Green and the executive board of the AFL. By the summer of 1937 Local 5 had considerable influence in the AFT. Of the seventeen members on the executive council of the AFT, six were supportive of Local 5: Charles Hendley, of course, Mary Grossman, of Philadelphia, Doxey Wilkerson of Howard University, George Axtelle of Chicago, Hugh DeLacy, of Seattle, and Allie Mann of Atlanta. Although not a member of the Communist Party, as president of the TU local Hendley did not want it expelled. Grossman was rumored to be a Party member. Wilkerson was sympathetic to the Communists and would eventually join the party. Axtelle was supportive of the TU in 1937 but would later join the opposition. Mann was supportive of the CIO and, therefore, of Local 5's position on that new federation of industrial unions.[4]

Only six executive council members voted against the TU, John Connors of New Bedford, Maine, Arthur Elder, state secretary of the Michigan Federation of Teachers and an organizer of the AFL, Michael Eck, secretary of the Ohio Federation of Teachers, Mary Herrick of Chicago, Joel Seidman, professor of economics at the University of Chicago, Paul William Preisler, a professor of biochemistry at Washington University, and Stanton Smith of Chattanooga, Tennessee. The remaining five members of the council were not partisan in the fight over Local 5, therefore not hostile to the TU. Jerome Davis, president of the AFT, was not supportive of ousting the TU because he had become a strong advocate of academic freedom after he was denied tenure at Yale Divinity School and was defended by Local 5 as well as the AFT.[5] The union should have been able to survive a vote.

However, Stalin's purges and the Hitler-Stalin nonaggression pact fueled opponents of the TU, and Local 5's decision to shift its rhetoric from popular front to imperialist war convinced many the union was a Party front. In March 1941 when Simon Beagle, a teacher at PS 83 in Manhattan and a former member of the TU executive board, was asked by the Rapp-Coudert Committee why he had resigned, he declared that the union was Communist dominated: "they paralleled the political line of the Communist Party." Philip Locker, a teacher at Lafayette High School and a member of the executive board, told the Rapp-Coudert Committee he suspected that the TU leadership was associated with the Communist Party, citing its "affiliation with the American League for Peace and Democracy, and affiliation with the American Labor Party," as well as its involvement in the emergency peace mobilization convention in Chicago the last weekend in August 1940. The convention, organized by the American Communist Party, protested FDR's policy of providing military and financial aid to the enemies of Nazi Germany. The TU's participation was a clear indication that it had joined the Party in abandoning the antifascist campaign.[6]

The TU's failure to take a more independent position helped to discredit it among AFT members. But there were other reasons for its loss of support within the national. The left had become a target of state and local government committees investigating Communist control of organizations. One such committee was the Rapp-Coudert Committee, whose investigations caused fifty professors, most of them from the City University of New York, to lose their positions. Although few public school teachers were fired, the committee obtained the TU's membership list, called a number of teachers before it, and created files on several TU members, noting their affiliation with the Communist Party. These files would become crucial in the Board of Education's campaign against the TU in the 1950s. The committee also investigated a number of teachers affiliated with Nazi and fascist organizations.

The executive board of the AFT had not been hostile to the Communist Party in the late 1930s, when it adopted a resolution calling for the release of Industrial Workers of the World members Tom Mooney and Warren Billings, who were serving life sentences for setting off a bomb in San Francisco's Market Plaza. When Mooney was pardoned in 1939, the AFT's newspaper, the *American Teacher*, published an interview of Mooney by Haakon Chevalier, president of the University of California Local. Another AFT resolution called for the release from prison of Fred Beal, a member of the Communist Party convicted of killing a police officer in Gastonia, North Carolina. However, when Beal decided to leave the Party, a member of Local 5 successfully had the resolution removed before a vote was taken.[7] TU opponents of the resolution were able to convince the majority of AFT members that the leadership of the AFT was controlled by Communists and was opposed to the interests of teachers. George Counts, a supporter of the guild and a close associate of the president of the International Ladies Garment Union, the fierce anti-Communist David Dubinsky, ran for president of the AFT in 1939. Counts managed to defeat Jerome Davis, a supporter of the TU, by fourteen votes; however, the new president then had to deal with a split council. Before the election the executive council consisted of seventeen members, six opposed to taking action against Local 5, seven in favor of expulsion, and four who were neutral. TU supporters Mary Grossman, who was head of the Philadelphia local, Hendley, and Doxey Wilkerson were reelected to the council in 1939, assuring the TU's security.[8]

Counts raised the red issue to convince teachers of the dangers of Communist infiltration in the union, asserting his opposition to Communism and other totalitarian, antidemocratic ideologies. Count's campaign was helped by the strong anti-Communist atmosphere in 1940. Appalled by news of the nonaggression pact, even Roger Baldwin, head of the American Civil Liberties Union, took action to root out Communists from that organization's ranks. Although he had resisted joining the anti-Communist camp, pressure within the ACLU convinced Baldwin to support a resolution barring people who belonged to "any political organization which supports totalitarian dictatorship in any country." The resolution, which was adopted by the body, specifically noted the Communist Party.[9]

In May 1940 the TU suffered another major blow when a number of teachers formed the Independent Group, dedicated to eliminating Communist domination of Local 5. While the leadership of the local boasted that membership in the TU had increased since the defections of 1935, the Independent Group claimed that teachers were leaving the union, without offering any evidence for its assertion. Still, the fact that a large number of unmarked ballots had been returned supported the accusation. The problem was a growing distrust of TU leadership. The Central Trades and

Labor Council had made it clear that it would only reconsider reconciling with Local 5 if Communists were removed from its leadership. The Central Trades and Labor Council's position, supported the Independent Group's argument that Communist domination isolated the TU from the trade union movement.[10] The Independent Group argued that the union leadership "fell in line" with the Communist Party by supporting "Stalin's agents" in the American Labor Party, subverted the economic interests of teachers for the political benefit of the Communist Party, and zigzagged on issues in order to suit Party policies. During the popular front era, for instance, the TU, like the CPUSA, supported Mayor LaGuardia and "soft pedaled the campaign against the Mayor's slash in the budget." When the Communist Party broke with LaGuardia, the TU also reversed itself and created picket campaigns against the mayor's policies. Although the TU accused its critics of red-baiting, the union's actions reinforced the claim that it was more than willing to adopt the Communist Party's positions. [11]

The Independent Group backed George Counts and accused the TU of a "character assassination campaign against the AFT president, designed to help Communists to gain control of the national organization." The Independent Group argued that the Communist-dominated TU administration could not maintain control "if all the union members made it their duty to participate in union meetings and activities."[12] Despite the Independent Group's crusade, it was unable to attract enough people to run a full slate in the union election of 1940, fielding no candidates for president and vice president and campaigning instead for the executive board and delegates to the AFT. The Communist leadership continued to control the TU, but Local 5 was becoming increasingly isolated. The resignations of teachers from the TU meant that the union was becoming less politically diverse, and it was simply left in the hands of those who shared the same political ideology. While the Independent Group could not muster a full slate or wrest control from the leadership, its campaign should not be seen as a failure. Clearly, it met one of its objectives: to weaken Local 5 at the national level by reiterating that the local was Communist controlled and that action needed to be taken against it.

To assure a victory for anti-Communist forces at the upcoming AFT convention, a new caucus was created to run viable candidates for the council and offices. The Joint Progressive Caucus, headed by Counts, nominated a number of familiar names for regional vice presidents such as Michael Eck,

John Connors, and Mark Starr. Although famed African American political scientist Ralph Bunche ran for vice president at large, he was not an AFT member in good standing, and his name was eventually withdrawn. Layle Lane, once on the executive board of the TU, ran in his place. One name on the Joint Progressive Caucus slate was surprising, George Axtelle, a former supporter of the Teachers Union who had come to the conclusion that the union was dominated by Communists and followed the dictates of the Comintern. In its campaign literature, the Joint Progressive Caucus contended that it opposed Communists and other groups whose aims were to bring the organization under the control of subversive foreign or domestic influence. All sixteen candidates representing the Joint Progressive Caucus were elected to the executive board of the AFT in 1940 at the national convention in Buffalo, replacing a number of Communist-leaning teachers and sealing the fate of the TU.[13]

The new leadership of the AFT did not immediately take action to remove Local 5. Instead, the national organization arranged a meeting between the TU and the Teachers Guild, with the former hoping to work out a compromise between the two groups. The *New York Times* (September 22, 1940) announced that a meeting between the guild and TU would take place at Counts's home with some AFT executive council members present. Failing a merger, the TU hoped that both groups would agree to work cooperatively, opposing cuts to state aid and teacher salary reductions and fighting to reduce class size. But it opposed granting a charter to a rival union. In a letter to executive council members and heads of AFT union locals, Hendley warned that another union competing for membership in the same schools where the TU operated would lead to confusion. Taking a swipe at the AFT executive council, he declared, if splinter groups formed, that "no local in the American Federation of Teachers can feel secure." However, guild officials insisted: unless the TU was willing to "clean house" and the "Communist leadership" resign, there would be no merger or cooperation.[14] The TU made offers to entice guild members: the merger would place each union on an equitable basis; Local 5 would assume the responsibility for Linville's pension, and it agreed to work out a plan of representation satisfactory to both organizations.[15]

Despite the Teachers Union's efforts, there was no merger. Rebecca Simonson, president of the guild, rejected the merger offer, arguing that the same issues that led to the walkout were still plaguing the TU: "Communist Party line dominated Local 5, and . . . political factionalism persisted. The same ground was again covered in the discussion at Professor Counts' home. . . . Since no changes have taken place in Local 5 and since the basic philosophies of the guild and the union remain widely divergent, the guild representatives once more rejected the merger proposal."[16]

To the dismay of the TU and to the delight of those calling for revocation of the union's charter, eighteen members who identified themselves as "leaders" of the organization publicly announced their resignation in the fall of 1940. The TU issued a statement accusing the opposition of dual unionism and using the public resignations to make it seem as though Local 5 was "disintegrating."[17] The TU refuted the assertion by those who resigned that they were prominent leaders; only six of those identified by the *New York Times* were active in union affairs or attended union meetings, and only two or three would be recognizable to the membership. Despite these protestations, the resignations boosted the efforts by those in the AFT who were in favor of granting a charter to the guild and revoking the charter of the TU. The resignations were more evidence that Local 5 was Communist dominated.[18]

The union did not directly address the charges of close ties to the Communist Party. It did, however, accuse the opposition of using the red issue to damage it. Opponents of the TU distributed the *New York Times* article in schools on the same day the TU issued a leaflet requesting contributions from teachers for its lobbying campaign in Albany. Most of all, the union leadership feared the resignations would intensify the attack by the Rapp-Coudert Committee. In fact, TU officials argued that the committee was attacking Local 5 because the union was taking the case of education to the public arena, undermining the state legislature's plans to gut public education.[19]

The TU gathered all its opponents into one basket, accusing them of being "reactionary and Fascist." Those who used the red issue were helping to destroy the trade unions and the civil liberties of the nation. TU officials did not distinguish between antitrade unionists, supporters of fascism, and those who were both pro-trade unionists and democratic but objected to the political agenda of the Communist Party. The union defended itself against the red charge by claiming that, of the thousands of acts taken by the Communist Party and the union, just three or four were repeatedly cited as proof that Local 5 was Communist controlled. The Teachers Union noted that its support of FDR in 1936, New Deal legislation, and "collective security in an attempt to stave off this World War" were used by its enemies to prove the Communist connection. Most Americans supported these goals, suggesting that the local had more in common with average Americans than with the Communist Party. In an attempt to demonstrate its independence, the union gave examples of how it differed from the Communist Party: the union held that true defense grew out of education and other social legislation, implying that the Communist Party only advocated a military solution; it condemned FDR's infringement on New Deal legislation, unlike the Party, which refrained from all criticism of the president; it never discussed the Hitler-Stalin pact, suggesting that it had no position on the issue. While the union did not deny supporting the left-wing American Labor Party and Michael Quill, its candidate for the City Council, it also supported "right-wing" candidates not supported by the Communist Party.

The union also denied that in order to conform to the shifting opinion of Communist Party it had changed its position on the Ludlow amendment, which called for a national referendum on any declaration of war by Congress. The Communist Party had not issued a public statement on the amendment. When Ludlow was first introduced in 1935, at the beginning of the popular front, it did not receive the support of the Communist Party and the Teachers Union. However, after the Soviet Union signed the nonaggression pact with Germany, the TU reversed its position. Not willing to address why it changed course, the union simply brushed off criticism and fell back on the familiar argument that red-baiting tactics were being used to convince people to leave the TU and join the guild.[20]

The TU argued that, since the Communist Party did not issue a statement on the Ludlow amendment, there was no way TU members could know the position of the Party. This position lacked credibility because the issue was most likely discussed in clubs and section meetings. While it is true that the union did not publicly discuss the nonaggression pact, the parallel timing of its shift and the Party's shift from popular front and collective security to anti-imperialist rhetoric was more than a coincidence.

Although the union repudiated the allegations of the opposition, which portrayed its supporters as progressives, independents, and liberals, it could not deny the losses in membership. However, the TU leadership did win a major victory at its September meeting, when a proposal calling for a dual union was defeated seventeen hundred to twenty. But this lopsided win was another strong indication that members who disagreed with the leadership had fled the union.[21] Defending the strength of the union, officials asserted that TU membership stood at sixty-three hundred, or one-fifth of the AFT, and that, at least half of the three hundred who had left the union were substitutes who had lost their jobs. The number of people in arrears was normal at a time when teachers were returning from vacation, and, in fact, the dues payment for September was above the previous year. The TU denied it had been expelled from the Central Trades and Labor Council because of Communism, attributing its suspension to a 1938 call for a conference of AFL locals to reopen negotiations with the CIO. The Communist charge came after the suspension and only when the opposition, which supported the petition for a resolution between the AFL and the CIO, began its red baiting. But the Central Trades did refuse to accept the TU among its ranks, charging the local was Communist dominated.[22]

With no chance of a merger between the guild and Local 5, the only way to assure the guild a charter was to revoke Local 5's. On December 29, 1940, the AFT's new executive council, meeting in Chicago, voted to investigate the Teachers Union, the College Union (Local 537), and the Philadelphia Teachers Union (Local 192), claiming all three were Communist controlled.[23] At the hearing, Charles Hendley spoke on behalf of Local 5; in spite of his testimony, the council voted to revoke the charter of the TU. There were a number of charges leveled at Local 5, among them, promoting dual unionism by assisting in organizing school custodians for a CIO chapter; accepting vocational teachers into its ranks, in spite of the fact that an AFT local existed for them, thus fostering factionalism within the chapter; bringing the AFT executive council into disrepute; being expelled by the Central Trades and Labor Council of Greater New York; and acting in ways contrary to democracy.[24]

In a thirty-five-page response, Local 5 noted that the effort to revoke its charter was not new.[25] Complaining that the AFT's investigation was "one-sided" and used materials it had taken months to gather while providing Local 5 with little time to answer the charges, the union pointed out that the investigation was being conducted at the same time as the Rapp-Coudert Committee attack. The fact that the press had received news of the charges before the local did was a "breach of trade union ethics." The investigation was based on a report of a committee created in August 1940 "to assist Local 5 of New York in securing reinstatement in the Central Trades and

Local Council." However, the committee members—George Counts, James Souba, and John D. Connors—all were opponents of Local 5 and staunchly anti-Communist. Connors, vice president of the AFT, actually became an informer, attending the New York State Communist Party's Convention and reporting back to the AFT. The three-person committee recommended giving charters to the guild and other anti-TU teacher bodies, creating a regency to run the affairs of Local 5, and revoking the union's charter.[26]

Local 5 declared that its expulsion would be a "flagrant violation of the letter and spirit of the constitution of the Federation," splitting the ranks and weakening the AFT during a period when unity was most needed to combat right wing attacks on education. Reviving old charges answered a decade earlier and dismissed by two AFT conventions was a legal as well as an ethical violation. Charges that Local 5 was a Communist front were hard to prove; allegations were repeatedly made. Such attacks, according to the union, revealed an "utter lack of constructive program" by the executive council. The council should reconsider its vote for revocation for the "sake of an effective and united American Federation of Teachers."[27]

Despite Local 5's protest, the council reiterated its charge that Communism was at the heart of the revocation battle. In the April issue of the AFT's *American Teacher*, the council proclaimed that so "long as the Communist Party is a significant force in the American Federation of Teachers, we can be united only under their program. It is, therefore, necessary to eliminate this influence."[28]

The article cited five charges against Local 5:

1. The union's internal affairs have led to factionalism and disharmony, and, as a result of this turmoil, the chapter lost hundreds of members through nonpayment of dues and massive resignations.
2. After the 1940 AFT convention, Local 5 sent to officers of locals communications attacking members of the executive council, using unfounded allegations.
3. Local 5's negative publicity aimed at the council led to decline in membership nationwide.
4. Local 5 had been suspended from the Central Trades and Labor Council of Greater New York, and William Green, president of the American Federation of Teachers, contended that the suspension was justified because of the conduct of the TU.

5. The local has participated in planned strategies that were adverse to democracy.[29]

The revocation resolution also included the college teachers' and the Philadelphia chapters, accusing them of being controlled by Communists. The three locals presented their case to the national membership in the April edition of *American Teacher*. In a lengthy draft of the April statement, Locals 5, 192, and 537 alleged that the executive council and pro-capitalist institutions, such as the New York State Chamber of Commerce and the Taxpayers Federation, were encroaching on democracy. The three unions portrayed themselves as a progressive force in the labor movement, drawing the ire of William Green. Their expulsion, they asserted, would result in a lackluster national union following a nonprogressive leadership. Attempting to discredit the charges, they hammered away at the theme that the affair was motivated by political concerns. The AFT was in excellent condition in August 1940, and charter revocations were not justified. Between 1936 and 1940 the national had experienced its greatest growth, thanks to the efforts of the three locals.

The three unions also denied engaging in an "undue amount of political activity" harmful to the AFT. Expulsion, they continued, would not lead to healthy relations with the AFL. The dual unionism charge was without merit. The executive council, not the three locals, was responsible for factionalism because it supported "small discredited factional groups in these locals." The executive council had relied on the testimony of former members and refused to accept statements from current representatives of Locals 5, 192, and 537. The locals were handicapped when preparing their statement because they did not receive a copy of the February 5 and 16 executive council minutes until March 10; they were required to submit a response to the national five days later, a short period of time for full-time teachers and those responsible for running their locals.[30]

The claim was unfounded that Locals 5, 192, and 537 were Communist fronts, whose only concern was the security of Moscow rather than of teachers, and that they were undemocratic. Besides noting their members' success as union activists, the three locals gave detailed accounts of their democratic procedures and practices. According to the unions, their constitutions gave their membership "absolute and unequivocal power to determine policy." They all claimed they held monthly membership meetings where "free discussion" took place and equal opportunity was given to opposing sides. The executive council meetings took place every two weeks, and their decisions were subject to review by the membership. Council meetings were open to the membership. Annual elections for officers and executive board members were held, and nominations were made from the floor of membership meetings. All elections were conducted by secret balloting.[31]

Pointing to their democratic procedures, Locals 5, 192, and 537 argued that such procedures made Communist domination impossible. The denial that Communists dominated the unions may have been true; however, some of the leading activists and officials of these organizations were members of the Communist Party. Moreover, the executive council pointed to a report given at a CPUSA convention claiming that there were several hundred Communists in Local 5. The TU's response that the claim was "greatly exaggerated" was not convincing. But because Communists were in key positions of leadership in the three locals, does it mean their aims were one and the same as those of the Soviet Union?

The unions' position on international and domestic issues was enough to raise suspicion about the motivations of the three unions. As a case in point consider that although Local 5 maintained it had dropped collective security after Hitler invaded Czechoslovakia, there does not seem to be any evidence to support this claim. Nowhere in its literature does it announce that it dropped collective security because of the invasion. The TU's assertion that it was joining other trade unions that worked to keep the United States out of the war seemed on the surface to be a valid point. John L. Lewis, president of the United Mine Workers, accused FDR of trying to involve the United States in the war and even endorsed Wendell Wilkie, the Republican candidate for president, in 1940. But Lewis had isolated himself from the rest of the labor movement. He had resigned as president of the CIO, keeping a promise that if labor went for Roosevelt he would step down as head of the industrial union. Indeed, labor did support FDR and his domestic and foreign policies. Besides the UMW, the other unions that opposed FDR's foreign policy were Communist dominated, such as the Fur Workers and the Transport Workers. So the TU's claim that it was joining those in the labor movement who were working for peace was not convincing.[32] When Hitler attacked the Soviet Union in 1941, the CPUSA again reversed its position and supported an antifascist alliance, so did Local 5. In the eyes of many, its changing position on the war made the union seem like a tool of Moscow and gave ammunition to its enemies.

The three locals refuted the charge that political activity resulted in unfavorable publicity, causing a reduction of membership. The unions denied that they were more political than other unions, and argued, in fact, that their political activities were in support of teachers. The activities in question included support of a resolution advocating aid to Loyalist Spain, affiliation with the American League for Peace and Democracy, affiliation with the American Labor Party, and participation in several May Day parades. It should be noted that Local 192 claimed that it was not involved in any political activity, while the other two locals confessed such involvement but claimed it was "directed towards strengthening the forces of labor and towards keeping our country at peace."[33]

Despite the three unions' efforts at self defense, at its 1941 convention, the AFT voted to revoke the charter of Locals 5, 537, and 192 and to grant a charter to the New York Teachers Guild.[34] Although it was kicked out of the AFT, the TU did not remain an orphan of the labor movement for long. After failing to repeal the AFT's decision to oust it, on September 19, 1943, the TU joined the ranks of the Congress of Industrial Organizations as the Teachers Union of the City of New York, Local 555 of the United Public Workers of America, CIO.[35]

The association with the CIO, a left-leaning union that organized local, state, and federal municipal workers, was a just fit because of the TU's identification with industrial unionism and emphasis on an organizing model. In its new constitution, the TU took the opportunity to codify its long-standing objectives of fighting bigotry and fostering working relationship with parents, community, and civic organizations as well as other labor unions. The union dedicated itself to expanding the "educational opportunities" of New Yorkers by working for a decent education budget and increasing services. It pledged to eliminate "discrimination in education on account of sex, color, race, religion, or political beliefs, or affiliations." After the revocation episode with the AFT, the inclusion of a clause disavowing discrimination due to one's political affiliation was no surprise. True to its type of unionism, the TU still pledged to work with community and civic organizations with the objective of assuring effective educational services. In its new constitution, the union promised to encourage "deliberation and action on social problems as a professional obligation" and promote the "active participation of teachers in organized labor's efforts to improve the standards of living and the conditions of work of all employees."[36]

As World War II approached, the Teachers Union, now affiliated with the left-leaning UPWA, would freely forge ahead with its brand of unionism, making issues of social justice a priority. In particular, the union led an intense battle against racial bigotry, linking it with the U.S. war effort.

4 / TO BE A GOOD AMERICAN

The New York City Teachers Union and the Issue of Race
During the Second World War

In 1942 May Quinn, a civics teacher at Public School 227 in Brooklyn, read to her class an anti-Semitic leaflet titled "The First Americans." The publication listed the names of "brave Americans" who served honorably during wartime. Jewish Americans were absent from the list, a particularly glaring omission in a city with a notable Jewish population. The leaflet also contained the names of Americans who performed dishonorable acts, and all those names that Quinn read from the leaflet that day were Jewish. Quinn also praised Hitler and Mussolini. She called Jews a "dull race," Italians "greasy," and she praised the cause of racial segregation.[1]

Fourteen teachers reported Quinn's actions to school authorities and the New York City Teachers Union highlighted the affair in its weekly publication, *New York Teacher News*, by placing it into a wartime context. In one issue of the paper it was reported that Quinn's fourteen accusers blamed her for inciting racial tension, creating disunity, and undermining the war effort. The fourteen also charged their colleague with spreading "defeatist propaganda and anti-Semitic slanders in the classroom." The *New York Teacher News* pointed to the fact that she was defended by the *Signpost*, the organ of the pro-fascist American Education Association, headed by Milo MacDonald, the principal of Bushwick High School, who was associated with the rabidly anti-Semitic priest, Charles E. Coughlin. *New York Teacher News* also pointed out that MacDonald wrote for the *National Republic*, a publication edited by Walter S. Steele, who U.S. Secretary of the Interior Harold Ickes claimed belonged to a "Fascist ring in America." Thus the union concluded that Quinn was in close contact with those whom the union labeled seditious forces, implying they were pro-Nazi fifth columnists conspiring with the enemies abroad.[2]

The union did not portray the Quinn incident simply as evidence of a bigoted school employee who should be fired for her outlandish acts. The episode was also described as a flagrant act of disloyalty during wartime. Quinn was depicted as an adversary of the American people who had committed treasonous acts, causing disunity and undermining the war effort. Her crime was more than an act of racial bigotry or upholding white supremacy; her transgression threatened the very existence of the United States during a time of crisis. May Quinn was characterized by the TU as un-American, for the union saw bigotry itself as un-American.[3]

Historian Leonard Dinnerstein notes that during World War II there was a "rising tide of anti-Semitism" in the United States as the country became more involved in European affairs. The Teachers Union was fully aware of the heightened anti-Semitism in the United States and therefore took action. Historian Ruth Jacknow Markowitz contends that "anti-Semitism caused many Jewish teachers to become sensitive to the invidious effects of bigotry of all kinds."[4] The explicit ideology of Nazi Germany, with its program of racial genocide, made the issue of race a prominent subject of discussion during World War II.[5] The war provided TU members who led its antiracist campaign with an opportunity to intensify their efforts. Nazism also gave the union's antiracist campaign an opening to point to the ongoing racial discriminatory policies and practices in the United States and the impact of institutional racism, particularly within the New York City school system.

From the late 1920s to mid 1930s, members of the Communist Party declared that African Americans were a nationally oppressed group that had the right to self-determination. The Party's theory for explaining the state of black America was referred to as the nation within a nation or the black belt thesis. The Communist Party argued that blacks should form a nation in the southern "black belt" where most blacks in the country resided. Moreover, blacks were also seen by the Party as a revolutionary segment of society who were essential in the working-class struggle.[6] Although it is not clear if the Rank and File caucus ever advocated the nation within a nation thesis, by 1936 and throughout World War II the union, in large part, shared the politics of the popular front. This movement, which began in 1935, was made up of a coalition of the Communist Party, the Socialist Party, independent socialists and leftists, the CIO and other labor groups, antifascist groups, social democrats, and the New Deal's left wing.

The movement championed several causes that included labor's right to organize, industrial democracy, the Loyalist government in Spain and an independent Ethiopia, refugees fleeing Hitler's Germany, and the abolition of lynching as well as other forms of racial terror.[7] The TU had diligently supported the black freedom struggle since 1935, when the union's Communist-led caucus gained control. Indeed, during the popular front years, Communists in the TU continued its crusade to save the lives of the young black men sentenced to death in the Scottsboro, Alabama, case, and it campaigned against lynching and other forms of racism. In particular, the union promoted black history and culture, and it argued that this history disproved the claim that African Americans were a detriment to the nation and had contributed little to America. Its approach was not only a means to prove that blacks were not inferior but also to highlight the role played by people of African origins in making America a great country. Moreover, the union argued that the fight against racism was important because racial discrimination not only hurt blacks but was also harmful to whites, partly because it deprived them of knowledge of the rich heritage of black culture and the greater contributions that blacks could make to the country if allowed to participate fully.

The Teachers Union effort on behalf of civil rights during the war years strongly suggests that American Communists, despite having adopted Moscow's position, were as diligent as ever in their challenge to racial inequality. By 1942 racism was not described by the union as simply endemic to American society and harmful to all Americans because of its denial of democracy. The TU argued, further, that racism was un-American. Racists were depicted as agents of Nazism and fascism who were working for the Axis powers in clear violation of the American principles of liberty, justice, and equality. The struggle to improve race relations between 1942 and 1945 was aimed not only at eliminating racism but also at helping to bring about national unity in order to defeat America's enemies at home and abroad. The union positioned the struggle for racial equality in a broad context, making fighting racism, anti-Semitism, and other forms of discrimination synonymous with patriotism. Consequently, for the TU antiracism became integrally linked to America's war effort.

Another important discussion during this period was on the best ways to eliminate racism. The union also advocated intercultural education for children, teachers, and community groups, informing them on the cultures of racial and ethnic groups in the United States and turning to cultural anthropology to further national unity.

During the war the union continued all its prewar anti-racist efforts. The Harlem Committee remained active and the union even helped form the Bedford-Stuyvesant-Williamsburg Council, a group made up of TU members and parents from the two Brooklyn neighborhoods. The organization pushed for replacing day-to-day substitute teachers with those who held regular licenses, a full day of children's instruction, an end to "discriminatory zoning," construction of a new school building, and providing hot lunches.[8] But the war changed the context of such antiracist efforts. Racism and bigotry were presented by the union as the intellectual property of fascists and Nazis. Their elimination was now part of a national war effort

RACE AND THE WAR YEARS

In March 1938 the union's monthly magazine, *The New York Teacher*, published an article by Doxey Wilkerson, a professor of education at Howard University, examining caste in America. Wilkerson argued that the New York City educational system assured that blacks would remain locked in America's caste hierarchy. Despite the lack of de jure racial oppression in the North, racism nonetheless was still a reality, and the institution where it reared its ugly head the highest was the school system. According to Wilkerson, "the most decrepit school buildings in the city" were in Harlem. He blamed the Board of Education for not remedying the horrible conditions.

In addition to having inferior school buildings, black students were relegated to vocational training instead of to an academic program that would allow them entrée into college. The concentration of black children in vocational schools and educational programs was not by accident but by design. School counselors who lacked an appreciation of the potential of poor black children and who were ignorant of black history and culture assumed blacks were incapable of doing vigorous academic work.[9]

Inferior facilities and the lack of opportunities were not the only type of bigotry that existed in northern schools. Wilkerson declared that a deliberate "mental crucifixion" of black children was taking place. In schools in Harlem black students were not allowed to use the swimming pools, were assigned seats in the back of the classroom, and were excluded from extracurricular activities and social events. "Thus, the Negro child is made to realize that he is not an integral part of the social group with which he is thrown, but rather, that he is a thing apart, isolated, ostracized, somehow not quite like his classmates."[10]

The problem of discrimination in both northern and southern schools was inherent in the structure of American society, Wilkerson suggested. This form of discrimination in the schools was maintaining a "horizontal division of the population on the basis of racial origin, into groups which are supposed to occupy *permanent positions* of superior or inferior social rank" (emphasis added).

The racial caste system was not only detrimental to blacks but to the entire society because it upheld American fascism. "To the furtherance of fascism in America, a great service is rendered by the persistence of educational and other forms of caste." Wilkerson did not tie this form of fascism to Hitler or Mussolini. Instead, he linked it to the American caste system.[11]

The Wilkerson article is indicative of the Teachers Union's emphasis on the struggle for racial equality, an emphasis it did not put on the back burner during the war. Rather, it continued to feature the Jim Crow issue in its publications, lashing out against institutional racism and the deliberate attempt to deny blacks the rights of full citizenship. For example, in the October 2, 1943, edition of the weekly *New York Teacher News*, the union contended that American democracy was clearly flawed because of the existence of the poll tax. It noted that eight southern states used this infamous Jim Crow method to deny black citizens the right to the franchise. In fact, the practice denied 99 percent of the population the right to vote in some places in the South.[12]

The Teachers Union did not limit its attack on racism and Jim Crow to the southern states during the war. It also continued to hammer away at northern racism. It accused the Hillburn, New York, school district, for instance, of trying to create "Jim Crow" schools by assigning fifty-six black children to dilapidated, segregated shacks serving as classrooms. The Board of Education in Hillburn was blamed for violating the law against segregation by gerrymandering and rezoning the district, thus forcing the black children to attend classes in the broken down building. The parents of the fifty-six black children refused to send them to the schools and instead paid for private instruction while they struggled against the school district. The NAACP represented the parents in court against State Commissioner of Education George

D. Stoddard. Calling the situation "Jim Crow North," the union praised the parents for their courage in not caving in to the threats by school officials to invoke the truancy law and other means of punishment.[13]

In addition to attacking racism in both the North and South, one cannot help noticing that in the war years the union also put the struggle against Jim Crow into a larger framework than previously. For example, in an October 2, 1943, *New York Teacher News* article on the poll tax, Senator Rankin of Mississippi was not only depicted as a racist but was also specifically referred to an anti-Semite. The TU argued that "the poll-tax will once more hamper our war effort," and that fighting the poll tax was more than a matter of racial justice; it was also a necessary strategy to defeat the Axis powers. It was clear that it was an American's patriotic duty to wage war against this undemocratic practice.[14]

The TU also labeled "northern Jim Crow" as Nazism and northern racists as allies of Hitler. In its criticism of those who claimed there was a crime wave in the predominantly black community of Bedford-Stuyvesant in 1943, the union argued that the charge was made to avert attention from the socioeconomic problems plaguing that community—poor housing, inadequate recreational facilities, dilapidated school buildings, and poverty. It specifically pointed its finger at the Hearst press, the *Daily News*, and the *Post* for concocting the notion of a crime wave. On several occasions the TU asserted that the publications of the Hearst press were pro-Nazi, and on one occasion it reported that Secretary of the Interior Harold Ickes named the Hearst- and the Patterson-McCormick newspaper "axis as among those 'powerful and active forces in this country that would rather see Hitler win the war, if the alternative is his defeat by a leadership shared in by the great Russian (Premier Stalin) and the great American (President Roosevelt).'" In an editorial titled "Hysteria-Fascist Pattern," the union also blamed Sumner Sirtl, head of the Midtown Civic League, for concocting the idea that there was a crime spree in Bedford-Stuyvesant. The union depicted Sirtl as a classic Nazi who, with his Midtown Civic Leaguers, advocated a fascist agenda that included pushing blacks out of Bedford-Stuyvesant and relocating them to Jamaica Bay, Queens. He also called for organizing armed white vigilante groups and gun clubs to protect whites against black people, leading the union to compare him to a Nazi who wanted to create a Brooklyn branch of storm troopers and SS men. It was Sirtl's fascist organization that petitioned the Brooklyn grand jury to take steps to stop the crime wave in Bedford-Stuyvesant.[15]

In addition to the Hearst publications and Sirtl, *New York Teacher News* also assigned responsibility for the crime wave concoction to John B. Snow of Hillburn, New York. According to the union, Snow never protested being labeled a "gentleman fascist," and the TU pointedly highlighted his use of Nazi rhetoric when he accused FDR of being a Communist and blamed Jews for causing World War II. The union also noted that he fought for "Jim Crowism in Hillburn." The union contended that Sirtl, Snow, the Hearst press and others who were pushing the crime wave story were creating disunity by scaring parents away from sending their children to schools in Bedford-Stuyvesant, clearly a way of hampering the war effort. The TU did not mince words when labeling those who headed the "Negro Smear." They were, it said, a "bigoted, fascist-minded interest and they have damaged the community and its schools."

Couching its argument in the language of patriotism, the union asserted, "we believe that the American way is best." The "American way" the union championed was its very own program, which it had advocated since before the war, to address poor conditions in black and Latino communities. "Provide better housing, more playgrounds, more nurseries, improve school buildings, reduce class size, give the children the care they need, and juvenile delinquency will be reduced. Concern for our neighbors inspires love and not race hatred."[16]

Along with equating Jim Crow with Nazism, the Teachers Union pointed to other overt acts of racism as evidence that a fifth column was functioning in the United States. Responding to the wave of anti-Semitic assaults that took place during the war, the union published on January 8, 1944 an article in its weekly titled "Anti-Semitism—A Call for Action." It claimed that recent anti-Semitic violence in Washington Heights, Brooklyn, and the Bronx was a "shocking reminder right in our own city that Nazis and their agents," operating in "our own country," were still trying to "change the outcome of the war by this [anti-Semitism] most potent of Hitler's weapons." The union pointed to a 1940 investigation disclosing that four hundred seven members of the New York City police department were members of the Christian Front, an anti-Semitic pro-Coughlin organization. As proof of the possible danger of further Nazi-style racist and anti-Semitic attacks and slurs, the union charged that twenty-three pro-fascists, who had been indicted by the government for sedition, were still at large and "carrying on their activities." Mayor LaGuardia and Police Commissioner Valentine, the

TU declared, should be forced to rid the police force of the pro-fascist element, and the U.S. attorney general, Francis Biddle, should prosecute those who had been indicted for sedition.[17]

The union praised *Facts and Fascism*, a book by investigative journalist George Seldes, for not only pointing out that "small-fry fascists have been magnificently exposed" in such magazines as *Sabotage* and *Undercover* but also for putting the spotlight on a group that Seldes claimed financed American fascism and other "native fascist forces," including the American Legion, Charles Lindbergh, and the *Reader's Digest*. Using a patriotic vernacular, the union claimed that the book's "significance in the struggle for victory lies in its challenge to those who love democracy to exert every effort of mind and will to fight wherever it becomes manifest."[18]

In its campaign to link racism and anti-Semitism in the U.S. to fifth-column activists, the union reported on a national conference to combat anti-Semitism organized by the American Jewish Congress in February 1944. At the conference, Attorney General Norris M. Little linked the work of racist and anti-Semitic groups in the United States "directly to Berlin." The union saw anti-Semitism and antiblack racism as two forms of fascism. Its critique emphasized the common cause between a union with a large Jewish membership and a city with a large minority and Jewish population.[19]

Many of the anti-Semitic actions taking place in New York City were being committed by boys age nine to seventeen who had no organizational affiliation. A special state investigation of anti-Semitic attacks in New York, headed by William B. Herlands, commissioner of the Department of Investigation, in 1943, pointed out that forty-one of the fifty-two anti-Semitic incidents in the city were the work of youths in that age group. The TU was well aware of the report. Despite the release of the Herlands Report, the union continued to argue that such attacks supported a fascist campaign to undermine the war effort. In a January 22, 1944, *New York Teacher News* editorial titled "Crush Anti-Semitism," the union warned of continuing racist attacks, including desecrations, assaults, and vandalism, and declared that these acts "have brought the leering visage of fascism close to us." Although acknowledging the Herlands Report and its finding that children were committing most of the racist acts, the union nonetheless linked the acts to a distant racist terror. It recognized the effort that many groups, including the Jewish, Catholic, and Protestant teachers associations, were making to fight anti-Semitism, however, it lamented that there did not seem to be a broad sense of urgency to create the unity necessary to address the immediate danger. In fact, while a coalition of nations was defeating Nazism overseas, "Hitlerism here at home may make our America the concentration camp of fascism."[20]

When Ralph Haller, principal of Andrew Jackson High School in Queens, issued a statement asserting that no student found guilty of taking part in racist activities would receive a diploma from his school, the union publicly praised him for taking tough action. An editorial in *Teacher News* featured a lengthy quote from the Jackson High School principal's statement asserting that he considered racist acts "totally in contradiction to everything that the America of today or the America which we hope to have tomorrow stands for." Haller said that he considered such activity "so completely un-American," he would not give his signature on a diploma to any student guilty of partaking in any racist activity. The union expressed delight that a school had met its responsibilities to let students know that racial intolerance was a "fascist weapon with which the enemy planned to conquer the world. It is against our own national interests, against our own safety to permit acts of violence against any minority group to pass unnoticed and unpunished."[21]

At the same time that the Teachers Union was pushing those in power to take an aggressive position against fascist enemies from within, it also adopted a rehabilitative approach, especially when it came to children, towards whom it clearly had a dual message. While it depicted youths committing anti-Semitic and racist acts as fascist sympathizers and advocated taking punitive measures to stop them, it did not seek to criminalize them completely. Instead, it stressed the rehabilitative effects of education. Nazis were not born, they were made, and with the proper de-Nazification curriculum they could be purged of their racist notions. Thus teachers had a special role in the fight for democracy; they were to use the best weapon at their disposal, education, in order to win the battle for the hearts and minds of students. The union even adopted the slogan "schools at war," and in March 1942 it published a pamphlet titled "Schools for Victory." The pamphlet emphasized the role that schools must play in the war effort, including teaching black history, as a way to fight fascism and win the allegiance of African Americans. Listing its accomplishments for 1945, the union declared that it had campaigned for the "fullest use of schools for the persecution of the war."[22]

In its educational campaign to combat anti-Semitism and "other forms of Nazi-inspired racist activities" in New York, the union created a Committee to Combat Discrimination. The committee met weekly with the specific purpose of proposing ways the union could address racism in city schools, neighborhoods, and the nation. The committee circulated a petition calling on the school board to create a program to fight racism, and it also established a subcommittee to collect data, work with civic organizations, and create a speakers bureau. It proposed a plan of action that called on the board to organize a conference of teachers, parents, and civic groups to work on a school curriculum that would inculcate ideals of equality and tolerance. The major objective of the committee was to build unity and help achieve "victory over Nazism."[23]

Remaining committed to the Communist Party's post-popular front line on the need to prosecute the war, the union reinterpreted its program of improving working conditions for teachers by arguing that the schools were a "bulwark of democracy," therefore requiring the unity of all "anti-fascist teachers and supervisors." Education, the union claimed, had been attacked by Hitler, and these attacks "will continue more sharply in an effort to extinguish enlightenment and culture and to pervert the schools to serve the needs of despotism and obscurantism." Teachers were obligated to ignore their "minor differences for the large objective to preserve and expand education as an integral part of the defense of American freedom and independence." The TU proposed that every aspect of school activity should be redirected toward achieving the maximum "contribution to the defense of freedom," including matters of curriculum, administration, and supervision for the war. "By affording living examples of democracy in action our schools can truly function as effective weapons in the arsenal of democracy." One way of guaranteeing the continued existence of democracy was to assure the health and welfare of children. In fact, the union contended, the Selective Service Medical Board's rejection of a number of young men for physical deficiencies was proof of the importance of children's welfare.[24]

The TU raised the issue of racial disparity by noting that health services were "particularly important in under-privileged communities such as Harlem, the Lower East Side, and other such communities." By singling out predominantly black and Latino communities, the union was indirectly accusing the board of neglect, but without proclaiming the school board was guilty of racism. Instead, it couched its argument in terms of the necessity of war preparation. It also argued that a strong democracy must assure all its citizens the same care and services.[25]

Besides pressuring board officials and government to take action that would address racial disparity and pushing for racial unity during the war, the TU also called on individual teachers to contribute to those objectives. The "teacher as a citizen" could "elect win-the-war candidates" and engage in "morale building" and rationing. Revising curricula to "stress the meaning of democracy" was also pushed by the union. This meant teaching "citizenship" by discussing and evaluating local problems, participating in get-out-the vote drives, and studying the contrast between "Hitlerism and democracy." One activity for older students suggested by the TU was to take a "census of nationalities" in their community, noting the contribution of each "to culture, as a basis for sponsoring a project on nationalities nights."[26]

Winning the war was a priority for the union, and it sought ways to convince the public that its program was not benefiting just teachers but the entire nation. Even the TU's annual conference reflected how the union framed its old concerns in the language of winning the war. In keeping with its seventh annual conference's theme, "Education for Victory in 1943," the union warned that a victory for the Axis "would destroy our national independence. . . . Conquered and enslaved by a ruthless invader, we would see swept aside every one of those pillars which [Thomas] Jefferson strove to establish and on which our way of life rests: equal justice, freedom of thought, of speech, of assembly and religion; and above all, the continuing heritage of public education." Moving away from the language used by a collective bargaining agency and substituting a war rhetoric, the union insisted that public schools were a "citadel and a fortress; a training-ground and a center of morale." The schools "must mobilize" for "victory," and, instead of educating, they had to "help in the training of thousands" who were going into the armed forces and the war industry. Moreover, each school had to "enlighten not only those within its walls, but the community which it serves" about the war.[27]

A crucial component part of the TU's emphasis at this conference was the fight against racism. One of the conference forums, "Through Unity to Victory," offered topics such as "The Negro in National Unity" and "Combating Anti-Semitism." Another forum, "Developing Manpower in the Secondary Schools," offered a discussion on "How Can Schools Help Eliminate the Discrimination Against the Employment of Negro Youth?" The union's annual award went posthumously to Dr. George Washington Carver (he died in 1943), whose work was "one of the highest expressions of the strivings of the Negro people" and a "granite monument" that would serve to disprove the "superior race theories and propaganda of the Nazis and inspire people everywhere to fight for victory and democracy."[28]

The Teachers Union insisted that the "Hitlerite poison of racism has taken a strong hold on our youth," but through education and providing students with information on blacks, Jews, and others Nazi ideology would be defeated.[29] The November 20, 1943 edition of *New York Teacher News* reported that a TU member and teacher at Mark Twain Junior High School in Brooklyn organized a school-wide student project examining issues of race and the war effort. Topics featured in the project were "Race Prejudice—A Hindrance to Victory," "Propaganda Analysis," race and racism, and the contribution of national and racial groups to America. The project praised America for being a "great democracy," but raised the question whether all its people are treated fairly and equally.[30]

The TU praised the United States government for organizing youth for the war effort by establishing a Junior Citizens Corps. "In time of war, when every available source of manpower is strained to the utmost, the importance of the energy of 14 million boys and girls cannot be overlooked." The Community Clearing House for War Services, which created the Victory Corps for Senior High Schools, formed the Junior Citizens Corps in order to organize preteens. The superintendent of schools authorized the Junior Corps in elementary and junior high schools. While participation was voluntary, the TU gave the program a ringing endorsement by saying this was an "opportunity for victory-minded teachers to vitalize and coordinate the war work in the schools." One benefit of mobilizing youth, according to the union, would be the reduction of juvenile delinquency.[31]

The TU called on the Board of Education to launch an all-out offensive and to "clean its own house" by investigating anti-Semitic employees, such as May Quinn and Milo MacDonald. In rallies held in the Bronx, Queens, and Manhattan in January 1944, Teachers Union representatives and others called for the Board of Education to create programs "of racial tolerance and understanding in the schools as well as Congress to pass anti-hate legislation."[32]

Practically all evils affecting the school system were now being couched in the language of hindering the war campaign. Rallies were held in the Bronx, Queens, and Manhattan by TU members, parents, and community organizations where teachers, leaders, and local legislators spoke out about the "threatening problems facing the community—anti-Semitism, anti-Negro discrimination, overcrowding and under manning of the schools." Overcrowding of schools and the lack of school personnel resulted in schools not being prepared to do their part for the war effort. Speakers for the union at the various rallies urged the Board of Education to create programs of racial tolerance and understanding in the schools and for those attending the rallies to support a number of hate crime bills including the Steingut-Wickman bill in the state legislature making it a crime to publish race-hate material.[33]

A major reason for the TU's fight against racism was its makeup. Although the union never kept records on its ethnic or racial makeup, by the 1930s an increasing number of Jews were entering the system. By 1940 56 percent of new teachers in the system were Jewish.[34]

Jewish Americans helped lead the fight against Nazism. As early as May 1933, the American Jewish Congress organized demonstrations against the persecution of Jews in Germany and the Nazi's burning of books by Jewish and non-Jewish authors. An estimated crowd of one hundred thousand demonstrated in New York City. Jewish leaders pressured President Roosevelt to take steps against the Nazi Final Solution.[35] Volunteers from fifty-two countries went to Spain to fight on the side of the leftist government during the Spanish Civil War. Between 25 and 30 percent of the international volunteers were Jewish. Of the three thousand American volunteers who served in the Abraham Lincoln Brigade, it is estimated that at least one-third were Jewish. Members of the Lincoln Brigade as well as those from other brigades joined because they saw it as an opportunity to fight Nazism and fascism.[36]

The union had carved out a space for itself and the public school system in the battle to defeat Nazi aggression and fight racism by advocating an educational program that would promote racial and ethnic harmony among children, parents, and communities. The effort to achieve national unity would assure that America's greatest resource, its people, would be behind the war effort to defeat the Axis powers abroad and Axis-style supporters at home.

INTERCULTURAL EDUCATION

The emergence of intercultural education in the 1930s provided yet another important way the TU could challenge racism. Intercultural education, the precursor to multiculturalism, emphasized that the teaching of the culture and history of immigrants and African Americans would lead to a better understanding and appreciation by the larger society of those groups. Intercultural education provided the union with a new language, new methods, and more innovative concepts for addressing bigotry in the schools and community. During the war, the TU called on the Board of Education to adopt an intercultural education plan providing teaching units appropriate for each grade level and course, and conferences for teachers and administrators.[37]

One of the most important promoters of intercultural education was Rachel Davis DuBois, a white Quaker born in 1892 and raised in southern New Jersey. Her politics and ideas were influenced by her friendly relationship with the African Americans who worked on her parents' farm as well as by her Quaker religious values. She was active in social reform movements, including the Grange and suffrage movements. After graduating from Bucknell College in 1914, DuBois began to teach at Glassboro High School in New Jersey. She attended the First International Conference of the Society of Friends in London in 1920, where she heard speakers describe British imperialism in India and Jamaica and the cruel treatment of African Americans in the United States, including during the 1919 race riot in Chicago and lynchings in the South. DuBois was so disturbed that she decided to take steps to heal the racial divide by seeking friendships across the color line. DuBois's views on race were also shaped by her travel to the South in 1921 where she witnessed Jim Crow first hand. In her autobiography she recalled seeing signs for "white" and "colored", reminders of how people of African origins were dehumanized in America. But she also had the opportunity to meet with the great African American scientist George Washington Carver, who impressed her deeply. She realized that she was in the "presence of not just a scientific genius, but a spiritual genius as well." She sat next to Carver at a dinner and attempted not to show her "ignorance." She later wrote that she could never forgive her "white social worlds for having sent me through high school and college, never preparing me for such experiences." Her encounters with Jim Crow and Carver would convince her of the need for intercultural education.[38]

Figure 4.1 Demonstration with sign asking for full employment and intercultural Education Program and Annual Salary for Subs. United Federation of Teachers, part 1, folder 521.

Her final inspiration was the work of W. E. B. Du Bois. (Despite their almost identical names, they were not related.) After reading Du Bois's "Race and War" in the *American Mercury*, Rachel DuBois claimed she had found her calling, one that she "must dedicate the rest of my life to." She contended that basic to the problem of peace and war is the problem of race. "I decided I must rid myself of my own ignorance about blacks in American life, not only reading books on the subject but by finding people in that group with whom I could become friends."[39]

Besides reaching across the color line for friendships, Rachel DuBois returned to teaching at Woodbury High School in New Jersey, where she decided to emphasize cultural diversity, with one effective avenue being the weekly assembly program. DuBois and other teachers in her school created the Woodbury Assembly Project, which brought an outside speaker representing a particular racial and/or ethnic group to an assembly and also presenting classes on the cultural contributions of that group. The idea was that the self-esteem of the featured races and nationalities would be bolstered while also making those outside the featured group more aware and appreciative of its accomplishments. DuBois did not limit her concerns to African Americans. She also included other racially and ethnically oppressed groups. "I suppose my sensitivity to the feelings of the black youth made me more aware of the other minority pupils—Jewish and the Italian Americans." DuBois did not agree with melting pot ideas that focused on the assimilation and "Americanization" of nationalities and races. Instead, her assembly programs recognized that all groups made important contributions to American life. They also went beyond the notion of tolerance, wanting instead to develop "sympathetic attitudes toward various races and nations" Rachel Davis DuBois's project of intercultural education stressed the "ethnic richness," history, and culture of immigrants and racial minorities. She was asked to develop intercultural assembly programs in other school districts including New York City. In 1934 she created materials to teach intercultural education through assembly programs in fifteen New York City high schools; in that same year she established the Intercultural Education Service Bureau, which provided lesson plans and the tools for replicating the intercultural education programs. The war brought her program additional support. She wrote in her autobiography that, after the spread of "Nazi prejudice" in New York City, school authorities issued an order that schools had to create assembly programs and classroom lessons on "tolerance and democracy." Dr Jacob Greenberg, associate superintendent of schools, approached her and asked her to teach in-service courses. She agreed and had teachers contact her bureau for assistance in setting up programs.[40]

As early as 1938 the TU was working with Rachel DuBois on devising intercultural education projects. The union used both DuBois's methods and her language. It agitated for assembly programs, developed materials on various racial groups, and spoke of the need for an intercultural perspective in the curriculum. It also emphasized intercultural education as a means of building national unity. In June of that year, the union's Harlem Committee organized an "experimental series of lectures on the Negro in American Civilization" to help teachers understand the problems of that community. Among those lecturing to hundreds of teachers were Doxey

Wilkerson, professor of education at Howard University and a writer for the *New York Teacher*; Max Yergan, the first African American to teach a course in black history at City College; and Rachel DuBois. The TU sought a broader audience for her program, saying "through schools, churches and other community groups we can give people mutually appreciative experiences. To the schools [the union] offers factual material on minority groups; as well as material on ways for promoting intercultural education, curriculum materials" that help to create "world mindedness."[41]

In January 1939 two TU members, Marion Milstein and Jenny L. Mayer, published an article in the *New York Teacher* titled "Schools for Tolerance." The authors praised the radio program "Americans All—Immigrants All," a show that was aired on CBS in 1939 promoting tolerance of the varied ethnic and racial groups in America. The radio program was the brainchild of Rachel DuBois. She believed radio was an important venue in which to counter the racist radio preaching of Father Coughlin. She convinced the commissioner of education, John Studebaker, of the need for such a program. Studebaker, who was concerned about rising tensions among ethnic and racial groups in the United States, was thrilled with the idea and saw radio as a way of "institutionalizing in his agency the newly politically valuable field of intercultural education." Together with a representative from the Illinois Governor's Committee on Citizenship and Naturalization, who was concerned about racial and ethnic tension in Chicago, Studebaker convinced CBS officials to air an intercultural education program.[42]

Milstein and Mayer called "Americans All—Immigrants All" a "significant achievement in the field of education for tolerance." Besides encouraging their *New York Teacher* readers to listen to "Americans All—Immigrants All," Milstein and Mayer urged the use of plays and films to promote tolerance in the assembly program. They reminded readers that the Board of Education recognized the value of the assembly program as a result of the union's effort. The union had adopted a resolution "urging assembly programs to be used to inculcate the ideals of democracy and tolerance." Milstein and Mayer reminded readers that, in response to that resolution, the superintendent of schools had sent a letter to principals instructing them to plan assembly programs to teach "these essential principles." They also suggested that language clubs "should make students aware of French, Italian, German and Hebrew ideals, ambitions, and creative efforts, and should help them see the human spirit underlying them all." They recommended that teachers and schools contact DuBois's Intercultural Education Service Bureau for materials and bibliographies on ethnic groups.[43]

While assembly programs and clubs were important vehicles for spreading intercultural education and promoting tolerance, they were not the only means. The union also encouraged academic departments to develop specific syllabi for teaching tolerance. "English, the social sciences, foreign languages, even the official period, offer many opportunities for such teaching. The spirit of democracy should permeate every classroom at all times."[44]

By the late 1930s and early 1940s intercultural education had become a major influence and cause of the union. It began offering courses in intercultural education, and individual union members were involved in such courses offered by community and civil groups. TU members were responsible for school assembly programs offering dramatic skits on black history and films on African American history and culture. The principal of Morris High School praised his teachers for creating an intercultural education program that included ethnic dances.[45]

During the war, education was intertwined with patriotism. When people attending the Intercultural Forum at Andrew Jackson High School in Queens recited the Pledge of Allegiance, the *New York Teacher News* reported that the salute to the colors was not simply a ritual but a vow to ensure the promises of the pledge. The major benefit of intercultural understanding and national unity was emphasized at the forum, which was organized by the school's student Intercultural Club, the Faculty Interfaith Committee, and other faculty. The theme of unity was echoed by a host of speakers, among them James Maxwell, principal of James Madison High School, Brooklyn, who declared that the "fascist enemy both" abroad and "native born, seizes upon the normal human tendency to be suspicious of that which is different and turns that suspicion into fear and hatred." Dr. Alphaeus Huhton, educational director of the Council of African Affairs, also spoke, stressing that justice for blacks was essential to the welfare of all Americans and necessary for world unity. The reason for racial friction, according to Huhton, was the ignorance and indifference of many whites and of newspaper, radio, and congressional figures who "preach the doctrine of a master race." Father Raymond Leonard of the Church of the Nativity, Brooklyn, emphasized at the forum that "man is one; civilizations are many." Dr. Paule Moody of the First Presbyterian Church, New York, begged that people of various faiths and skin colors attempt to attain understanding of one another by having closer contact.[46]

While national unity was an important focus, the promoters of intercultural education did not neglect its significance as a cure for racial animosity. To help teachers foster antidiscrimination intercultural education, the union created a reference room at its headquarters, providing lesson plans, magazines, booklets, and other material on "intercultural understanding." It also created courses on intercultural education for teachers and assisted in the formulation of the Board of Education's intercultural program and materials.[47]

As noted, the TU did not limit its focus on intercultural education to the study of black culture but examined a number of ethnic and racial groups. In the fall of 1945 the Association of Biology Teachers, the Association of Teachers of Social Studies, and the New York Association of Teachers of English (all TU-affiliated) organized an in-service program, "Minority Problems in American History," with a course schedule that was to run from late October to early December. The program provided expert scholars, including Columbia University professor of anthropology Gene Weltfish, who offered a course on "Native Abilities of Different Peoples of the World"; Doxey Wilkerson, who offered a course on "The Negro People in America"; Valia Hirsch, of the Commission of Jewish Writers, Artists, and Scientists, whose course was titled "The Jewish People in America"; Robert J. O'Donnell, executive secretary of the Committee of Catholics for Human Rights, who lectured on the "Irish People in America"; and anthropologist Gitel Poznanski of Columbia University, who focused on Native Americans and the people of Japan, China, and Mexico. Other courses addressed minority problems in American history and the interaction of native whites, blacks, and immigrants in American history. The final event was a group discussion among the participating teachers to develop intercultural cooperation in the classroom, school, and community.[48]

The TU's intercultural campaign extended beyond the school buildings; in March 1944 the Citizens Committee of the Upper West Side of Manhattan, a group in which TU members were active, organized a children's unity festival. The New York Teacher News reported that it was the "most significant work that we have heard of in the city getting right down to rousing fervor for intercultural understanding." Celebrities from the worlds of baseball, boxing, and Broadway attended, and a photo in the paper showed that white, African American, Asian, Latino, Jewish, Italian, and Polish children participated in the affair.[49]

The TU pushed for legislation to make intercultural education mandatory in schools. In 1945 it submitted a resolution to the state assembly specifying that schools should teach scientific facts about race, challenge racial myths, eliminate textbook bias, and train teachers in intercultural education. The union had some success in convincing the Board of Education to adopt intercultural education. It persuaded school authorities to grant in-service credit to teachers who took intercultural education courses, and by 1945, the superintendent declared his support for intercultural education.[50]

By the time the United States entered the war, the union had fully embraced the language as well as the aims of DuBois and intercultural education. In fact, intercultural education became the model teachers used to challenge racial intolerance. It was a means of gaining an appreciation of diverse cultures and challenging ethnocentrism and racism, as well as a way of gaining unity to advance the war effort. DuBois's strategies to spread intercultural education through the schools had its strongest advocates among the membership of the TU.

ANTHROPOLOGY AND THE TU

Anthropology was also an avenue the Teachers Union used to confront racism during the war years. By the early part of the twentieth century, Franz Boas and other anthropologists had challenged the notion that race was the decisive factor to determine intelligence and character. Boas saw culture as a set of customs, social institutions, and beliefs that characterize any particular society. Cultural differences were not due to race but to environment. Culture was also mutable, a fusion of a variety of cultures as they interacted over time. Boas's approach was known as "historical particularism." He argued that anthropologists needed to carry out extensive regional studies to understand the processes changing culture. With enough regional studies, it would be possible to make broad generalizations about the development of culture.

Soon after Hitler came to power, Boas dedicated a great deal of his time to challenging Nazi ideas on race, or what he called "Nordic nonsense." Incensed that, because of his views on race and because he was Jewish, his books had been removed from the library at the University of Kiel, in Germany, Boas undertook to locate jobs and fellowships at American universities and colleges for scholars fleeing Nazi Germany. He led a campaign to persuade learned scientific societies, including the National Academy of Sciences, to adopt resolutions supporting academic freedom and condemning the events in Europe. On December 10, 1938, Boas released to the public a scientific manifesto with the signatures of over 1,200 scientists at 167 universities and colleges. It challenged the pseudo-scientific findings of those who attempted to link race to intelligence. He also organized and became a head of the "Lesser League" to fight anti-Semitism. The league prepared newspaper and magazine articles and created a lecture bureau. Boas came to the conclusion that the battle with fascism was ideological and that the one sure way of combating it was through science and education.[51]

By 1936, Boas had stepped up his anti-Nazi activities, conducting scientific work to undermine Nazi ideology. He also traveled in the United States and abroad presenting his findings and views on race. It is thought that his anti-Nazi activity proved so intense that the stress contributed to his fatal heart attack in 1942.[52]

Boas's political work won the respect and admiration of many, including the New York City Teachers Union, which so appreciated it that the union awarded Boas its annual award in 1940 and recommended his work to teachers. In honor of his work, Herbert Chaimes, a TU member and biology teacher, organized the Franz Boas Workshop for teachers in 1943, the purpose of which was to create programs for fighting racism. The workshop also created courses on race problems for the Board of Education staff, parents, and civil organizations and organized forums on the contributions of racial and ethnic groups. In addition, it examined textbooks for biased materials, recommending to the board that it either revise the books or in some cases eliminate them from the curriculum.[53]

Relying on Boas's own arguments, the Franz Boas Workshop helped organize events at which some of the questions he studied were addressed. Leon Kaiser, principal at Mark Twain Junior High School, credited the Franz Boas Workshop for helping to organize a school-wide event focusing on "Hitler's Secret Weapon," mentioned earlier in this chapter.[54] The Franz Boas Workshop was also given credit for creating a bibliography of books on Jewish immigration and the contributions of Jews as a group and as individuals to "our American culture."[55]

Boas was not the only anthropologist influencing the TU. After his death, two of his students, Ruth Benedict and Gene Weltfish, both from the Anthropology Department at Columbia University, decided to "carry the banner on the race question." At the request of the United Service Organization Inc., a voluntary civilian multiprogram social service agency that helps meet the needs of United States armed services personnel and their familes, they wrote a pamphlet, *The Races of Mankind*, for members of the armed forces who found themselves fighting next to people from different countries and different cultures. The pamphlet was also used later in Germany's de-Nazification program.[56] In October 1943 a nonprofit educational organization, the Public Affairs Committee, published Benedict and Weltfish's thirty-two page pamphlet for the American public. The pamphlet was as much a political manifesto as it was scientific literature. The two anthropologists argued that, since it had become a central issue of World War II, the findings of science on race should be widely studied, which was their purpose in writing the pamphlet at what they labeled a "crucial moment in history." Like their mentor Franz Boas, they did not contend that race was a social construct, rather, they rejected the racist notion that race determines intelligence, character, and customs.[57]

Benedict and Weltfish showed that the world's races have similar anatomical structure and that race had no bearing on height, the size of the brain, or blood types. They challenged the Nazis' erroneous racial classifications by contending that groups such as Jews were not a race but rather a religious affiliation. What differentiated such groups was culture, which was socially constructed. Degrees of intelligence had more to do with environmental factors such as education. They offered as proof scientific and historical examples, among them the fact that northern blacks scored higher on tests than southern whites. Likewise, they noted that Africans and the Chinese had created advance civilizations and that "all races have made their contributions to human knowledge." Turning to the United States, they argued that various cultures have contributed to the country's greatness. "Our country would be poorer in every phase of its culture if different cultures had not come together here, sharing and learning the special contributions each had to offer."[58]

Benedict and Weltfish contended that although racial prejudice had a long history, its continued existence was not inevitable. In one of the most controversial sections of the pamphlet, they claimed that their proof of this was the Soviet Union. "The Russian nation has for a generation shown what can be done to outlaw race prejudice in a country with many kinds of people. They did not wait for people's minds to change. They made racial discrimination and persecution illegal. They welcomed and honored the different dress, different customs, different arts of the many tribes and countries that live as part of their nation." For the two anthropologists, no aspect of the Soviet Union had "greater success than their racial progress."[59]

Although several groups attacked it as subversive, and it was banned from the library of the armed forces, the pamphlet sold like hotcakes. Civic groups, churches, and school districts bought thousands of copies. Thanks to the TU, it was a hit among New York City school teachers as well. In one Manhattan high school alone, three thousand copies of *Races* were distributed to the student body. Just a few weeks after it was issued, every copy had been sold, and it remained unavailable for weeks. Finally, in December 1943, the *New York Teacher News* announced that the pamphlet had been reissued at only ten cents a copy.[60]

One of the major reasons it sold out was the union's campaign to promote use of the pamphlet. A February issue of the *New York Teacher News* quoted the preface of the pamphlet: "We must know whether race is an inevitable barrier to any possible commonwealth of nations that guarantees the four freedoms to all men. We must know whether the diversity of races and ethnic groups in America must inevitably mean that this is a country divided against itself. No subject you study in school today is more fraught with consequences than this subject of race. We shall examine it from every angle." In another edition of the paper, the union contended that what made *Races* an invaluable work was that it presented "scientific" material on the subject of race. The paper also mentioned that a publication by the Council Against Intolerance in America used an illustration from the pamphlet (a pin-up page of people of various races titled "Meet Your Relatives") and encouraged its use. Anthropology had become a field through which the TU could challenge racist theories, and in this effort it carried positive reviews of books, encouraging teachers to read them. For example, a June 1938 issue of the TU's monthly magazine reviewed Bernhard J. Stern's *The Family: Past and Present*. This book consisted of essays by several well-known anthropologists describing the property, customs, and marriage and family relations of a number of nonwhite societies. The review praised the work for presenting, "vividly, the human factor."[61]

After the war, the union continued to stress the importance that inter-cultural education and anthropology could have in promoting a society devoid of racial and ethnic tensions. In the February 16, 1946, issue of *New York Teacher News*, the weekly column, Road to Peace (formerly Road to Victory), noted the release of new classroom materials for Brotherhood Week. Not only was the material deemed adequate for Negro History Week, but it also allowed teachers "the opportunity to broaden discussion so that students may become aware of the fact that Negroes, Jews and other minority groups face common problems." The material consisted of fifteen posters by the American Missionary Association that explained "the physical origins of racial groups and stress[ed] the cultural contributions of all peoples." The titles of some of the posters were "Why Are There Different Races?" "The Jews Are Not a Race," "Inventions Have Come from All Races," and the "Negro Is an Integral Part of Our Culture." These posters, the union stressed, could be used for plays, pageants, and assembly programs.[62]

In addition to the posters, the TU pointed out that the National Conference of Christians and Jews had a number of radio and assembly plays for elementary, junior, and senior high schools, "the themes of which are combating prejudice and improving intercultural relations." One program, "The America of Tomorrow," took place in a classroom where a teacher and her class decide, after a discussion, that "people all over the world, as well as the diverse groups in the United States, must learn to live in harmony."[63]

This chapter does not deny or ignore the Communist Party's influence on the thinking of the New York City Teachers Union. There is no doubt that the TU followed Moscow's line, but it also placed the fight for civil rights in a larger context. The move to support the policies of the Communist Party did not mean racial equality was no longer a priority. TU members sought ways of bundling the goal of winning the war with the fight against racism. No teacher organization in the city matched the TU's effort when it came to the struggle for racial equality. Without a doubt, race and race relations were central issues in New York City schools before the cold war because the TU remained just as passionate on this issue as it had been during the prewar years. The union's contention that fighting racism was inseparable from winning the war was an attempt to get Americans to think not only about their ideals but also their practices. The racist nature and objectives of the enemy provided the union with an avenue for winning people to the cause of equality at home as well as abroad. Juxtaposing the Axis's racist ideals to those of Americans, the TU asked Americans to distinguish themselves from both Nazism abroad and what the union called Nazi practices in America. The men and women who were members of the union should not be seen as dupes but as historical agents who addressed bigotry and sought ways to eliminate it.

TWO

5 / THE OPENING SALVO
Louis Jaffe, Taft-Hartley, and Minnie Gutride

By the late 1940s the world had divided into two hostile camps, the Soviet Union and its satellite nations on one side and the United States, Western European countries, and other anti-Communist forces on the other side. In part, the cold war was an international conflict that resulted in military tension between the two camps, including proxy wars. Thus wars and military clashes in Africa, Asia, Latin America, and Europe were not isolated events but took on cold war themes of Communism versus democracy.[1]

American citizens, like citizens elsewhere, grew increasingly fearful, thanks, to a large extent, to the propaganda campaign initiated by their governments in response to the Communist threat that seemed to them to be engulfing the world. The post-war takeover of Eastern Europe by the Soviet Union, the fall of China to the Communists, and the outbreak of the Korean War alarmed Americans about the aggressive nature of the Soviet Union. Communist aggression around the globe and United States' reaction to that aggression increasingly made the front pages of U.S. newspapers. Americans were engrossed by international affairs, and many backed their nation's effort to halt the Communist's international belligerence.

But the cold war was also a domestic affair that took center stage in the United States when, fearful of Communism, people in power and ordinary citizens organized to stamp out what they believed was widespread infiltration by subversives of institutions and organizations bent on destroying the American way of life. Federal, state, and local governments and agencies joined with industry, civic and labor groups, religious bodies, and cultural organizations, as well as individuals, to fight what they called the Communist menace. Not only the Communist Party and its members but also groups labeled as fronts and those struggling for civil rights and liberties came under attack. One of the groups targeted by the anti-Communist network was the New York City Teachers Union.

The New York City Teachers Union twice faced investigation for what was labeled un-American acts, first by the state legislature in 1919, when the union was led by the social democrats, and again in 1940 when it was under Communist leadership. Even within the ranks of labor, action was taken against the union because of its association with the American Communist Party. But in every case it managed to survive the attacks, including the revocation of its charter by the American Federation of Teachers. In fact, the TU remained throughout most of the 1940s the largest teachers union in the city, an affiliate of the CIO with an estimated fifty-six hundred members.[2] However, by the late 1940s as the cold war set in, the radical union was about to face what proved to be an insurmountable challenge to its existence. The New York City Board of Education—with the support of various federal and local governmental agencies, teachers' unions, and civic organizations organized to eradicate Communists and Communist groups and individuals—launched a massive campaign to stamp out the union, accusing it and its members of being part of the larger worldwide Communist conspiracy.

This assault against the Teachers Union differed from earlier attacks that were aimed specifically at the union and involved tactics such as revocation of its charter (the AFT, 1935, 1937, and 1941) or calling individual members before an investigative body (Rapp-Coudert). The new tactic was for a large number of groups to attempt to separate the radical union from the labor movement through a variety of means: hearings and investigations, new state statutes, Board of Education resolutions, and a fierce propaganda campaign. Although the Teachers Union mounted a painstaking fight against the campaign, the prevailing cold war atmosphere assured the success of its opponents. In the resulting purges close to four hundred TU members were fired, forced to resign, or compelled to retire. The Louis Jaffe case, the Taft-Hartley hearings, and the Minnie Gutride incident represent significant events in the campaign.

THE LOUIS JAFFE INVESTIGATION

The first individual union member investigated during the cold war, in 1948, was Louis Jaffe, a social studies teacher who had been employed for his entire seventeen-year career at Samuel Tilden High School, Brooklyn. A member of the executive board of the Teachers Union and a scholar who had coauthored a pamphlet on academic freedom published by the Teachers Union in 1948, Jaffe had also written articles on the Soviet Union for the TU publication *The Bulletin.* Moreover, a few of his lesson plans had been published in *High Points,* a Board of Education publication, and he had been on several panels at professional conferences. Michael Glassman, chair of Jaffe's department, had observed Jaffe nine times and rated the lessons from good to excellent. The fact that, over the two years prior to March 1948, Glassman had visited Jaffe's classroom only once a term indicated his confidence in the teacher. Louis Jaffe was a dedicated professional who was respected by his colleagues and administrators.[3]

In March 1948 Glassman observed Jaffe in the classroom on two separate occasions. What started as a normal observation procedure exploded into a major confrontation that eventually involved the superintendent's office and the Teachers Union. On March 23 Glassman walked into Jaffe's American history class, U.S. 225, for high school seniors who had been classified as slow learners. Jaffe's subject was "To Study the Veto Question in the United Nations' Security Council."[4] Glassman's observation report included a summary of the lesson, an explanation of the process used by Jaffe to accomplish his goals, commendations, and a lengthy section of recommendations. The supervisor criticized the social studies teacher for failing to use the blackboard to list an outline for the students who, he emphasized, were "slow" learners. He also raised concerns about Jaffe's reliance on just a few of the students in the class for answering questions and not engaging the rest of the class, an objection tied to the most serious criticism: "It seems to me that you were consciously attempting to direct the class to accept the necessity for a justification of the veto." In Glassman's opinion, an objective treatment of the subject should not be a defense but a criticism of the veto, because the veto made a "mockery of the UN." The supervisor took a clear anti-Soviet position. "Emphasis should also be laid on the fact that the U.S. has recently tried to modify it, but Soviet Russia has not only barred any modification but has attempted to still further extend it." Despite his criticism, Glassman concluded that it was a "fair lesson."[5]

The following day, during a lesson contrasting the different views of the atomic bomb by the Soviet Union and the United States, the supervisor once again took issue with Jaffe over content. He accused the teacher of arguing that the Soviet Union was in favor of giving the Atomic Energy Commission power of inspection, as the United States had done when it supported the Baruch plan. The Baruch plan, designed by Bernard Baruch, also called for nations to exchange important scientific information, guarantee peaceful use of atomic energy, and eliminate atomic weapons created for mass destruction. According to Jaffe, the only difference between the two superpowers was that the Soviet Union wanted the United States to agree to immediately destroy all its atomic weapons, but the United States refused. The facts, Glassman said, did not support that argument. Glassman accused Jaffe of not telling his students that the Baruch plan received the support of all the members of the UN save the Soviet Union and its satellites, and the USSR's Gromyko plan did not receive any support (he did not bother to mention that it was supported by the Soviet Union and many of its allies). Again, even with the harsh criticism, Glassman rated the lesson satisfactory.[6]

The principal of the school was Abraham Lefkowitz—a former leader of the Teachers Union who had fought bitterly with the Communist-dominated Rank and File caucus and led the walkout of seven hundred TU members in 1935 that helped create the Teachers Guild. Lefkowitz intervened in the Jaffe matter. On May 12 he wrote the social studies teacher a letter informing him that Glassman's observation reports made him (Lefkowitz) "apprehensive as to his [Jaffe's] understanding of academic freedom." The principal was disturbed by the teacher's failure to discuss all differences between the Soviet and American plans concerning control of atomic energy; he rejected Jaffe's explanation that his goal had been to show the difficulty of the deadlock in the UN over the issue of atomic energy.[7] Jaffe wanted his students to think critically and engage in discussion, not merely take the U.S. position. But, in the atmosphere of the cold war, to express a view that could be deemed objective when it came to the Soviet Union would be considered anti-American. As a founder and officer of the guild, Lefkowitz was not unbiased, and he continued to oppose the TU. The principal saw Jaffe's lesson as an attempt to indoctrinate students and push the Communist Party's line. The ensuing discussion between the principal and teacher did not go well. In fact, Jaffe would later claim that Lefkowitz told him that there were going to be "investigations, possible accusations and the need of principals to have 'records on file' about 'certain' teachers."[8]

Fearing that he was going to be one of the teachers investigated, Jaffe responded in writing to Glassman, accusing his chairman of lacking objectivity and criticizing the pedagogic observation reports. The notion that the veto made a mockery of the United Nations seemed to the veteran social studies teacher to "contradict the accepted principles of teaching controversial subjects in the social studies." The major emphasis should be on students learning how to understand and evaluate different viewpoints, arriving at conclusions on the basis of their own reasoning and judgment. To support his argument and, in addition, to embarrass Glassman, Jaffe quoted the Board of Education's Curriculum Bulletin no. 6, 1947–48: "Teaching which cannot distinguish between fact and opinion or which lacks either the intelligence tack or skill requisite for the presentation of controversial material or which . . . habitually seeks to impose upon the public special theories and interpretations of life of events, or government, can only be characterized as unsatisfactory and incompetent."[9] Without any explanation, Glassman ordered Jaffe to collect his students' notebooks and immediately send them to him—probably a fishing expedition to try to prove that Jaffe was indoctrinating his students. To avoid being accused of insubordination, Jaffe obeyed the order. He would later get the notebooks back, again without any explanation.[10]

In a written response to Jaffe's letter, Glassman accused Jaffe of peddling propaganda for the Soviets, arguing that the teacher refused to understand his criticisms of the two lessons and in all of his lessons on the Soviet Union and the U.S. he was prejudiced "for the Soviet position." Glassman informed Lefkowitz that he would do everything possible to help the veteran teacher to do a better job, "provided that he cooperates."[11] While Glassman seemed to strike a conciliatory note at the end of his letter to Lefkowitz, the fact that he accused Jaffe of always taking the position of the Soviet Union left the impression that the teacher was more interested in pushing propaganda than in teaching. It was unlikely that Jaffe, who considered himself a scholar and an expert on the Soviet Union as well as an excellent teacher, was going to admit that he was incompetent and needed guidance from anyone.

Instead of submitting to Glassman, Jaffe again sent the chair a letter, this time accusing him of violating academic freedom. Jaffe's June 8 letter to Lefkowitz said that Glassman's suggestion contradicted accepted principles of teaching controversial issues and that Glassman had attacked his "character and integrity." Maintaining there was no evidence that he had ever violated the high standards set for a social studies teacher, Jaffe cited passages from earlier observation reports by Glassman. In four years as chair of the department, Glassman had never pointed out in his written observation reviews of Jaffe's lessons any trouble or consistent pattern of speaking propaganda. In fact, the chair, for the most part, had praised the teacher for his professionalism and high academic standards. Glassman wrote that there was "constant probing for cause and effect relationships" and that Jaffe's "questioning was usual[ly] quite challenging and thought provoking." The students "were given excellent guidance as to know how to do research work and how to report on it," and Jaffe's "insistence on exactness in statements of pupils concerning voting arrangements in the Security Council was commendable." Glassman praised Jaffe's fine preparation, use of "excellent quotations," "good class management," and the "fine relationship between yourself and your pupils." These and other statements written by Glassman supported Jaffe's claim that he had not deviated from the responsibilities of a social studies teacher and had maintained the highest level of professionalism.[12] In the letter to Lefkowitz Jaffe insisted that the controversy between Glassman and himself was a matter of the teaching of "controversial issues," and they could simply continue to discuss the matter at the department level for clarification. This attempt to defuse what he called a disagreement was an effort at conciliation designed to stop what was rapidly becoming a crisis.[13]

Lefkowitz was not interested in conciliation; he was ready to take punitive action against the social studies teacher. In a letter to Jaffe, the principal said that his, Jaffe's, statement on June 8 "fools no one—not even yourself. The issue is not as you stated it, but one of slanting the lesson in the direction of your political inclination by omission of vital aspects or over emphasis of certain points." But the teacher's alleged actions had come into play. The principal told Jaffe that he objected to his method of undermining school unity by conducting a whispering campaign against the administration; if Jaffe had a grievance he should have submitted it to the Welfare Committee of the school instead of spreading rumors.[14] Lefkowitz announced he was sending the entire file to the Board of Education for a decision. Unlike Glassman, who had suggested cooperation, the principal concluded that he had a subversive in his school who was going to have to be removed. By June 11 Glassman's effort to cooperate with Jaffe had come to an end. In a letter to Jaffe, the social studies chairman accused the teacher and his friends of carrying on a "whispering campaign of misrepresentation, mudslinging and character assassination against me." There was even a rumor that he, Glassman, was a "warmonger" who opposed academic freedom. It was an attempt, Glassman declared, to intimidate him into silent submission so he would falsify reports about Jaffe's work in the department. He reminded Jaffe that he had rated the lessons satisfactory with both commendations and recommendations.

This small-scale confrontation resonated in the context of the nation's cold war anxieties. What infuriated the chairman against Jaffe was an editorial that had appeared in the *New York Teacher News* criticizing the Mundt-Nixon Bill, sponsored by U.S. representatives Karl Mundt and Richard Nixon in 1948, requiring Communists to register with the U.S. government and barring them from holding office. The bill eventually became the McCarran Act. That same paper also contained an item that noted that an administrator had ordered the collection of high school student notebooks for the "purpose of checking on the loyalty of a teacher." Fully aware that the piece referred to him, Glassman declared in a letter to Jaffe that the accusation in the editorial was a "malicious and deliberate falsehood." The collection of the workbooks was Glassman's call and had had nothing to do with Lefkowitz. Justifying his actions, the social studies chair claimed that the "supervisory device of collecting homework" was a legitimate technique and needed no defense.[15]

Glassman then attempted to make Jaffe the guilty party—"An honest teacher not only does not fear it but welcomes [the] supervisory device"—and accused Jaffe of doing him a great disservice by having the piece published in the *New York Teacher News*. As the social studies chair he had gone out of his way for the teacher, including shielding Jaffe when he "deserved official reprimand." Jaffe, according to Glassman, had "forfeited every right to" his friendship and tolerance. "I shall no longer bend backwards or appease. Thus I put you on notice here and now that if you force the issue I am prepared to meet it."[16] If Lefkowitz and Glassman's letters were meant to frighten Jaffe into submission, they failed. The social studies teacher denied conducting a whispering campaign, but admitted speaking to colleagues asking for their advice. Despite's Glassman's claim that collecting notebooks was not unusual, Jaffe insisted that it had never happened to him before the March observations; such an action was not routine practice in the department. He also claimed that it was Glassman who attacked his integrity and what was developing was a campaign to intimidate him by using "unsubstantiated and unfounded accusations."[17]

Infuriated, Lefkowitz wrote to Jaffe declaring that he considered him dangerous and was determined to stop him. The slant Jaffe put on his lessons was in line with his "left-wing orientation." Although Lefkowitz continued to complain about a whispering campaign, the bigger issue was Jaffe's "left-wing orientation." Lefkowitz wrote: "The issue is not one of academic freedom and you know it only too well. No point of view has ever been outlawed at Tilden. But academic freedom can't b[e] used by you or another teacher at Tilden to overemphasize a point of view contrary to that of America and the United Nations to favor the Soviet Union and her satellites, without a protest or a recorded warning from a loyal Head of Department or any one who witnessed it."[18]

Not willing to handle the dispute with Jaffe at the school level, Lefkowitz requested that Superintendent of Schools William Jansen step in, hoping he would take action against the teacher. Jansen assigned the investigation to Assistant Superintendent David Moskowitz, who heard from Jaffe, Lefkowitz, and Glassman. The principal sent all documents to the superintendent's office, and Jaffe prepared a long brief explaining his side of the story.[19] Jaffe did not want the matter to be settled at the superintendent's office, where, he believed with good reason, he could not receive a fair hearing. Moreover, the appeal process weighed heavily in favor of the administration; essentially, labor had to appeal to management and ask it to rule against another branch of management. Jaffe was skeptical of the entire process, a sentiment evident in his additional brief to Moskowitz. On June 28 the beleaguered social studies teacher wrote to Associate Superintendent Frederic Ernst requesting that he direct Glassman to provide him, Jaffe, with information about his charges against him, including prejudice in favor of the Soviet Union's position and a lack of intellectual honesty.[20]

Ernst suggested a way out of the mess: Jaffe should request a voluntary transfer, since his position was unsustainable at Tilden. The compromise, on the surface, seemed a reasonable solution. As long as he remained in a school with Lefkowitz and Glassman, Jaffe would be constantly embroiled in confrontation. But Jaffe rejected the solution, telling Ernst that he did not believe that this "controversy on pedagogical principles with my chairman has placed me in an untenable position nor should it be a basis for continuing friction." A voluntary transfer would indicate wrongdoing on his part, something he could never admit to, and suggested the board was condoning intimidation. Jaffe wanted his record cleared of the charges of slanting the truth and intellectual dishonesty. More important, a transfer would not address the central issue, the right to teach a number of viewpoints on controversial issues had been undermined by Glassman's insistence that his own view was the right one.[21] Unable to convince Jaffe, Ernst decided to issue him an involuntary transfer, forcing Jaffe to go to Erasmus Hall High School in Brooklyn. Disappointed with the action, Jaffe appealed to Superintendent Jansen to defer the transfer until a full hearing, with Glassman present, could take place. Jansen did not stop the transfer.[22]

Jaffe's transfer did not settle the matter. The battle at Tilden evolved into a confrontation between the Teachers Union and the Board of Education over core issues: academic freedom versus the right of administrators to ban what they interpreted as propaganda in the classroom. In a brief on behalf of the social studies teacher, legislative representative of the TU Rose Russell argued to the Board of Education that democratic principles as well as "constructive supervision" were violated by the principal and chair, creating a chilling atmosphere of intimidation among social studies teachers. How, under such conditions, were they to teach controversial issues in accordance with established principles and implement the Board of Education resolution declaring that public schools should be used as instruments to maintain peace in the world? She argued that a single point of view should not be imposed on students. Teachers, Russell insisted, should help their students arrive at valid conclusions and learn how to think critically: "This can only be achieved through the impartial presentation of conflicting viewpoints in the classroom." For Russell, Lefkowitz and Glassman were "promoting a spirit of hatred and war propaganda in the classroom."[23]

In addition to the union leadership, Jaffe received support from ninety Tilden teachers, who petitioned the board protesting the decision to transfer him and advocating that the conflict be handled within the school through dialogue and understanding. This approach, according to the petitioners, was far better than interference by board officials because it would promote unity and uplift morale at Tilden.[24] Getting those ninety teacher signatures was rather a remarkable feat, for it had meant convincing half the school's staff to sign regarding a highly charged matter and to do so only a few days before the summer break. Just as significant, those who signed were willing to risk possible retaliation and the severance of cordial relations with their principal and others in the school for what they argued was unfair treatment of a colleague by the principal.

Despite these efforts, Jaffe's fate was sealed. The superintendent responded that the case had already been heard by Associate Superintendent Ernst and by assistant superintendents whom he would not overrule. However, an appeals committee would be appointed in the fall so that Jaffe could present his arguments. In the meantime, the decision to transfer him would be upheld, allegedly for his own benefit because he could get a fresh start and be given an opportunity to disprove the allegations against him.[25]

The union did not give up the fight. In a letter to Jansen, Russell challenged his claim that the interview Jaffe had had with Ernst and the assistant superintendents had been a formal hearing. Ernst, according to Russell, had referred to the interview as informal. Jaffe should not be transferred, Russell claimed, because of some allegation of "strained relationship." The very fact that half the faculty signed a petition was a strong indication that an internal resolution could restore unity.[26] To bolster his claim that the attack on him had nothing to do with his competency as a teacher, Jaffe reproduced a February 5, 1948, letter of recommendation written by Glassman. In it there is no accusation that Jaffe slanted the truth or revealed a biased attitude, as he is characterized in the March 23 and 24 observation reports. Short of praising him, the chair found the social studies teacher professional, "thoroughly competent and reliable." In spite of Jaffe's efforts to remain at Tilden, he was officially transferred to Erasmus Hall High School on September 9.[27]

The Tilden High School controversy in 1948 was not a struggle over pedagogical methods but a reflection of the cold war. Lefkowitz defended his actions in an open letter dated October 11, 1948, and titled "My Last Will and Testament on the Teachers Union and the Jaffe Case." He did not describe a disagreement on teaching approaches. Instead, he portrayed the battle between himself and Jaffe as one between the forces of Communism and democracy. Jaffe's pro-Soviet view was tantamount to treason, "weakening the case of the United States" by omitting facts. Indeed, Jaffe's union had developed lying into a "fine art"; it was simply following the "Lenin Line" by urging its followers to use "cunning, unlawful" methods and evade the truth. The principal was continuing the fight with the Teachers Union that had erupted in the 1930s and culminated in the walkout and formation of the Teachers Guild, in 1935.[28] Lefkowitz argued that Jaffe "placed Russia above his own country." Unable to find evidence of bias in Jaffe's record, Lefkowitz took aim at the TU by citing its record, noting that it had been ousted by the AFT for following the party line, the same policy that Jaffe embraced. In fact, Lefkowitz wrote, the TU was nothing more than a Communist organization. It consistently supported Communist fronts such as the Jefferson School, which was on the attorney general's list of subversive organizations, and followed Moscow's line, first attacking FDR as a warmonger, then changing its position a few months later, when the Nazis invaded the USSR, for a second front.[29]

Lefkowitz focused on what he claimed was Jaffe and the TU's subversive behavior. Jaffe and the TU's odd interpretation of academic freedom, Lefkowitz insisted, meant "the right to protect its members who followed the official Leninist Line which is as follows: only when teachers have mastered Marxism-Leninism will they be able skillfully to inject it into their teaching at the least risk of exposure and at the same time, conduct struggles around the schools in a truly Bolshevik manner." Still, Lefkowitz oddly asserted that he demonstrated great patience in the face of seditious conduct and pointed out that, in his last ten years as principal no one had made a complaint that he was unjust. He concluded his piece by challenging the union to prove that he had violated academic freedom. In Lefkowitz's view, it was the union's dishonesty and Communist bias and its attacks that were the problem. Clearly, his entire justification for claiming that Jaffe was dishonest rested on the social studies teacher's affiliation with the TU, a group he attempted to demonstrate was a Communist Party front. The bigger fight for Lefkowtiz was not this individual teacher but the very organization that he still blamed for the split in the teachers union movement.[30]

Lefkowitz's years of inaction against the TU may have had less to do with patience than with a lack of opportunity. Despite the efforts of the Rapp-Coudert Committee, the New York City Board of Education avoided attacking the union in large part because of the World War II alliance between the United States and Soviet Union. By the late 1940s, however, the cold war campaign to eradicate the American Communist Party and Communist fronts created the opportunity for board officials to take aim at the largest and most militant teacher organization in the city. Jaffe was not fantasizing when he mentioned Lefkowitz's plans for investigations and lists of suspect teachers. The *Journal-American* reported that on October 8 Jansen said,

"There may be a need for legislation on the broad problem [of Communist teachers in the system] we are confronted with, and we are giving the problem careful consideration." Jansen was joining the anti-Communist network by thinking of a way to purge Communists from the system. In fact, the state legislature would respond to his statement by passing the Feinberg Law (see chapter 6).[31]

Jansen's remarks to the *Journal-American* worried Russell so much that she issued an open letter to the superintendent, reminding him of both his and Board of Education President Andrew G. Clauson Jr.'s testimony before the subcommittee on the House Committee on Education and Labor claiming they had no knowledge of Communist teachers in the public school system; now they were advocating legislation for a "non-existent peril." But it seemed that Jansen was preparing to take action against what he was beginning to see as subversives in the school system. Lefkowitz never addressed the question that both the veteran social studies teacher and Russell kept raising: why did the principal keep giving Jansen annual satisfactory ratings? Russell also suggested that Lefkowitz was disingenuous when he claimed that he was reluctant to raise the "Red line." He had been making that argument since 1935, when he and others seceded from the TU.[32]

Although Jansen refused to rescind Jaffe's transfer, he did agree to hold a formal hearing on October 28, 1948. The hearing committee, which was made up of three associate superintendents, issued its report on December 1, 1948. After months of battle, Jaffe was vindicated by the committee when it found that he had not slanted his lessons.[33] Jaffe would have no time to celebrate his victory. A week before the committee's report was issued, he was called for an additional hearing, before the same committee of associate superintendents, inquiring into his "activities as a teacher" and "certain other matters." At his second hearing, Jaffe was interrogated for two hours on his "opinions, beliefs, and activities and associations outside of the classroom." The associate superintendents asked if he believed there was freedom in the USSR and if Stalin was an enemy of the United States. He was also asked about his views on World War II and his involvement with the Jefferson School. It was evident that Jaffe had become a target of board officials.[34]

On January 14, 1949, the TU issued a letter to its members titled "The Case of Mr. Louis Jaffe: A Threat to the Security, Tenure and Academic Freedom of All Teachers." The letter accused Jansen of going after Jaffe because, in March 1946, he had represented the TU in criticizing the Board of Education's American history syllabus for its portrayal of American-Soviet relations. Jaffe was asked to write an article for the Social Studies Association to generate discussion among history teachers about how textbooks and the New York City social studies curricula treated the Soviet Union. The TU lodged a formal complaint against the October 28 hearing for a number of reasons. Such procedures denied teachers the right to know in advance of the exact nature of a hearing, the right to appeal a negative rating without being subjected to probing into their political beliefs, and the right to publish in professional journals articles that criticized administrative practices. The board of superintendents, the TU letter said, was tacitly claiming the right to probe into teachers' opinions and after-school activities.[35]

TAFT-HARTLEY

Although the Jaffe incident signaled Jansen's intention to move against Communist teachers in the system, it was the House Committee on Education and Labor's hearings that confirmed the superintendent's fears of Communists in the school system. Owners of the Radio Electronic School in Manhattan complained to the committee about the TU's role in a strike by teachers, asking it to investigate the Teachers Union as a Communist front. Hearings were held in New York starting in September 1948, and the committee subpoenaed the leaders of the union. The decision by the House Committee was a devastating blow for the Teachers Union. Although it had been investigated before, this was the first time a United States agency turned its attention to the union's activities. The union went on the defensive by claiming that the committee's objective was to destroy the labor movement. Before the hearing, Rose Russell issued a public statement blaming the "gutter press" for red-baiting the union, making it a target of the committee. In a statement approved by twelve hundred TU members, Russell accused the committee of being anti-education because it "bottled up a bill for federal aid to education." According to Russell, the committee had tried to destroy the Congress of Industrial Organizations by investigating an auto strike at Allis-Chalmers from April 30, 1946, to March 24, 1947, seeking to find out if the striking autoworkers belonged to a "Communist-inspired" group.[36] The committee's attack on the TU,

Russell said, persecuted teachers for their political beliefs, especially during a period of war, providing grounds for "heresy-hunting." The committee wanted to silence teachers and create a faculty that would impose self-censorship and submit to a nameless terror.[37]

Despite the union's efforts, the committee began its hearings on September 27. Colonel William B. Campbell, co-owner of the Radio Electronic School, told the committee the trouble began when the union helped organize twenty-seven staff members and began negotiating a contract with him and the other two owners, R. L. Duncan and Edward M. Kirby, who had created the school in 1946. Both Campbell and Duncan had been involved in radio technical education since the end of World War I. Kirby was in charge of public relations for the National Association of Broadcasters. The three men established the school because it seemed like a good financial opportunity. Testifying before the Taft-Hartley Committee, Campbell claimed that the school was paying salaries above the going rate for private school teachers, with a three-week vacation. Despite that, on June 24, 1948, he received a letter from Alfred Katz, an organizer for the Teachers Union, Local 555, asserting that the vast majority of the teachers in the school were TU members and that the union was their sole collective bargaining agent. Katz called for the school to recognize the TU, provide dues checkoff, and give preference in hiring to the TU and union members when vacancies occurred.[38]

The owners claimed to have been bargaining in good faith to create group and individual contracts. However, after thoroughly investigating the TU, they decided not to recognize it as the collective bargaining agent. In retaliation, the TU launched a strike. Campbell claimed that, while he was negotiating with both individuals and groups "as the men want it," a picket line was created on August 18, and, he insisted, the picketers were not school employees. The picketers called the students scabs as they entered the building. When asked by a committee member what other names picketers called students, Campbell said, "'rat,' 'scab,' and 'skunk,' you hear all those sort of things." Having decided not to deal with the TU, and denying that there had been a collective bargaining election, Campbell argued that the school was under no legal requirement to recognize the union.[39]

According to Campbell, the teachers in his school were "loyal" and did not want to join the picket line. He claimed that the four or five who joined the line "resigned" their position by just walking out, and "we have not seen them." However, he confessed he didn't know how many teachers were members of the union, raising the question how he could be certain that none wanted to be represented by the TU. He suggested the committee invite all the school's teachers to appear in order to find out if they were members of the TU, clearly a way for the owners to intimidate their employees and get rid of union members. Any teacher going before a United States congressional body and admitting that he or she was a member of a union being investigated as a Communist front would invite trouble.[40]

Campbell claimed that, after investigating the TU, he discovered that it did not qualify as a legitimate union under the Taft-Hartley Act because its officers did not sign the requisite non-Communist affidavits. The Taft-Hartley Act, passed by Congress in 1947 over President Truman's veto, amended the National Labor Relations Act and emphasized the right of employees not to join a union and not to participate in collective action. It required, in part, that union officers sign affidavits asserting that they were not members of the Communist Party. The Communist-dominated union, Campbell argued, employed "threats, coercion, and intimidation" of the faculty and student body, tried to sabotage laboratory equipment at the school, and endangered national defense by picketing the school on a day that a reserve unit of the United States Signal Corp was to be created there. In Campbell's escalating rhetoric, this indicated a "deliberate effort by this Communist-dominated union to sabotage this unit of our national defense at a time when international relations with Russia were very grave and strained almost to the breaking point." Even the TU's effort to help train and rehabilitate veterans was depicted as an attempt to undermine loyalty by trying to disseminate "subversive propaganda."[41]

The Taft-Hartley Committee was hardly impartial. The counsel for the committee, Irving McCann, told his colleagues Campbell had told him, "Some of the students were driven away or blocked out because of the threats to members of their families, or a statement such as this 'you have a sister working at such and such a place, remember?'" McCann asked Campbell if he could name any particular student willing to testify that he did not cross the picket line because he was threatened; the colonel responded that he would need time to get the person, because he did not know his name.[42]

Bella Dodd testified before the Taft-Hartley Committee, lending weight to the charge that the union harbored Communists. Despite her eventual decision to leave the TU (discussed in Chapter 6), she did not turn against it at the Taft-Hartley hearing. When asked by a committee member if she had become a member of the National Committee of the newly formed Communist Political Association, she refused to answer. She affirmed, "I am proud of my political life in this city and state," adding she did not think any committee had the right to inquire into a person's political opinion: "Surely, you may think my political affiliation is unpopular, but that is where you must defend the American Constitution." Although she admitted that her political association was public record, on principle she believed a person should not be investigated about her affiliation. Pressed by the committee, she did admit that she spoke at the twenty-fifth anniversary of the Communist movement in 1944 and that she represented the Communist Party in Albany as the district legislative director. She refused to answer when asked if she was a vice-president of the New York State Political Association or currently a member of the Party.[43] In spite of Dodd's refusal to denounce the TU and the Communist Party, she admitted that while serving as legislative representative for the union she had been in the Communist Party and the Communist Political Association.

Abraham Lederman's testimony on behalf of the union was particularly damaging to it. Lederman, who was a junior high school math teacher, joined the union in 1933 and was elected to its executive board three years later. He interrupted his teaching career to serve in the U.S. army in 1942. Returning from military duty, he resumed his career as a teacher and was elected secretary of the TU in 1946 and president in 1948. The newly elected president of the TU claimed that there were fifty-six hundred members of the union, six hundred to eight hundred substitute teachers, and some forty-four hundred with regular licenses.[44]

Lederman criticized the committee for inviting Lefkowitz, Board of Education member George Timone, and others to testify as experts on the TU because, he claimed, they knew little about the union and its officers. Committee members were only interested in proving that the union harbored Communists. One committee member, Representative Ellisworth Buck, Republican from Staten Island, noted that Isidore Begun, who was fired by the school board in 1933 but stayed on the union's executive board until 1936, and Bella Dodd, who was also on the executive board, were members of the Communist Party. In a weak defense of the union, Lederman said that two avowed Communist Party members did not constitute Communist control. Buck, sensing he had trapped the TU president, argued that Begun and Dodd were not ordinary members: they were in leadership positions, members of the executive board. Dodd was the legislative representative and spokesperson for the organization. Buck lashed out at Lederman: "Bella Dodd is a Communist. Then you sit there and say that we are witch-hunting when, or if we even assume that Communists have had anything to do with the teachers union."[45]

Lederman dug himself in deeper when he said he knew nothing about Dodd's Communist affiliation because, when she was the legislative representative, he was in the army. Buck took full advantage of this opening by asking if Lederman would have been in favor of keeping Dodd in her position after she announced her membership in the Communist Party. "That is a hypothetical question," the union president said. Buck retorted, "I am asking your opinion." But Lederman still avoided giving a direct answer, claiming that he did not like responding to "iffy" questions and arguing that the union's constitution did not "inquire into the political beliefs, religious beliefs, or discriminate in any way about any teacher who wants to be a member." Buck's tactical interrogation helped foster the view that the union was controlled by the Communist Party.[46] Lederman admitted that, if he disagreed with the TU's constitution, its program, and decisions made by the membership, he would not have been elected president: "I think one can say, with perhaps exceptions here and there, that the position of the Teachers Union would represent my own position." These positions, Buck asserted, included the belief in Communism, knowing full well that if he were not willing to state whether past members were Communists he would refuse to reveal the political affiliation of present board members. McCann asked Lederman if there were Communists on the executive board and received no answer. Lederman asked to read a statement, but the committee was not done with its questions.[47]

Unable to get Lederman to discuss the political affiliation of union leaders, McCann asked if he had been a member of a committee to nominate the Communist Isidore Begun for a New York City Council seat in 1937. Lederman declined to answer and invoked the First and Fifth Amendments. McCann then asked the formula question that was used by anti-Communist investigative committees to suggest witnesses were guilty: "Are you now or have you ever been a member of the Communist Party?" And, as so many witnesses did before these committees, Lederman declined to answer.[48] The committee eventually allowed the TU president to make a statement, but only after it had created the impression that he was lying and covering up his Communist connection. Lederman claimed that teachers had been subjected to "thought control and attempts to deny them normal civil and personal liberties." As leader of over five thousand teachers, he had an obligation to the Constitution: "If we are to safeguard our rights as Americans to be truly free, to speak and think without fear, we must resist any demands—including congressional committee—that we divulge those beliefs."

Despite Lederman's awkward experience, the dynamic between freedom and democracy is illuminated by his testimony. The Taft-Hartley committee's notion of freedom was a popular one of the cold war. While committee members and other anti-Communist forces embraced the Constitution, they saw the nation as being at war, threatened by enemies who, they believed, wanted to destroy the "American way of life." Their job was to defend that way of life and the nation against all who were labeled as enemies. Because the nation was at war, the anti-Communists argued, constitutional rights could not be extended to those posing the threat. There was a blurring of the line between political affiliation and actions; just being a member of the Communist Party was close to treason.

The witnesses for the Teachers Union had a more expansive definition of freedom rooted in the belief that the Constitution protected freedom of speech, association, and thought. They were not enemies of the state, but dissenters whose activities, they contended, were protected under the Constitution. The political climate of the time dictated that they could not confess their membership in the Party and expect to be depicted as anything but subversive. Lederman and other TU witnesses invoked the First and Fifth Amendments, arguing that under American jurisprudence a person had to commit a crime and be tried and convicted before being classified as a criminal.

Rose Russell was also subpoenaed by the subcommittee. She cleverly avoided falling into a trap when asked if she had been a member of the Civil Rights Congress. Instead of responding to the question, she requested the same privilege afforded to Campbell, Duncan, Jansen, Clauson, Lefkowitz, Timone, and others, who were sworn in and given a chance to speak with few interruptions. She wanted to answer what she labeled false accusations and slander against her and the union. Since she was the last witness and aware that her time would be limited, she wanted to control the discourse and defend the TU instead of allowing the committee to hammer away at the red allegation. Despite objections from McCann, the chair of the subcommittee allowed her to make her statement.[49] Russell told the committee that the TU's main area of organizing was in the public sector and colleges. Private schools were only organized by request of the faculty, usually because of a grievance that could not be settled. The union mostly focused on increasing salaries for teachers, reducing class size, getting more sick leave for its members, and improving sanitary conditions for children.[50]

Russell refuted the claim that the TU's 1945 book, *Education for One World*, was subversive, noting the sources used to compile the work. She pointed out that Timone had cited some sources on the attorney general's list of subversive organizations but ignored others such as the NAACP, the Bureau for International Education, the National Education Association, the Urban League, the American Jewish Committee, and the American Jewish Congress. According to Russell, it was a "well balanced list, providing students with all sides on the issue of education.[51] In an attempt to convince committee members that the TU was not a subversive organization planning to assist Moscow in overthrowing the government, Russell pointed out that the TU was the first teachers union to offer an annual conference. The conference had become so prestigious that Mayor William O'Dwyer, the Board of Education president, Andrew Clauson Jr., U.S. Senator Claude Pepper, and Secretary of Commerce Henry C. Wallace had all participated in the events. President Roosevelt sent a letter on April 10, 1945, congratulating the union on its annual conference.[52]

Despite Russell's efforts, she failed to persuade the committee that the TU was a professional organization for teachers rather than a tool of Communist propaganda. McCann asked if she had participated in a conference sponsored by the Civil Rights Congress. After consulting her attorney, Russell decided not to answer the question. Because the event had been sponsored by an organization listed by the attorney general as subversive, it would have undermined her efforts to paint the union primarily as representing the interest of teachers. When McConnell asked if she had attended the meeting as a representative of the union, Russell said she did not recall. Undaunted by her refusal to answer the question, McCann asked if she had signed a 1945 petition for Ben Davis, Communist Party candidate for a city council seat. Once again, Russell declined to answer.[53]

McCann, McConnell, and other members of the Taft-Hartley Committee pressed the line of questioning. Russell's repeated refusals to answer made her look guilty, accomplishing the committee's goal of linking the TU to Communist organizations. McCann asked Russell if she were a sponsor of the Jefferson School and if there were any Communists among the leaders of the TU. "I decline to answer," Russell responded. However, she asserted, the union never inquired into the political affiliations of its members. When committee members asked Russell if the union would dismiss known Communists, she would only state that requirement for membership was being a teacher. "If the teacher was on a street corner advocating the overthrow of the government by force or violence, would you expel them?" McConnell asked. Russell doubted that would ever occur and emphasized that TU members did not advocate violence or the overthrow of the government.

McConnell accused Russell of ducking his question about whether being a Communist Party member threatened free institutions. She contended that the "tenets of Anglo-Saxon Jurisprudence" regarded a person as a criminal only if he committed a crime, not on the basis of thought or association. Russell characterized the committee as a bunch of marauders trampling on the Constitution. McCann demanded to know if Russell were or had been a member of the Communist Party. "On the advice of counsel," Russell responded, "I decline to answer."[54] Despite Russell's skill at handling the committee, her refusal to disclose whether she was a party member was considered tantamount to an admission of guilt. If she had nothing to hide, why wouldn't she answer the question?

Both Superintendent of Schools Jansen and Board of Education President Clauson had testified before the Taft-Hartley Committee before Russell was called, refuting the claim that the union was Communist dominated. Jansen told committee members there was no evidence that Communists were operating in the 750 schools of New York City. The superintendent admitted to "occasional problems" with members of the TU who, it was discovered after they left the system, were members of the Communist Party; and he noted his relation with the union was "sometimes pleasant and sometimes not so pleasant." But Jansen did not criticize the teaching performance of union members or suggest that TU members were pushing leftist doctrine in the classroom: "no one has presented any evidence to me that warranted bringing any individual case before the Board of Education." But Jansen left the door open by asserting that, if he did receive "strong evidence" that a teacher was a Communist Party member, he would refer the case to the board and request a trial. For her part, Russell contended that, despite the TU having disagreements with the Board of Education, both Jansen and Clauson "led [the committee] to conclude that we [the TU] are a responsible organization; that our members are satisfactory teachers indeed, that our proposals on professional questions have frequently been of a very high order."[55]

The testimony of Jansen and Clauson exposed a divide within the leadership of the Board of Education. Board member George Timone, who also testified before the Taft-Hartley Committee, emphatically stated that the TU was a Communist organization, claiming that the *New York Teacher News* praised and defended Communist fronts, advocated the use of publications from organizations that the justice department listed as Communist, and promoted Communist causes. Moreover, Timone maintained that the union had never criticized any policy of the Soviet Union or a Communist front group, citing materials from the National Council of Soviet-American Friendship, the American Committee for the Protection of the Foreign Born, and the Council of African Affairs that were "recommended in the pages of the [*New York*] *Teacher News*, official organ" of the union. Timone accused *Teacher News* of urging parents to take courses at the Jefferson School of Social Science, considered a Communist front group. In contrast to his characterization of the TU as Communist, he emphasized that the vast majority of teachers in the system were "splendid, loyal" Americans.[56]

Jansen and Timone's testimonies demonstrated that, as late as September 1948, they disagreed about the TU's supposed Communist bias. Even during the Louis Jaffe affair, Jansen stopped short of targeting the Teachers Union, even though he was clearly concerned about some Communist teachers in the system. But Jansen had drifted into the Timone camp by early October, after Samuel Wallach testified before the Taft-Hartley Committee. Samuel Wallach, a thirty-nine-year-old social studies teacher at Franklin K. Lane High School and former president of the Teachers Union, was questioned about whether he was a member of the Communist Party or if the TU was led by Communists. Instead, Wallach stressed his patriotism as a "proud American Teacher" who had attempted to instill in his students a "deep devotion for the American way of life, our Constitution and Bill of Rights." He also insisted that hundreds of his students served in

Figure 5.1 TU's President Samuel Wallach at podium. United Federation of Teachers, part 1, folder 521.

World War II due in part to patriotism "inspired by my teaching and the Bill of Rights."[57] But Wallach also argued that the Constitution and Bill of Rights obligated him to oppose the committee's violation of American ideals: "As a teacher and a believer in fundamental principles, it seems to me that it would be a betrayal of everything I have been teaching to cooperate with the committee in an investigation of a man's opinion, political belief and private views." Even when Representative Buck reminded Wallach that he was an employee of the Board of Education in front of a United States congressional committee, Wallach refused to cooperate, cited both the First and Fifth Amendments.[58]

Wallach's testimony seems to have ushered in a dramatic change in the relationship between the TU and Jansen. The Board of Education had already dismissed Alexander Koral, a sanitary engineer, for refusing to say whether or not he was a Communist. Koral was not a teacher however, so his testimony did not hurt the TU. Dodd had never worked for the Board of Education, and Rose Russell resigned her position with the board, but Lederman and Wallach were current employees of the system and key figures in the union. The cumulative weight of public testimonies by TU officials, especially their refusal to answer if they were Communist Party members, probably convinced Jansen that the union was a Communist front and that he had to take action. Representative Samuel K. McConnell, Republican from Pennsylvania, said, at the end of the hearings, that his job was to find "links between any Communists in the union and Communists in other countries." The committee found enough links between Communists and the TU to convince Jansen to act. Receiving advice from the corporation counsel that a teacher's refusal to answer when asked if he was a Communist Party member by a congressional committee was a breach of the city charter, Jansen told the law secretary of the board to obtain a copy of Wallach's testimony.[59]

The union immediately realized Jansen's maneuver had large implications, signaling a shift from seeing the TU as a "responsible organization" to one dominated by Communists. If action were taken against Wallach, it would mean action could be taken against other members. On October 7, 1948, the union issued a leaflet, "Support the Teacher Who Is Defending the Bill of Rights." Citing Wallach's remarks as evidence that he was defending the Constitution, the union argued that pressure was mounting on the Board of Education to fire the fifteen-year veteran using Section 903 of the City Charter. However, Section 903, the union contended, was aimed at official misconduct of public officers, specifically graft. In a letter to union members the following day, Russell warned that Wallach was in danger of being brought up on charges or dismissed from his position because of his political views; the TU itself was in danger of becoming a target. The subsequent Minnie Gutride event brushed away all doubts that board officials were now targeting the Teachers Union.[60]

MINNIE GUTRIDE

Minnie Gutride arrived at Public School 21 in Staten Island on the morning of Tuesday December 21, 1948. Gutride, a seventeen-year veteran teacher and a member of the New York City Teachers Union, was already under a great deal of stress because she was suffering from cancer. That day she was called out of her classroom of first graders by her principal, taken to the teachers' room, and questioned about her affiliation with the Communist Party. Superintendent William Jansen had sent Assistant Superintendent John F. Convey, Nicholas Bucci, law secretary for the Board of Education, and a stenographer to interrogate Gutride at P.S. 21. Also present at the interrogation was Gutride's principal. No one was available to represent her at this surprise hearing.[61] To make matters worse, the interrogators did not wait until her class was over. In this extremely intimidating atmosphere, Gutride was questioned about alleged Communist Party meetings she had attended in 1940 and 1941.[62]

Gutride was so distressed by the ordeal that, when her workday was done at P.S. 21 she went directly to the office of the Teachers Union to complain and ask for assistance. In a letter to the Board of Education and the superintendent Russell claimed that the elementary school teacher was "visibly shaken" when she arrived. In a letter to the union Gutride described the "terrifying atmosphere" of the ambush interrogation and defended her long record, pointing out that her teaching and service had been rated "highly satisfactory" and no fault was ever found with her conduct or professionalism. She strongly protested the "complete disregard for safeguards which had been established for teachers against this type of treatment" and argued it was improper to remove a teacher from her class and "subject her to this type of questioning without any warning or prior notice of opportunity to consult with anyone for advice as to her legal rights."[63] But writing the letter did little to lessen the trauma. The fear and embarrassment she suffered exacerbated the other problems she was facing. On the evening of December 21, Minnie Gutride committed suicide in her apartment at 200 West 16 Street, by placing her head in the gas oven. The body of the forty-year-old elementary school teacher was found two days later.[64]

The tragic death of Gutride was dramatic evidence of the cruelty and injustice implicit in the investigation of teachers suspected of being Communists, an immediate example of the lives ruined by cold war paranoia. The Gutride incident was a perfect case for the union's argument that the superintendent would stop at nothing, even pulling a widow (her husband had died fifteen years earlier in a car accident) with cancer out of her classroom and interrogating her without providing an opportunity for a defense. The Teachers Union took immediate action.

On December 23 the TU's executive board adopted a resolution condemning the witch hunt in the schools. The following day, Rose Russell sent a letter to board members and the superintendent informing them of the executive board's resolution. She also reported that Abraham Lederman had been summoned to Jansen's office on December 22 and warned that, if he did not appear, the superintendent would consider it an act of "insubordination." Both Lederman and Gutride deserved better. "It is, therefore, very clear that performance in the classroom and service to the children," Russell stressed, "are no longer regarded by Superintendent Jansen as criteria for judging teachers. Instead, political tests are to be applied, such as probing into thoughts, opinions and associations." Russell took note that the surprise interrogation of Gutride and the summoning of Lederman took place "just before the Christmas holidays." She summed up: "The manner in which Mrs. Minnie Gutride and Mr. Abraham Lederman were questioned without prior notice and without any opportunity to prepare or to get legal advice showed a shocking disregard of all humane consideration and all rights and safeguards which teachers on tenure have won through the years." The union feared that a campaign to "intimidate and silence every teacher of independent judgment on school matters and other affairs" was under way. Blaming Gutride's suicide on Jansen, Russell declared, "This terrible event should serve as a warning to the Board of Education as to the atmosphere of fear and intimidation which will permeate the schools in the wake of the witch-hunting which the Superintendent seems ready to launch."[65]

Jansen was now faced with a public nightmare. The union was going to pin Gutride's death on him and try to undermine his investigation of Communists in the school system. Faced with questions from reporters about the suicide, Jansen expressed regret but refused to take responsibility: "In the course of my duty as Superintendent of Schools, it occasionally becomes necessary for me to conduct inquiries into the conduct of one of our 37,000 teachers." He told the press that he had recently received information regarding Gutride's alleged Communist activities, justifying sending two of his assistants to question her. Jansen admitted that it was "regrettable when any human being takes his life. It is particularly so when a teacher on active duty does so." Jansen denied he had driven Gutride to suicide. He intended to continue his investigation of Communists in the school system.[66] The Teachers Union pressed its case. On December 27 Russell sent a letter to Mayor O'Dwyer urging him to put an end to Jansen's "witch hunt." "It is imperative that you as mayor of New York," she pleaded, "not allow the philosophy and methods of the Un-American Committee [HUAC] to become official policy of the Board of Education and the Board of Superintendents." Fear and chaos were inevitable if the investigation continued, and teachers had to be reassured that they would be free of unannounced visitation by school authorities. That same day, the union issued a press release with the text of Russell's letter to the mayor.[67] Another press release on the following day reported that the union continued to receive messages expressing anger over the Gutride incident. Jansen suggested that it was the TU's protests, rather than his behavior, "which sow fear and hysteria among our teachers and the people of this city." Russell defended the skilled professionals targeted by the board because of their political leanings, ignoring their service to the children of the city, and she dared Jansen to show a blemish on the seventeen-year record of Minnie Gutride or the twenty-two-year record of Lederman.[68]

The union alleged that Gutride was targeted by Jansen because the *Journal-American* fed him lies. Lederman and Russell, in a communiqué titled "New Year's Message to the Superintendent of Schools and Members of the Board of Education," reiterated the accusation that Gutride's suicide was "caused by the shock she had suffered from the sudden inquisition to which she was subjected to on Tuesday, December 21st" and that teachers returning to work on January 3 would be upset and bewildered by the tragic act. On the day of Gutride's funeral, December 26, the *Journal-American* boasted that what convinced Jansen to question Gutride was information provided to him by the newspaper several months earlier—specifically, that she had attended Communist Party meetings in September 1941, September 1942, and May 1942.[69]

Jansen never revealed the source of his information on Gutride, but it was clear that even her suicide was not going to derail the investigation. Jaffe, the Taft-Hartley hearings, and the Minnie Gutride episode were all evidence that the union had become a prime target of the anti-Communists at a time when cold war paranoia trumped academic freedom and civil liberties.

6 / THE FIRST WAVE OF SUSPENSIONS
AND DISMISSALS

Though most of my teachers were white, many were black. And some of the white
teachers were very definitely on the Left. They opposed Franco's Spain and Mussolini's
Italy and Hitler's Third Reich. For these extreme opinions, several were placed in
blacklists and drummed out of the academic community—to the everlasting
shame of that community.

—James Baldwin, "The Price of a Ticket"

On December 27, 1948, the *New York Sun* reported that Superintendent Jansen was looking for Communists in the school system, although he claimed to be investigating only three or four teachers out of forty thousand. The following day the *New York Times* quoted the superintendent regarding the necessity to "investigate communistic activities." Still, he denied that there was a system wide investigation of Communists in New York City schools.[1] Despite Jansen's reassurances, the TU knew it was the target of the probe. In a January 8, 1949, letter to Jansen, TU President Lederman accused the superintendent of "pursuing a course which I believe runs counter to the philosophy and spirit as to the letter of our Constitution as interpreted by the highest Court of our Land" and cited two Supreme Court decisions, Virginia State Board of Education v. Barnette and Thomas v. Collins. In both cases the court upheld the protection of individual liberty against the abuse by the state. "I believe any attempt to probe into the political and personal beliefs of teachers," Lederman wrote, "is a violation of the constitutional principles embodied in these decisions."[2]

Signaling that he had no intention of calling off his investigation, Jansen created the Committee to Strengthen Democracy, which declared its aims in a publication titled "Strengthening Democracy": to strengthen "teaching for democratic living," to instill in students "American Ideals," and to emphasize the significance of "democratizing teacher-pupil classroom relationships." While the TU claimed that it had no quarrel with these stated goals, it objected to the committee's position that teachers could not be "neutral in the world struggle between democracy and any form of totalitarianism" and were obligated to "carry the fight against Communism." The TU saw the committee as a loyalty test, a part of Jansen's campaign to remove members of the union.[3]

The committee was laying the groundwork for dismissal of teachers simply because of their political views, another episode in a long history of suppression of teaches. The board had already victimized one teacher, who had appealed against an unjust charge of slanting the truth, and pushed another to suicide. How could teachers believe that it wanted to emphasize democratic traditions? The "uncritical anti-Communist aspect" of the committee's stated objectives would encourage reactionaries to intimidate teachers, forcing them to stay away from controversial subjects.[4]

Jansen was not acting in a vacuum. In the spring of 1949 the New York state legislature passed, and Governor Dewey signed, the Feinberg Law. Under Feinberg, the State Board of Regents had to come up with rules overseeing the dismissal of teachers and other school employees who belonged to groups the regents labeled subversive.[5] In May the newly elected president of the Board of Education, Maximilian Moss, publicly supported the effort to remove teachers belonging to subversive groups from the school system and noted that he had "confidence" in Jansen in his task.[6] In September Jansen explained the procedure the school system would use to determine if teachers and other Board of Education employees belonged to subversive groups. Principals would have to file reports on all teachers and clerks, and two lists would be maintained. Principals would certify on one list the employees for whom there was no evidence demonstrating membership in subversive groups. The other list would consist of special reports on employees who were suspected of belonging to subversive organizations.[7] Although there would be court battles over the Feinberg Law, with it Jansen gained an important tool in his fight against Communism.[8]

On May 3, 1949, when the New York Times reported that Jansen was investigating "six" teachers regarding their membership in the American Communist Party, the Superintendent denied to the paper that he was carrying out a "witch hunt." To ease the anxiety, he wanted to clarify what he said were "false" charges and "loose talk" by the union. Six teachers were questioned about their affiliation with the Communist Party because they had refused to answer before the Taft-Hartley Committee; another was questioned because colleagues reported that he had admitted his membership in the Communist Party.[9] According to Jansen, one teacher admitted membership in the Communist Party, but the other five refused to answer. He did not reveal the names of any of the teachers, saying that everyone should be presumed innocent until proven guilty. He had a duty to investigate, but declared that most teachers should not be concerned.[10] If the evidence was strong enough, Jansen would present it to the Board of Education, which then would proffer charges and try the teachers. The *Times* reported that the Board of Education and the corporation counsel authorized the investigation under articles 23 and 25 of the State Education Law, which would "allow the prosecution of teachers who do not fulfill their obligations." Although Jansen did not reveal the names of those questioned, Celia Lewis Zitron, a TU executive board member and its secretary, admitted to the *Times* that she had been interrogated.[11]

THE SYLVIA SCHNEIDERMAN CASE

But it was not Zitron and the others who would first become known to the public as suspected Communists but a first grade teacher at P.S. 3, Brooklyn, Sylvia Schneiderman. In late December 1949 Schneiderman received a letter telling her to report to the superintendent's office on January 6 to discuss her application for a regular license. Schneiderman, finishing her probationary period, was just a few months from receiving appointment as a tenured teacher. Jansen wanted to question her about a claim in her application that she had never been a member of the Communist Party. Schneiderman, the mother of a six year old and an infant, wrote to the superintendent on January 3, noting that she had recently been on maternity leave. Because P.S. 3 was located in the "heart of the Bedford-Stuyvesant section" of Brooklyn and could not attract substitute teachers, at her principal's request she had willingly returned to the school before her maternity leave was up. Schneiderman told Jansen she would be unable to make the meeting because she could not make child care arrangements for that day.[12]

Undoubtedly, Schneiderman was avoiding interrogation by the superintendent. She never proposed an alternative date. Jansen wanted to move against her because her probationary period was drawing to a close: as a tenured teacher, she would be entitled to a formal hearing. While she was still a probationary employee, she could simply be fired by the Board of Education. Schneiderman managed to avoid a meeting with board officials for three months. On March 6 she was called to her principal's office to answer a telephone call from Jacob Greenberg, associate superintendent, telling her to report to his office either that afternoon or the following day to discuss a matter affecting her license. Once again, she claimed she could not arrange for child care and for another teacher to accompany her.[13]

When Schneiderman reiterated her excuses the following day, Greenberg ordered her to appear, warning her that her "professional life" was at risk. Schneiderman's letter of response once again noted her positive performance in a so-called problem district, citing "excellent" relationships with her students, "all of whom are Negroes." She accused Greenberg of abuse: "I am so physically and emotionally upset by your summons and threatening message as to be unable to think coherently [about] this whole thing." She even compared herself to Minnie Gutride. "I can appreciate now what led Mrs. Gutride, after years of teaching, to take her life after such an experience. I am distressed and upset by this terrible thing, I feel myself utterly unable to respond." Because of what she labeled Greenberg's "inhumane" treatment, she was too emotionally upset to return to work for a few weeks or to go through an interrogation.[14]

Jansen, with only ten days left of Schneiderman's probationary period, made his move, informing the media that he was recommending to the Board of Education that Schneiderman be fired. He did not notify her of his recommendation but provided the press with details about her, including her address. On March 9, photographers and reporters "invaded" Schneiderman's home, according to Rose Russell, who also said the news people barged into the teacher's bedroom where she lay ill. Russell accused Jansen of "violating basic decency" in his effort to rid the system of Communists. "Your lack of consideration speaks louder than your frequent words about dignity of the teacher and of the individual."[15]

In an effort to stop the Board of Education from firing Schneiderman, the union issued a press release calling Jansen's action a "vindictive heresy hunt." He had refused to wait a few days and give her the protection and rights of a tenured teacher. Juxtaposing Schneiderman to Jansen, the TU portrayed her as unselfish, a dedicated teacher who voluntarily shortened her maternity leave to return to a school in the predominantly black community of Bedford-Stuyvesant.[16]

The TU sought and received backing from a number of groups and publicized their support in order to put pressure on Jansen. The letters of support portrayed Schneiderman as a selfless, caring, and dedicated educator who deserved better treatment. The Teachers' Interest Committee of P.S. 3 sent Maximilian Moss a letter supporting their embattled colleague, pointing out that Schneiderman's classes contributed to charities and participated in patriotic celebrations. No one on the faculty ever heard her "utter a word of disparagement concerning our government."[17] Schneiderman's class had acted on behalf of the underprivileged, collecting toys for the "needy" at P.S. 3. Her actions clearly demonstrated her "self-effacing, modest, democratic and wholesome Americanism." The committee requested that she be given a hearing to defend herself.[18] Edward S. Smith, executive director of the National Teachers Division of the United Public Workers of America, in a letter to the *New York Times*, maintained that there was no contention that Schneiderman had ever been derelict in her obligations as a teacher or used the classroom to promote any political view. Smith wrote,

> For those who cling to traditional American practices of jurisprudence and common decency, the lesson of the Schneiderman case is clear. The determination of a teacher's fitness must be neither political association nor answers on an application blank regarding political association—itself an act of effrontery. Rather it must rest on a finding of whether the teacher is, in fact, a good teacher. Has he made the classroom a forum for indoctrination of ideas, political, religious or whatever? If so, he is an unfit teacher; if not, he is entitled to all the protection of freedom of thought, speech and association guaranteed to all citizens by the Bill of Rights.[19]

Academic freedom, performance in the classroom, and constitutional rights became major arguments in defense of those targeted by the board.

Even the TU's arch nemesis, the Teachers Guild, criticized the superintendent. Rebecca C. Simonson, president of the guild, opposed the procedure used in the Schneiderman case and called Jansen's actions a violation of due process. It was clear that it did not matter whether a teacher was on probation or on a permanent tenure line: "every teacher against whom charges have been made is granted the fullest judicial protection." Due process included full judicial protection, including notice of charges, reasonable opportunity to prepare a defense, notice of hearing, right to be represented by counsel at the hearing, right to cross-examination, right to present witnesses in his or her own behalf, and the right to notice of the decision by the Board of Education.[20] The guild was not rushing to the aid of the TU in a demonstration of solidarity. Instead, the TU's rival was making an argument for the protection of due process. If the board were allowed to fire a teacher who was a member of the TU without explanation, what stopped it from firing guild members or others?

Despite the TU's effort to save Schneiderman's job, Russell informed union members in a March 18, 1950, letter that the "opening gun in the Board of Education's announced witch-hunt against teachers was fired" when the first grade teacher was dismissed.[21] Although the battle to save Schneiderman was lost, there was a larger struggle underway. In an attempt to galvanize the public and teachers, Russell issued a March 24 letter urging parents to take action to stop what she called a witch hunt. Their children were entitled to the best teachers, and they needed to stop the "flagrant assault against progressive teachers" due to their political beliefs and affiliation. Jansen and the board were specifically targeting teachers with "progressive" views and "superior teaching records," when racist and anti-Semitic teachers like May Quinn were left alone. Schneiderman was the "first victim," but clearly would not be the last. Russell urged friends of the union to send letters to Moss requesting that he put an end to the "undemocratic inquisition."[22]

The reaction of the TU and its supporters was not hyperbole; they had every reason to be alarmed. Speaking before the Women's City Club, Jansen stated that he believed Communists should not be permitted to teach in the New York public school system. Although he had made a similar statement before the Taft-Hartley Subcommittee, the context was quite different. His testimony before the subcommittee also included friendly remarks about the TU. But his remarks before the Women's City Club occurred when he was launching an investigation against teachers. He claimed to have questioned ten teachers and to have "complete proof that they were in the Communist Party." The Board of Education was vigorously hunting for Communists in the school system, and TU members were the prime targets.[23]

THE SUSPENDED EIGHT

In the spring of 1950 Jansen demanded that Louis Jaffe, Isadore Rubin, Celia Lewis Zitron, David Friedman, Alice Citron, Abraham Feingold, and

Figure 6.1 Eight suspended teachers. *Left to right:* Louis Jaffe, Alice Citron, Celia Lewis Zitron, Abraham Lederman, Abraham Feingold, Mark Friedlander, Isadore Rubin, and David L. Friedman. United Federation of Teachers, part 1, folder 522.

Mark Friedlander come to his office on April 24, with Abraham Lederman summoned for the following day, for questioning. Harold Cammer, of the law firm Witte and Cammer, hired by the union to represent the teachers, sent the superintendent a letter accusing him of violating basic procedure in his investigation, including refusing to give reasonable notice to those being investigated and not allowing them to have adequate representation. Cammer argued that teachers should be accompanied by an attorney—not a colleague as the superintendent had ruled—and that they should receive at least a week's notice.[24] Cammer's letter had no impact. Instead, Jansen would move ahead with his investigation. In his "Material for Questions of Seven Teachers," Assistant Corporation Counsel Michael Castaldi provided Jansen with a strategy for interrogation. First, the superintendent would inform the teacher that he intended to ask questions "concerning your conduct, character, and fitness as a teacher." The "Material for Questions" warned Jansen that he should expect the seven to be evasive, refusing to answer questions about their membership in the Communist Party; therefore, he should assert, "as Superintendent of Schools, I direct you to answer the questions 'yes' or 'no.' I shall consider your failure to do so insubordinate conduct."[25]

On April 24 Jansen questioned Citron, Zitron, Jaffe, Rubin, Friedlander, Friedman, and Feingold. The superintendent released a press statement claiming that those interviews were "merely a continuation of an investigation of membership in the Communist Party I have been conducting for some time." The following day, he questioned Lederman about his political affiliation. These were not investigations of ordinary teachers. Jansen was targeting important leaders in the largest teacher's organization in the city. On May 3 Jansen sent a letter to the members of the Board of Education informing them that he had formally charged Citron, Feingold, Friedlander, Friedman, Jaffe, Lederman, Rubin, and Zitron with insubordination and conduct unbecoming a teacher and had suspended them without pay, effective at the end of the day. The superintendent told the press that he had received "sufficient information about each of these teachers to cause me to call them in for questioning about their present or past membership in the Communist Party." But he was careful to point out that they were suspended for refusing to answer questions about their political affiliation with the Party, rather than for actual membership. Formal charges against the eight were filed on May 9. The Board of Education's next step was to appoint a trial examiner.[26]

THE TU'S PUBLIC CAMPAIGN

Almost immediately, the union launched a campaign to win public support. The union's legislative representative, Russell, called on the board to lift the suspensions, arguing that the charge of conduct unbecoming a teacher was bogus. Claiming that all eight teachers had an "unimpeachable record of faithful and superior service to the children, to our school system and to our country," Russell was not only laying out the public campaign but also the defense strategy for the teachers. Their superb records, which Jansen claimed were "irrelevant," were at the heart of the TU's case. The union contended that teachers should be judged by their actions in the classroom and not by their beliefs or convictions.[27] The board's violation of the core values of academic freedom and freedom of opinion became a major theme of the union. Teachers should be evaluated solely on their conduct and performance in the classroom, not on their outside affiliations. Isadore Rubin declared, on May 4, 1950, "If teachers are to be questioned on what they do outside the classroom, it will mean second class citizenship."[28]

Another claim by the TU regarding Jansen's actions had to do with the union's challenge to board policies. Russell accused the superintendent of trying to destroy the union because it "exposed the conditions that have produced the present crisis," pointing to the TU's "constructive suggestions" for improving conditions for children as well as teachers. Russell's opinion of the cordial relationship between the TU and Jansen, expressed at the Taft-Hartley hearings, changed after the suspensions. "Early in Dr. Jansen's administration, a group of officers from the Teachers Union met with him to offer our cooperation, but it soon became clear that Dr. Jansen was interested in 'unifying' the teaching staff in a spurious unity that actually meant docile conformity. As a result, efforts to make suggestions generally turned into controversies." Tension arose from specific policies and actions, such as Jansen's decision to scrap an in-service course on techniques in intercultural education, the banning of books and periodicals, including the *Nation* magazine, "Races of Mankind," and *Gentlemen's Agreement*, and the light treatment of May Quinn and other racist teachers. She also mentioned the union's objections to racist textbooks, including some written and edited by Jansen and other school officials.[29]

But the TU's strategy had no impact on Jansen. In fact, the suspension of the TU members and the ensuing publicity threatened the union, which found it difficult to address the tactic of trying to remove individual members from the school system. The union had been investigated several times and its AFT charter revoked. Now it had to defend individual members with a legal campaign, creating a potential financial crisis. Jansen made it clear that his investigation was not going to end with the eight, telling the press that several more schoolteachers were going to be investigated.[30]

Realizing that Jansen was planning a deeper probe, the TU sent individuals and organizations a list of things they could do: send resolutions of protest to O'Dwyer, Jansen, and Moss, have the members of the organizations sign postcards and petitions protesting the suspensions.[31] Supporters of the TU echoed the union's main arguments, calling for judging teachers on their professional records and their political beliefs, and saying the board's actions were an assault on academic freedom and the dismissal of the teachers would have a negative impact on children. Some noted that the board's suspension of the eight was a clear violation of civil liberties and academic freedom and constituted an attack on labor. Abraham Edel, professor of philosophy at City College, wrote to Moss protesting the suspensions as a gross violation of academic freedom, a well-established principle that included the right to free exercise of civil rights. How could the board of the largest school system in the country violate this treasured tradition? William Cartwright, president of the Academic Assembly of the University of California, called on President Moss to end the "hysteria of political inquisition and the pernicious doctrine of guilt by association; and insist that teachers be judged on performance of their classroom duties. Competence in such performance is, and if academic freedom is to survive, must be the only test for fitness to teach."[32]

Although the United Parents Association did not support the suspended eight, individual PTAs protested Jansen's actions. The executive board of the PTA, Junior High School 115, Manhattan, condemned the suspension of teachers whose excellent records were "relevant and the only basis for judgment." It juxtaposed May Quinn, who was guilty of racist acts in the classroom, to the eight, who had "unblemished classroom records and excellent past ratings." The PTA of P.S. 86 in the Bronx adopted a resolution asserting that all citizens have the right to their political beliefs. Only when a teacher tried to indoctrinate students, to push a philosophy or ideology contrary to American democracy, should the teacher be disciplined.[33] Fifty parents whose children attended schools in Washington Heights and the Inwood section of New York sent a letter to Jansen protesting the suspensions.[34]

The TU also received international support. Educators from abroad criticized the Board of Education for damaging the image of United States as a paragon of democracy. Fernand Petit, a teacher and member of the Lausanne, Switzerland, city council, declared his solidarity with teachers worldwide and protested against "an action which dishonors the school authorities of a nation which pretends to be the champion of principles of liberty and democracy throughout the world."[35] The Spanish Federation of Educational Workers (UGT), made up of anti-Franco university professors, high school teachers, librarians, and other educators, called the suspension of the eight teachers "violation of the most elementary democratic rights and of the respect that every teacher deserves."[36]

The TU continued emphasizing the stellar teaching record of the suspended teachers in the hope of winning public support. In a pamphlet titled *What Kind of Teachers for Your Child? The Facts Behind the Suspension of 8 Excellent Teachers,* the suspended eight are described as "exemplary" professionals devoted to children. The pamphlet never denied that the eight were Communist Party members, because Party membership was irrelevant and did not determine the fitness of a teacher, but it noted the superintendent could not cite any evidence the eight conducted themselves in an unprofessional manner.[37] *What Kind of Teachers* noted the superb service record of each suspended teacher. A twenty-three-year veteran, Lederman was the only classroom teacher serving on the Standing Committee on Junior High School Mathematics of the Board of Education. Celia Lewis Zitron, a twenty-seven-year veteran who taught Latin at Washington Irving High School, receiving praise from supervisors, also taught the first course in Hebrew at Abraham Lincoln and sacrificed her summer vacation to help prepare curriculum and teaching materials. Alice Citron, a teacher for eighteen years, struggled for opportunity "for Negro children and against every form of Jim Crow."[38] In a leaflet titled "Your Children Have Lost Eight of Their Best Teachers," parents and others were asked to write to Moss and O'Dwyer insisting the teachers be reinstated.[39] Despite TU's arguments citing academic freedom and focusing on the records of the suspended teachers, it did not stop Jansen from moving ahead with the hearings. The larger issue for the superintendent was Communist infiltration of the schools, and he was determined to rid the system of that menace

"TEACHERS ON TRIAL"

Although the TU could not stop the hearings, it decided to discredit them by portraying them as trials. The union distributed a pamphlet, *Teachers on Trial,* claiming that the Board of Education needed the "trials" to "put across the militarization of the schools," part of a larger campaign to destroy the rights of all citizens. The pamphlet cited examples such as forcing a peace organization to register as a "foreign agent," passing the Wood-McCarran Bill, "which aims to set up a police state and concentration camps" in the United States, and rearming "Nazis who only recently slaughtered six million Jews and countless millions of other innocent people." Anti-Communist hysteria threatened to eliminate the civil liberties of all people. To "stop the plot against" children, the union called on parents and others to write to Moss demanding that he stop the "witch-hunt and reinstate the teachers."[40]

In publications such as *Teachers on Trial* and *Teachers Fight for Freedom: Eight New York City Teachers on Trial* the TU painted the hearings as *trials,* suggesting the teachers faced the loss of their freedom. Of course, the Board of Education did not have the power to conduct legal proceedings or to decide if someone had committed a crime and pass sentence. Its powers were limited to determining if an employee had violated the contract, by-laws, or state and city statutes relating to his profession. But union leaders were not the only ones to use the term *trial.* Jansen and the Board of Education embraced attempts to portray the hearings as trials. In their estimation, these were not ordinary disciplinary hearings of teachers who committed wrong doings in the classroom. The teachers had committed a criminal offense by joining the American Communist Party.

Even though the hearings were not legal proceedings, they played into the board's effort to criminalize the union and its members while ignoring their right to academic freedom. The board conducted the hearings as if they were criminal proceedings. Corporation Counsel John McGrath suggested a legal strategy that was a carbon copy of the one United States attorney general Tom Clark used against Party members in criminal trial. J. Edgar Hoover, director of the FBI, had argued that outlawing the Communist Party would only make members martyrs.[41] However, Clark attempted to prove that American Communists' loyalty was to the Soviet Union rather than the United States and that American Communists were part of an international movement to overthrow democratic governments and establish Soviet-style governments in their place.

The U.S. government's case against the Party members relied on the testimony of "expert" witnesses, former members of the Communist Party, along with informants. The charges leveled at Eugene Dennis, the general secretary of the Communist Party, and eleven members of its National Committee included violating the 1940 Smith Act, which made it a crime to teach or advocate the overthrow of the government. There was no evidence the accused were actually engaged in any scheme. Instead, citing the writings of Marx, Lenin, and Stalin, the government argued "Marxism-

Leninism" advocated the overthrow of the United States government. Membership in the Party was enough to prove that the defendants were involved in a conspiracy against the United States. The government also forced the defendants to commit contempt of court by demanding they name others in the Party, knowing full well that they would refuse.[42]

Using the same approach as Clark, McGrath presented the charges with supporting arguments that he believed would apply specifically not only to the eight cases but also to other teachers. Membership in the Communist Party—an organization that cultivated adherence and allegiance to specific doctrines, beliefs, and ways of teaching that were contrary to the ideals, purposes, and standards of behavior required by the Board of Education—rendered the accused "unfit to be continued in the employ of the Board of Education." Thus, the board's duty would be to prove the teacher was a member of the Party while employed as a teacher, was "engaged in advancing the interests" of the Party by attending "secret Communist meetings," and participated in other party-sponsored activities, such as recruitment and persuading both teachers and students to adhere to the principles of the CPUSA.[43]

According to McGrath, the eight accused teachers were practicing deceit by concealing their Party membership, damaging the interests, reputation, and welfare of the Board of Education and those entrusted with management, operation, and control of the system. The Communist Party was designed to benefit a "foreign power;" it mandated "unequivocal obedience" to its commands, no matter how inconsistent or antagonistic to the ideals, purposes, established policies, and standards of conduct of teachers employed by the board. The Communist Party required that members lie or deny their membership, or withhold information pertaining to the identity of other Party members or the nature of the Communist Party, even under oath.[44]

To bolster his case, McGrath pointed out the Rapp-Coudert Committee's findings that membership in the Communist party was an "overt act incompatible with public service." Benjamin Gitlow, once one of the highest ranking members of the Communist Party, had testified before Rapp-Coudert that the Communist Party was a "secret, conspiratorial and deceptive organization" controlled by the Soviet Union and that the autocratic nature of the Party would lead to a "totalitarian government." According to Gitlow, teachers could not be Party members and perform their duties. The member was not a "free individual to do as he sees fit" but was under the "direct orders and discipline" of the Communist Party. McGrath cited passages from the writings of Lenin, Stalin, and other Communists to prove his point that the Communist Party was part of an international conspiracy.

The Board of Education moved quickly against the eight teachers, attempting to select a "trial examiner" to oversee the hearings. Jansen and the board knew that their hearings, if successful, would serve as a precedent. The union, also aware of the consequences if Jansen was successful in dismissing the teachers, continued to try to stop the hearings. When the board selected Theodore F. Kiendl, a prominent attorney, as examiner, the union and its allies strongly objected, accusing his law firm of racial basis. A special public hearing was conducted on June 12, 1950 to hear the views of those who supported or opposed the appointment of Kiendl. At the hearing Lederman said, "Not one of the scores of partners in the firm, past or present, has been Jewish." Moreover, the firm had defended railroad companies that contended they had a legal right to discriminate against blacks. The railroad companies did not deny discriminating. On the contrary, "the firm maintained in those cases, that the railway had the legal right to practice such discrimination." Although Lederman did not accuse Kiendl personally of anti-Semitism, he argued that the trial examiner and his firm must be above reproach. Before any group with "legislative jurisdiction," Kiendl would be disqualified. Accused teacher Louis Jaffe argued that a special trial examiner was not necessary because there was no need for a trial. Instead, he insisted that the teachers be reinstated. Arthur Newman, representing the Better Schools Committee, a parents organization located in the South Bronx, also spoke against the appointment of a trial examiner, contending that it was unnecessary to go outside the ranks of the board. Arthur Schutzer, executive secretary of the New York State American Labor Party, called the trial examiner a "witch-hunt specialist." Despite the opposition, the board voted to appoint Kiendl.[45]

The corporation counsel tried David Friedman first. He was charged not only with insubordination but also for acknowledging that he was a member of the Communist Political Association and the Communist Party of the United States. Proving his membership would be straightforward. McGrath argued that Friedman violated "Education Law" by being a member of the Communist Political Association and the Communist Party of the United States, which required that he obey its principles and doctrines, including performing acts that were "contrary to the standards of conduct for teachers employed by the Board of Education." A third charge was that he evaded and refused to answer questions concerning his "conduct, character, fitness, and loyalty as a teacher."[46]

The board also pursued another important strategy, proving that being a Communist violated academic freedom, making Party members unfit to teach. The board was not the first to use this strategy. The Rapp-Coudert Committee had argued that Communist professors in the City University system violated academic freedom by either denying their membership or evading direct questions, thus throwing into question their integrity. In January 1949 the Board of Regents of the University of Washington, on the recommendation of President Raymond Allen, fired three professors on the grounds that two were in the Party and one was carrying out the Party's work, even though there was no evidence that he was a member.[47] The firings set off a wave of protests. Allen maintained that a Communist Party member was "not a free man" and free teaching and research were essential components of the academic profession. A Party member was "instead a slave to immutable dogma and to a clandestine organization masquerading as a political party." The Communist professor did not have the freedom to accept or reject theories or notions on his own independent research, experience, or thinking: "his mind is chained to that theory which is written into Communist Party dogma."[48]

Allen was not the first person in academia to make this argument. Sidney Hook, professor of philosophy at New York University, argued that Communists were unfit to teach. Early in his career Hook offered courses in Marxism and wrote several books on Marxist philosophy, including *Towards the Understanding of Karl Marx*, in which he argued that Marxism was an objective science.[49] However, Hook became disillusioned with the Soviet Union once he learned of Stalin's purges. In 1934, at a conference with Bertrand Russell and John Dewey, he presented a paper, "Communism Without Dogma," which did not denounce Communism but repudiated the Third International. His falling out with the Communist Party occurred when Hitler came to power and Hook called on the Party to end its attacks on social democrats and socialists. "I had come to the conclusion that the Communist doctrine that the socialists were the chief enemies of Germany, played directly into the hands of Hitler." When he learned that the Soviet

Union had entered into "financial and industrial relations" with the Nazi regime, Hook publicly attacked the Soviet Union and the American Communist Party.[50]

By the mid 1930s Hook had become an outspoken critic of Communism. Testifying before the Rapp-Coudert Committee in May 1941, Hook took aim at the New York City Teachers Union, declaring that the Brooklyn College chapter had Communists and that the Party was "cultivating the academic people." As proof, Hook told the committee that CPUSA founder Earl Browder attempted to "enroll" him by arguing he would be very valuable in "building a strong following in the cultural and educational field." It was the very fact that the college section of the Teachers Union was made up of Communists, Hook insisted, that made it a dangerous organization:

> In any college where you have a group of people organized in a conspirational manner, who take their instructions from a foreign power—because the basic value and allegiance of the Communist power is oriented toward Russia, and that can be documented in a thousand details where you have such a group who publishes newspapers, organizes the students, aims to inculcate a point of view which is laid down by a foreign power, and then the very pre-supposition of educational freedoms are undermined. . . . So that I think there can be no question but that if conspirational groups of that sort existed on the campus, it would make impossible the work of education of the university or college as such.[51]

Eight years after his testimony, Hook was still hammering away at the dangers of allowing Communists to teach. In the February 27, 1949, *New York Times*—a piece that Raymond Allen pointed to in his argument as to why Communists should not be allowed to teach—Hook argued that membership in the Party was "prima facie evidence that a teacher does not believe in or practice academic freedom." Communist Party members forfeited their rights to teach.[52] Hook had made the argument before the suspension of the eight New York City school teachers that dismissal of Communists did not violate academic freedom.[53]

McGrath argued in his opening statement that Friedman's conduct violated sections 161 and 162 of the penal law, which made it a felony for a person, group, or organization to advocate the violent overthrow of the United States government; section 12a of the Civil Service Law, which disqualified a person who advocated the violent overthrow of the government from a public service job; section 23a of the Civil Service Law; section 3021 of the Education Law, which dismissed a licensed public employee from employment if he advocated or performed "treasonable" or seditious acts; and the Feinberg Law, which made belonging to a group that advocated the overthrow of the government grounds for dismissal by the Board of Education. "These statutes and Court decisions," McGrath said, "reflect a common recognition by the American people that the doctrines and activities of the Communist Party threaten our existence as a free nation and our entire way of life."[54]

McGrath then turned to the literature of the Party, contending it was a guide to action. The mission of the Party was to "recruit, organize, train, and prepare its members as professional revolutionaries who shall engage in unceasing struggles to undermine and weaken capitalist states by every possible means." The first duty of Communists was to the Soviet Union.[55]

McGrath quoted Lenin, Stalin, and William Z. Foster, a leader of the CPUSA, to bolster his theme that the Communist Party called for the violent destruction of the government of the United States and the establishment of Soviet America. Leaders of the American Communist Party "subjected themselves to the authority of its Russian master." Turning to David Friedman, McGrath asserted that the teacher was an officer in the United Nations Club of the Communist Party, supported the revolutionary program of "Lenin and Stalin," adhered to party discipline, and concealed his party membership. By following the writings of Lenin and Stalin, Friedman had become a "professional revolutionary, a Marxist and a disciplined member of a quasi military organization." The writings of Soviet leaders were "guides to action, blueprints of what is to be done, strategies to be employed in the coming revolutions."[56]

The most sensational part of McGrath's opening statement, the heart of his argument, was the assertion that Communist teachers attempted to indoctrinate children. McGrath argued that he would prove, using Communist periodicals, that a Marxist teacher was required to "guide and direct that spirit of rebelliousness" in students. An expert in Marxism-Leninism could "skillfully inject these doctrines into his teaching without risk of exposure," influencing the "minds of pupils in the public schools" by adopting what they labeled an objective view on controversial topics.[57]

Testifying at the hearing was undercover police officer Stephanie Horvath, who in 1944 and 1945 had attended meetings of the Communist Party and joined the United Nations Club of the Communist Political Association where Friedman was a member. The August 24, 1957, edition of the *Tablet*, published by the Brooklyn Catholic diocese, reported on "an undercover police woman who has infiltrated the Communist party." Horvath testified that Friedman presided at some of the meetings in support of various Communist activities. On December 12, 1944, when Friedman was serving as chair of the UN Club, members referred to him as "comrade Dave." Friedman was nominated for and accepted a position as educational director, which he declared was a good position for him, because it did not jeopardize his civil service position. A copy of the ballot for educational director was introduced in the case as exhibit 48. Horvath claimed that other candidates for the position eventually withdrew their names and Friedman was "unanimously elected." At the January 23 meeting Friedman, according to Horvath, urged his fellow comrades to help distribute 250 copies of "L'Unita del Popolo," a Communist Party publication aimed at the Italian American neighborhoods.[58]

Friedman had participated in club activities and even attended a May 9 Communist Party celebration. Horvath, a member of the same Communist Party club, said Friedman supported renaming the Communist Political Association to the Communist Party at a meeting on June 5, 1945. Citing an article by French Communist Leader Jacques Duclos (see Chapter 9) criticizing American Communists under the leadership of Earl Browder, Friedman argued that Communists should reject "revisionism and opportunism" and embrace the principles of Marxism-Leninism. According to Horvath, at a June 26 meeting Friedman promoted the principle of "democratic centralism," which required all Communists to "obey and carry out the decisions of the Party's leaders even if they happen to doubt their correctness." Friedman had attended Communist Party meetings throughout 1947, pushing the Marxist-Leninist line.[59]

The testimony of Joseph Zack Kornfeder was also a crucial element of the Friedman hearing. Kornfeder joined the Communist Labor Party (later the American Communist Party) in 1919 and served on its central committee from 1920 to 1927. Between 1928 and 1930 Kornfeder was a student at the Lenin School for Advanced Communist Studies in Moscow; he was an international representative of the Comintern in Columbia and Venezuela from 1930 to 1931. Growing disillusioned and breaking with the Communist Party in 1934, he would eventually become an expert witness for the government, providing it with information on the party and key leaders. Kiendl noted that Kornfeder "attended the most important secret councils of the Party, both here and in Moscow, and the testimony which he gave bore directly on the issue as to whether the Communist Party, among other things, advocated the violent overthrow of the government."[60] Kornfeder testified that the American Communist Party joined the International in 1920 and accepted all its conditions of membership, including advocating the "violent overthrow of the government of the United States." Members, he alleged, agreed to defend the Soviet Union and embrace "democratic centralism." Non-nationals who were agents of the Comintern became officers in the Communist Party of the United States and "supervised and directed the activities of the leaders" as dictated by Moscow. In 1921 the Communist Party advocated the "violent overthrow" of the U.S. government and in 1925, at its national convention, the toppling of the government. The U.S. Party circulated resolutions at the World Congress that called for overthrow of capitalist governments and following the Soviet Union as a model "when the time was ripe."[61]

When Kiendl asked the corporation counsel if there was any evidence for Friedman's inappropriate behavior in the classroom, McGrath admitted there was no "proof of any specific classroom act," nor had he "heard of any conduct unbecoming a teacher." Taking as a given that the Party called for the overthrow of the government, the case against Friedman hinged on whether he was a member of the American Communist Party. He was on trial not for his actions in the classroom but for his political views and political activities outside the school system. The defense attempted to present as witnesses "experts on academic freedom," such as Thomas I. Emerson—a constitutional scholar and professor at Yale University School of Law, later cofounder of the Emergency Civil Liberties Committee, which defended the rights of American Communists. Kiendl denied them permission to testify, arguing that academic freedom had nothing to do with the proceeding.[62] The TU complained that Kiendl refused to consider teacher morale, bias, bigotry, and pending investigations of corruption in the repair of school buildings. Serving as a member of the defense team, Rose Russell challenged all McGrath's accusations, including that Friedman accepted the "iron discipline" of the Communist Party or was a professional revolutionary, a "disciplined member of a quasi-military organization" required to inject Marxism-Leninism in the classroom and involved in establishing a "fifth column" in the country.[63]

Despite the testimony of Horvath and Kornfeder, neither McGrath nor Jansen found any fault with the twenty-five-year veteran's teaching. According to Russell, Friedman was threatened with dismissal "not for anything he did or said, not for the actual influence that he had upon his pupils, but because of what his words and acts were assumed to be, because of what others said certain doctrine was alleged to mean." Jansen had evaded his responsibility by allowing the corporation counsel to determine what was conduct unbecoming a teacher. By delegating power to McGrath and hiring Kiendl as trial examiner, Jansen shifted in Friedman's case from educational polices to narrow legal issues, excluding expert witnesses on the issue of academic freedom.[64] Russell also condemned the school system's practice of using spies and informers, creating an unhealthy atmosphere in public education. Russell took full advantage of her closing statement to quote the findings of the Public Education Association of New York, thirty years earlier, arguing that the repression in the schools right after World War I damaged intellectual freedom and led to a "reign of terror against those teachers suspected of independent opinion."

When Kiendl asked Russell if she considered a teacher "bordering on the possibility of indoctrinating" students to be dangerous and incompetent, she replied that actions were more important than unproven accusations. Kiendl argued that a Communist teacher is dangerous because "he is prepared, when, if and as in the opinion of that party it becomes propitious and advisable to follow the Party Line." Russell suggested he would have to extend that assumption to other groups with rigid doctrines, such as Jehovah's Witnesses and Catholics.[65] Cammer argued that Marxism-Leninism itself was on trial, but theory and doctrines could not be proven in a court of law or hearing to be good or bad.[66]

Despite the cogent arguments raised by Russell and the lawyers representing the teachers, Kiendl recommended that Friedman be fired. Informers and expert witnesses had established he was a member of the Communist Political Association and reorganized CPUSA. McGrath had demonstrated persuasively that the Communist Party advocated violent overthrow of the United States and that Friedman "approved of, assisted and participated" in the Party's subversive activities.[67]

Friedman, Kiendl argued, was guilty of neglect of duty, conduct unbecoming his position, and violation of other provisions in New York State Education Law 2523 and the Board of Education bylaws. It had been proven that he supported the Duclos article, criticized "Browderism," and called for a return to Marxist-Leninist principles, "democratic centralism," and the "dictatorship of the Proletariat," which Stalin said would come about by "smashing of the bourgeois" state. Kiendl wrote, "American Communists unquestionably adopted these views" and took them to be "Party gospel." Many principles of "Marxism-Leninism," Kiendl continued, were unpatriotic and illegal. Communist Party members participated in a "semi-military organization" to recruit, organize, train, and prepare themselves as "professional revolutionaries who shall carry on constant bitter class struggles, to undermine and weaken capitalist states until war, depression or other favorable situations promises a successful outcome."[68]

In his role as trial examiner, Kiendl quoted extensively from Communist Party literature. In the "Manual of Organization" J. Peters wrote that the Communist Party of the United States must lead the American working class in the struggle for the "revolutionary overthrow of capitalism, for the establishment of the dictatorship of the proletariat, [and] for the creation of a socialist republic in the United States." The program of the Sixth World Congress openly advocated "violent Communist insurrection" and asserted that the first duty of Marxist-Leninists was to defend the "fatherland" against the United States. The American delegation to the World Congress in 1928, headed by William Z. Foster and Jay Lovestone, accepted the program calling for the "violent overthrow" of the capitalist countries; they "participated and joined in the opening proceedings wherein all of the delegates pledged loyalty to Stalin and idolized him as a Communist deity, in terms which are nauseating to free men."[69]

According to Kiendl, the New York constitution required public school employees to take an oath of office. Once public school employees take the oath they are obligated as officers to support and defend the Constitution and government." The government had the duty to assure the loyalty of its employees for its own protection.[70] The dismissal of Friedman, Kiendl argued, did not violate his constitutional rights. Civil liberties as assured by the constitution were not "absolute" but were limited by the need to maintain public order. Words as well as actions that posed a "clear and present danger of detriment to public order" were a good reason for limiting

the guarantees of the First Amendment. Nevertheless, the proceedings con-
formed to the principle of due process. First, the charge of advocating the
overthrow of the government was specific, not vague, according to cases
such as the People v. Gitlow (1922), U.S. v. Foster (1948), and Lederman
v. Board of Education (1950). A "constitutionally permissible influence of
future evil conduct" was highly plausible for a member of the Communist
Party, and removing Communist Party members would eliminate the opportunities for such evil activities.[71]

The criminalization of the Communist Party and its members had already
been established. Kiendl essentially used the same arguments for Friedman's
dismissal. He claimed there was sufficient evidence that all Party members
owed allegiance to every detail of the Communist program and had assumed
an active duty to help execute it. Congress could, on similar conspiracy principles, charge each member with responsibility for the goals and means of
the Party and for having entered into a "criminal conspiracy."[72]

The hearings of the seven other teachers followed Friedman's, and in all
of the proceedings a number of witnesses spoke on behalf of the respon-
dents. The chairman of the mathematics department at Manual Training
High School, where Feingold taught, said that the math teacher was "a very
capable teacher, sincere, very much interested in children, anxious to do a
complete job for them," and "ready to cooperate in anything I asked him to
do." Harry Eisner, once Feingold's chairperson, described him as "cooperative, conscientious and competent. He has shown particular skill in handling
slow students, slow learners. . . . He has never turned down an assignment,
and he has always been very glad to help in any way that he could." In some
cases parents took the initiative. Although no prominent minister or politi-
cian expressed support for Alice Citron, fifteen black parents at P.S. 84 in
Harlem came forward on her behalf. The president of the PTA said, "We love
Alice Citron because she has fought for us and our children.[73] Another parent, Edith Joell, said that Citron was 'known all through our community"
as "unstinting in her time and efforts." Citron was credited by one parent
with getting needed books, while another declared, "She is everything to
our neighborhood, to the community as a whole." Ida Wessa, chair of the
Department of Foreign Languages at Washington Irving High School, said
Celia Zitron was "an excellent teacher," and her former chair at Abraham
Lincoln High School called her "a superior teacher in every way, in preparation, results, achievement, and especially in her influence on her pupils."[74]

Russell and the attorneys for the eight also demonstrated that Jansen had not considered the performance of the teachers in the classroom. When Russell questioned Jansen, the superintendent admitted he had no information that Friedman "advocated the violent overthrow of the government" or "uttered any treasonable words" or performed any treasonable or seditious acts. Friedman's supervisors had brought no evidence of him trying to "inculcate the Communist doctrine into pupils in the public schools." Despite testimony supporting the professionalism and dedication of the teachers, the trial examiner endorsed the superintendent's report and recommended that they "should be removed as public school" teachers. They had refused to answer or were evasive when Jansen posed questions concerning "character, fitness and loyalty, including questions regarding [their] membership and activities in the Communist Party," even when they were warned that their refusal to answer "would be considered an act of insubordination." For Kiendl the refusal was proof of conduct unbecoming a teacher.[75] On Febuary 8, 1951, the board dismissed all eight teachers.

The first wave of suspensions not only helped established the procedure that would lead to the purging of numerous members of the Teachers Union from the school system; it also was evidence of the mindset of the Board of Education. The cold war helped foster a worldview that the professionalism of teachers in the classroom was of no consequence when deciding if they were fit to teach. In fact, the professionalism of the teachers who fell victim to the purge was never in question. The reason they were purged had to do with their political views and affiliation. It was immaterial in the eyes of board officials and others that these views were never expressed in the classroom. The fact of affiliation with the Communist Party was enough to label a teacher subversive. This state of mind among its officials would help the board foster a close relationship with law enforcement agencies and other anti-Communist forces in the campaign against the New York City Teachers Union.

7 / BANNING SUBVERSIVES

The New York City Board of Education joined the campaign to make America safe from "subversives." The board attacked the New York City Teachers Union, using a variety of methods: investigations, interrogations, charges of conduct unbecoming, and dismissal hearings.

In 1951 Superintendent Jansen suspended eight more teachers: Dorothy Bloch, a high school teacher of English for fifteen years; Mildred Flacks, a teacher of first grade children for twenty years; Cyril Graze, a high school teacher of mathematics for nineteen years; Hyman Koppelman, a Spanish teacher for twenty-five years; Julius Lemansky, a high school social studies studies for seventeen years; Arthur Newman, a high school English teacher for the seventeen years; Dorothy Rand, who taught elementary school for twenty-two years; and Samuel Wallach, former president of the TU and a social studies teacher for eighteen years.[1] Like the eight before them, this second group was charged with insubordination, found guilty, and fired from the system. By April 1954 forty-three teachers had been "dismissed" and ten had resigned because of the board's investigation. By May 1955 two hundred thirty-nine teachers and other board personnel had been forced out of the system.[2] But suspending, interrogating, firing, and forcing teachers to resign were not the only means used to eliminate Communists from the school system. By depicting the union as a group working on behalf of Moscow, the board and the union's enemies launched a campaign to strip the TU of its right to represent teachers before management. It would be a mistake to portray the story of the campaign to ban the TU as one of a powerful force preying on a helpless entity. The union and its supporters fought back fiercely for the TU's survival, galvanizing many to support their cause and helping to make New York City and its school system an important cold war battleground. The fight to ban the TU involved a coalition of anti-Communist forces consisting of Catholic lay and civic organizations, veteran's groups, Board of Education officials, labor, school administrators, teachers, and prominent individuals. The TU supporters were made up of parents, civic groups, teachers, labor, and clergy. The battle was fierce because the stakes were high—if the TU were banned, that would finish its attempt to build a form of social unionism.

GEORGE TIMONE

One of those urging that the TU be banned was George A. Timone, who had been appointed to the Board of Education in March 1946 by Mayor William O'Dwyer. The forty-two-year-old attorney had attended parochial schools in Manhattan and graduated from Regis High School, which offered a Jesuit College preparatory education. Timone received his bachelor's degree from City College, his law degree from Columbia University, and attended Fordham University's School of Business. At the time of his appointment to the Board of Education, he was a member of the law firm Latson and Tamblyn. Timone served as chairman of the New York chapter of the Knights of Columbus, a Catholic fraternal service organization, and was a member of the National Catholic Community Service of the Archdiocese of New York as well as the New York Foundling Hospital's Adoption Services.

Although he told the *New York Times* that he was enthusiastic about the new position, Timone voiced surprise over his appointment.[3] Others expressed shock and anger. Dr. William J. Schieffelin, founder and chairman emeritus of the Citizens Union, urged O'Dwyer to ask for Timone's resignation, asserting that the appointment did not match the mayor's statement concerning the qualifications for appointments to the Board of Education, which he made in a campaign speech in October 1945. According to Schieffelin, O'Dwyer had said he would appoint independent thinkers "free from political influence." Schieffelin contended that Timone had supported a Christian Front meeting organized by Mervin K. Hart. The Christian Front was an anti-Semitic organization that had chapters throughout the United States. The Front blamed Jews for starting World War II, advocated boycotting Jewish merchants, and accused Jews of Communism. The Christian Front openly supported Francisco Franco and Fascist Spain. According to

Schieffelin, Timone had been a member of the "general mass member committee" that organized the "Great Pro-American Mass Meeting" held on February 19, 1939. A leaflet for the meeting listed both the Christian Front and the *Tablet,* a newspaper published by the Brooklyn Diocese, among those selling tickets to the event. But organizing a meeting is one thing, being a member of a fascist organization is another. Despite his participation in the "Great Pro-American Mass Meeting," there was no evidence that Timone was a member of the Christian Front.[4]

Two hundred and fifty people, representing numerous civic and labor organizations, demonstrated at City Hall against Timone's appointment. At the same time, the demonstrators also protested the board's decision to retain May Quinn, accused of anti-Semitic, racist, and un-American remarks, and to transfer her to P.S. 220 in Brooklyn. Timone denied that he was a member of the Christian Front: "I never attended, and I was never invited to their meetings. I have never knowingly met a member of the organization."[5] Despite his denial, ninety teachers signed a petition, sponsored by the American Jewish Congress, calling on Timone to resign.[6]

Although O'Dwyer never publicly explained his selection of Timone, his decision to do so sent a message to New Yorkers that he was embracing the anti-Communist agenda. Communism had become a major issue in the 1945 mayoralty race. When he decided to run for mayor, O'Dwyer, then Kings County district attorney, sought and won the endorsement of both the Democratic Party and the politically leftwing American Labor Party (ALP). However, Bronx Democratic leader Edward J. Flynn demanded that all Democratic candidates reject the endorsements of the ALP, which he considered a Communist front. Bronx Democrats were urged to disassociate themselves from O'Dwyer. What bothered Flynn and other Democrats was their party's endorsement of the ALP candidate for the Harlem City Council, Benjamin Davis, an avowed Communist. In fact, the Democratic Party's endorsement of Davis meant that he was on the ticket with their candidate for mayor.[7]

Fearing a major backlash, O'Dwyer put pressure on Edward V. Loughlin, leader of Tammany Hall, the Democratic Party's political machine, to withdraw the Democratic Party's support for Davis. The controversy continued. Thomas F. Cohalan, temporary chair of the Committee for Fusion candidate Jonah Goldstein, charged that O'Dwyer's silence on the Davis issue proved an "irrevocable alliance" with the Communist-dominated ALP.

Cohalan charged that O'Dwyer had simply been forced into disassociating himself from the Communist Davis: "The harmonious relationship between Tammany and the Communists has by no means been ended by the window-dressing divorce from Benjamin J. Davis Jr. Only the protests from Democratic circles, which mounted in fury from day to day, prompted this rescinding of the Davis designation. O'Dwyer failed to go on record with a direct public repudiation of Davis." Members of the more conservative wing of the Democratic Party continued to hammer away at what they called the Democratic Party's Communist connection.[8]

In an attempt to demonstrate his anti-Communist position, O'Dwyer took part in the Ninth Annual Pulaski Memorial Day Parade in Manhattan. Politicians frequently show up at parades, but this one turned into an anti–Soviet Union event, with participants carrying signs that read "We Want Free Elections in Poland," "Russian Influence Must Leave Poland," and "Communism Will Be America's Cancer." O'Dwyer adopted the prevailing political tone: "There seems to be a clear-cut expression by the Polish people that when the peace is written, Poland should get a fair break. Every American who loves freedom and justice will be with them." Although the statement seems straightforward, it implicitly challenged the ALP's position, which called for cooperation with the Soviet Union.

O'Dwyer defeated Jonah Goldstein in the election, receiving 685,175 more votes. Democratic and American Labor Party candidates won every assembly district in the city except Manhattan's Ninth AD, a Republican stronghold, and the fifteenth, which Newbold Morris of the No Deal Party won. The Democratic–American Labor Party line won, despite the red-baiting. The decision to give Ben Fielding, executive secretary of the American Labor Party, the position of commissioner of licenses was indicative of the ALP's success.[9] Yet O'Dwyer soon made decisions that would lead to the disintegration of the coalition. The mayor-elect appointed two allies of Edward Flynn to key positions: Harry B. Chambers, as president of the tax commission and head of the tax department, and Louis Cohen, a former councilman from the Bronx, as assistant to the mayor. Placing two Flynn allies in his cabinet sent a message to those against the American Labor Party that the mayor-elect was moving in a different direction.[10]

The 1945 election proved to the mayor that he did not need ALP support to win. The appointment of Timone was connected to O'Dwyer severing his ties with the ALP and reaching out to anti-Communist liberals and more conservative forces. The mayor's action demonstrated to New Yorkers that he had veered away from the Communist faction in the ALP and allied himself with the enemies of the left. Timone was an outspoken anti-Communist crusader. In a 1942 Columbus Day speech for the Columbia Association of the Department of Sanitation in lower Manhattan, Timone told an audience of three thousand that the nation must fight its enemies at home because they were as "deadly as Hitler's Panzer divisions." He specifically pointed to Communist Party members, who, after Germany attacked the Soviet Union, "suddenly put on the masquerade of super-patriots." Timone singled out New York City's Teachers Union: "Remember, too, that a year ago the Teachers Union was kicked out of the American Federation of Teachers upon the ground that it is Communist controlled." Timone's appointment was due, in large part, to the political maneuvering and realignment of political forces in New York City.[11]

The protest over the Timone appointment persuaded the Mayor's Committee on Unity to step into the fray in June 1946. Created to promote interracial harmony, in line with O'Dwyer's 1945 campaign for mayor, the committee appointed a subcommittee that met with Timone and announced it would give his critics the opportunity to present evidence of his right-wing bias.[12] To the dismay of Timone's opponents, the mayor's committee publicly announced in October that the charges against him were unfounded, noting that, to the contrary, Timone had worked for the improvement of interracial and interfaith relations and there was no evidence of "anti-Semitism, anti-Negroism, bigotry or bias in interfaith or interracial relations." There no facts had been presented to "justify an inference of any such attitude unless it may legitimately be derived from his association with the two mass meetings." Elated, Timone declared that the committee had done an "exhaustive investigation and the report speaks for itself." The campaign to vilify him, he argued, was "Communist inspired and its intent was to confuse and create division among New Yorkers."[13]

The report by the mayor's committee cleared the way for Timone to carry out his major objective, to rid the school system of any Communist influence. But he did not immediately go after his main rival, the New York City Teachers Union. His first target was the book *Citizen Tom Paine* by Howard Fast, a prolific novelist who had joined the American Communist Party in the early 1940s. In February 1947 the Board of Education's Committee on Instructional Affairs, which consisted of board members James Marshall,

Harold C. Dean, and George Timone, voted in support of the Board of Superintendents' recommendation to ban the book from school libraries because it contained "vulgar passages." Despite the publisher's protests, the Board of Education voted to uphold the superintendents' ban. The only board member to object was Maximilian Moss, who told the press that he considered the book a good one overall. Timone and other board members claimed they would accept the book if the objectionable passages were removed, but the author would not agree to any changes.[14] While the effort to ban Fast's book did not directly raise the issue of Communism, focusing instead on "vulgar language," Timone and the committee had scored a victory over those who argued for academic freedom.

The first major fight directly aimed at Communists took placed in October 1947, eight months after the Howard Fast episode. The Catholic War Veterans of New York, a staunchly anti-Communist group, demanded that the Board of Education make public its policy regarding the physical use of public schools by groups it considered subversive. The precipitating event was the issuing of a permit for the American Youth for Democracy (AYD) to meet at Theodore Roosevelt High School. The Bronx chapter of the Catholic War Veterans accused the board of allowing the AYD, which it considered a Communist organization, to use school buildings. Timone, representing the Catholic War Veterans, told the press that the board was considering the issue. Exactly one week later Timone, who had become head of the Board of Education's Law Committee soon after his appointment, proposed a resolution banning the Communist Party, the Socialist Party, the AYD, and the Nazi Party and fascist groups from using public school buildings for meetings. Among those supporting the resolution were the American Legion, Veterans of Foreign Wars, the Catholic War Veterans, and numerous civic groups. The Teacher Union joined other labor unions, the ALP, the ACLU, the American Veterans Committee, and the Communist Party in opposition to the measure.[15]

The New York City school system became a major battleground during the early period of the cold war. Labor, civic, and civil rights organizations, alarmed by news of the Timone Resolution, requested permission to speak at the October 23, 1947, board meeting. Anti-Communist groups also geared for battle. During the six-hour meeting, ten police officers, a police sergeant, and a deputy police inspector were on hand in case trouble erupted.[16] John Reidy, "Commander" of the Catholic Veterans group, said to the two hundred people in attendance that the AYD was listed on the U.S. Department of Justice's subversives list and by allowing Communist organizations the right to use school buildings, the board "has already stirred up the righteous indignation of great numbers of loyal Americans." One speaker declared that inroads into the country by "termites of the Kremlin" would be challenged "with our naked hands if necessary."[17]

The supporters of the resolution were not the only ones to use vitriolic and sensational language. Councilman Michael J. Quill, while acknowledging that there were good people who supported the resolution, also identified "confused people" and "Fascists" as supporters. He asserted that some who declared that they were experts on Communism were "more familiar with alcoholism." If the board voted for the resolution, it would be "on the road to Hitlerism."[18]

Timone, calling the Communist Party a "subversive, disloyal, conspiratorial group committed to the destruction of the very ideals which our school organizations are striving to foster," maintained that he was not questioning any group's right to free speech, to publish, to rent space, or to seek a permit for a "soapbox meeting." However, America "should not fall into the trap of giving subversive groups what amounts to our imprimatur and of providing them with a sounding board and a pulpit to ensnare the unwary. We have the duty to exclude them from our schools."[19] But Timone could not persuade the majority of members, and the first Timone Resolution went down in defeat by a five to two vote, with Clauson, Anthony Campagna of the Bronx, Joseph D. Fackenthal of Brooklyn, Maximilian Moss of Brooklyn, and James Marshal of Manhattan all voting against the anti-Communist motion. Besides Timone, only Harold C. Dean of Queens, former vice-president of Consolidated Edison, supported the resolution.[20]

Although the five board members voting against the resolution saw themselves as standing up for the Constitution, anti-Communist groups perceived the vote as a declaration of war. The board's decision resulted in a number of groups expressing their anger. Daniel J. O'Neil, commander of the Veterans of Foreign Wars, lashed out, asserting that Timone's opponents had "proved themselves un-American and in so doing have made a contribution toward the warping of the minds and morals of American youth."[21] Catholic Church leaders were in the forefront of the struggle to deny Communists the use of school buildings. Speaking at the annual Communion Breakfast of the Catholic Teachers Association, Msg. John S.

Middleton, secretary for education of the Roman Catholic Archdiocese of New York, ridiculed the board's vote against the Timone Resolution. "Not only as Catholics but as true Americans," Middleton told the audience of eleven hundred, "we do not give license of speech to those who would destroy our constitutional right to real freedom of speech." Among the dignitaries present at the breakfast was George Timone.[22]

The board had upheld a civil libertarian argument in 1947 when it came to the issue of banning Communists affiliated groups from the schools, but had changed its attitude by January 1949, when at a board hearing it voted to ban the International Workers Order. At that hearing Timone argued that it was "common knowledge that the subversive organizations are presently making a special effort to offset their losses in organized labor by gains in the field of education." Only six of the nine board members attended the meeting. Timone was able to persuade four to vote to bar the IWO from the city's public school buildings, making it the first time since World War I that the Board of Education had banned an organization because of its political leanings. Timone, who had included the IWO among the organizations listed in his failed October 1947 resolution, was elated by the decision. Sensing that he was in a strong position, he announced that he would make an effort to bar all Communist groups from using public school property. Timone began his new effort at banning Communist groups in early 1950, and unlike his 1947 attempt, it would include the New York City Teachers Union.[23]

ANTI-COMMUNISM AS A SOCIAL PROTEST MOVEMENT

Building support for what became known as the Timone Resolution was, in large part, a grassroots effort. Numerous organizations and individuals joined the 1950 crusade to stamp out what they saw as an international conspiracy to destroy the United States. The anti-Communists who supported Timone's campaign to ban the Teachers Union from operating in the schools, were a diverse lot, made up of war veterans' organizations, the American Legion, the Jewish League Against Communism, the Knights of Columbus and other groups associated with the Catholic Church, governmental officials, law enforcement agencies, teacher organizations, and ordinary citizens. In some cases they used tactics similar to those of social protest movements—printing and distributing leaflets, flyers, and other literature, sending letters to board members, and appealing to the general public. Reacting to a perceived threat to the security of the nation, they called for drastic measures, including denying the very rights and liberties they claimed were imperiled by Communists. They fought for what they believed were universal values, freedom, and democracy. The people involved in the anti-Communist movement were not part of an irrational mob; they were highly organized and sophisticated, taking advantage of resources indigenous to their community, such as local Catholic churches, civic organizations, and charismatic leaders.[24]

Labor was an important component of the anti-Communist movement. By 1946 Communists were playing prominent roles in fourteen Congress of Industrial Organizations unions, with a total membership of 1.4 million. Communists held leadership positions in a number of unions, including the United Electrical, Radio and Machine Workers Union, the Food, Tobacco Allied Union, the International Longshoremen's and Warehousemen's Union, the Transport Workers Union, and the United Public Workers of America. However, thirteen CIO unions, with a membership of over 2.6 million, were in the anti-Communist camp. Phillip Murray, president of the CIO (1940–1952) had initially tolerated Communists, but by 1946 was moving closer to the anti-Communist unionists. Murray pushed through a resolution proposing that the CIO reject efforts by the Communist Party and other political parties to interfere in labor's affairs, based on his view that Communists were more loyal to a brutal state that murdered millions, including workers and unionists, than to the United States.[25]

Communists and Soviet sympathizers within the CIO backed Progressive Party candidate Henry Wallace's bid to be U.S. president, and they publicly opposed the endorsement of Harry Truman by Murray and the CIO leadership. For Murray and other anti-Communists, third-party politics was a way to back the Soviet Union. Walter Reuther, president of the United Auto Workers and one of the staunchest anti-Communist leaders in the CIO, accused Wallace backers of embracing the program of the Communist Party of America. To purge the CIO of Communists, the executive board of the body voted between 1949 and 1950 to expel eleven Communist-dominated unions, including the United Public Workers of America, of which the TU was an affiliate.[26]

On March 1, 1950, Morris Iushewitz, secretary-treasurer of the New York chapter of the CIO, informed Mayor O'Dwyer that the United Public Workers of America had been expelled from the CIO's national executive board for consistently supporting the "program and the purpose of the Communist Party rather than the objectives and policies set forth in the CIO Constitution." Iushewitz declared the UPWA to be "outside the ranks of organized labor" because it had "been exposed as an instrument of Communism;" and O'Dwyer assured Iushewitz that his administration would have nothing to do with the UPWA.[27] A few days after Iushewitz sent his letter to O'Dwyer, Raymond Hillard, commissioner of the Department of Welfare, issued Executive Order No. 291, withdrawing recognition of the UPWA and ordering all units under New York City's Department of Welfare not to have dealings with any UPWA group. Since the department did not recognize the Communist Party, it could not recognize a group that was an "instrument" of the Party.[28]

The CIO's action gave opponents of the TU new ammunition. Although credited to George Timone, the 1950 resolution to ban the Teachers Union was the creation of the Joint Committee Against Communism, a coalition consisting of the New York State Department of the American Legion, the New York State Department of Veterans of Foreign Wars, the New York State Department of the Catholic War Veterans, and the Veterans Division of the American Jewish League Against Communism. On March 10, 1950, the Joint Committee issued a public statement. Claiming to represent fifty million Americans in patriotic, fraternal, and religious organizations, it addressed "Communist infiltration into our school system." The TU had been ousted from the AFL in 1941 and the CIO in 1950 for being "Communist-dominated," and recognition of the union constituted "an implied approval of a pro-Communist organization." The TU's *New York Teacher News* had been used to disseminate the "Communist Party line among teachers and students." The group called on the Board of Education to take steps to bar the union from the schools—"withdrawing at once any recognition, privilege, or consideration heretofore extended to it or its representatives, at public or private meetings of the Board of Education"—and from holding meetings in the public schools.[29]

The resolution was supported by thirteen American Legion groups, four American Veterans (AMVETS) groups, ten Catholic War Veterans groups, and four Veterans of Foreign Wars Supporters organizations, crossing religious, ethnic, and racial lines and including Catholics, Protestants, Jews, Italians, Irish, and at least one African American. The black conservative and correspondent for the *Pittsburgh Courier*, George Schuyler, signed the resolution and was listed as a representative "of the Negro Community." Alfred Kohlberg, the national chairman of the American Jewish League Against Communism, also signed the resolution, along with Mrs. Earl French, former president of the Young Women's Christian Association. The Joint Committee attempted to portray itself as a multicultural organization, and it challenged the TU's argument that its movement was launched by the Catholic Church. The committee maintained that the issue was not race, religion, or ethnicity but ideology.[30] The conservative *New York Daily Mirror* joined the anti-Communist crusade, publishing, on March 14, an editorial calling the UPWA one of the "rottenest and lowest-down of low-downest organizations ever." It praised Hillard for his actions, but warned more had to be done to drive Communists from city government, calling for tightening civil service laws. Although the paper did not mention the TU, it was clear the union was being targeted. The *Mirror* called on the appellate court to rule in favor of the Feinberg Law, the legality of which was being challenged by the union.[31]

THE TIMONE RESOLUTION

On the day that the *Mirror* released its editorial, George Timone informed Jansen and Associate Superintendent Greenberg that he had requested that the school board's law committee consider a resolution regarding the Joint Committee Against Communism's call for banning the Teachers Union. Timone asked the law secretary, Nicholas Bucci, to invite the corporation counsel to the meeting or send a representative. Timone also invited all members of the Board of Education to the meeting. In preparation for the meeting (first scheduled for March 30 but pushed back to April 6), Timone asked Jansen to prepare a report addressing several questions, including what was meant by recognition of a teacher organization and what were the various activities and services such organizations performed for their members.[32]

To support his case against the TU, Timone sent an additional memo the following day to law secretary Bucci and board members Jansen and Greenberg calling their attention to Commissioner Hillard's executive order. He included Iushewitz's letter to O'Dwyer.[33] The full text of the Timone Resolution first appeared on March 20, when the head of the Law Committee sent a copy of the resolution to board members Jansen, Greenberg, and Bucci. It read:

> Whereas, Teachers Union, Local 555, United Public Workers, is not a bona fide professional or labor organization and has been expelled from responsible professional and labor groups upon the ground that it is an instrument of the Communist Party and
>
> Whereas, the action and tactics of said Teachers Union over a substantial period of time have been and are calculated to cause discord and confusion to impair public confidence in our schools and to reflect discredit on the high professional and ethical standards of our teachers and to interfere with the proper administration of this board, now, there, be it
>
> Resolved, that effective immediately, neither this Board, nor its supervisors or administrators shall negotiate, confer, or deal with or recognize the said Teachers Union Local 555, United Public Workers, or its agents or representatives, in relation to any teacher grievances or any personnel or professional problem, nor grant to said Teachers Union any of the rights or privileges accorded to any teacher organizations, provided, however, that this order shall not deprive any person of the opportunity to address a public meeting of this Board in accordance with the rules and customs of the Board; nor shall it affect the right of privilege of any individual employee to present, through appropriate channels, any personal grievance or problem.[34]

The Timone Resolution was the greatest challenge the TU faced in its thirty-four-year history. The schism fifteen years earlier, while serious, did not endanger the union's existence as a collective bargaining agency; in fact, within a year union membership had grown. The revocation of its charter in 1941, another enormous challenge, presented the union with the opportunity to join the more militant CIO. Even the union's dismissal from the CIO in 1950 did not stop it from functioning in schools as a representative of teachers. The Timone Resolution, if adopted, would bar the TU from negotiating and filing grievances on behalf of teachers and holding meetings in school buildings. The TU would immediately stop functioning as a union and become a voluntary membership organization with little power.[35]

The Teachers Union was not officially notified that the Law Committee considered banning it. When Timone warned new teachers, at the dismissal hearing for teacher Sylvia Schneiderman on March 16, 1950, to stay away from certain teachers' organizations, it was his first public challenge to the TU. The union wasted little time before responding. At a membership meeting on March 17, 1950, a resolution on the right of teachers to join organizations of their own choice passed unanimously. The union accused Timone of carrying out a campaign of intimidation, calling upon the board to repudiate his unwarranted attack and assure teachers they had the right to join any teachers group they desired without fear of reprisal. The union contended that organizing was the "most fundamental democratic right" and any attempt to interfere with that right should not be "tolerated in a democratic school system."[36]

Even as late as March 22 the union was not referring specifically to the proposed resolution. However, the TU leadership understood that Timone intended to ban the union from the school system. If it was going to survive as a labor representative for teachers, it had to take action. On March 22 union leaders sent a letter to union and nonunion teachers, warning them of Timone's threat at the Schneiderman hearing. The letter, signed by Lederman, Russell, Zitron, and Samuel Greenfield, the union's treasurer, argued that, for the first time in the history of the Board of Education, a board member had dictated to teachers what union they should join. Timone targeted the TU because it was the only teachers organization in the city that directly challenged the board's policies. The union also reiterated its charges that linked Timone to Gerald K. Smith, founder of the virulent anti-Semitic political party called America First Party, later named the Christian Nationalist Crusade. The union also once again claimed that Timone was linked to the fascist radio personality Father Coughlin.[37]

THE SCHOOL SYSTEM AS BATTLEGROUND

The effort to ban the Teachers Union was no small dispute between a union of a few thousand teachers and their employer. The battle over the resolution galvanized a large number of people and organizations on both sides, reflecting the national fight over Communism and dividing New Yorkers into two camps. One camp fought to eliminate what they labeled a menace to children and national security; the other camp claimed to be protecting academic freedom, labor's right to select its own representatives, and democracy. At the April 6, 1950, Board of Education meeting, over sixty speakers presented their case on the Timone Resolution.

Resolution supporters represented a variety of groups, including Catholic laity, teacher organizations, and civic groups. Edward Lyman, president of the Coordinating Committee of the Archdiocese of New York, spoke for a "Catholic Lay organization" made up of twelve member-groups representing "one million" people in the New York area. According to Lyman, three hundred thousand Catholic children attended the New York City public schools, and their parents wished them to have a "proper, moral and intellectual upbringing" and "true knowledge of our American heritage, with an appreciation of our liberty and our system of government, with an unshakable faith in our decency as a nation and a loyalty above all . . . with a reverent belief" in God. Acknowledging that most New York City schoolteachers were "God-fearing Americans," he protested any recognition of an organization dedicated to "undermining every decent ideal of morality and good citizenship."[38]

According to Theodore McDonald, chairman of the Law Committee, Court Attaches Guild, which claimed to represent 1,675 members, the TU was being used by Communists to further their objectives and had no place in the public school system. Although it did not attend the meeting, the St. John's Alumni Association sent a letter voicing its support for the Timone Resolution and condemning TU tactics, including "vilification and character assassination," that "emanate from Moscow." No teachers' group "whose party line is dictated by the leaders of Communism should be permitted to air its propaganda in the democratic halls of the Board of Education."[39] A number of speakers from the Joint Committee Against Communism spoke in favor of the resolution. Mrs. Norman Hugh Cain, for instance, representing the Women's Division of said Joint Committee, contended that the officers of the TU were "in accord" with the policies of Lenin. Another representative of the Joint Committee, A. E. Bonbrako, protested that Timone received credit for the resolution when it was her organization that came up with the measure and sent it to board members. Theodore Kirkpartrick gave three reasons for supporting the measure: the Teachers Union was not an "American union," was not democratic, and was not a legitimate union. Otherwise, it would not have been thrown out of the CIO.[40]

To no one's a surprise, the New York City Principals Association came out in support of the Timone Resolution. The association's president, Katherine E. Sullivan, described the TU as a "menace to the safety and welfare of pupils and the orderly functioning of schools." Although the vast majority of representatives of teacher organizations spoke against the resolution, a few supported Timone. Dennis Hayes, representing the anti-Communist Teachers' Alliance, argued that although he supported a teacher's right to organize, the TU did not represent teachers. His group was "firm in its belief that Communists cannot be good teachers in a democracy. Any organization that is dedicated to the spread of Communism is inimical to our country and to free education." Mae Adres Healy, representing the executive board of the Joint Committee of Teachers' Organizations, cited loyalty to the country as a paramount qualification for a license to teach American children, claiming that the TU had been discredited by its peers both in teacher organizations and the labor movement.[41]

Attempting to separate Jews from Communism, Alfred Kohlberg, speaking on behalf of the Jewish League Against Communism, applauded the attempt to deny the union recognition: "No anti-American organization, no fifth column of Stalin should have the right to tell an American Board of Education what to do. . . . As Americans and also as Jews, we would oppose any privileges being extended to Nazi, Hitlerite, Fascist or other subversive groups. We know that Communist-dominated groups are just as bad, and no consideration should be extended to them." Kohlberg emphasized his Jewish heritage: "As members of the Jewish faith, we are alarmed at atheist Communism and its campaign to enlist our youngsters." Children were not represented as the only victims: "A Communist teacher in a public school is bad enough. But there are many innocent teachers in the Teachers Union receiving instruction from the Teachers Union about classroom tactics. In this way even a teacher who is not a Communist can be led to indoctrinate children with pro-Communist propaganda stemming from the Teachers' Union."[42]

Representatives of veterans groups made up the largest pro-Timone contingent. Matthew Shevlin, spokesperson for a coalition consisting of the American Legion, Veterans of Foreign Wars, Catholic War Veterans, the AMVETS, and the Servicemen's Division of the American Jewish Legion Against Communism, claimed credit for activism on behalf of the Timone Resolution: "I don't hesitate to say we represent not hundreds, not thousands, but millions of people in our city." Shevlin called the TU a "counterfeit union" devoted to pushing a dangerous ideology in the school system, nothing more than "Stalin's fifth column," already "convicted as a Communist-dominated organization" by the AFL and the CIO. Those opposing Timone were "dupes" and liars. William H. O'Neill, past county commander of the Queens County Catholic War Veterans, accused the TU of "Communistic tendencies, Communistic leanings and writings and we cannot subscribe to Communism or cannot subscribe or compromise with it one iota."[43] James F. Reilly, second vice commander of the Department of New York, Queens County AMVETS, said that his group was "proud to support the resolution to ban the Teachers Union. Just look at what the Teachers Union has printed, what they have said—the double talk, the distortion of the facts." Thomas F. Flynn, vice chairman of the Americanism Committee of the American Legion, Kings County chapter, proclaimed that "we want American teachers" and put the union on notice: "They will be watched—perverts, Communists, traitors—We don't want them here."[44]

SOCIAL PROTEST TO SAVE DEMOCRACY

Those supporting the Teachers Union at the April 6 meeting included school faculty members, PTAs, and religious, labor, and civil rights organizations, reflecting the union's successful effort at social unionism. Defenders of the union challenged the anti-Communist narrative that depicted the TU as a servant of Moscow. Instead, they portrayed it as an organization dedicated to children, fighting racial and ethnic bigotry, and standing up for labor.[45]

To help build a support campaign, the leadership of the union reached out to members, teachers, and other allies, urging them to derail the Timone Resolution by sending letters, telegrams, petitions, and resolutions to board members. Board members were inundated with expressions of support for the TU. Seventy-six of the ninety faculty members from Samuel Gompers High School (main building) and nineteen of the twenty at Gompers Annex signed a petition urging a no vote on the Timone Resolution. Fifty-five of the sixty-one staff members at Junior High School 109, Brooklyn, wrote to the board strenuously objecting to the resolution. Seventy percent of the teachers at Textile High School, Manhattan, presented a petition defending a teacher's right to select an organization, pointing out that the TU represented a significant number of teachers in the school: "We

Figure 7.1 Fired teachers with children picketing, Brooklyn 9. United Federation of Teachers, part 1, folder 522.

are personally acquainted with various individual members of the Teachers Union who have worked sincerely and energetically for the common good of our entire faculty here at Textile High School, and we believe that it is undemocratic to bar their organization from full participation in the life of the school system."[46]

Parents and representatives of PTAs supported the campaign to save the Teachers Union. Enid Tyler, a representative of the Bedford-Stuyvesant and Williamsburg Schools Council and a parent of three children, emphasized the strong relationship the Teachers Union had developed with parents whose children attended schools in depressed areas: "We have had a wonderful experience in working with the Teachers Union in the Bedford-Stuyvesant area." Tyler asserted that the union had displayed its "sincerity" by providing information, making its surveys and other materials available to parents, and making them aware of prejudicial passages in children's textbooks. The TU, Tyler said, had spoken on her behalf and given her the opportunity to speak out against Board of Education practices and polices: "When the Teachers Union published an article about the bias and prejudice, we in the schools council sent a report of just that same type of thing to the school board." Adopting the undemocratic resolution would be a form of discrimination, and the board, Tyler claimed, would better spend its time "cleaning up some other overt acts of prejudice in the schools rather than harassing" the TU.[47] Martha Knight, president of the PTA of P.S. 63 in the Bronx, claimed that the TU worked in the "interest of our children and this strengthened our efforts." The PTA had "always" received the full cooperation of the TU: "The Teachers Union is on twenty-four hour duty if it means there is something to do to benefit the schools." Knight underlined a more important reason for rejecting the resolution: the act would kill democracy because it denied people the right to join an organization of their choice. Arthur Newman, co-chair of the Better Schools Committee of the southeast Bronx, also praised the TU: "The parents in our area want more schools and they want smaller classes and they want adequate health facilities. They want remedial teachers. Throughout the city parents had discovered that the TU was one of the "sincerest and strongest allies on these issues." Helen Wortis, chair of the Child Care Commission, Congress of American Women, Parents Association of P.S. 8, Brooklyn, described the Teachers Union as being in the "forefront always in explaining to us the needs and helping us to get better things" for the children.[48]

The popular image of PTAs in the 1950s has been that they were made up of housewives whose main function was to raise money for schools by holding bake sales. However, the testimony of PTA representatives paints a picture of politically astute activists, working to improve the education of children and willing to challenge administrators. They were not only concerned about educational issues but also intellectually and actively engaged in the cold war debate. Parents argued that the TU was fighting for their children and for democracy. Joseph Pelkoy, of the Brooklyn Community School PTA, saw the resolution as a "continuation of witch hunts" and as the Board of Education undermining the rights of both teachers and students. The question before the board, Pelkoy claimed, was would it recognize as "servants of the people" the democratically elected representatives of the TU. Anna Baronofsky, president of the PTA of P.S. 234, stressed the democratic right of teachers to join the organizations they wished to represent them.[49] One parent, representing the executive board of the Parents Association of P.S. 165, Brooklyn, likened the board's actions to "Hitler tactics of banning and destroying trade unions under the guise of fighting Communism." Milton J. Goell, president of the Brownsville Neighborhood Council, praised (in a letter read by an associate) the TU's work for underprivileged children, attempting to get them hot lunches, milk, and better after-school activities. According to Goell, most of the children in his community were Jewish, and anyone who tried to weaken the trade union movement was simply siding with fascism.[50]

The union estimated that, of the 128 speakers that day, 100 spoke in support of the union and against the Timone Resolution, a record number, as board member Maximilian Moss acknowledged. Speakers waited over six hours to express their views. Hundreds of TU supporters waited outside the auditorium, while hundreds more demonstrated outside the building. Even supporters of the resolution acknowledged the overwhelming support of parents for the union. Edward Lyman, president of the Coordinating Committee of the Archdiocese of New York, said that he was "sorry to see so many parent organizations approve the Teachers' Union's irresponsible, disruptive, and hate-mongering influence."[51]

Labor was another important ally of the union. Leon Sverdlove, business representative of the International Jewelry Workers Union, Local 1, denounced the Timone Resolution as opposed to "every concept of free trade unionism," granting the employer unilateral rights to decide which union would be legitimate for workers, a clear violation of the Constitution and labor laws. Aaron Schneider, representing the United Labor Committee to defeat Taft-Hartley, argued that the board was trying to set up a company union. Edward Glotz, representing the Retail Drug Employees, Local 1199, condemned management's encroachment on the right of workers to pick their own union, in "violation of principles established for labor relations in this country." Ewart Guinier, secretary-treasurer of the United Public Workers of America, went on the offensive, criticizing the American Legion and the Catholic War Veterans as undemocratic and antiblack organizations. (Both the American Legion and the Catholic War Veterans excluded blacks from their New York City chapters, although there were a million blacks in the city.) Ferdinand Smith, executive secretary of the Harlem Trade Union, declared that "as trade unionists, we are opposed to management dictating who shall be our representatives."[52]

Members of the clergy also voiced their opposition to the Timone Resolution, which Rabbi Max Felshin of the Radio City Synagogue called "an affront to all decent-minded citizens who believe in freedom. It violates the fundamental concepts of American fair play and collective bargaining. . . . Let us not, as true Americans, willfully sound the death-knell of our free educational system of our mutual trait and confidence in peaceful associations in our trade, labor and professional organizations." Orthodox rabbi Jonah Caplan argued that "teachers have equally the right to organize." According to Dr. John H. Lathrop, a minister, no one had the right to disapprove of the Teachers Union except its members. Rev. John W. Durr Jr., a Protestant, declared that the resolution was an "assault upon fundamental human rights" and challenged veterans organizations' right to dictate to New York City school teachers.[53]

To no one's surprise, the Communist Party disapproved of the measure to ban the union. Victoria Lawrence, representing the New York State Communist Party, condemned Timone's efforts "to destroy the fabric of democracy in the school system." She continued, "To defend democracy for all, this Board must defend the rights of the teachers to join any union of their own choosing and the rights of the American people to join any organization of their own choosing." Other political groups also opposed the resolution. Sam Kantner, of the Kings County American Labor Party, argued that the real subversives undermining American democracy were bigots such as May Quinn, whom the board allowed to perpetrate discriminatory practices. Bronx assemblyman Bernard Austin identified himself as a friend of the Board of Education but noted he had also been associated with officers of the Teachers Union for sixteen years: "I regard them as a group of intellectuals, fair-minded, free-thinking, liberty-loving and genuine patriotic American citizens."

The Teachers Union also gained the support of civic and civil rights groups. Louis Zimmerman, counsel for Free Sons of Israel, the oldest and largest Jewish fraternal order in the country, called the resolution "a serious infringement upon justice, upon democracy, which your board is endeavoring to teach to our children." Lea Nelson, speaking for the Emma Lazarus Division of the Jewish People's Fraternal Order, protested the resolution because Jews "must not forget what happened to our people in Europe. And we must not forget whenever democracy is weakened the lives of the Jewish people are at stake." Abraham Hillman, a representative of the Bronx Civil Rights Congress, restated the argument that teachers had a right to select their own representatives for collective bargaining, adding that Timone and his supporters were targeting the militant TU. The Progressives of America opposed the resolution because, according to Executive Director Richard Lindheim, "it is the most Fascist thing that I have heard or seen." Comparing New York to the South, Lindheim expressed surprise that the resolution was actually being considered: "I didn't know such things could happen in a state like New York. Down there, you know, you have . . . the Ku Klux Klan, and other Fascist-minded people." His parents had left the South so that their child would escape its racial horrors, yet they were "coming up here and finding the same thing—in other words, this is 'Up-South' with a bill like this."[54]

The most cogent defense of the union came from Rose Russell, who argued that the resolution "would deny teachers and other employees of the public schools the right to freely join any organization of their own choosing," thus destroying "every vestige of independence." According to Russell, the board was using the issue of Communism to cover up its real objective: huge budget cuts that would deny teachers' salary increases, increase class size, burden teachers with a heavier workload, and perpetuate the policy of seasonal unemployment from hundreds of substitute teachers. The resolution was an attack on labor's right to organize.[55]

Challenging any group to "match our 34-year history" of fighting for better schools for children, Russell cited a litany of achievements: enrichment of the curriculum, efforts to eliminate discrimination and safeguard academic freedom, the battle against budget cuts, the struggle for veterans' pensions and improvements in the retirement system. Russell told the crowd that the TU had brought ten thousand teachers to city hall on October 2, 1946, forcing the Board of Education to announce a salary increase for teachers that same day. The union helped thousands of members and nonmembers address their end-of-term ratings, salary credits, and pensions, and had filed grievances against unfair practices by supervisors. It had been, Russell asserted, the union of choice for thousands of New York City schoolteachers. TU members and officers had "irreproachable records of classroom and professional services." Russell contended that the TU's tireless efforts on behalf of teachers, opposition to censorship, and combating racism were the real reasons for the attack on the union.[56] Countering the charge that the union was totalitarian, she characterized it as the "most democratic of all teacher organizations," citing its annual elections by secret ballot of union officers and executive board members, and monthly delegate assembly and membership meetings. "It is a thoroughly classroom-teacher-dominated organization," Russell proclaimed. Its militancy had aroused the anger of the "enemies of public education, of authoritarian school officials," and those who wished to frighten teachers into silence and deny their rights guaranteed by the Constitution.[57]

While Russell's strategy included responding to the charges made by Timone and the enemies of the TU, she knew a defensive approach, simply denying allegations, would permit opponents to define the union. Instead, she tried to define the enemy as dangerous right-wing fanatics who distorted the truth to fit their agenda and were out to take away constitutional rights, destroy unions, and rob workers of their hard-earned rights, including the right to organize. Russell also placed the attacks against the TU in an international context.[58]

THE FIGHT MUST CONTINUE

The union claimed a victory when, at the close of the hearing, the Board of Education postponed making a decision. The TU leadership noted the large turnout at the hearing in an April 12 letter, but stressed that there was no time to waste. Postponement by the board demonstrated the impact of effective mobilization, but the campaign had just begun. The union encouraged its members, allies, and supporters of civil liberties to write to the board, contribute to what it labeled its Freedom Fund, and increase their activities against anyone who was trying to destroy the Teachers Union.[59] Clergy, PTAs, and unions continued to send letters protesting the resolution.

The largest group of TU supporters was teachers. Seventy-six members of Samuel Gompers High School sent a petition to the board urging it to vote against the resolution. Fifty-seven members making up 78 percent of the faculty at P.S. 116, Brooklyn, wrote to the board, declaring that teachers should not be denied the right to choose the organization to represent them. Shirley Weinraub, chair of the Interest Committee of P.S. 93, Brooklyn, representing thirty-two of thirty-nine faculty members, offered a resolution supporting teachers' rights and urging rejection of the Timone Resolution. In a twenty-eight to six vote, the faculty of P.S. 5, Manhattan, urged members of the board to vote against Timone, arguing that its adoption would mean other organizations could be barred. Rebecca Solinger, chair of the Teachers Interest Committee of P.S. 25, Brooklyn, informed board members that forty-nine members of the faculty voted in favor of a resolution opposing the Timone Resolution, arguing that it would deprive teachers of their democratic right to select an organization of their choice, a "step toward destroying the foundations of a democratic school system." Thirty-two of the thirty-nine teachers at P.S. 61 contended that teachers should determine who should represent them. Other schools that protested the resolution included P.S. 106, Bronx, Thomas Jefferson High School, the Bronx Vocational High School, and Tilden High School.[60]

The anti-Timone forces were not the only ones pressuring the board. The union's detractors campaigned to get the resolution passed. In an April 16 editorial the *New York World-Telegram and Sun* challenged the TU's claim that it was the only true union representing teachers, asserting that, for "all its troublesome noise," the union was just one of sixty groups representing thirty-eight thousand public school teachers. The TU's secretary-treasurer, Samuel Greenfield, had reported before a congressional committee that the union had only three thousand members. The passage of Timone would be a "wholesome brake on Commie propaganda" but would not hinder teachers' freedom of speech.[61]

The vast majority of letters, postcards, petitions, and resolutions from teachers expressed opposition to the Timone Resolution, but a handful of teachers supported the measure. Eighteen teachers from Alexander Hamilton Vocational High School signed a petition commending George Timone for his resolution. Myra G. Fleming, claiming to represent the Women Teachers Association of New York, endorsed the resolution. Jessie Bolton, identifying himself only as a teacher in the city school system, said TU representatives had been guilty of conduct unbecoming to teachers, allowing an "avowed Communist" to speak at an April 4 demonstration.[62]

The board again tabled a decision on the Timone resolution at its April 27 meeting, moving the discussion and vote to its June meeting. The TU took full credit for the postponement, crediting an organizing drive that, it claimed, led to the largest picket line outside the board since 1947. In a letter to members of the union's delegates assembly, Abraham Lederman paid tribute to the demonstrators, noting the "fine spirit with which our union members have rallied to the fight against the Timone Resolution." He also spelled out the union's strategy: if the resolution were tabled at the next meeting, it might be expected to die. The delegate assembly would focus on campaigning against the measure.[63] Board officials again received thousands of resolutions, petitions, and letters. Between April 29 and May 23, President Moss's office received five thousand 790 postcards urging the defeat of the Timone Resolution. Postcard writers emphasized the constitutional rights of teachers as citizens, calling for the defeat of a resolution that would deprive teachers of their "democratic rights to be represented by the organization they have voluntarily joined."[64]

One of the most eloquent statements against the Timone Resolution made at the June 1 meeting came from board member Charles Bensley, who argued the resolution was "alien" to basic rights and did "violence to our democratic procedures." The Board of Education was in no position to tell teachers who should represent them, and those who embraced democracy should not weaken it by implementing undemocratic procedures. If the Timone Resolution passed, Bensley asked, what would stop a member of the board who disagreed with another teacher organization from issuing a resolution banning it? "The issues of the moment, however grave they may be, must not blind us so that we would sweep aside basic rights inherent in our American democratic heritage." Despite Bensley's statement and the support the TU received from labor unions, clergy, civic and political organizations, and their colleagues, the Timone Resolution passed on June 1, with Bensley the only board member voting against it. (It should be noted that Board member James Marshall was out of the country and did not vote.)[65]

Two days later, Lederman told the delegate assembly that the union would go on functioning. TU representatives would still appear at board meetings; the union would continue to "take action" on behalf of its members and assist them with individual problems and grievances. The TU, its president insisted, would issue a plan of action and "turn more and more to parents, trade unionists and other citizens," informing them of the "scandalous situation" in the city schools, and would use outside pressure to make the Board of Education response to its demands.[66] The union reached out to its allies on June 8, when Russell and Lederman sent out a letter describing the board's recent actions, including passage of the Timone Resolution. They pledged to continue to fight for better schools; but, for all of Russell and Lederman's assurances, with the Timone vote the union had been transformed from a legitimate labor organization to one whose purpose was ambiguous. The Timone Resolution was by far the most devastating measure taken by the board against the union. The campaign against Timone and defense of the suspended teachers had put a serious financial strain on the TU. Russell and Lederman told supporters that the union needed money. "We need all kinds of help—we need your financial support. How much can you give?" This was a desperate plea.[67] The resolution and the continued purges raised a crucial question: how could the union continue to function without the ability to represent teachers?

In May 1956 the Board of Education produced a list of teachers who had been "suspended, dismissed, resigned or retired" as a result of its investigation into subversion. Of the two hundred seventy-three names on the list, forty-seven had been dismissed. The majority, one hundred thirty-nine, had been forced to resign, seventy-one retired, seven had been suspended, and the remainder either had to surrender their license, were substitutes who had their license cancelled, or, in one case, did not receive an appointment. All of the teachers on the May 1956 list were members of the TU, and the vast majority were Jewish. The purging of TU members from the school system brought to the forefront the issue of anti-Semitism. The TU contended that the suspensions were, in large part, due to the anti-Semitic sentiment of Jansen, Timone, and other opponents of the union. Some who opposed the union made it clear that they hated people of Jewish heritage, and many even participated in an anti-Semitic and racist antiunion letter-writing campaign that equated Jews with Communism and advocated solutions to the Communist threat that ranged from dismissal to murder.[1]

But the issue of anti-Semitism, in relation to the attempt to remove Communists from the school system, was far more complicated than people simply expressing hatred of Jewish teachers. While all but a few of the letters were, indeed, vicious anti-Semitic attacks, the writers also attempted to construct a personal identity as loyal, patriotic citizens. Anti-Semitism was also a tool used by the union in its fight against the Board of Education's campaign to remove Communists from the schools. There is no evidence that a hatred of Jews motivated board officials to remove TU members. In fact, the data strongly suggest that anti-Communism was the key factor. Some Board of Education officials, who were Jewish, insisted that the TU was a Communist front that had to be eliminated. The Teachers Union nevertheless highlighted the board's "double standard," interrogating and driving Jews out of the system, while not taking the same action against teachers who expressed racist, anti-Semitic, and fascist sentiments. Indeed, charges of anti-Semitism and bigotry became as important in the defense of the TU as the issue of academic freedom. But the TU and its supporters were not alone in raising the issue of anti-Semitism. Going on the defensive, the union's opponents attempted to convince the public that the TU was using the accusation to divert attention from the real issue, the union's Communist affiliation. This chapter examines the issue of anti-Semitism: how it was used by anti-Semites, by the union, and by those ideologically opposed to Communism.

"THE TROUBLESOME JEW"

After the suspension of Alice Citron, Abraham Feingold, Mark Friedlander, David L. Friedman, Louis Jaffe, Abraham Lederman, Isadore Rubin, and Celia Lewis Zitron, the union and the individual suspended teachers started receiving virulently anti-Semitic and racist letters and postcards. Historian Marjorie Murphy contends, "Some of the attacks on Jewish teachers were frightening reminders of Nazi hatred." Writer David Alison notes, "One of the first by-products of the suspension of the eight Jewish teachers was the scurrilous activity of certain groups who were quick to seize the opportunity to incite anti-Semitism of the most depraved kind." To bolster his argument about depraved attacks, Alison cites an anti-Semitic sticker entitled, "Who Are the Communists?" found on New York City subway cars in the summer of 1950:

LOOK ABOUT YOU NOW AND OBSERVE THE HOOK-NOSED, IMMORAL, MONEY-HUNGRY, ANTI-CHRISTIAN MONGRELOID PARASTIC LEECHES AND VERMIN OF DELANCY ST SEWERS. DO YOU NOT SEE MORE DISLOYAL AND DEPRAVED SCUM OF THE ISADORE RUBIN, JUDITH COPLON, HARRY GOLD, ABRAHAM LEDERMAN, DAVID FRIEDMAN . . . ILK? EVEN TO THIS DAY THIS REPULSIVE VULTUROUS SWILL WOULD BARGAIN FOR ANOTHER 30 PIECES OF SILVER.[2]

While the rhetoric certainly expressed hatred, it would be a mistake to dismiss it as purely bigoted ranting. The hate writers were part of a well-organized campaign to construct a dichotomy between the suspended teachers and self-styled patriotic Americans. They reached back to racist caricatures of Jews in order to argue that Jews' very presence in the U.S. was a source of imminent danger. Letter writers painted themselves as patriotic Americans battling to save the nation from satanic elements. Thus Jews as a group were condemned as unpatriotic, Communists, and traitors unappreciative of the opportunity that America provided. One letter called Jews ungrateful "cowards" and warned of another "Hitler" on the rise. The writer, whose views echo those of the anti-Semitic *Protocols of the Elders of Zion* from the late nineteenth century, asserted, "All Jews . . . have always made trouble in every place of the world," arguing that Jews were a global threat. Another writer advocated a Nazi-like approach, contending that a Hitler in New York City was needed to "fix the Kike."[3] Although not explicitly advocating genocide, another hate mailer, commenting on a May 5, 1950, *New York Times* photo of the eight suspended teachers, argued that Jews were unpatriotic, hateful, and responsible for the existence of anti-Jewish sentiment: "What a fine looking bunch of patriotic Americans. Jews all of them. [I]t seems nowadays a Jew can do no wrong[.] What's the matter, can't they take it along with other individuals that go to make up this nation known as the United States[?] . . . To bad Jews . . . you have made yourselves the curse of the earth, or the cancer in the earth[.]" One writer who signed himself Ted Ramsday called the teachers "real mockie" Jews, "ungrateful pigs" hated "the world over."[4] "You Commie Jew," scolded another writer, "you are biting the hand that feeds you [and] brought you to America." A writer signing himself Tom Sealey complained that Jews refused to assimilate to America society, following the old racist accusation that Jews were tribal and stuck together.[5] Jewish teachers were specifically targeted by the letter writers: "You try to ruin our children's minds towards their own gov[erment]," which, according to the writer, should be punished by "hang[ing] every one you." Among the letters was a sketch of two men, depicted with stereotypically large noses, one saying to the other, "Oy-Yoy, Thanks comrade." The other responds, "We Jews must stick together." Just above the characters are two flags, one with a skull and anvil and the other with a Star of David. The hate mailer, echoing Nazis literature, calls Jews "termites" and adds, "This is why we had Hitler," and, referring to the Holocaust, "[we'll] have it here only worse."[6]

One recurring theme was that Jews were spies for the Soviet Union who, when exposed as traitors, cried anti-Semitism. One writer, addressing the suspended teachers as "Comrade Muscovites," asserted that Americans were growing intolerant of their traitorous activities: "They are even saying Exterminate the Rats." Another attacker mailed a *Los Angles Times* illustration of a robust man smoking a pipe, wearing a sweater emblazoned with the Communist Party emblem, a hammer and sickle, and the words "Campus Reds." The illustration by Bruce Russell is captioned, "One View of the Communist Teachers Issue—Uncle Joe College." The caricatured man's large nose, clearly disproportionate to the rest of his face, could be seen as an attack on Jews. Sending a copy of the illustration to the suspended teachers made it clear the sender perceived them as traitors whose loyalty was to the Soviet Union. The hate mailer wrote that the best solution to the problem was for Jews to repatriate to "Palestine."[7]

Jews themselves were blamed for anti-Semitism. Teacher Minna Finkelstein, who was dismissed in April 1954, received a letter soon after her suspension accusing her of hiding her affiliation with the CPUSA. "And especially these days with [what] Stalin is doing to the Jews—you people bring it on yourselves, make others hate you—for you think only of yourselves—your rights, etc . . . as long as you like Communism I would give you a lot of it" (shipping them to the Soviet Union). A similar letter to Mildred Grossman argued that there would be "less Anti-Semitism in this world if the Semites would learn to be decent and not do the things that make people, right thinking, hate them."[8]

Another letter signed by "Ann Knight, An American Mother," used cartoonist Abner Dean's illustration "Orwell's Strange World of 1984," published in *Life* on July 4, 1949. The illustration featured Joseph Stalin overseeing workers at grueling labor with the caption, "Big Brother is Watching You." In the background a pyramid is inscribed with slogans: "War is Peace," "Freedom is Slavery," "Ignorance is Strength." Dean was using George Orwell's *1984* to criticize the Soviet Union, but sending the illustration to TU members skewing the message toward anti-Semitism. Knight charged that this was the "kind of world you communists would turn America into. The trouble with Jews is they have no roots, no loyalty." Emphasizing the foreignness of Jews, the writer expressed a fear of miscegenation, mixing the "Jewish race" with pure Americans. In this dichotomy, Americans were loyal, rooted in the Judeo-Christian tradition, and willing to defend their country. Jews, on the other hand, were deemed to have none of these qualities. "Your kind have deserted the religion of your fathers." The modern secular Jew was cut off from the Old Testament heritage and described by Knight as a "Godless Jew." "Ann Knight, An American Mother" was, on the other hand, God-fearing as well as patriotic.[9]

However inexcusable it was as a tactic, this virulent rhetoric had a political context that went beyond racism. Relying on epistemological notions of the cold war, the hate mailers justified their campaign as part of the U.S. battle against the Soviet Union and its allies at home and abroad. This form of pseudo-patriotic anti-Semitism also had a gender component. Some letters attacking Jewish teachers raised issues of family security. Children were seen as vulnerable because of their direct exposure to teachers. Teachers affiliated with the Party would attempt to fill children's heads with Communist propaganda and should therefore be removed. The nineteenth century cult of domesticity relegated women's sphere of influence to the home. Their principal duty, raising children, included taking responsibility for children's education. In the cold war context, this translated into standing up against any teacher's attempt at Communist indoctrination. Letters signed by Ann Knight charged that American mothers did not want their children educated by "Jews who think Russia is a better place than the U.S. Now you have your own country Palestine why don't you go there." The writer's signature juxtaposed a loyal and patriotic "American mother" to Godless Jewish Communists.

Another letter, signed by "Indignant American Mother," contended that all Jews were Communists and it was her duty to oppose them and to fight the cold war battle in the nation's schools. Moreover, the adjective *indignant* emphasized intolerance as an important virtue in the battle for the souls of American children. Yet another letter asserted: "American mothers don't want their children taught by Communist[s] who worship the God Joseph Stalin or by Jews who have denied the religion of their fathers." The writer in this case differentiated between Communists and Jews. The former worshiped Joseph Stalin; the latter, denied the religion of their Judaic heritage. Gender was used as a political weapon. Many teachers and several of the TU leaders were Jewish women.[10]

Most of the letters mingled racism and patriotism. However, there were exceptions. Evelyn Johnston disclaimed racism and embraced freedom in her letter, which was sparked by finding "your commie circular on the subway." Appalled by the subversive TU circular, the writer called the union members "miserable traitors" who were corrupting "the children of this free country." Claiming to be a "colored girl" but also a "free girl in this country," the writer scolded the suspended teachers for their "wicked, filthy capers." This letter illustrated another theme in the largely anonymous letter-writing campaign. Johnston shifted the terms of the attack on Communist teachers by arguing that America offered opportunity to all, even a "colored girl." In the propaganda war between the United States and the Soviet Union, the U.S. accused the USSR of enslaving its citizens, while the Soviets portrayed the United States as a country that denied millions of African Americans the right to full citizenship. The Johnston letter, a defense of U.S. racial policies by an African American, undermined that Communist claim.

The hate mail sent to suspended teachers and the TU, was a deliberate tactic by the writers to win the battle at home against what many saw as a dangerous threat to their country. Their anti-Semitism was enmeshed in patriotic fervor. The debate about purging the union from the New York City school system extends far into the social and political life of the United States.

THE DOUBLE STANDARD CAMPAIGN

Despite the anti-Semitism expressed in the letter writing campaign, there is no evidence that anti-Semitism played a role in the drive to remove teachers identified as members of the Communist Party. In fact, some of the board officials who took part in the effort were Jewish, including Assistant Corporation Counsel Saul Moskoff and President Maximilian Moss, who served as New York City's community representative for the American Jewish Committee. The motivating factor for board officials was anti-Communism. The TU nevertheless accused the Board of Education of a "double standard," pointing to harsh punishment for Jewish teachers accused of Communism and the lenient treatment for non-Jews accused of anti-Semitism, racism, and other forms of bigotry.[11]

In a March 9, 1950, press release, Rose Russell declared that Jansen's interrogation of Minnie Gutride, the firing of Sylvia Schneiderman, and his investigation of other TU members illustrated his "vile anti-Semitic double standard towards teachers." She contrasted the "protection of May Quinn whose bigoted statements in the classroom brought only a mild, apologetic rebuke and the treatment of similar cases that are regularly covered up and hushed up with the sadistic Gestapo method employed a year ago against Mrs. Minnie Gutride who was terrified into committing suicide." According to Russell, children were "entitled to the best teachers," those who "demonstrated their love for students." She contended that the "first victim" of the board's witch hunt was Sylvia Schneiderman.[12]

The union tried to rally its supporters to the March 16, 1950, board hearing on Schneiderman by distributing a flyer protesting the school agency's plan to dismiss her while protecting "May Quinn who defended segregation of Negroes." The flyer, which had the heading "Superintendent Jansen Guilty of Anti-Negro Prejudice," also demanded an "end to bigotry in the schools." Abraham Lederman noted that the *Jewish Day* (*Der Tag*) carried an editorial titled "A Jewish Teacher Also Deserves a Trial." According to Lederman, the editorial contrasted the leniency with which board officials dealt with the "anti-Semitic, anti-Negro teacher, May Quinn, and the ruthless manner in which they dismissed Mrs. Sylvia Schneiderman without a hearing." The *Jewish Day*, Lederman contended, called the contrast "subtle anti-Semitism." He insisted that, in particular, the Jewish community take the *Jewish Day* editorial seriously because Quinn was a "notorious bigot" who during World War II forced her students to copy verbatim portions of an "anti-Semitic Christian Front leaflet, and who was charged with asking one of her Jewish colleagues where she could get a copy of the Talmud so that she could see where it said that Jewish men may rape Christian girls over the age of three."[13]

In a letter asking Nathanial Kaplan, magistrate of the domestic relations court, Brooklyn, for his support in the Schneiderman case, Russell described the behavior of Quinn's supporters at the March 16 board hearing: "Never before have I seen or heard at such close quarters so murderous a collection of anti-Semitic hoodlums as our school officials assembled in the Board's meeting hall to bolster up the dismissal of Sylvia Schneiderman. You're well out of it but still you might feel impelled to do something at least to put a stop to the shame of Jews fronting for the Christian Front."[14] Ann Filardo, a young elementary school teacher and member of the TU, attended the meeting and recalls the viciousness of many anti-Schneiderman attendees, who used anti-Semitic language in their attack on Rose Russell and others. The nasty attacks sent shivers down the teacher's spine.[15]

TU officials were not the only ones making the charge that the Board of Education's suspensions of union members were anti-Semitic. The board was openly accused of anti-Semitism by Abraham Edel, a City College philosophy professor. In a May 7, 1950, letter to Moss, Edel focused on academic freedom but also leveled the accusation that the suspensions of the first eight teachers were bias related. The charges against the eight, he correctly pointed out, had nothing to do with their performance in the classroom. In contrast, those who were accused of making racial and anti-Semitic remarks in the classroom were treated with respect. Edel asked, "Is it surprising that this is widely seen as evidence of a 'double standard' in the treatment of Jews and non-Jews in New York? Can you and I, as Jews ourselves, honestly be without misgivings on this score in the light of what has happened?"[16]

B. Z. Goldberg, a columnist for *Jewish Day*, also raised the anti-Semitic flag in a May 24 article translated into English and distributed by the TU. According to Goldberg, the teachers' suspension "tells the world that Jewish teachers are to be suspected of Communism, and it frightens Jewish teachers into silence and inaction in exposing what fascists and anti-Semitic teachers carry on in their classrooms." May Quinn was still in the classroom, Goldberg wrote, because the "Catholic organ of the Brooklyn bishop, the anti-Semitic *Tablet*, defended her." The Catholic Church was "capitalizing on the current hysteria to make its hold on the school system more absolute. To this end it terrorizes Jews in the school system and seeks to keep Jews and Protestants from uniting to secure a really 'balanced' school system—one that is free of the control of the Brooklyn bishop and the *Tablet*."[17]

Indeed, the double standard argument became just as important as academic freedom. In its pamphlet *What Kind of Teachers for Your Child*, the union reprinted Ted O. Thackery's May 7, 1950, *Sunday Compass* editorial "Sinister Pogrom." The journalist listed several things the eight suspended teachers had in common, including the fact they were Jews, and pointed out that the bulletin of the Commission on Christian Social Relations of the Protestant Episcopal Diocese of New York had requested an inquiry addressing the Brooklyn *Tablet's* control over Board of Education policies. Also mentioned was that the editor of the *Catholic Daily*, Father Edward Lodge Curran, "was eastern representative for Father Coughlin's Social Justice."[18]

What Kind of Teachers for Your Child contained a section titled "Double Standard," highlighting the actions of May Quinn, and another teacher, Agnes Driscoll, who had "terrified her sixth grade pupils by calling them 'un-American' and 'Communists' and telling them that 'a plane leaves the airport every hour' and they had 'better go back where they came from,'" as well as the "slurs against the foreign born" by a third teacher, Gladys Laubenheimer. But, the publication stressed, Jansen had decided to suspend only the eight teachers of Jewish heritage.[19]

The TU asked parent teacher associations, civic and other organizations to take action against board members because of the double standard policy, and parent teacher associations responded urging Jansen to reinstate the teachers. In May 1950 eight people who identified themselves as citizens whose children attended New York public schools sent a letter to Jansen criticizing him for suspending "eight of the most outstanding teachers in our city—those who have devoted themselves unstintingly to the welfare of pupils, their schools, and the communities in which they teach," while retaining teachers who made "vicious, anti-Semitic, anti-Italian, anti-Negro, Anti-American utterances in the classroom." The parents expressed their anger at the "twisted double standard" and urged the board to lift the suspension.[20]

The double standard argument bolstered the TU's argument that the Board of Education was trying to remove the union as the legitimate collective bargaining agency for thousands of teachers. In a March 22 letter, Lederman warned that Timone's warning to teachers—especially newly appointed ones—not to join the TU was an effort to make them subservient to the board and the superintendent. The TU was the only organization "conducting a real salary campaign; the only organization which fought so strenuously against the substitute evil," the only teacher union "which is exposing anti-Semitism and anti-Negro bias in textbooks," the "only organization which effectively helps individual teachers with their problems and grievances," and the "only organization which opposes political inquisition and insists that teachers be judged on the basis of their professional merit and performance." Lederman argued that it was because of the TU's militancy on behalf of teachers that top board officials tried to destroy it.[21]

The day that Jansen announced the suspension of the first eight teachers, Rose Russell along with the eight suspended teachers, held a press conference where she leveled several accusations at the superintendent, including trying to break the union and intimidating schoolteachers. But the charge most prominently reported in the press—the one that got under Jansen's skin—was that the suspensions were motivated by anti-Semitism. According to Russell, she mentioned anti-Semitism neither in her press release nor in statements to the press. Apparently, Abraham Lederman, president of the union and one of the suspended teachers, issued that accusation, but Russell never disavowed it. She realized it could benefit the eight in their fight to save their jobs.

Charged with anti-Semitism, the normally cool-headed superintendent reacted angrily, claiming that it was "an absolute lie." He realized the potential impact of the accusation. Despite Jansen's attempt to deflect the charge, the union had thrown a body punch that hurt the school leader. All eight teachers were Jewish, and, by publicly claiming (after the press conference) that the suspensions were anti-Semitic, Russell and the union found the one element that could undermine the Board of Education's crusade to crush the TU—public opinion.[22]

Up to this point, Jansen had tried to win over the public by playing to cold war sentiments. Communism was a charge he could use against a union that had been aggressive on issues of salary, class size, and racial discrimination. But the public charge of anti-Semitism was potentially damaging because of the liberal political ideology that had come to dominate postwar New York. In the fields of labor, housing, employment, and race relations, New York's liberal elite had made major strides, including providing public housing for the working class and the poor, codifying antidiscrimination policies in housing and employment, and recognizing public workers' right to bargain collectively. Portraying public school officials as anti-Semitic could undermine the city's liberal image and cause the city to lose support among New York's liberal establishment.

The TU had been on the defensive against the Communism charge. When asked by reporters at the May 5 press conference if any of the eight teachers were members of the Communist Party, the teachers claimed that membership in the party was irrelevant; they should be judged on their performance in the classroom and not on their outside affiliations; all had been praised by their supervisors. But deflecting the question only raised suspicions of ties to the CPUSA. On the other hand, anti-Semitism was an issue the suspended teachers could use in their battle to defeat the suspensions. The fact that the anti-Semitic claim appeared in the same May 5 edition of the *New York Times* that announced the suspension of the eight helped to rewrite the anti-Communist narrative. It was not Communism that led to their suspension but hatred of Jews.[23] Responding to the article, Lester J. Waldman, director of the New York Anti-Defamation League of B'nai Brith, wrote to Russell to inform her that the league was concerned with problems of anti-Semitism and welcomed the opportunity to explore the evidence she had for the charge.[24] Waldman's letter, coming from one of the leading Jewish organizations in the city, was encouraging.

But Russell had a problem, since she had never officially made the charge that Jansen's actions were provoked by anti-Semitism. This was, she told Waldman in a May 10 letter, a "serious omission" on her part. To keep Waldman from losing interest in the case, Russell informed him that, even though anti-Semitism may not have been a "primary factor," it nevertheless played a role in the suspensions. Russell emphasized the double standard argument.[25] Why was Russell making such careful distinction? The accusation was a serious one, and she did not have the evidence to make a strong case. On the other hand, she was confident she had ample evidence of a double standard. The double standard argument was a gamble, because motivation had to be proved for anti-Semitism. Board members contended that Communist subversion was the motivating factor; it was a coincidence that those suspected of being members of the Communist Party were Jewish. In fact, Jansen made this very point when responding to Russell's complaints about the vicious anti-Semitic mail, suggesting that he was deliberately targeting TU members and teachers of Jewish heritage. Jansen claimed he was unaware that any of the eight teachers were members of the TU, which was untrue because he had been so informed by police informers. Trying to move the confrontation from the realm of religion to that of ideology, Jansen maintained that he had received letters of support from many Jews who resented the TU's accusation that he had suspended teachers because they were Jewish. Attempting to wrap himself in a flag of –blindness to religion, Jansen sounded merely insensitive: "I don't ask anyone his religion and I doubt if they are Jews." In a city with a significant Jewish population and the headquarters of several Jewish national organizations, as well as an increasing Jewish representation on the Board of Education, Jansen had to feel uneasy about the anti-Jewish accusation.[26]

Russell and union members still hoped that the double standard charge would persuade Waldman that the board's action was anti-Semitic and that the league would come to the TU's defense. The league's support was crucial and would make it more difficult for Jansen to carry out his campaign to eliminate the union. Russell requested a face to face meeting with Waldman so that she could use her skillful oratory to convince him. Waldman must have sensed her urgency but nonetheless declined the meeting and asked instead for a memorandum detailing anti-Semitic acts. If the memorandum pointed to the need for discussion, he would be happy to arrange a conference.[27]

Although Waldman's response to Russell was not a complete brush-off, it was clear he wanted contact between the TU and the league to remain as formal and detached as possible. He was not ready to leap into a cold war battle where one accusation of being a red could create havoc. He needed ample proof of anti-Semitism.

A DIVIDED COMMUNITY

Some people of Jewish heritage remained skeptical about TU claims regarding the board's anti-Semitism. When the Teachers Union learned that the Eternal Light Committee of the New York Theological Seminary of America as going to give board president Maximilian Moss an award for his "devoted and active leadership in furthering mutual understanding among peoples of diverse faiths," Russell wrote to Benjamin Browdy, chair of the committee, expressing amazement. Russell did not accuse Moss of being an anti-Semite or a self-hating Jew. Instead, she claimed he was influenced by anti-Semitic elements such as George Timone, Hearst's *Journal-American,* the *World-Telegraph Sun,* and the *Tablet.* Russell argued that giving such an award to Moss was inappropriate. The TU considered the award "an affront to all those fighting with all their might to stamp and root out these evil influences from American life." The conflict between the board and the union, Russell continued, was larger than job security. The TU, the largest teachers' union in New York City, was not only the "staunchest fighter for better schools" but also had a record of "exposing and opposing all forms of bigotry and discrimination" that was "second to none." The union's militancy prompted the board's attempt to eliminate it; if the school agency were successful, there would be dire consequences for New York. Moss's values were incompatible with those of the Eternal Light Committee.[28]

Realizing that it would be embarrassing for the committee to reverse its decision, Russell pointed out that B'nai Brith had canceled its invitation to a Mr. Butenweiser after discovering that his prepared speech was an "apologia for resurgent Nazism." In what seems to be an act of desperation, Russell then issued a threat: if the committee refused the union's request, the TU would use "every means at our command" to expose Moss at the event. Union members might not behave peacefully. Raising the specter of a violent confrontation, Russell claimed, "Moss participated in organizing a mobilization of Christian Fronters at the Board of Education meeting on March 16, 1950. That meeting was an anti-Semitic demonstration deliberately arranged in order to provide a semblance of public support for the summary dismissal of Mrs. Sylvia Schneiderman, an excellent young teacher just completing her probationary period but dismissed one week before superintendent Jansen would have been obliged to prove his charging that she had given a false answer on her license application."[29]

On June 14 Russell received the not unexpected news that Browdy would not rescind the award, which he contended had nothing to do with the Teachers Union and its predicament. The Jewish Theological Seminary, a beneficiary as well as a sponsor of the event, had not taken a position on the battle between Moss and the TU. Clearly, not every New Yorker of Jewish heritage was convinced that the union was a victim of anti-Semitism.[30]

The Jewish Teachers Association voiced its support of the board's actions, which prompted one union member, an H. Katzen, to write a letter criticizing the JTA for not defending the fired teachers against anti-Semitic attacks. In a letter responding to Katzen, the JTA did not dispute the fact that the fired teachers were Jewish, but it contended that all those teachers were found to be "insubordinate and with conduct unbecoming a teacher or being charged with these two." According to the JTA, Katzen had not mentioned that Jews and non-Jews resigned or retired to avoid standing trial for insubordination. Although Katzen charged Jansen was anti-Semitic, he provided no evidence for the claim.[31]

After reading the New York Times on May 5, 1950, Alexander Eiseman, head of Eiseman Industrial Corporation, became so incensed at what he thought was an unfounded charge of anti-Semitism that he sent a letter to Abraham Lederman, whose statements "are meat for the real anti-Semites." Eiseman said his own efforts to eradicate anti-Semitism were undermined by the "clumsy accusation by some of our fellow Jews." While Lederman had gone out of his way to point out that "all eight of the teachers who seek to hide their past associations are Jewish," the anti-Semitic charge was nothing more than a smokescreen to divert the real issue, Communist af-filiation and subversive behavior. Eiseman declared it was also a disservice to announce publicly (during the board's special hearing to appoint a trial examiner for the first eight suspended teachers) that none of Theodore F. Kiendl's law partners was Jewish. Such an accusation reminded Eiseman of "some ungracious-spoken Jews to scream anti-Semitism at every oppor-tunity thus creating anti-Semitic feeling where it never existed before. We used to joke about people like you when we hailed an empty taxicab which failed to stop, 'Anti-Semitic driver.'"[32]

Lederman lashed out at Eiseman in a June 17 letter, accusing him of con-tradicting himself by telling the union to keep quiet while advocating that Jews "discard the old hush-hush psychology" and of misreading history by ascribing anti-Semitism to Jews who exposed it. Had Eiseman "forgotten that the Nazis also declared that Jews created anti-Semitism by their poor manners, their avarice, their radicalism, etc.?" A person of Jewish heritage should not blame anti-Semitism on Jews instead of on the bigots.[33]

Lederman then turned to the subtle allegation of a double standard, characterized as the "policy of the Board of Education under the influence of board member George Timone, well-known associate of Christian Front elements in New York." The message was clear. Lederman did not directly claim that all the board members were anti-Semitic; he pointed to the one person who had the strongest ties to groups the union considered anti-Jewish. The implication was that the board's policies were being shaped by anti-Semitic forces.[34] For Lederman, radicals of Jewish heritage should not be labeled subversive but should be celebrated because of their defense of the nation. "I believe Jewish people should be proud that these eight Jewish teachers are defending the basic American freedoms guaranteed in the Bill of Rights and are battling for the fundamental principle that teachers and others should be judge on the basis of their actions, not their beliefs or as-sociations." The dismantling of these rights will lead to "doom" for Jews in the United States.[35]

The exchange between Eiseman and Lederman highlights the divi-sions among Jews over the issues of anti-Semitism and Communism dur-ing the cold war period. Scholars have noted that anti-Semitic attacks had declined in the 1950s and that American attitudes toward Jews had become more tolerant since the 1940s. Historian Leonard Dinnerstein points out that polls commissioned from 1940 to 1959 by the American

Jewish Committee showed "increasingly favorable attitudes toward Jews."[36] During the cold war period a person's ideology had become more important than his/her racial, ethnic, and religious origins. For more and more Americans citizenship was being defined less by a person's genetic makeup than by political associations. American Jews had been successful in climbing the economic and social ladder. According to historian Jonathan Sarna, by the mid 1950s Jews in the United States "had become fundamentally middle class, their proportion in non-manual occupations exceeding that of the general population." They were well represented in law, medicine, journalism, engineering, architecture, and academic professorships, while at the same time the number of Jews involved in manual labor had dramatically decreased.[37]

Eiseman did not dispute the existence of discrimination against Jews; however, he saw America as a land offering great opportunity. Involvement by Jews in what he perceived to be subversive activity jeopardized that opportunity. Lederman, on the other hand, viewed the anti-Communist forces as comprised of people driven by racial bigotry and hatred of Jews, attempting to derail any group or individual laboring for peace and racial and ethnic harmony.

The debate between Lederman and Eiseman was over how deep anti-Semitism ran in the United States and what Jews' proper response should be. Eiseman essentially denied that the union's problems were due to anti-Semitism. There was a legitimate way of fighting discrimination in the United States, and becoming part of a movement that was considered un-American was not appropriate. Affiliation with the Communist Party only hurt the larger Jewish community because Americans would conclude that all Jews were dangerous Communist subversives. Lederman's response was also an argument over appropriate behavior for Jews.

The American Jewish League Against Communism was even tougher on the TU than Eiseman. The league was formed in 1948 by Alfred Kohlberg, who had acquired enormous wealth importing Irish linen embroidered in China. Disturbed by the growing power of the Chinese Communists, seen as a threat to his economic interest, he became an ardent supporter of Chiang Kai-shek and the major financial backer in the United States of the "China Lobby," a group that accused Communists in the State Department of "losing" China to the "Red" Chinese. Kohlberg became a Communist hunter, attempting to expose Communists and Communist Party fronts in the United States. He financed a number of Republican politicians, anti-Communist groups, and *Counterattack*, a publication that alerted its readers to Communists operating in the United States. The league, located at 220 West 42 Street in Manhattan, claimed its major function was "to voice to America the anti-Communist feeling of its Jewish citizens" and to "rid Jewish life of whatever pro-Communists remain."[38] The American Jewish League Against Communism aggressively pursued groups it considered subversive, alerted officials to the safety risk of a "Red Polish" steamship using New York piers, and provided information about the "Pro-Red infiltration" of radio and television. Informing radio and television network sponsors and advertisers about subversive "singers of folksongs" such as the popular folk group the Weavers, the league—along with the American Legion, Disabled War Veterans, Catholic War Veterans, and other groups—requested in its 1951 newsletter that Mayor Impelitteri investigate radio station WNYC to uncover the "grave" situation at the station.[39]

The league became the fiercest Jewish opponent of the TU, pushing the Board of Education to ban it at every level in the public schools. Kohlberg was praised in a May 24, 1951 *New York World-Telegram and Sun* editorial for protesting the continued use of the public schools by the "Communist Party, the International Workers Order, and allied groups." The league took credit for the Board of Education's decision to oust these organizations from the schools and for preventing the "pro-Red" Teachers Union from holding meetings at public high schools.[40] Testifying before the Board of Education in the Schneiderman hearing, Benjamin Shultz, a reform rabbi from Yonkers and executive director of the league, stated that the Teachers Union "has devoted itself to making every important issue a phony racial issue—a Negro issue or a Jewish issue, or both." But he warned his audience that it should not ignore such a tactic:

This is a serious matter. If not controlled, it can lead to chaos in our schools and the disruption of our city. It is a Communist tactic. The Reds introduce a racial issue wherever possible. They do this deliberately. By stirring up races against one another they hope to create chaos so that America will be softened and weakened by confusion and some day Stalin can walk in because we are weakened and softened. This is no guess of mine. The Reds write the pamphlets for each other and I have read them. The writing of Lenin and Stalin are full of these instructions and in 1948 Alexander Bittelman wrote a book "To Secure Jewish Rights" in which he told the Communists how to fool the Jewish people.

The rabbi assured the anti-Communist faithful they did not have to doubt the patriotism of Jews or their hatred of Communism: "we Jews have not been fooled. . . . There is no more loyal American than the average citizen of Jewish faith." Jews, Shultz persisted, were more than willing to do their fair share in the civil defense of the nation: "We're prepared."[41] Jews were not confused by the TU's false accusation of anti-Semitism. The Communist Party, the rabbi insisted, was trying to equate anti-Communism with anti-Semitism. "The Commies are putting Communists and Jews in the same category. We repudiate this. We deny this. We are the enemies of Communism and the Communists are enemies of ours. We despise the Communist party and the Communist-dominated Teachers Union. Throw this so-called Teachers Union out!" To be sure, Shultz was addressing an ardent anti-Communist crowd that appreciated voices from the Jewish community that were ideological soul mates in the cold war battle. But his message resonated with those who were, at best, not sure where Jews stood in the battle against Communism and who, at worse, considered all Jews Communist traitors by nature. Shultz and Kohlberg were attempting to convince American society in general that Jews were indeed loyal citizens fighting for the survival of the nation.[42]

The Teachers Union did not see the members of the American Jewish League Against Communism as patriotic Americans but rather as servants of the American Legion and others on the "roster of racists and anti-Sem- ites." In a press release responding to Shultz's testimony, the union ar- gued, "Those who try to buy protection by lining up with the worst ene- mies of their own people are well fitted to be co-sponsors of this shameless document [the Timone Resolution], whose utterly undemocratic and truly subversive character is flagrantly revealed by its attack upon the right of teachers to join organizations of their own choosing and select represen- tatives to appear on their behalf before the Board of Education and other official agencies."[43]

Criticism of the union's accusation of anti-Semitism did not come only from those who considered the TU subversive; at least one supporter also disapproved of the tactic. Sylvia Sternberg, who described herself as a member of the union, argued that the suspensions were motivated more by anti-unionism than anti-Semitism. In a June 16 letter to Russell, Sternberg noted that Maximilian Moss was Jewish. "He [Moss] is not acting as an anti-Jew," she told Russell, "but as an anti-unionist and anti-liberal and would be equally fascistic in his attitude toward a non-Jew in the same position as our eight officers." The accusation of anti-Semitism was "unfortunate" because it only clouded the issue.[44]

Sternberg's rebuke did not force Russell to back away from the anti-Semitic charge. The action against the teachers was political, Russell admitted, and the eight were battling against the "destruction of academic freedom as a part of the Cold War hysteria." But, she insisted, there was also evidence of a double standard. The school system faced pressure directly from Cardinal Spellman's office, the *Tablet*, and officials such as George Timone. Moreover, "many teachers" who were guilty of flagrant racist acts were either shielded or if caught exonerated, not just because of the precedent of May Quinn "but also and precisely because they are Catholics."[45]

The TU's double standard argument did help it win outside support. Ervin Wagner, president of Fur Workers Union Local 64, complained to Maximilian Moss that his eleven-thousand-member local was "outraged recently to learn that Miss May Quinn, a teacher who had been proven guilty of the most vicious, bigoted statements in the classroom," had been given a mild reprimand while Jansen intimidated and terrorized "teachers with outstanding records of service."[46] Matt Vincent, president of the eleven-hundred-member United Mechanics Union, accused the superintendent of not taking any real action against May Quinn, who had been "deliberately poisoning the minds of our children with her bigoted, un-American propaganda" and, at the same time, sought to remove teachers who had "earned the love and respect of their students."[47] Despite the TU's double standard allegation, it could do nothing to stop the board's campaign or its enemies from pressing for its elimination.

THE *TABLET* AND ANTI-SEMITISM

One of the fiercest enemies of the Teachers Union was the *Tablet,* the official organ of the Roman Catholic Diocese of Brooklyn and one of the first Catholic newspapers in the country, established in 1908. The *Tablet's* second editor, Patrick Scanlan, held that post from 1917 to 1968 and followed a mission to defend the Catholic faith in a secular world. He helped make the paper a tool in the war against Communism, proclaiming in one of its advertisements that the great battle of the human race was "Communism vs. Religion: Numerous Articles on this subject appear each week in the *Tablet*."[48] The *Tablet* presented the battle against Communism as not just an ideological conflict but a theological one, a battle for the human soul between morality and religion, on the one hand, and a godless doctrine enslaving millions around the world, on the other. Individuals, institutions, and groups linked to the iniquitous forces had to be eradicated. One force linked to such evil was the New York City Teachers Union.

The *Tablet* became one of the leading voices in the fight to destroy the TU in the 1950s, denouncing the union as a Communist front and praising the Board of Education for trying to ban the militant union. A major backer of George Timone when he was recommended to the board, the paper advocated the adoption of the Timone Resolution and other measures aimed at the Teachers Union. A January 29, 1950, issue praised the board's banning of the union, noting that it had been kicked out of both the AFT and the CIO for being a Communist front.[49]

The *Tablet* consistently portrayed the actions of the TU as treasonable. On March 25, 1950, covering the Sylvia Schneiderman case, the paper sided with the school superintendent, arguing the teacher did not deserve a license because she had committed perjury by denying ever having been a member of the Communist Party and had refused to go to Jansen's and Greenberg's offices when summoned. Ignoring the testimony of pro-Schneiderman speakers, the paper offered lengthy excerpts from those in favor of Jansen, such as George Timone. On March 25, 1950, the *Tablet* reported that Timone had lashed out against the TU: "It is the same group which the Rapp-Coudert Committee in 1941, the House Sub-Committee on Education and Labor in 1948 and the Senate Judiciary Committee in 1949 have branded as a Communist-dominated organization that slavishly follows the Kremlin line." As further proof that the TU was a Communist front, Timone cited the 1935 walkout of one hundred TU members protesting the growing Communist presence in the union, its expulsion from the Central Trades and Labor Council and, in 1940, from the AFT and CIO. It was the union's disruptive behavior that led to its ousting from these "responsible labor and professional organizations."[50]

The Teachers Union and its supporters attacked the *Tablet*, asserting that it was virulently anti-Semitic and supported fascism. The paper took on controversial causes, including the support of fascist Spain. It published transcripts from the radio program of the rabidly anti-Semitic priest Charles E. Coughlin, an enthusiast of the corporatism of Mussolini and creator of the Christian Front (first called the National Union for Social Justice), an organization that became a mouthpiece for Nazism. Coughlin accused Jewish financiers of engineering World War II, and his magazine, *Social Justice,* published the racist *Protocols of the Elders of Zion,* a bogus work that claimed to depict a secret Jewish plot to take over the world. Citing a Judeo-Bolshevik threat, he argued that the Soviet leadership was entirely made up of Jews.[51] "If Jews persist in supporting Communism directly or indirectly that will be regrettable," Coughlin threatened in November 1938. "By their own failure to use the press, the radio and the banking house, where they stand so prominently, to fight Communism as vigorously as they fight Nazism, the Jews invite the charge of being supporters of Communism." On January 30, 1939, he asked, should the "entire world go to war for 600,000 Jews in Germany who are neither American, French, nor English citizens but citizens of Germany?"[52]

Like Coughlin, the *Tablet* linked prominent Jewish figures, organizations, and politicians to Communism. A February 25, 1950, article titled "Einstein Backed Pro-Red Fronts" linked the physicist to alleged front organizations, including the World Peace Conference, the Congress of American Soviet Friendship, the National Council of American-Soviet Friendship, the American Committee for the Protection of the Foreign Born, the North American Committee to Aid Spanish Democracy, and the Appeal of the Joint Anti-Fascist Refugee.[53]

In his column, "From the Managing Editor's Desk," Scanlan challenged Jewish organizations to take action against those who misrepresent the "Jewish people as Communists" and brand anti-Communists "anti-Semites."[54] In an article titled "10 Jewish Groups Oppose Loan," the *Tablet* listed the groups—the American Jewish Committee, American Jewish Congress, Association of Jewish Chaplains in the Armed Forces, B'nai Brith, Jewish Labor Committee, Jewish War Veterans of USA, National Community Relations Advisory Council, National Council of Jewish Women, Synagogue Council of America, and Union of American Hebrew Congregations—all of which had warned that a proposed loan to Franco's Fascist government would aid the Communist propaganda machine. The ten groups labeled Spain a "totalitarian tyranny" as evil as any Communist regime. In defense of Spain's fascist government, the *Tablet* contended that such an accusation would surprise many Jews. "Jewish individuals and organizations have expressed their gratitude to Spain for religious and social liberty" and for "providing a haven to thousands of Jews who would otherwise have been murdered by Hitler's gangsters."[55] The *Tablet* blamed the "ten Jewish organizations" for stirring up bad feeling between Spain and Jews: "The denunciation of the country by the United States Jewish groups is being widely printed here and has occasioned ill feeling." The *Tablet* claimed that several daily papers in Spain, notably *El Diario Vasco*, claimed that the "opposition by the United States Jews was based on the strong anti-Communist character of the Spanish government."[56]

Scanlan claimed that the Jewish groups had not opposed giving billions of dollars to the Soviet Union, "the worst dictatorship in the history of the World and a menace to the United States and all other civilized countries." The managing editor asked, "What hate does such discrimination take? What disregard of humanitarianism does it manifest?"[57] Scanlan also targeted lawmakers, including three prominent Jewish politicians—U.S. representative Emmanuel Celler of Brooklyn and New York senators Jacob Javits and Herbert Lehman—claiming that, regarding Franco, all shared the same view as "Paul [Joseph] Goebbels, most important and influential Nazi leader after Hitler." Goebbels's diary had described Franco as anti-Bolshevik, but suggested the Nazis did not expect much from him because he was not in a position to enter the war. These "attacks" on Franco by Goebbels were similar to those made in the U.S. Congress, according to the editor, who ignored the fact that both Hitler and Mussolini provided Franco with support during the Spanish Civil War. Scanlan's comparison of three American Jewish leaders to the Nazis revealed both disregard for the historical record and insensitivity to the Jewish community.[58]

The paper bought Father Coughlin's line that too many Jewish groups, leaders, and intellectuals were apologists for Communism. On October 7, 1950 Scanlan reported that the annual Pulaski Day parade, which took place on October 1, had attracted "40,000 Americans of Polish descent" and drew protest from "Communists" because of the presence of alleged anti-Semite General Wladyslaw Anders, who blamed the *Daily Worker* for whipping up a hate campaign. In defense of Anders, and to demonstrate the "falsity of the smear," Scanlan pointed to the large number of Jewish officers who had been under the general's command in Italy. To stress the absurdity of the charge of anti-Semitism, candidates for political office attended a September 30 dinner held for the Polish general. Scanlan claimed that the left protest "was a sad spectacle, but sadder still was the stupidity of people who enjoy the freedom of America and yet permit the Communist party to direct their actions and to fool them with such faked smear slogans as ant-Semitism."[59]

The *Tablet* concluded, as did many Americans, that Jews—more than other religious, racial, or ethnic groups—were attracted to the Communist Party and should be viewed as enemies of the United States and the Catholic Church. Subtle and sometimes blatantly outright attacks grew out of what the Catholic newspaper argued was the defense of Communism by too many Jews and their stringent opposition to supporting anti-Communist measures. Scanlan saw it as his duty to challenge all supporters of subversion, even if it meant being labeled anti-Semitic. But he was also determined through the *Tablet* to fight the charge of anti-Semitism.

One way the *Tablet* challenged the TU's accusation that the paper was anti-Semitic was to turn that accusation back against the union, calling it a Communist plot used to divert attention from the real issue. When Rose Russell labeled the sponsors of the Timone Resolution racists and anti-Semites, the *Tablet* charged that Russell, by making the claim, was acting in a "typical Communist style."[60] The *Tablet* published extensive excerpts of speeches by anti-Communist crusaders. It barely mentioned the arguments of TU members except to characterize the union as a pro-Communist, intolerant, and bigoted organization that used charges of anti-Semitism to deceive the public. An April 1 article, "Teachers' Union Gives Support to Red Charge," accused TU members and supporters at a March 16 meeting of the board of character assassination, vilification, and disruption. Attacking an "imaginary Christian Front," the union had used the charge of anti-Semitism to divert attention from Schneiderman's perjury and the union's Communist affiliation. Union literature distributed in schools and on subways called for the firing of May Quinn, labeled as racist and anti-Semitic, an end to discrimination and bigotry in the school system, and a stop to the political witch hunt of teachers. The union raised irrelevant issues such as Schneiderman's record as a good mother and affectionate teacher to avoid addressing her act of perjury.[61]

Outrageously, the *Tablet* even claimed the union's "diversion" was a Nazi tactic: "Following the policy of Hitler that a lie repeated often enough will gain credence, the Communists, who read the *Tablet* and know the truth, circulate such falsehoods among people who do not read it and who are thus susceptible to being deceived." The union stirred up racial hatred and religious bigotry. The union's claim that the Board of Education's refusal to permit use of a school building by the "Jewish People Fraternal Order" was an anti-Semitic act was proof, the *Tablet* proclaimed, of how a Communist-dominated organization used bigotry for its own ends. According to the paper, the Jewish People Fraternal Order was a "Communist outfit."[62]

The *Tablet* hammered away at its opponents, excerpting in June 1950 Kiendl's response to Abraham Lederman's charges. "It is unworthy of you," Kiendl scolded the president of the TU, "and those on whose behalf you purport to act, to raise against me the ugly claim of anti-Semitism and racial prejudice." Kiendl portrayed himself as an "advocate" for those of the "Jewish faith." No one except Lederman had ever accused him of being bigoted, and he was sure that "many distinguished Jewish leaders in the city, familiar with my professional career would not hesitate to denounce publicly anyone who attacks me as anti-Semitic or otherwise intolerant in any respect whatever."[63]

The *Tablet* took the offensive in the propaganda war, accusing the TU of using anti-Semitism as a "ruse" to create dissension. For example, reporting on the trial of David L. Friedman the *Tablet* characterized Rose Russell's cross-examination of Jansen as an attempt at "smearing Dr. Jansen with the anti-Semitic brush." Russell "gratuitously" argued that Jansen discriminated against Jewish teachers, while non-Jewish teachers guilty of serious transgressions were never seriously punished.

Russell asked the superintendent if he recognized names like O'Brian, Wilson, O'Bannigan, Quinn, Mitchell, and Graham as non-Jewish. Jansen responded, "I happen to know some people with some of those names who are Jewish." Russell continued: "You would not recognize that names like Levy, Cohen, Goldman, Shapiro, Seltzer, Moscowitz and so on are the names of persons who are Jewish?" Jansen replied that he knew a "Levy who is not Jewish." Kiendl ended what the paper called "irrelevant questioning" by posing the obvious question to Russell: "What difference does it make . . . if [Jansen] is not influenced by the fact that the names happened to be Friedman and whatever. . . . If all you have on this question of bigotry is that these names are names that are usually connected with those of the Jewish faith, I would leave the subject entirely." The *Tablet* ridiculed the attorney for the suspended teachers, Cammer, for proclaiming that Jansen was "guilty of discriminatory treatment of Jewish teachers." The attorney asked the superintendent if he had ever interrogated a Catholic teacher for misconduct. The corporation counsel objected to the question, and the objection was upheld by the trial examiner. The *Tablet* further polarized the controversy by claiming that Cammer's line of questioning was "anti-Catholic" and pointed out that a non-Jewish teacher, May Quinn, had been questioned in her school for misconduct. The *Tablet* contended the teachers' counsel continued to "filibuster" and "persisted in trying to caricature Dr. Jansen into an anti-Semite."[64]

In summing up this strident debate, several facts are clear. Those who participated in the anti-union letter-writing campaign were anti-Semitic. The Board of Education practiced a double standard, punishing Jewish teachers who belonged to the Communist Party but taking little action against teachers who made racist statements. And the *Tablet* fanned the flames of anti-Semitism in its fight against Communism. Nevertheless, the Teachers Union failed to convince the public that anti-Semitism was the major reason it had been targeted by school officials. One reason the TU could not get traction is the shift that had taken place in the country away from ethnic to civic nationalism. By the end of World War II, civic nationalism—which based citizenship on a common purpose and common beliefs and recognized every person's inalienable right to life, liberty, and the pursuit of happiness—was becoming the norm. Ethnic nationalism, in contrast, defined citizenship in ethnoracial terms, recognizing blood and skin color. According to historian Gary Gerstle, a major reason for the growing popularity of civic nationalism was that the cold war provided a new common threat, Communism, that trumped old concerns about racial and ethnic conditions. In fact, the struggle against Communism united Americans of different racial, religious, and ethnic backgrounds in a fight to protect the country. Historian Barbara Ransby notes that "liberal-left coalition work took on new meanings during the postwar period, when virulent anticommunism spread through the organized labor movement, partisan politics, the U.S. government, and even the civil rights movement."[65]

Board of Education officials used the language of civic nationalism to frame their opposition to the Teachers Union, staying clear of overt anti-

Semitic or racist rhetoric. They repeatedly assured the public that members of the Teachers Union had embraced a doctrine that was anathema to freedom and threatened all Americans. By dichotomizing the conflict with the TU as a choice between a union that was part of the Communist international conspiracy and "freedom," Jansen and other board officials evoked what scholar Godfrey Hodgson has described as the ideology of liberal consensus. That ideology held that "American capitalism was a revolutionary force for change" and that, throughout American society, there was little dissent from the "broad axiom of consensus."[66] Those who were critical of this notion were marginalized.

Some of the union's most vocal critics crossed racial and religious lines, underscoring the strength of civic nationalism and the ideology of liberal consensus of the 1950s. This philosophy helped undermine the union's credibility when it argued that anti-Semitism was the major reason for the board's attacks. The great fear of the cold war period for millions of Americans was Communism. The Communist threat narrative—which included news of the dangerous exploits of the Soviet Union and its allies as well as Communist espionage in the U.S.—was constantly fed to the general public. This narrative assured that any organization affiliated with the CPUSA was also going to be seen as a danger.

In the spring of 1957, Josephine Ann O'Keefe, a young substitute social studies teacher, gave her eighth grade class at Simon Baruch Junior High School,
Manhattan, an assignment to gather information on foreign countries. She
instructed the students to write to foreign embassies requesting information
on history, geography, economy, and other pertinent data. Only the British
and Soviet embassies responded and sent packages including magazines and
brochures. The twenty-six-year-old teacher placed the foreign magazines in
a rack in room 404 of the school, which was used by the social studies class.
In the pre and post–cold war era the incident would have seemed harmless;
in the mid fifties it set off a wide-spread investigation.[1]

Detective Mary J. McDonnell, shield 520 of the New York City Police Department's Bureau of Special Services and Information Agency, was teaching
an evening graduate course in police science in room 404 at Simon Baruch
JHS when she spotted the Soviet magazine. McDonnell immediately reported to her commanding officer, Lieutenant William P. Brown, that she had
found Communist literature in the school. Brown interviewed the school's
principal, Carl Cherkis. Together they went to room 404, where they found
the magazine and two "Communist propaganda pamphlets hidden behind
other magazines." A display of pictures and magazine clippings also caught
their eye. Titled "The Aftermath of the Civil War," it chronicled events in
the South, mostly using pictures from *Life* magazine. The pictures demonstrated incidents of racial intolerance: "Aside from one rather small section
on the recent interracial difficulties in Mississippi, the largest part of the
display concerned the Ku Klux Klan and other organized groups persecut-
ing Negroes." The pictures included images of blacks being shot or lynched
and a close-up of a man being burned.[2]

After interviewing O'Keefe, Cherkis attempted to defuse the situation, declaring he was convinced that she was guilty only of "bad judgment." He assured Brown and Assistant Superintendent of Schools Clare C. Balwin that the teacher would not be allowed to use Soviet material in her class. Nevertheless, Brown reported the incident to William DeFossett of the Bureau of Special Services. Details of the affair would eventually reach the office of the assistant corporation counsel of New York City. O'Keefe was in danger of being investigated by Saul Moskoff, who had been assigned to the Board of Education in 1951 to oversee the anti-Communist investigation.[3] Clearly fighting to save O'Keefe's career, Cherkis contacted John Dunne, assistant to Moskoff, to point out that O'Keefe was devoutly religious and quite patriotic, implying that such a person could not be a Communist. Cherkis asked Dunne not to call her in for questioning since there had already been an internal investigation. The teacher believed that she had no choice but to display their work because she had promised her students she would do so. Concerning the picture display, which the principal confessed he, too, found offensive, O'Keefe explained that the students had brought the pictures to school, making her feel obligated to place them on the bulletin board. O'Keefe was a dedicated teacher, and there was nothing of a "Communistic" nature in her lessons. In the end, O'Keefe was not called before Moskoff, and she managed to hold on to her job.[4]

The O'Keefe affair demonstrates the level of surveillance in the New York City Public School system during the cold war and how fear could impinge on academic freedom. Despite Cherkis's defense of O'Keefe, he never raised the issue of academic freedom in the interview with Brown and Balwin. During the cold war period, activities of teachers in New York City schools were being monitored by the police, with collaboration between the board and the New York City Police Department. The fear of Communism helped to determine what children learned, a decision traditionally left to educators. Police and those invoking the need for national security had a strong voice in deciding what was educationally appropriate for students. If teachers exercised independent judgment, they risked their careers. Even the subject of lynchings and racism could be eliminated from a teacher's lesson plan because it was seen as supporting Communist propaganda. Academic freedom became subordinate to the concerns of the security state.

This chapter examines how the New York City Board of Education relied on an elaborate network of undercover agents, informers, and cooperating witnesses to closely monitor public school teachers considered subversive. Academic freedom and freedom of thought became casualties of the anti-Communist crusade in the schools.

POLICE AND UNDERCOVER AGENTS

The Board of Education's success in purging the school system of teachers who were Communist Party members was due primarily to its collaboration with law enforcement. The superintendent interrogated the first wave of teachers based on the records of the New York City Police Department, which had been spying on the suspended teachers for years. According to the document titled "Material for Questioning of Seven Teachers," written by Assistant Corporation Counsel Michael Castaldi in early 1950 to prepare Jansen for interrogating the teachers, police records identified Alice Citron as an active member of the Communist Party, most likely in the Harlem branch, living at the same address as Isidore Begun, an "exposed Communist." She also went by the alias Alice White. Because there was no record of her having married Begun, the superintendent could make "quite a good case for conduct unbecoming a teacher on the grounds of having been Begun's mistress." Layle Lane, former executive board member of the TU, was listed as an informer who helped provide detailed information on Citron.[5]

Another witness named teacher Abraham Feingold as a member of the Parkside Club of the Communist Party. According to the NYPD, Feingold held party meetings in his house, was the editor of a Communist pamphlet distributed to club members on February 28, 1946, was also a member of a number of Communist fronts, such as the American Labor Party and the American League for Peace and Democracy, and participated in a Communist Party demonstration at the Japanese consulate. Mark Friedlander was listed as a member of the Central Committee of the Yorkville district of the party and registered with the American Labor party. Louis Jaffe confessed at a departmental conference that he was a Communist and admitted to another teacher, also in the department, that he was a Communist. He was also listed as an instructor at the Communist Party's Jefferson School in 1946 and was affiliated with the American Labor Party. Lederman, discharged from the Navy as an "undesirable," had refused to answer questions before Taft-Hartley. Police department records listed Rubin as a member of the Flatbush club and noted that the *Daily Worker* called him "our own Isadore Rubin."[6] Part of Jansen's strategy was to shock the teachers into submission. For example, it was suggested that, while interrogating Citron, Jansen should buzz Layle Lane in the office and tell her "never mind, you don't need to send for Miss White now." Citron would be convinced that informants had revealed her activities and she should confess.[7]

The police agency that provided the board with the greatest support was the NYPD's Bureau of Special Services and Investigation, BOSSI, which came into existence in 1946 and infiltrated the Communist Party by having police agents pose as members. These agents kept copious records that proved crucial in charging teachers. In a letter to Police Commissioner William P. O'Brian in early May 1950, Jansen recognized the board's reliance on the BOSSI. It was due, the superintendent told O'Brian, to the "splendid cooperation" of the agency that he was able to gain what he called sufficient information on all eight teachers.[8]

Jansen's decision to rely on the city's police apparatus proved that he saw his campaign in the context of fighting crime. The hearings of the first eight teachers charged were not just disciplinary procedures but criminal trials. He declared to the police commissioner that the cases were going to be "prosecuted" by the corporation counsel, who assigned Michael A. Castaldi, Esq., assistant in charge of the division of education, to handle the task. By using an attorney, instead of board officials, Jansen sent a message that the teachers were criminals. Castaldi had advised Jansen that the testimony of "Police Operator Number 51," assigned to the BOSSI, would be crucial in establishing the guilt of two of the eight teachers. Jansen requested that the police commissioner allow the undercover agent to testify in the "trials." The superintendent argued, "were the teachers to win their cases[,] my long efforts to expose and oust Communists from the school system would come to an unsuccessful end. The Communists and their sympathizers would resume their pernicious activities with new confidence, feeling themselves immune from legal sanction." A "successful prosecution" on the other hand, would be a victory for the thousands of loyal teachers who wished to free the schools of Communists.[9]

Collaboration between the board and police department seemed to be an established routine. Whenever school officials or the corporation counsel wanted information on teachers, they submitted their request to police authorities. At times the board submitted lists of teachers, requesting information on their "subversive" activities. Jansen was unconcerned with the civil liberties and rights of teachers. He asked Police Commissioner George P. Monaghan in January 1952 for department files on Gustave Jaffe (not to be confused with Louis who had been dismissed from the board in 1951), at 245 Hawthorne Street, Brooklyn, a teacher employed by the Board of Education and a member of the Parkside Club of the Communist Party. "Of course, I do not expect," Jansen proclaimed, "that the identity of your undercover operator would be revealed." Any teacher was subject to surveillance, thus making the schools into police states. In February Jansen submitted a list of names to the police department asking for information. Acting Lieutenant Thomas F. Crane of the BOSSI informed him that, of all the names, he had files on only three teachers, including Katherine Miller, who registered for the Party in 1936. In one instance, Jansen submitted a list of thirty names of employees under investigation for subversive activities.[10]

The police investigation of teachers had been going on for at least a decade. In May 1952 Monaghan told the superintendent that his request for the files on three teachers, based on reports submitted by "Operator 51", could not be granted: "Operator 51 has been affiliated with Communist party for the past ten years and to date is not definitely or positively identified by the rank and file of said party. To divulge the information requested would of necessity expose [the] accumulation of information gathered during that period of the time which is most vital to the security of this nation and would identify subject Operator 51 to subpoena in the event of hearing on the matter." The commissioner was worried about legal action being taken against the department's BOSSI.[11] Operator 51 continued to report on Board of Education employees. In a 1952 memo to Moskoff, Dunne reported that the BOSSI provided important information on seventeen board employees, including David Flack, one of the editors of *New York Teacher News*.[12] But in cases where the department determined there was no jeopardy to its work, undercover agent identities were revealed. In a November 1953 letter to Monaghan, Moskoff noted that the "excellent cooperation" between the board and police department helped him prove Paul Seligman was a member of the Young Communist League. Moskoff wanted to know if Detective Margaret Disco, shield no. 923, assigned to the BOSSI, could testify at the Seligman hearing, since Disco had been expelled from the YCL and the CP and there was no need to keep her identity secret. Monaghan told Moskoff that Disco would be available to testify in the case of the "subversive activities of Paul Seligman."[13]

The BOSSI, which had thoroughly infiltrated the Communist Party, assigned specific agents to trace teachers, report on party gatherings, and provide other "vital" information to help the board. Detective Disco, Moskoff informed Police Commissioner Francis W. H. Adams in February 1955, was "completely cooperative at all times and displayed a remarkable understanding of the operations of the Communist Party with which she became connected in the performance of her duties." While the work of Disco and "others like her who made such sacrifice" to gather information "concerning the Communist conspiracy" was not known to the public, nevertheless, they had been of "tremendous assistance in cleaning our school system of those who affiliated themselves with the agency of a foreign power."[14]

There were dozens of informers who went by code names. One of the most important undercover police agents for Moskoff's investigation was Detective Mildred V. Blauvelt, known as Operator 51 or "Blondie," who had been assigned to Moskoff's office on March 27, 1953, at the request of the board. An undercover operator in the Communist Party for almost a decade, Blauvelt obtained valuable information that led to the firing or resignation of several teachers who were identified by her as CP members. Blauvelt helped cultivate the bonds not only between the corporation counsel and NYPD but also with other "government agencies engaged in security work." In a 1953 Christmas Eve letter to George A. Loures, head of the BOSSI, the assistant corporation counsel singled out the "exceptional character" of Blauvelt's service, which included noting that she worked as an undercover agent providing the "means to detect and uproot subversive teachers." The dismissals of Sylvia Schneiderman, the first victim of the purge that began in 1950, Isadore Rubin, and Abraham Feingold were the result of information gathered by Blauvelt. In an October 7, 1957, letter to Jansen, Moskoff wrote: "Det. Blauvelt has been the greatest single source of information in the positive identification of teachers known to be Communists."[15]

Blauvelt initiated investigations of fifty teachers by tracing "relationships of suspects, references, nominating petitions and voting records" and membership in front organizations. She also assisted in the investigation of one hundred teachers suspected of being in the Party. Moskoff remarked:

"It is hoped that through her efforts an ever expanding number of Communists within the school system will be detected until the school system is rid of every subversive." Blauvelt also worked with the Department of Investigations, the Immigration and Naturalization Services, HUAC, the Justice Department, the Subversive Activities Control Board, and other city, state, and federal agencies.[16]

Blauvelt's reports did not uncover any plots to overthrow the government. Paramount among the issues discussed were racial discrimination, including what the Party labeled the "The Negro Question," gender bias or the "Women's Question," U.S. foreign policy, and the working class. The individuals she reported on wanted to influence politicians' votes, work for pro–Soviet Union candidates, and persuade lawmakers to take a more favorable position toward the Soviet Union. In a March 31, 1953, memo "Operator 51" reported that Leo Auerbach, a high school social studies teacher and TU member, stated that United States foreign policy was heading in the wrong direction and that the Soviet Union's knowledge of making atomic bombs was beneficial to world peace. Auerbach also insisted that it was the job of the teacher to help educate the children of the working class. In an April 11, 1953, memo Blauvelt noted that the Flatbush, Parkside, and Kensington clubs were planning to send a delegation to the office of their local congressman, James Heffernan, on December 15, to convince him and others in Congress to take action against the foreign policies of the Eisenhower administration.[17]

No matter how benign or unattached to classroom activity attending a club meeting seemed, for Jansen, affiliation with the Communist Party was enough to taint teachers as subversive. Sylvia Schneiderman's Communist Party membership prompted her dismissal. In her summary of information on Sylvia Schneiderman, Blauvelt described a February 26, 1946, meeting of the Parkside Club in Scheniderman's apartment at 409 Parkside Avenue, Brooklyn. The eight "comrades present" made plans to distribute leaflets regarding the Freeport Case (Ferguson Brothers), excluding Schneiderman and another teacher from distributing the material because of the danger they faced as public employees. Schneiderman criticized the leaflet as too "wordy" and dull for workers. Blauvelt reported other meetings that Schneiderman attended, including one on April 24, 1946, where she circulated a petition to rebuild P.S. 3. None of Schneiderman's activities constituted a treasonable act. On May 6, 1955, Congressman Willis of Louisiana noted that Blauvelt's work was "very commendable" and expressed his gratitude to the New York City Police Department.[18]

Blauvelt was not alone in being credited by Board of Education officials. Moskoff gave credit to detective Margaret Disco for the resignation of Paul Seligman. Ann Zarchin of BOSSI did such crucial undercover work identifying several New York City teachers affiliated with the Young Communist League that in March 1954 the assistant corporation counsel requested that Police Commissioner Francis W. H. Adams permit him to interview Zarchin, who was on maternity leave. In a spirit of cooperation, Adams directed Chief Inspector Kennedy to make the arrangements for the interview.[19] The surveillance of teachers was not limited to meetings and other Communist Party gatherings. The police also infiltrated parent-teacher associations. In a March 1954 memo to Moskoff the police claimed that the PTA of P.S. 98 was Communist controlled and provided thirty-eight names, suggesting that Moskoff check the list to see if any teachers were named.[20] Even children's assembly programs were monitored for possible subversive activities. A March 26, 1955, program at P.S. 349, Brooklyn, became controversial when it was suggested that the school auditorium had been rented by Herbert Kruckman, a children's entertainer. Police records on Kruckman "contained derogatory" information and the event had been allegedly advertised in the *Daily Worker*. When Associate Superintendent of Schools Edward J. Bernath investigated, he discovered that the PTA had received permission for the event, not Kruckman. The associate superintendent promised Moskoff he would alert the Elementary School Division of the incident.[21]

Blauvelt, Disco, and other undercover agents were very successful. In late May 1956 the assistant corporation counsel sent Lieutenant Thomas F. Crane of the BOSSI a list of 284 teachers who had resigned, retired, been suspended, or dismissed since the start of the investigation, with dates and reasons for their leaving. Of the 284, 161 had resigned, 70 had retired, 48 had been dismissed, 4 were suspended, and 1 had not been appointed.[22] Although these numbers represented just a fraction of teachers in the city's public schools, they sent a message that teachers were being watched, both in the classroom and outside, and were in danger of losing their jobs if they joined the Teachers Union.

The purge succeeded in large part because Moskoff developed such a strong relationship with police, assisting them in the larger patriotic endeavor of rooting out Communism. That assistance became personal at times. Ed Fitzpatrick, one of the detectives Moskoff relied on for his investigations, asked Moskoff for a favor, and Moskoff wanted to help him in order "to cement our relationship with BOSS." Fitzpatrick's wife wanted a job as a lunchroom employee in a parochial school, Blessed Sacrament, located in the Bronx. Knowing the strong tie that Timone had with the Catholic community, Moskoff asked the board member if he could assist her.[23] The assistant corporation counsel also asked Assistant Superintendent of Schools Samuel Levenson to assign the daughter of Detective Walter Upshur to Junior High School 210. "The nature of the duties of Detective Upshur with the New York Police Department," Moskoff wrote to Levenson, "is such as to make it possible for him to be extremely cooperative with our Board of Education."[24]

The NYPD was not the only police agency involved in the investigations. The New York State Police provided Moskoff with reports and data on individual teachers and allowed him to examine the Rapp-Coudert Files. On December 24, 1952, the assistant corporation counsel successfully petitioned Francis S. McGarvey, chief inspector of the New York State Police, requesting that he and Dunne be allowed to research the Rapp-Coudert Committee records. The State Police also sent Moskoff copies of signed Communist nomination petitions for state office to check against the names of New York City teachers. In April 1954 Moskoff asked to look at a petition for Israel Amter, a leader of the New York district of the Communist Party who was running for governor of New York. He wanted to check if the Harold Collins who signed it was the same individual who applied for employment with the Board of Education.[25] By gathering information on individual teachers' political affiliations, the state agency became a willing partner in the purge.

The exchange of letters between Moskoff and members of the state police chronicles a strong bond. On January 28, 1955, Moskoff congratulated Everett C. Updike on his promotion to chief inspector of the Bureau of Criminal Investigation of the New York State Troopers, adding that he would continue to assist him in "any manner whatsoever." Updike assured Moskoff of his own continued cooperation. Moskoff informed McGarvey, who had been promoted to superintendent of the state police, that their information had been "extremely effective in enabling us to oust from our school system the members of an organization which has been determined to be an agency of a foreign power." Moskoff was particularly indebted to a

Sergeant Davis for continued cooperation. McGarvey responded by thanking Moskoff "for your kind letter commending this division. It is indeed gratifying to learn of the efficient aid and cooperation in the matter of mutual interest."[26]

Moskoff also attempted to provide favors for state police. In July 1955 Moskoff reached W. Bernard Richard, assistant corporation counsel in charge of the division of legislation, with a request to help state trooper Kevin Clare, "who has been rendering extremely valuable service to our office in connection with my official duties." Clare had a "personal problem involving his sister," a former employee of the department of hospitals, and Moskoff thought that Richards could introduce the trooper to Commissioner Matzkin "with a view to assisting his sister."[27] The relationship with law enforcement agencies was not merely a professional one; Moskoff was cultivating a fraternity of those dedicated to protecting the security of America.

New York officials even appealed to the Federal Bureau of Investigation in their campaign. John Dunne met with the special agent in charge of the New York bureau, Donald E. Moore in March 1956, because the board wanted the assistance of the FBI. A nationwide policy prevented such collaboration, but Moore assured Dunne he was "completely sympathetic" with the school agency and hoped to continue their existing relationship. Bureau agent Robert L. Latchford told Moskoff that he was conducting an investigation of two teachers, Morris and Gertrude Lipschitz, and wanted his assistance. The relationship between the Board of Education and the FBI was a reciprocal one.[28]

Although unable to foster the strong alliance with the FBI that they had with New York police agencies, Moskoff and Jansen received a great deal of support from the House Committee on Un-American Activities. As early as March 10, 1950, Jansen informed Louis J. Russell, senior investigator for HUAC, that he was sending two of his assistants, John R. Fenety and Stuart C. Lucey, to Washington, D.C., to discuss his own investigation of New York City teachers. One person either from the superintendent's office or from the office of the corporation counsel met (on an unspecified date) with Benjamin Mandel, research director for HUAC. Reporting on the meeting, the person wrote that Mandel gave him access to files and even assigned one of his assistants to elaborate on procedures. Mandel was unable to identify any New York City teacher as Communist and had no knowledge of Alice Citron or Celia Zitron's involvement in the Party. However, he claimed that

Ben Davidson, Rebecca Simonson, and Abe Lefkowitz had knowledge of CP teachers. Mandel also suggested that a statement be prepared pointing out every teacher's duty to assist in exposing Communists.[29]

The House Committee on Un-American Activities shared its information with the board on teachers in the Party, including Dorothy Funn (who will be discussed later in this chapter). Moskoff asked to examine the official reports of the 1940 and 1942 New York State nominating petitions and a list of petition signers filed by the Communist Party with the secretary of state, which had been printed for the confidential use of HUAC. HUAC clerk John W. Carrington sent them to Moskoff, with the understanding that they were to be returned to the committee. Blauvelt sent Don Appell, an investigator for HUAC, a list of teachers divided into three categories: those dismissed by the Board of Education for insubordination for refusing to answer questions in connection with the school agency's investigation of subversives, those dismissed under the provisions of section 903 of the New York City Charter for refusing to answer questions before a congressional committee, and those who resigned while under suspension on charges of insubordination. The first list had thirty-four names and included the first group of eight, the second sixteen names, and the third four names. Even after dismissal the teachers' troubles were not at an end. More important, Blauvelt's letter to Appell indicated that eliminating Communists from the school system was part of the larger national and international fight against the red menace, and New York City officials saw themselves as part of that fight.[30]

Immigration and Naturalization Services also became involved. New York district director Edward Shaughnessy was carrying out an investigation of people who might be deportable or whose citizenship might be "amenable to cancellation" due to their affiliation with the Communist Party. Shaughnessy asked Moskoff for information on teachers and other board employees who were party members, foreign-born, or naturalized as U.S. citizens who had resigned during the past two years while under investigation. The board submitted over sixty names, noting date and country of birth; whether they had retired, resigned, or were dismissed; marital status; and whether they were named as Communist Party members or "known to be" Party members. Included in the list were Celia Zitron, born in Russia in 1899; Abraham Feingold, born in Russia in 1917; and Meyer Case, born in Russia in 1904 and dismissed by the board in 1953.[31] Although the three were never deported, this collaboration demonstrates that the union had become a focus of several governmental entities. Moskoff had successfully brought city, state, and national agencies together in a crusade to remove teachers from the New York City school system for no other reason than their political leanings.

Forcing people to relinquish their careers as public school teachers was not enough for Moskoff and Jansen. They were bent on assuring that Communist teachers be banned permanently from teaching. Jansen became aware that some of "our teachers who resigned" found employment at the Elizabeth Irwin High School, the "Little Red School House," on Bleecker Street. Founded in 1921, Elizabeth Irwin High School was a place of progressive education, applying the principles of John Dewey to a racially and ethnically diverse New York City community. Psychologist and journalist Elizabeth Irwin was the guiding spirit of the school, which influenced teaching methodologies and curricula at universities and colleges. Elizabeth Irwin High School, which became completely private in 1932, hired a handful of teachers who had been forced out by the board.[32]

Under Jansen's directives, John Dunne identified several teachers who had resigned and were later employed at Elizabeth Irwin High School, including Morris Salz and Sarah Abelson. Police Department records indicated that Abelson, who held a substitute license, sent a letter protesting the Feinberg Law (which she had every right to protest) and did not tag her as a Communist Party member. Nevertheless, the mere fact that she opposed the Feinberg Law suggested to Dunne that she was a Communist sympathizer. Another teacher employed at the private school, Leo Shapiro, was listed in Police Department records as a member of the American Labor Party in 1951. Adele Lithauer, another teacher at the Little Red School House who was thought to be a Communist, had a temporary license to teach in kindergarten but was never appointed. She refused to answer questions concerning past or present membership in the Party before the Senate Internal Security Committee.[33]

EXPERT WITNESSES AND INFORMERS

The Board of Education and the corporation counsel also relied on expert witnesses and paid informers, with little distinction made between those categories. In fact, in some cases people who provided information to the board were, at various times, called both informers and expert witnesses. Expert witnesses had usually climbed to high positions in the Party and professed to know how the movement operated, both in the United States and worldwide. Informers, on the other hand, were not necessarily experts on the functioning of the Party but had information on individuals and organizations. Expert witnesses also were known to the public, while informers remained anonymous. But the categories were used interchangeably.

Witnesses and informers gave authenticity to the view that Communist Party members were engaged in an international conspiracy to eradicate Western democracies and create Soviet-style regimes. Although HUAC's research director, Benjamin Mandel, claimed he had no knowledge of Communists in the Teachers Union, Board of Education documents labeled him a source. In one such document, "Thomas Jefferson High School," Mandel placed Israel Wallach, who was on the minority slate for secretary-treasurer of the TU in 1935, on his list of Communists. Mandel also identified as Party members Irving Adler, Meyer Case, Alice Citron, Louis Cohen, Samuel Greenberg, Eugene Jackson, Jacob Lind, Julius Metz, and Rose Olson.[34] Another expert witness was Louis Budenz, who had joined the party in 1935, eventually becoming managing editor of the *Daily Worker*. Disillusioned with the Party and under the guidance of Bishop Fulton Sheen, he joined the Catholic Church in 1945. Offering J. Edgar Hoover his expertise, Budenz was the lead witness in the 1949 trial of Eugene Dennis and other Communist Party leaders. In a "confidential memorandum," from Jansen's first assistant Stuart C. Lucey to Jansen dated April 1950, Budenz is listed as an expert witness who identified Lederman, Celia Zitron, Mary Bernikov, Sarah Gross Hertz, and others as members of the Communist Party.[35]

Usually informers did not reveal their identity because they worked undercover. Instead, informers were assigned code names. Parachute, Sprint, President, Chubby, Frankfurter, Cigar, Crime, Sad Sack, Siesta, Spinach, and Sugar were just a few of the code names for teachers who served as undercover agents. A person identified as "Doctor" reported that Lucille Spence, a "Negro" who was teaching at Franklin K. Lane High School, had been accused by Layle Lane, "another negro teacher" who was an anti-Communist, of being a leftist who traveled with a well-known Communist group. "Doctor" also named at least seven other people as Party members. The document on Spence noted that "Doctor" was not the only expert witness reporting on her, Layle Lane was considered an expert witness because of her credentials, race and ideology. Lane's race gave her legitimacy due to the fact that she was identifying another African American as a Communist. Hence, one would be hard pressed to claim she was motivated by race hatred. An undercover agent, code name "Falcon" (Bella Dodd), made it clear that her identity had to remain secret so she could not testify in public. However, she was willing to give Moskoff information on teachers in the Communist Party.[36]

Many informers and witnesses were actually paid by the Board of Education. In April 1950 Jansen's assistant Lucey, contacted Charles Gilman, auditor for the Board of Education, reminding him that he needed to confer with John Huber (undercover name JH), noting Huber's rate was $25 a day. Maurice Malkin, "an expert for a period of one month," starting May 22, was paid $225; Herbert Romerstein (undercover name "Italy") was owed $20 for June 1951; and Mrs. Sigmund Dobbs was paid $75 per week for services in the Friedman case. She provided thirteen weeks of work and received $1,158.82. For providing his expertise to the Board of Education, former CP member Louis Budnez was paid $70,000.[37]

Others volunteered information to Moskoff and the Board of Education. A teacher at William Cullen Bryant reported that Edit Vanderward Needleman of Benjamin Franklin was the "brains of a radical movement" and was referred to by teachers in the school as "Stalin." An anonymous informer claimed that "I admire your efforts to rid our schools of Communist teachers. Please look into the politics of Miss Pauline Thorner and Mr. Meyer Case who used to teach in PS 189 Brooklyn and were great admirers of everything Communists."[38] A teacher at New Utrecht High School in Brooklyn, Henry Appel, reported to Moskoff on subversive statements by colleagues. A conference was held at that school on September 23, 1952, between investigators and Appel and Harvey S. Hirsch, another voluntary informer who taught at New Utrecht. Hirsch reported that Samuel Applebaum, a teacher of French, was heard to say in November 1950 "that the United States did not belong in Korea and that he was happy at the destruction of the American forces in Korea." Hirsch also asserted that a Mr. Morris Jacobs had been present and could verify Applebaum's statement. Appel told investigators that, the day after Budenz announced his reconversion to Catholicism, William Shulman asked Applebaum in the men's room of the school, "What do you think about that wife-slayer and pimp?" Applebaum, Appel declared, had agreed with Shulman's remarks. The report also noted that a student allegedly stated in the classroom, in the presence of "Mrs. Baker and Mr. Cohen," that President Eisenhower and Secretary of State George Marshall were "Fascists." Baker made no attempt to challenge the student.[39] Appel had a long history of informing on his colleagues. On January 11, 1941, he testified at the executive session of Rapp-Coudert that another teacher had told him Henry Felix Mins, a teacher at New Utrecht, had joined the Communist Party and Harold Collins, yet another teacher, was present at a Party meeting. Others "volunteered information" alleging board employees were in the Communist Party, supported by varying degrees of detail.[40] One teacher at Benjamin Franklin claimed that a colleague, Frederick Field, "praises Russia to the sky" and his name appeared on the masthead of the *East Harlem News*.[41]

Parents also became voluntary informers. One parent complained that her son, who attended Lafayette High School, told her about the Communist view of his teacher, Benjamin Malamud, who was so far to the left that he was known in the school as "Stalin's man." Moskoff had been informed by the corporation counsel that a Mrs. Dorothy Tekel, active in the PTA of P.S. 234, claimed that a February 20, 1952, meeting would be where "you will meet some of the people there that you are interested in." A Mrs. Anna Baronofsky brought Isadore Rubin to speak at a PTA meeting and sought to have the PTA protest the death of Minnie Gutride. Tekel also asserted that Samuel Mehlman, a tenant in the building where she lived, was a teacher and was a Communist, claiming that there were barrels full of papers and literature in his apartment. She also claimed that he had hosted meetings of six to ten people. Apparently, Tekel was not on good terms with Mehlman after he called the police to complain about a loud party. In a November 17, 1959, letter, a parent from Far Rockaway, active in the neighborhood PTA in Bayside, alleged that the principal of P.S. 205, the school psychologist, a guidance counselor, and members of the PTA were all Communists and part of a conspiracy against her because she was anti-Communist.[42]

Anonymous communications, too, were taken seriously by board officials. One letter sent to board officials named Leda Goldway of P.S. 90 as a Communist stirring up trouble through the Committee for Better Schools for Harlem. Two anonymous letters received by board leaders reported on the "Communist" activities of Peter Nunan of P.S. 43 in Manhattan: he signed a nominating petition for Israel Amter's bid to be New York's governor in 1939, was a member of the Irish Reading Circle and Irish American Fellowship, and wrote a Christmas carol with the line "For the Reds they are fighting these rights to maintain."[43]

Expert witnesses and informers helped convert schools from institutions of learning and academic freedom into places where practically no one dared oppose the government's point of view. When teachers saw it as their duty not to speak out for freedom of expression and academic freedom, but rather to inform on their colleagues for expressing unpopular and controversial views, they became part of the effort to create a de facto police state.

BELLA DODD

One of the most celebrated expert witnesses and informers was Bella Dodd. Dodd had risen to high ranks in the Party and in the Teachers Union, knew the key players and the union, and helped formulate policies. Born Maria Assunta Isabella in Southern Italy in 1904, Dodd came to Harlem during a period when millions of southern and eastern Europeans immigrated and attended New York City public schools. At Evander Childs High School she came across the socialist publication the *Call* and, as she noted in her autobiography, *School of Darkness*, she became interested in socialism, with its stress on improving the conditions of humanity. Attending Hunter College in Manhattan, she majored in political science, joined a group of young women who considered themselves avant-garde, and dedicated her time to working for social justice. In her senior year at Hunter she was elected president of the student council.[44]

After graduating in 1925 she briefly became a substitute teacher at Seward Park High School, then accepted a position in the political science department at Hunter College. While working, Dodd earned a master's degree at Columbia University in 1927 and entered New York University Law School. She earned her law degree in 1930 and went on to pass the state bar examination. On a trip to Europe she met John Dodd, and the two eventually married. During the Depression, Dodd helped organize the Hunter College Instructors Association and was elected representative to the faculty council. The 1930s was the heyday of American Communism, especially in the labor movement and on college campuses, when it was a leading force in antifascist campaigns. The Party's Young Communist

League was active at Hunter and City College, attracting both faculty and students. Dodd attended meetings of the Class Room Teachers Association and was an eyewitness to the factional struggles that erupted in the Teachers Union. She saw the Communist-led Rank and File caucus gain strength in the union, in large part because of its successful campaign to organize unemployed teachers, eventually taking over the leadership from the Linville and Lefkowitz faction.[45]

The Communist takeover of the Teachers Union did not disturb Dodd, who was "grateful for Communist support in the struggle of the Instructors Association. I admired the selfless dedication of many who belonged to the Party. They took me into their fraternal circle and made me feel at home." The rise of fascism and Nazism also sparked her interest in Communism. Dodd, like many whose politics were on the left, saw the Soviet Union as the one true opponent of Franco, Mussolini, and Hitler. A colleague in the political science department, Harriett Silverman, confessed in 1932 to Dodd that she was in the Communist Party and asked her to join an antifascist literature committee. When Dodd asked Silversman to provide proof, her colleague took her to meet Communist Party leader Earl Browder. Impressed with Browder, and supportive of the antifascist cause, Dodd agreed to join and raise money for the committee.[46]

In 1935 Dodd was asked to serve as legislative representative of the Teachers Union, which automatically made her a delegate to the American Federation of Labor Central Trades and Labor Council of New York. She held that position from 1936 to 1944. She wrote: "I now became a member of the Communist Party Fraction in the A.F. of L. This meant that I would meet regularly with Communist Party members of the A.F. of L and the leaders of the Party in order to push A.F. of L. policy toward the Communist line." Dodd would later claim she had been responsible for the growth of union membership after the 1935 schism and walkout of seven hundred teachers. Testifying before a subcommittee of the United States Senate Committee on the Judiciary on September 8, 1952, Dodd contended that the TU spearheaded the Communist Party's work in the AFL. She faced opposition in the AFL because it became known that the TU was a Communist-dominated organization.[47]

Dodd claimed that between 1936 and 1939, when the TU parroted the Communist party's antifascist campaign, the union grew dramatically; among Local 5, the college teachers' Local 537, and the WPA Local 453, there were ten thousand members. Dodd claims that although, during this period, there were only one thousand Communist Party members in the TU, they were in leadership roles and had complete control over the union by 1936. The Party made sure that Party members attended the conventions of the AFT and AFL so they could support resolutions favorable to Party programs and recruit new members. In her autobiography Dodd wrote that she "consciously" built new Party leadership in the TU after the 1935 schism by surrounding herself with young CP members who were less rigid in their "Marxist patterns." By the late 1930s the union's prestige had grown among teachers and public officials because of its numerous campaigns, including fighting for issuing regular licenses to substitute teachers. Dodd's reputation among teachers grew, and she was recognized as a leader in the teacher union movement. She was nominated for a state assembly seat in Greenwich Village in 1938.[48]

Despite her success in the union and in the Communist Party, Dodd claimed that she became disillusioned after witnessing the "opportunism and selfishness" of leading Communist Party members, who purchased expensive clothes, lived in "fine apartments," and went to vacation spots provided by the wealthy. In 1943, Gil Green, the New York State chairman of the Party, suggested that she publicly declare her membership. The Communist Party under the leadership of Earl Browder was moving away from class analysis and revolution to reform. In this period of what would later be called Browderism, openness was emphasized. Party members had to work aboveground and not hide their identity. Dodd never explained why, despite having become disillusioned, she accepted Green's suggestion and officially joined the Communist Party. She resigned her position as the TU's legislative representative, although she remained a union member, and became a paid employee of the Party, earning fifty dollars a week. But, she told the U.S. Senate judiciary's subcommittee in September 1952, her involvement in the Party had nothing to do with money. It was her desire, like others who joined, to "help make a better world."[49] Claiming to be an "elder statesman," she selected Rose Russell, identified as a member of the Party, to be her replacement as legislative representative and helped train her. Most of Dodd's time was spent at Party headquarters, attending politburo meetings where "Browder seemed the undisputed leader." She organized the legislative program for the Communist Party in January 1944 and announced her membership at its 1944 convention.[50]

Dodd backed Earl Browder's efforts to "Americanize" the United States Communist movement by dissolving the Communist Party and creating the Communist Political Association. For her loyalty, Dodd was elected to the National Committee of the CPA, the top leadership in the United States. Dodd dedicated herself to implementing Browder's program while continuing to "exercise control over the communist teachers" in the TU. She also became a member of the New York State Board of the Communist Party and a member of the New York State Committee of the Party in the mid 1940s. She notes that she was "second to Gil Green in charge of political campaigns." Despite her claims of disillusionment, Dodd remained supportive of Browder's program, hopeful that the U.S. Communist movement could be reformed.[51] But Dodd's new optimism was tested in the spring of 1945 when French Communist leader Jacques Duclos criticized the reformist position in "On the Dissolution of the Communist Party of the United States," first published in *Cahiers du Communisme* and later translated into English. Duclos wrote that Browder had destroyed the United States Communist Party as an "independent political party of the working class in the US," saying that, while proclaiming Marxist principles, Browder took a revisionist path, emphasizing "the suppression of the class struggle in the postwar period and harmony between labor and capital." Interpreting the 1943 Teheran declaration (in which the Soviet Union, the United States, and England agreed to work together during and after World War II) not as a diplomatic document but as a "political platform of class peace in the United States in the postwar period," Browder had suggested in a December 1943 speech that capitalism and socialism could coexist and collaborate. According to Duclos, many international Communists rejected Browder's positions, some even publicly arguing that he had "swerved dangerously from the victorious Marxist-Leninist doctrine whose rigorously scientific application could lead to but one conclusion, not to dissolve the American Communist Party but to work to strengthen it under the banner of stubborn struggle to defeat Hitler Germany and destroy everywhere the extensions of fascism." Duclos warned that the "material bases" for fascism is monopoly capitalism and pleaded that the "forces of democracy and progress do not shut their eyes to the economic and political circumstances which engender fascism."[52]

Browder was in trouble. William Z. Foster joined with other proponents of "Marxist Fundamentalism" to oust the leader of the Communist Political

Association. Even early Browder supporters such as Gil Green and Israel Amter now joined the anti-Browder forces. According to Dodd, Green and Amter asked her to write a public statement repudiating recent policy changes and label them errors. Although Dodd claimed she was confused, she did not desert Browder. Dodd committed a sin in the eyes of anti-Browder forces at a meeting of the National Committee when she approached Browder, who was being castigated, and shook his hand, urging him to defend himself. He refused, calling the assaults "leftwing sectarian nonsense." Dodd criticized Benjamin Davis, who had accused Browder of abandoning blacks in the South when he dissolved the Communist Party. In response, Davis charged Dodd with white chauvinism, a charge supported by other "black comrades" on the National Committee, including William Patterson. According to her friend Annette Rubinstein, Dodd, as legislative representative for the Party in Albany, was critical of the condescending responses of Communist leaders and asked them to be more respectful to state legislators. Her criticism did not endear her to these leaders.[53]

Despite the infighting, Dodd was named to the Committee of Thirteen, charged with interviewing the members of the National Committee to "estimate the extent of their revisionist errors" and recommend to the National Convention which members should be dismissed. William Z. Foster was named chair of the Committee of Thirteen, proving that he had regained power and that Browder's fate was certain. Eventually an emergency convention was organized; it met in late June 1945 and elected a new National Committee. After Browder addressed the convention, Dodd applauded him. The convention dissolved the CPA, reestablished the CPUSA, and voted to intensify "Marxist-Leninist" education and oust Browder from the Party.

Dodd was in a difficult position. As its legislative representative, she had to push the Party's new line, even when she disagreed with it. When she opposed the Party's move against New York Councilman Michael Quill, because he voted in favor of a resolution to greet Archbishop Spellman on his return to New York, she was rebuked by New York district leader Bill Thompson. She accused Party investigators of invading her law office and home and claimed that her secretary was reporting on activities in her office. Dodd also asserted she was further isolated by her criticism at a 1947 national committee meeting of a decision by the Party leadership to support a third party in the upcoming national elections only if Henry Wallace ran as a third party candidate. Eventually, Dodd stopped going to Party meetings. In 1948 she was summoned to appear before the Party's discipline committee, but no action against her was taken. The event that led to her expulsion was a legal case in which Dodd represented tenants who accused their landlady of overcharging them. While Dodd could have won the case, the landlady offered to voluntarily pay back the tenants if Dodd would drop a demand for jail time. Dodd agreed to the request and was eventually expelled from the Communist Party on the charge that she had defended a landlord and sold out the working class.[54]

After her expulsion Dodd wrote that she felt alone and isolated. She was also penniless, since she had dedicated most of her time to the Communist Party and as an attorney usually represented the poor. Rubinstein contends that Dodd was so broke she had to lend her three hundred dollars. A friend suggested that Dodd see a priest, and under the influence of Monsignor Sheen at Catholic University and another Catholic theologian, she became a devout Catholic and a fierce anti-Communist. Feeling guilty about her contribution to what she now saw as the Communist menace, she began cooperating with investigating and governmental agencies.[55]

Testifying before a subommittee of the U.S. Senate's Committee on the Judiciary, Dodd detailed how Communist Party members in the TU organized a caucus to hold on to leadership. Although executive board membership was based on proportional representation, two-thirds of that body was Communist, Dodd testified. The Party used the union to persuade the AFL and AFT to adopt policies such as collective security and called for unity between the AFL and the CIO. Innocent teachers were duped by the Party's "humanitarian causes." Communists were placed in key positions. For instance, although TU President Charles Hendley did not become a Party member until after he stepped down from that position, his office manager during his presidency was a member. "We placed" in his office, Dodd declared, an office manager who made certain that "he saw the right reports." When he came to the office at TU headquarters, the manager would give him certain letters to sign and not show him others. Responding to a question, Dodd never said she saw the manager removing letters; it was a method commonly used by the Communist Party to control an organization. The office manager, Dorothy Wallace, was the sister of the vice president of the union, Dale Zysman. According to Dodd, Zysman was the "liaison between the Communist Party and the union."[56]

At times Dodd embellished and distorted the truth. In her autobiography she claims she was disillusioned with the Party before she joined it officially; in her testimony before the subcommittee she reports becoming disillusioned once she became an insider in 1944. She took responsibility for the TU's growth, but offered no details on how she accomplished that task. She had no evidence to support the charge that Dorothy Wallace controlled what Hendley read. In her autobiography she portrays the Party as an organized crime outfit, claiming that once you joined you could never leave. However, thousands of people joined and left the Party without fearing for their lives. When asked by the subcommittee of the U.S. Committee on the Judiciary if there was a Party line, she maintained that no member could be a "free agent," but she could not specify how teachers distorted their lessons in order to push Communism.

Dodd's decision to become an informer was devastating to the Teachers Union. The anti-Communist forces got what they needed, a high-ranking insider willing to testify that the Teacher' Union was nothing more than a Communist Party front. Her characterization of the Communist Party as a "conspiracy . . . an extra legal and an illegal apparatus" working for a "Marxist-Leninist victory in America" tarnished the TU.[57]

"AIN'T WE GOT FUNN"

Dorothy Bloch burst into tears in 2001 when recalling her firing from her teaching position by the Board of Education almost fifty years earlier. Bloch had gone on to have a successful career as a children's psychoanalyst practicing on the Upper West Side and a training therapist at the National Psychoanalysis Professional Organization and the Manhattan Center for Psychoanalytic Studies; she wrote an acclaimed book, *So the Witch Won't Eat Me: Fantasy and the Child's Fear of Infanticide* (1978). But she was still raw from what happened to her a half century earlier. Recalling her interrogation by Saul Moskoff, the ninety year old told an interviewer, "I am still terribly affected." Asked if she knew Dorothy Funn, she expressed shock and anger, replying "What made you ask that question? ...She is the one who reported me. . . . She was the informer."[58]

While Bella Dodd became the most well-known witness for the campaign against Communist teachers in the schools, the testimony of Dorothy

Johnson Kilso Funn was just as significant. Funn provided not only names of key figures but information on the inner workings of Communism in the union. Funn is barely mentioned in writings on teachers and Communism, yet no testimony reinforced Moskoff's notion of the criminally conspiratorial activities of Communist teachers more than this African American's. Despite historical neglect, Funn's story offers insights into issues of anti-Communism and race in America.

Born on July 7, 1903, in Brooklyn, Funn attended P.S. 5 and Girls High School in Brooklyn, then enrolled at Maxwell Training School for Teachers. She started teaching in 1923 in the public schools but did not join the Teachers Union until 1938. She claimed that the incident that persuaded her to join was the case of a principal accused of mistreating black children. One of the teachers organizing a protest was a TU member, and Funn was impressed with her initiative and courage. Funn remained inactive in the union until 1939, when she was transferred from a school in Queens to P.S. 3 in Bedford-Stuyvesant, a center of Teachers Union activity. Union members held regular meetings and were active in the community, working with parents to help organize a viable parent teacher association. The PTA of P.S. 3 launched a campaign to end discrimination and overcrowding, to get experienced teaches assigned to the school, and to make repairs on the physical plant. TU members at P.S. 3 were also pivotal in organizing the Bedford-Stuyvesant and Williamsburg Schools Council, which consisted of parents, teachers, community, and civic leaders. The council fought to have licensed teachers in all classrooms in the prominently black and Latino communities of Bedford-Stuyvesant and Williamsburg instead of day-to-day substitutes, a full day of instruction for children, an end to discriminatory zoning, and new school buildings.[59]

Morris Salz, a member of the TU on the executive board of the School Council of Bedford-Stuyvesant and Williamsburg, approached Funn at a P.S. 3 meeting. Salz confessed to her that he was a Communist Party member and asked her if she would like to join, but she was not ready. Over a six month period Salz provided Funn with Communist Party materials, including the *Daily Worker*, in an attempt to prove the Party was the only group diligently fighting on behalf of African Americans. Salz also introduced Funn to Robert Campbell, the section organizer for the Bedford-Stuyvesant area. Funn joined the Party in May 1939, becoming an active member of the Bedford-Stuyvesant Professional Group, made up of eight to ten teachers in the community. They met every Tuesday at the homes of the various members but were advised not to attend section meetings, which would jeopardize their positions. The meetings of BSPG were divided into two segments. The first was a forty-five minute discussion devoted to Marxist-Leninist theory, current events, and their impact on the Communist Party's program. Books used in the discussion included Lenin's *State and Revolution*, Stalin's *Foundations of Leninism,* and J. Peters's *Manual on Organization.* Funn declared, in an interview with a Board of Education investigator, that the BSPG's discussion was designed to "indoctrinate the teachers with the tenets of the philosophy," although she confessed that she was never instructed to indoctrinate students. However, as Marxists, they were expected to be disciplined in their work and submit themselves to the program of the Communist Party.[60]

Funn attended a Communist Party sponsored camp in June 1939, where the participants read the writings of Marx, Lenin, and Stalin and were told that the Soviet Union was the vanguard of the working class. When Funn joined, she knew almost nothing of Marxist-Leninist principles, but the meetings of BSPG, Communist Party literature, and the camp convinced her that the Party was a militant force for racial justice.

In 1940 Funn joined the National Negro Congress, created in 1935 to put pressure on Congress to pass civil rights legislation. The group represented several organizations, including the American Communist Party. Funn moved to Washington but did not give up her residence in Brooklyn. She became the legislative representative of the NNC, drawing a weekly salary of $172.92. Bill Taylor, chair of the D.C. branch of the Communist Party, told Funn that her sole function was to promote the Party. At a September 12, 1946, NNC meeting, Dorothy Funn spoke on an upcoming mass meeting on the American Crusade to End Lynching. On October 23, 1946, Funn made a report to the Negro Commission of the Communist Party, arguing that the NNC was the only national Negro organ that followed the lead of the CP. She sent invitations to a luncheon for feminist organizer Elizabeth Gurley Flynn at a mass rally held by the Communist Party on November 8, 1946, at the National Press Club.[61]

Besides working for the NNC, Funn served as the representative for the New York State CIO Political Action Committee and as executive secretary for a Committee on Unity working to eliminate the causes of the 1935 Harlem riot. Despite her meteoric rise in Communist Party circles, by

1946 Funn had changed ideologically, having come to the conclusion that the Party was undermining the fight for racial equality. "I had joined and thought I was going on the right path for economic and social and political freedom for the Negro," Funn told members of HUAC in 1953. "Working in the organization I found that we were really a puppet of the Communist Party and there was truly no interest in furthering Negro rights." Funn told HUAC that she "found great insincerity [in the Party]. I found untruths. I found that there was no one thing that I could latch onto as something that the Communist Party was sincere about, other than socialism for America and doing away with the . . . democratic government that had been established here for years and years and years."[62]

In 1947 Funn left Washington, claiming that she no longer wanted a "part of it" (the American Communist Party). She went back to teaching in Brooklyn and stopped attending NNC meetings. Unlike Dodd, who volunteered to become a witness, it is clear from her correspondence with Jansen that Funn had no intention of coming forward. On May 23, 1949, Funn wrote a response to Jansen's May 19 request that she come to his office to discuss her alleged membership in the Communist Party. Funn, asserted, "I do not believe it is within your province to probe into my personal beliefs or my associations. Your request for such a discussion seems to me to violate one of the basic tenets upon which our American democracy has been built. In fact, it has been my faith in our democratic principles that led me to work for the inclusion of the Negro in every phase of America's life." Funn maintained that her accomplishments were "well known to thousands of people in and out of New York." She had taken a group of black and white representatives to Washington, D.C., to discuss the lack of black captains on the Liberty boats bringing arms to U.S. allies overseas during war: "As a result, Captain Hugh Mulzac [an African American] was appointed under the War Shipping Administration." Emphasizing her patriotic credentials, Funn declared that she had been able to "convince trade unions and management that to win, all Americans had to put to work making the weapons for victory. My work in conjunction with thousands of others led to jobs for Negroes in the war industries." Funn cited her role in organizing the Negro Freedom Rally at Madison Square Garden in June 1943, which attracted twenty thousand people, as secretary to a 1944 conference working for the establishment of unity in New York City, and in assuring the successful passage of a law creating the New York State Committee Against

Discrimination. She also contended that she had satisfactorily served the New York City school system.[63]

But Funn changed her mind. In a June 3, 1949, letter to Jansen she contended that she wanted to dispel any doubts about her "Americanism" and compared herself to Supreme Court Justice Hugo Black, who was questioned about his membership in the Ku Klux Klan. He publicly admitted his error as a young man in joining the un-American organization. She, too, had made a "grave error when I joined the Communist Party in May 1939." Although she first believed that the Party was working on behalf of African Americans, she eventually realized that the "Communist pronouncements for the rights of Negro Americans . . . were a snare and delusion." She had been "duped" by an organization that used all means to "further its own nefarious ends," even appealing to the desire of blacks to become equal citizens. However, even during her time in the Party she had never taken part in any activity that could be considered treasonous or un-American. "I have never pledged alliance to any other country but the United States, the country of my birth." She was even willing to declare under oath that she never committed herself by "word or deed to un-American activities."[64]

On January 11, 1950, Funn sent Jansen a detailed description of her activities after she resigned from the Board of Education until February 1947, including her work as the legislative representative of the National Negro Congress from November 1943 to December 1946. She emphasized her meetings with mainstream political labor representatives, rather than Communists. "I had to meet personally with Congressmen and Senators on matters of legislation affecting the American people as a whole as well as that affecting Negro Americans," she wrote, adding that she also saw legislative representatives of the "AFL and CIO, the NAACP, the National Committee for a Permanent FEPC, the Non-Partisan Alpha Kappa (one of the two largest Negro sororities in the United States) lobby, the National Committee to Abolish the Poll Tax, farm and industrial groups." Funn was on a committee set up by "Congressmen" for the passage of legislation concerning rent control, price control, federal aid to education, free lunches, and housing. Her litany of activities did not include her connections with the Communist Party.[65] A major reason she did not raise the Communist Party issue was because she was attempting to convince Jansen that, even though she admitted to being a Party member, her activities were not unpatriotic. But

Jansen was only concerned about her activities while in the Communist Party: was she willing to name names?

Despite Funn's attempt to present her activities as mainstream, she confessed to Jansen before March 30, 1950 that she had joined the Party in May 1939, leaving in June 1946 because the "Communist Party was interested in using any and all means to further its own nefarious ends." In a March 31, 1950, confidential memorandum to Jansen, Lucey recommended that Funn should be "called in and asked to assist us in any way she can on the basis of her own professed disillusionment." Jansen asked Funn if she would "kindly come to my office on Friday afternoon, June 2nd at 3:30 in order that Mr. Lucey and I may discuss with you certain matters connected with the Communist Party." The tone of the letter was nonthreatening.[66]

Funn testified in August 1950 before Jansen. Her testimony was devastating to the Teachers Union. Funn's testimony identified TU members who were in the Party and explained how the Party controlled the union. She reported that Morris Salz, identifying himself as a Communist, had recruited her. She revealed the names of the teachers involved in the Bedford-Stuyvesant branch of the Party, such as Salz, whom she described as the organizer of the group, and Jules Lemansky, who was the literature director. Funn claimed that the objective of the study group was to "indoctrinate the teachers with the basic tenets of Marxist-Leninist philosophy." Communists were expected to submit themselves to the Party's program and were told for whom to vote in TU elections. The workings of the union were often discussed at club meetings, and the slate supported by the CP would usually win the election. She admitted there was opposition in the union to the Communist Party-supported slate after 1935, but eventually the opposition left the union. All the teachers in her club were employed by the New York City Board of Education.[67]

At an August 24, 1950, meeting with Jansen, Harold F. Hay, and John R. Fenety, Funn reported attending a Communist Party school near Kingston, N.Y., in the summer of 1939, along with Arthur Newman, Martha Lepowski, Charlotte Wacker, and Rose Olson, a New York City School teacher who came on weekends. The names of Mildred and David Flacks, Dorothy Bloch, and many others were given to investigators by Funn. According to Funn, the literature distributed at the Kingston school was devoted to "general Communist political, social and economic philosophy." Although Funn was giving testimony behind closed doors, Jansen told her she might be called on in the "forthcoming trails." "Mrs. Funn did not express any unwillingness to respond to such a request."[68]

Funn's decision to become a witness aroused disappointment and hostility. On January 4, 1950, Funn informed Jansen she had received an angry postcard:

> Dear Dot,
>
> I just heard that you are doing so well with your hired job against your fellow teachers that you bought a new house. Well, I didn't think undercover work would pay so well. Will you tell me how I can get in on the racket. Sure, what do I care what people think of me, stoolie or no stoolie, I am looking for security.
>
> Very sincerely yours, Max[69]

There is no evidence Funn received a financial reward for turning informer. In June 1950 Jansen claimed that Funn had freely discussed her past involvement in the Communist Party and had "sided [with those investigating] the activities of that Party in the public schools." He was satisfied that she had left the Communist Party in 1946, that she was no longer sympathetic to its cause, and that "we may count on her loyalty to her country and to the public school system."[70]

In May 1953 Funn testified before HUAC, and provided names of TU members who were in the Communist Party, including Salz, Ruth Finkelstein, a clerk for the Board of Education and sister of Jeannette Finkelstein, Ann Nechemias, Beatrice Goldberg Pelham, Hyman Koppelman, Mildred Flacks (who had earlier been dismissed by the board based on Funn's testimony), David Flacks, Edna Rosenberg, a teacher at Girls High School, Robert Cohen, a teacher at P.S. 35, Sarah Gilman, a clerk at a school in Brooklyn, and Stanley Chapman, who also taught in a school in Brooklyn. She pointed out that there were other Communist Party school groups, but said she had little knowledge of those organizations.[71]

Funn's testimony before HUAC would lead to the firing of teachers. When teacher David Flacks was called before HUAC, the committee noted that Funn had identified him as a Communist Party member. "You heard the testimony here yesterday by Mrs. Funn in which she identified you as a member of the Communist Party during the period in which she was a member. Have you ever at anytime been a member of the Communist

Party?" Flacks declined to answer the question. "First, I don't believe this committee has any right to ask me that question." Although he attempted to finish his statement, he was interrupted by a committee member who ordered him to answer the question directly. Flacks declined, arguing that it violated his rights under the first, fifth, sixth, ninth, and tenth amendments. The New York City Board of Education used David Flacks' testimony before HUAC to fire him.[72]

Dodd's close friend, Annette Rubinstein, insisted that Dodd was selective in whom she named. Questioned about Rubinstein's membership in the Party, Dodd, according to Rubinstein, protected her by claiming she had no knowledge of her party membership. But Funn was not always so reserved. In 1988 Mildred Flacks still expressed disbelief that it was Funn who had revealed that she and her husband David were affiliated with the Communist Party. When the committee asked about a particular person, Funn was more than willing to give as much detail as possible, noting if the person was a member of the party, BSPG, or other fronts, how active the person was in the Party or front, and the position held in the school system. Funn portrayed the BSPG as a clandestine organization; therefore, a member did not have to bother using an alias. Funn also named the members of the Bedford-Stuyvesant branch of the Communist Party, including Salz, Clara Rieber, Sylvia Elfenbein, and Mildred Grossman. Funn did not spare even Communists who were not members of the BSPG. Although Maurice Riedman was not a teacher in the BSPG, Funn contended he gave lectures to the group on aspects of Marxism-Leninism.[73]

What were Funn's motives? Her desire to make up for being "duped" by the Party and to serve the cause of the fight against Communism were factors, but she also wanted a position as a guidance counselor. Saul Moskoff, who had taken over the investigation of Communists in the school system, wrote to Jansen in September and October 1953 asking if he would consider assigning Funn to a guidance counselor position in P.S. 129. Funn asked Moskoff if the superintendent had made any decision concerning her request.[74]

As an African American, Funn reinforced the accusation that the Party used race to manipulate black America. Funn testified from her perspective as a former legislative representative of the National Negro Congress, which she labeled a civil rights organization. However, unlike the NAACP, which attracted the black middle class, the NNC drew from the black working class. The goal of the Party was to develop a "mass organization of tremendous membership," which would be "built up of working people interested in eliminating the social, economic and political inequalities of the Negro here in America." But the Party and its fronts were nothing more than a lie, according to Funn.

By supporting arguments that Communist Party campaigns against discrimination and lynching were designed to dupe black people, Funn publicly undermined the view that the Party stood for the rights of labor and blacks. When HUAC member Kunzing asked her if the Communists were "furthering the cause of the groups they were representing" or the cause of the Communist Party, Funn responded that the goal was a Communist revolution. Responding to another question, Funn said, "my feeling and conclusion is that the Communist Party took this great need that Negroes in America feel as a basis for exploitation of their wants, desires and the things that they were looking for, which were not for complete justice and equality for the [N]egro but it lends itself beautifully to an emotional tie-up." The Party, she claimed, was not really interested in the plight of black people: "I think they [Communists] will take every opportunity today or tomorrow, any time to gather forces around them for their support." Funn also exposed black Communists, including Max Yergan, Doxey Wilkerson, Bob Hall, and Ferdinand C. Smith, among others.[75]

Funn's testimony before HUAC highlights issues of race and Communism during the cold war period. Funn helped deracialize the anti-Communist movement, while fostering cynicism about the Communist Party's and the Teachers Union's programs for racial equality. Funn used her status as a Party insider and an African American to refute the Communist claim of racial leadership. The black conservative George S. Schuyler celebrated what he saw as a victory in a May 16, 1953. "Views and Reviews" column for the *Pittsburgh Courier*: "Well, well! Ain't we got Funn—Mrs. Dorothy K that is!" Gloating over the testimony of "this little colored Brooklyn school teacher," who was at one time "deep in the heart of Moscow's machination in America," Schuyler wrote that, while many were complaining about the attack on academic freedom, Funn deserved credit for unveiling that "behind the Fronts, many of them professing to rescue African-Americans" were simply "spreading racial ill-will." Schuyler challenged educated blacks who were prominent in the Party to step forward like Funn and "name names."[76]

The New York City Schools had become a cold war battleground, where informers and witnesses were used against teachers. Dodd and Funn and a host of others helped foster the view that the Communist Party, the TU, and other "front" organizations were part of a conspiracy that needed to be eradicated. However, no evidence was uncovered that the teachers who were victims of this domestic spying were guilty of incompetence or indoctrinating children. Using informers and witnesses violated the constitutional rights of teachers, but that meant little to those carrying out the campaign to eliminate the TU. One of the many unsavory aspects of this cold war effort was how it pushed the school system in the direction of becoming a police state.

THREE

10 / CRUSADING FOR CIVIL RIGHTS

In a letter to the February 1, 2007, edition of the *New York Teacher*, Phyllis Murray, a member of the New York State Teachers Union, wrote: "As we prepare to celebrate Black History Month in February, we must not forget that Black history is American history. Therefore, it is incumbent upon educators and all people of good will to work toward infusing this history into all American history textbooks, all American historical societies and all chronological accounts of American history."[1] This call for the inclusion of black history in the American experience was not a new one among teachers. Sixty years earlier, the New York City Teachers Union fought diligently for inclusion of the history of black Americans in New York City's school curricula. In fact, the promotion of black history became an important component of the agenda of the union.

By the end of 1950 the New York City Teachers Union was in the worst position in its forty-four-year history. Thanks to the Timone Resolution, it could no longer operate as a collective bargaining agency for New York City public school teachers; it could not represent faculty in grievances or hold meetings in the public school buildings. Moreover, the New York City Board of Education's purge of TU members was on-going. After 1935 the TU claimed that it became the largest teachers' union in the city. However, there is no doubt that the purges led to a dramatic decline in membership, the direct result of the board's campaign to eliminate the union.

Despite its inability to represent teachers officially, the New York City Teachers Union did not fold in 1950. In fact, it would continue to exist for another fourteen years. To its credit, during the period of rapid membership attrition in the 1950s and 1960s, the union refused to move to the margins but remade itself instead into a politically connected pressure organization fighting for several causes. The issue that received the greatest attention from the union was civil rights. As the school integration battle heated up in New York and civil rights leaders and organizations fought to eliminate segregated schools in the city, the TU carved out a space for itself as an important ally in the civil rights struggle. It became one of the most outspoken advocates for racial equality in the city and the nation.

Recently, some scholars have made a distinction between the civil rights struggles of the 1930s and 1940s and those of the 1950s and 1960s. Earlier battles, they argue, were led by popular front labor organizations and members of the left, especially the American Communist Party. Later, a number of civil rights groups, such as the NAACP, sought legal remedies, while religiously based organizations of the black working and middle classes fought for integration of schools, black enfranchisement, and public accommodation by using a number of tactics, including nonviolent resistance. "Historians see the civil rights movement in the 1940s," historian Anthony Badger asserts, "as different from the movement in the 1950s and '60s; it was a class-based movement, powered by leftist and biracial trade unions and focused more on economic rights than legalistic civil rights. This era of the civil rights movement, however, was brought to a halt by McCarthyism. The civil rights movement that emerged after 1955 was a church-based, cross-class movement that stressed legalistic civil rights."[2]

The TU's story after 1950 throws into question the argument that popular front unionism in New York City was eradicated during the civil rights struggles of the cold war period. Despite the decimation of the left and popular front unions that championed civil rights by anti-Communist forces, the TU did not back away from the struggle for racial equality. Indeed, it now devoted most of its energy to supporting the civil rights crusade in New York City. Given that it could no longer directly address the Board of Education as a legal representative of teachers or wage its campaign as part of a collective bargaining unit, its tactic was to attempt to force the board to end racial discrimination through applied pressure. It turned to the strategy of creating a popular front, organizing community, civil rights, labor, and progressive politicians. Clearly, the TU's World War II formulation of racism as unpatriotic because it caused disunity in a time when unity was needed to defeat fascism would no longer apply; however, it still maintained that racism was a threat to American democracy. Racism, the union claimed, distorted the contributions African Americans, Latinos, and other nationally oppressed groups made to the democratic project. Racism helped create structures that dramatically limited the opportunities for blacks and Latinos to succeed in America.

Arguing that racial equality and democracy were essential for education, the TU launched a campaign that made New York City schools an arena of the civil rights struggle. The TU's civil rights crusade was waged on four fronts: it campaigned to rid the school system of biased and racist textbooks, it fought to force the Board of Education to hire more black teachers, it promoted black history, and school integration.

The TU's platform went beyond the liberal consensus that called for equal opportunity and an end to employment discrimination, making a case for the importance of taking steps to hire blacks. Moreover, it did not rely on electoral politics or legislation. Instead, it adopted mass organizing to place pressure on the board and other agencies, exposing the Board of Education's policies and practices with an impact on children across racial lines.

CIVIL RIGHTS IN NEW YORK CITY: THE TEXTBOOK CAMPAIGN

The Teachers Union linked its New York City struggle for racial equality to the southern wing of the civil rights movement. In a 1963 letter to the National Association for the Advancement of Colored People, Rose Russell noted the TU's financial contribution to that organization, asserted that the TU had a long history of fighting bigotry in the New York City school system, and said it would continue to cooperate in every way in the fight against de facto segregation. In 1963 the union also contributed money to the Congress on Racial Equality, the Southern Christian Leadership Conference, and the Southern Conference Educational Fund, as well as the campaign to integrate a Brooklyn junior high school.[3]

One of the TU's most important initiatives was the attempt to remove racist textbooks from the public schools. The drive to eliminate biased textbooks goes back to the 1930s, when African American historians W. E. B. Du Bois and Carter G. Woodson brought to the nation's attention the texts' derogatory images of people of African origins. In his monumental work on Reconstruction, Du Bois analyzed how high school text-

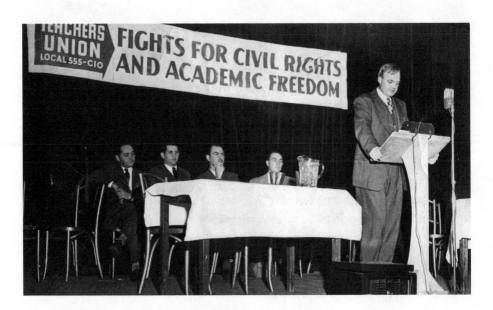

Figure 10.1 Speaker addressing TU membership meeting, September 1947. United Federation of Teachers, part 1, folder 518.

books presented this period in history, noting that they either ignored the subject or depicted it as a tragic era. Adopting the arguments of historian William Dunning, authors of high school textbooks portrayed the period as one in which white northerners and incompetent blacks gained political power only to prove that they were incapable of governing. Reconstruction governments were depicted as bent on punishing white southerners. Woodson also provided an analysis of the racism in American history textbooks in the March 1939 issue of the *New York Teacher News*. He noted that board officials selected books for use in the classroom despite the fact that they were filled with racist depictions of people of African origins.[4]

The struggle against racist textbooks was part of a larger attempt, launched in the 1930s by Rachel DuBois and proponents of intercultural education, to promote positive images of blacks, immigrants, and other ethnic and racial groups. DuBois emphasized the importance of teaching children about the cultural contributions of immigrants and African Americans in large part in order to foster the self-esteem of those groups. In 1939 the NAACP published a pamphlet titled *Anti-Negro Propaganda in School Textbooks*. In 1944 a delegation of black leaders met with Board of Education officials to discuss the racist portrayal of blacks in books used by children in the public schools. The delegation, which included New York City Councilman Benjamin Davis and the publisher of the *Amsterdam News*, argued that books that praised the Ku Klux Klan for removing blacks from state governments during Reconstruction could have originated from the United States' fascist enemies. Thus it would be incorrect to argue that the TU initiated the textbook campaign.[5]

The union's campaign to ban biased textbooks was reinvigorated by its effort to end the Board of Education's ban on such books as Howard Fast's *Citizen Tom Paine* and Laura Hobson's *Gentlemen's Agreement* as well as journals like the *Nation*. The union consistently put questions to the board and public challenging why books that demeaned races and cultures were allowed to remain in schools while politically progressive material was banned. It was this question—and the union's broader commitment to fighting bigotry—that stirred it to challenge the board's pervasive hypocrisy.

The TU's textbook campaign was undoubtedly broader than the NAACP's and those of African American leaders: it included an analysis of pernicious images of Jews, immigrants, colonial subjects, and labor. Borrowing the methods and arguments of the NAACP, the TU issued a pamphlet, *The Children's Textbooks*, in April 1948 identifying several books used by New York City schools that made children "prey to anti-Semitism, Jim Crow and racism." Recapitulating its World War II campaign against racism, the TU contended that the books led to division among peoples, promoting war and fascism.[6] The TU group that took the lead in the textbook campaign was the Harlem Committee, a racially diverse group that, since its inception in 1935, had challenged racial stereotypes in books as a threat to democracy. In 1950, when the purges were well underway, the Harlem Committee, under the leadership of Norman London, issued a more comprehensive analysis titled, *Bias and Prejudice in Textbooks in Use in New York City Schools*. The twenty-six-page pamphlet grew out of a 1949 study conducted by London and the Harlem Committee and was first published in the *New York Daily Compass*. The document was both a study and a political commentary on how African Americans, other people of color, and immigrants were depicted in textbooks approved by the Board of Education and the Board of Superintendents. Many of the books were authored by board officials. All of the books discussed in the pamphlet frequently used vicious racist representations of people of color and the foreign born.

The committee made a distinction between censorship, which it did not support, and the elimination of "racist stereotypes, distortion of historical and scientific fact, and bias." The latter were a violation of the democratic rights assured all Americans. The objective was to challenge racist images, which helped reinforce a sense of inferiority and distorted the truth about the role of blacks in American history. The union wanted to introduce the "study of Negro history not as a mere gesture one week out of the year but as a basic phase of the development of American culture and traditions."[7]

The various sections in *Bias and Prejudice* explored the manner in which textbooks treated blacks, "Colonial Peoples," and other "minority groups." Millions of school children were presented a distorted image of blacks as, for example, "carefree, lazy, banjo strumming, watermelon-eating" slaves suited for the "peculiar institution." *Our United States*, approved as a textbook by the Board of Superintendents, contained the following sentence: "It was often a happy life for the slaves. They had no cares except to do their work well." Another text, for sixth graders, authored by former assistant superintendent James J. Reynolds, contained a reproduction of a painting of an African American playing a banjo with the caption, "How do you know these Negroes lived a happy, care-free life?" School textbooks presented the treatment of slaves as benign and free of brutality. A passage in *United States in the Making*, by Leon H. Canfield, Howard B. Wilder, Fredric L. Paxson, Ellis Merton Coulter, and Nelson P. Mead, noted that "slaves of the South were considerately treated. . . . They were in most cases, adequately fed and cared for and they submitted in general to their lot without protest. They probably did not work any harder than the northern hired man, and at least they had fewer worries than un-employment and the insecurity of old age."[8] The Harlem Committee saw such passages as evidence of a systematic effort by school officials to deny the cruelty of slavery and present the treatment of blacks in the antebellum period as paternalistic. *Bias and Prejudice* noted that school textbooks either distorted or ignored black resistance. Thus, Nat Turner, leader of an 1831 slave rebellion, was described as "ignorant," "illiterate," and "a religious fanatic." The benign image of slavery was symptomatic of the larger problem of institutional racism in the North. The very institutions that were supposed to educate children were perpetuating lies by demeaning a large portion of the student body. The racist texts endorsed by the Boards of Superintendents and Education were promoting white supremacy and black inferiority.

The black image fared no better in the sections on Reconstruction in approved textbooks, which adopted William Dunning's view that blacks were unable to govern when provided with political power in the South, leading to a period of massive corruption and chaos. Some of the textbooks approved by school officials contained passages that defended the Ku Klux Klan. In their eighth grade textbook, *The Treasure Chest of Literature*, editors Edward J. Kehoe and Charles G. Eichel, who were both New York City public school principals, and Ignus O. Hornstein, assistant director of New York City public evening schools, included a piece by Thomas Nelson Page that the TU characterized as an apologia for the Ku Klux Klan. Page wrote: "The degradation and suffering of the old leaders of the South were pitiful. Deprived of their homes, bankrupt, terrorized by the Negroes and Carpetbaggers, they finally organized, for the protection of their families; the famous Ku Klux Klan, which although wrong in principle and contrary to law, gave them some relief from their suffering."[9]

This blatantly racist passage portrayed freedmen and freedwomen as the cause of violence in the South, whereas the Klan was depicted as nothing more than a group of innocent southerners defending themselves against black attacks. A passage in *Our Country* by W. H. Yarbrough and Herbert F. Hancox accused the United States Congress of passing "a number of harsh laws to punish the South," including one law disfranchising white men and giving the vote to freedmen. Another of these laws sent northern troops to police southern whites. "To make matters worse for the South, some of the soldiers were Negroes." An assistant superintendent assigned to the high school division, William Hamm, coauthored *The American Story*, a textbook expressing admiration for the Klan. According to the authors of *The American Story*, in 1867 hundreds of local Klan groups united in the Invisible Empire of the South, under the leadership of General Nathan Forest as its Grand Wizard. "Its purposes were patriotic, but its methods cannot be defended. . . . Unruly Negroes were whipped."[10]

Although the major focus of *Bias and Prejudice* was on how blacks were portrayed in textbooks, the work also included a small section on other "Minority Groups." Mexicans, Latin Americans, and the "foreign born" in the United States were also portrayed in degrading fashion in texts approved by the school system. Fredrick K. Branon, in *Social Geography*, contended: "Nicaragua and Guatemala are very much alike in that about 85 per cent of the populations is Indian or lower class Spanish of mixed race. These people are quarrelsome and therefore lacking in progress." In another textbook the author asserted that many among the foreign born "did not even learn to speak English. Some people do not make good American citizens." Superintendent William Jansen's work contended that Mexican farmers "are not greatly interested in their work and seem satisfied as long as they have enough to eat." *Bias and Prejudice* also noted that no attention was paid to Jewish contributions to American society in most of the history texts approved by the boards.[11]

Bias and Prejudice demonstrated the pervasiveness of racism in the system. School leaders in New York were the ones perpetrating racist stereotypes. The union cited as an example *A History of My Country*, coauthored by the acting chair of the Board of Examiners, David S. Muzzey, which depicted emancipated blacks as simpletons and slavery as a benevolent institution and argued that once slavery was removed, blacks reverted to savagery. One passage in a sixth grade textbook, *Reading for Appreciation,* compiled by former associate superintendent of schools William E. Grady (who would later have a school named after him) and Paul Klapper, read: "At night Whitney loved to hear the Negroes singing the old plantation airs as they sat in front of their cabins picking seeds from the vegetable wool. . . . There were, however, the holiday times when banjos were brought out and all the evening was given over to merry making—to singing and dancing and a feast of watermelon and roasted corn."

Of all the school officials noted in *Bias and Prejudice,* William Jansen received the most attention. The Jansen administration was responsible for the controversial banning of *Gentlemen's Agreement, Citizen Tom Paine, Focus*, the *Nation,* and other publications. As noted, under Jansen TU members were being fired, forced to resign, or compelled to retire because of their political affiliation, and the TU was eventually banned in 1950 from the school system. The union had reason to claim it was under attack because of its challenge to the school agency. *Bias and Prejudice* was not merely a fact-finding report but also a political document designed to weaken Jansen's position and bolster the image of the union.

The superintendent's thirteen geography books, ranging from the fourth to the eighth grade and all on the Board of Education's approved list, were filled with racist and ethnocentric notions. "Because the native people of Africa, most of whom belong to the Negro race," Jansen asserted, "are very backward, the greater part of the Continent has come under the control of European nations since its opening up began." In another text coauthored by Jansen, *The Distant Lands*, Ethiopians are referred to as "backward and of mixed race." The Harlem Committee also noted Jansen's embrace of imperial rulers. Jansen and coauthor Nellie Allen Jansen wrote in *Our Own Lands*, "since Puerto Rico has been our possession, we have aided the people in building good roads, establishing schools and hiring good teachers, and living in a more healthful way." The committee concluded that the highest-ranking administrators, including the superintendent, were not impartial when it came to judging the contents of textbooks. The board refused to eliminate racist texts because they themselves were biased, and racism operated "likewise in the victimization of teachers (particularly leaders of the Teachers Union) who have fought against the policy of the Board of Education in regard to intercultural education, the banning of books and numerous instances of undemocratic practices of Dr. Jansen and his subordinates."[12]

The images of blacks, Puerto Ricans, and colonized people in the textbooks endorsed the view that they were intellectually inferior beings. The union was challenging these efforts by the school system and exposing the board's racism, which was having a detrimental impact on black children. This civil rights effort was just as important as the right to vote because it attempted to put an end to the systematic psychological destruction of children. According to the committee, biased textbooks fostered "profound prejudices in the very young." The images of "shiftless, irresponsible, chicken-stealing Negroes" were instilled in the "minds of impressible children." The Harlem Committee cited in *Bias and Prejudice* a mother at a Harlem conference who reported that her child had looked at his first grade reader and asked, "Where am I?" However, the Harlem Committee did not define its major objective as psychological change; instead it used a political argument. The textbooks were promoting white supremacy and thus undermined American democratic principles of equal opportunity and fair play. Moreover, the language of the biased texts distorted historical and scientific truths, contradicting the findings of such prominent scholars as W. E. B. Du Bois, Carter G. Woodson, and John Hope Franklin.

TU activists were aware that, if the union was to have any chance of forcing the Board of Education to remove biased textbooks from the schools, it had to have mass support. Thus the union launched a public campaign. It distributed copies of *Bias and Prejudice* throughout the school system and to trade unionists, the press, and civil rights groups. The TU also handed out an advertising leaflet offering a copy of the pamphlet for fifteen cents and describing it as a "detailed study of textbooks approved by the Board of Superintendents for use of our children." Employing a provocative tone, the TU claimed that readers would find "shocking proof" of the board's textbook policy, which allowed "disgraceful insults" against minorities and immigrants and ignored their contribution to the country's democratic heritage. The union raised the question how leaders who were responsible for such ugly depictions of blacks, Puerto Ricans, Mexicans, and other groups could impartially judge the appropriateness of textbooks. School officials had provided no plausible rebuttal to the union's charges. How could they promote Brotherhood Week and democracy at the same time the board's top administrator was guilty of advancing racist propaganda in his own publications?[13]

To pressure the board further, in April 1950 the union sent copies of *Bias and Prejudice* to Jansen and all the board members except Timone accompanied by a letter informing them that the TU had written to the publishers of the textbooks cited in the work, encouraging them to delete or revise objectionable passages. The letter to Jansen told him that it was his responsibility to "make certain that books which hinder the development of a truly American outlook on the subject of minority groups are not permitted in our classrooms."[14]

The TU continued its public campaign at a July 20, 1950, Board of Education meeting, at which Norman London, chair of the Harlem Committee, spoke about the treatment of racial, religious, and national minorities in texts on the approved list of the Boards of Superintendents and Education. London cited examples of racist and prejudicial phrases and argued that the books did not point out the contributions of these various groups. In response, President Moss asked London to send Andrew Clauson, chair of the Instructional Affairs Committee, materials supporting this claim. London's presentation had forced a high-ranking board official to respond to the TU. In addition, the community and parent leaders issued an open statement expressing their concern. Despite criticism from the NAACP, the American Council on Education, and the TU's *Bias and Prejudice,* the Boards of Superintendents and Education did not, at this point, remove the majority of the offending books. In an open letter to the Board of Education in October

1950 parents working closely with the TU in the textbook campaign declared that "school officials have frequently made declarations of the importance of teaching brotherhood and interracial understanding, bit the presence of biased and antidemocratic texts in the hands of our children belie[s]" the statements of the school officials.[15]

Not only did the TU try to gain support among teachers, it also attempted to get them actively involved in the campaign. In January 1951 the TU issued a *Guide for Research in Bias in Books*, asking teachers to provide the title and publisher, author, and illustrator of books they found to be biased, along with a brief summary of the work and description of the characters, indicating their gender, economic class and race, creed, and national origin. The guide requested that the reviewer point out stereotypes, "e.g. Negro maids or porters," and raised the issue of gender stereotypes, focusing on activities "typically associated with male or female" and instances where only "women and girls were portrayed in inferior roles." Reviewers were to note if dialect was used and when colloquial expressions were used to designate racial, national, religious, or economic groups. One important objective in the effort to get teachers involved in the campaign was to raise their consciousness. The union assumed that teachers often paid little or no attention to images in textbooks, thus, asking them to scrutinize these works to see how people were portrayed might make them aware of racist images.[16]

IMPACT OF THE TEXTBOOK CAMPAIGN

The Board of Education did not directly respond to the union. It never acknowledged the existence of *Bias and Prejudice* because its Timone Resolution forbade the TU from having any official dealings with board officials. But it was clear that the union had publicly embarrassed the school administrators. The union revealed to the public that the Board of Education and the Board of Superintendents were feeding children books with racist and offensive depictions of blacks, Latinos, Italians, and other groups. When the school integration campaign started in the 1950s, administrators maintained the façade that there was no deliberate attempt to segregate children based on race, pointing instead to neighborhood patterns. When it came to the issue of biased texts, however, there was no feasible explanation for allowing children to be subjected to such material. By becoming a leading force in the textbook campaign, the union gained credibility and a certain prestige that it would have been denied had it become simply a voluntary teacher organization. Just as important, it found a way to promote its brand of unionism, which connected the concerns of the union with those of parents and civic organizations.[17]

The union's effort garnered the support of political, civic and labor groups. The Bedford-Stuyvesant and Williamsburg Schools Council joined the TU in its textbook campaign. Ada B. Jackson, president of the council, requested a meeting with Jansen so they could discuss "anti-Negro teaching in our city's schools." When she received no response, she wrote to him on January 25, 1950, urging the superintendent to consider the recall and revision of every textbook that violated the principles of Negro History Week, Bill of Rights Week, and Brotherhood Month, all celebrated in February. She took a swipe at Jansen by noting that his own geography textbook series stressed the superiority of whites and the inferiority of blacks. "White superiority concepts are repeated again and again and again so that these are drilled into the minds of the children." The books, Jackson said, also omitted important facts on culture which "bring out the basic equality of peoples," as well as information on segregation and the exploitation of people.[18]

Albert Pezzati, the 1940 American Labor Party candidate for the New York State Senate and a former member of the International Union of Mine, Mill and Smelter Workers executive board, sent a letter to the superintendent and board members registering an "emphatic protest" against the biased textbooks approved by the school system. He accused the board of being a "party to the pollution of the minds that you are supposed to nurture." Invoking the impact on American democracy of such texts, Pezzati asserted that as a citizen of New York he did not want his child to "unlearn" the decent virtues she learned at home by being subjugated to racist literature. Leon Straus, executive secretary of the Fur Dressers and Dyers Union, notified Jansen that several locals representing seventy-five hundred union members had adopted a unanimous resolution calling on the Board of Education to remove the biased textbooks from its approved list. Straus contended that his union was "aware of the fact that the circulation of these books helps to plant in the minds of our children the seeds of bigotry and intolerance which should not be countenanced in a democratic school system." His argument emphasized the notion that such literature challenged a democratic society because it instilled antidemocratic views in the nation's future leaders.[19]

By March 1951 the union had won a major victory. At a March 22 board meeting Charles Bensley requested evidence that textbooks approved by the board were racist. Like Norman London who convinced Moss at a 1950 hearing to ask for evidence of the union's charge, Bensley was also compelled to respond to the union's accusations.[20] The union also met with success in its fight against anti-Semitic textbooks on the board's approved list. In early May 1951 the union cited the inclusion among the approved textbooks of a transparently anti-Semitic play, *The King's English*, by Herbert Bates. The one-act play included a "cannibal chieftain" and a person of Jewish heritage who had a heavy Yiddish accent, mispronounced English words and mixed Yiddish into his sentences.[21] The *New York Daily Compass* reported on May 29 that the textbook committee of the board had dropped *The King's English*, clearly a victory for the Teachers Union.[22]

The board's Committee on Instructional Affairs studied the problem and in 1952 announced the removal of eight of the offensive books from its approved list. By April the union's Anti-Discrimination Committee claimed that some books listed in *Bias and Prejudice* and others later noted by the union had been removed from the approved list.[23] The board's decision was a victory for the New York City civil rights movement. Although a handful of books were removed from the list of approved textbooks, the board's action was an acknowledgment of the TU's accusation, if of not all the works at some were racially and ethically offensive

Although the major emphasis of the union's campaign was on race, religion, and ethnicity, labor was also included in the mix. In January 1952, Lederman reached out to trade unionists, informing them of a "vicious anti-labor" publication, *T-Model Tommy*, which was on the 1951–1952 board's approved list for high schools. Tommy, the hero in the book, is a strikebreaker portrayed in a positive light, while strikers are depicted as "disreputable characters." Lederman contended that the book failed to discuss what caused workers to strike; the images only reinforced anti-labor and antiunion sentiments. Well aware that the board would ignore any request the TU made without the support of a highly organized campaign, the union reached out to its follow unionists.[24] As part of the drive to remove *T-Model Tommy* from the public schools, Lederman issued directly to Jansen a letter that was made public urging him to remove the anti-labor book. New York

City, the union leader told Jansen, had a reputation as a "trade union city," and many of the parents of children who attended the city's public schools were trade unionists. *T-Model Tommy* was an insult to these parents. Lederman used the same argument the union had used in calling for the ban of textbooks containing racist, anti-Semitic, and anti-immigrant passages: the biased view of strikers was damaging to American democracy.[25]

The TU managed to gain some union support in the *T-Model Tommy* effort. Hyman Gordon, president of the Paper, Bag, Novelty, Mounting, Finishing and Display Workers Local 107 of the International Brotherhood of Pulp Sulphite and Paper Mill Workers protested to Jansen about the "vicious anti-labor book," which characterized strikers as "tough law-breakers and thugs," while strikebreaker T-Model Tommy was portrayed as "100% American." He requested that Jansen "stop this spread of poison which infects the minds of our children." Pheter A. Geis, recording secretary of Automobile Lodge 447 of the International Association of Machinists sent a letter to Betty Hawley Donnelly of the Board of Education complaining that the book portrayed workers in a "ridiculously unfavorable light" and urging her to use her influence to have the anti-union propaganda removed from the approved list.[26] On February 20, 1952, Ethel F. Huggard, associate superintendent and chair of the Committee on Textbooks and Supplies for the Board of Education, acknowledged Victor Teich's complaint about *T-Model Tommy* and notified him that its publishers had offered to withdraw the book from the approved list; the Board of Superintendents approved the publisher's request.[27] Neither the Board of Education nor Jansen contacted the Teachers Union. Such a move would have been a tacit acknowledgment of the pivotal role the union played in the crusade. To his credit, Victor Teich called attention to the TU's contribution in a February 29 letter to Huggard: "It was the vigilance of the Teachers Union, an affiliate of the United Public Workers, which brought this book to our attention, and we are fortunate in that there are teachers in the school system who are sufficiently alert to this sort of anti-labor divisive material."[28]

While the campaign to eliminate racist textbooks was a continued effort to connect the TU's plight to the black and Latino communities, the successful *T-Model Tommy* fight helped the union keep its identity as a defender of the working class. Both efforts reflected its vision of American democracy and were part of its larger civil rights struggle. The civil rights campaign in New York City involved, to a large degree, members of the working class.

Derogatory images of these workers were part of an effort to create views of people who did not deserve full citizenship, thus impeding democracy.

Although the Board of Education would not remove most of the offensive textbooks until the 1960s, the Teachers Union's protracted campaign has to be given credit for raising people's consciousness and helping pressure school officials to eliminate some of the offensive texts. The TU's campaign helped move to the foreground discussion of the role of negative images and why removing them was important in the fight for equality.

PROMOTING BLACK HISTORY

As part of the push for racial equality, the Teachers Union campaigned for what it labeled Negro history. The teaching of Negro history in institutions of learning had been advocated by scholars and activists well before the TU's efforts. One of the most prominent figures championing such a study was African American historian Carter G. Woodson. Woodson, who received a doctorate in history from Harvard in 1912, became the director of the Association for the Study of Negro Life and History in 1915 and editor of the ASNLH's journal in 1916. Woodson argued that the researching, writing, and teaching of black history could be used to oppose the myths of black inferiority propagated by white America. Negro history could also help bolster black esteem, which was constantly under attack by the dissemination of racist lies. These lies, according to Woodson, were harmful to the well being of a country whose intrinsic promise was life, liberty, and the pursuit of happiness. Woodson also invoked the psychological argument by claiming that for black children the study of black history would provide psychological protection against white racism.[29]

Using Woodson's arguments, the Teachers Union connected the promotion of black history to its textbook campaign by contending that it was not enough to remove negative images. The textbooks used by children had distorted the record of people of African origins, so remediation was necessary. By letting students know the contributions blacks made to America and the world, teaching black history could undo the damage caused by racism. Because of their role as educators, teachers, more than any other professional group, were in a position to address the distortions and myths that students heard and correct the record. Teaching history could provide a corrective because it challenged views of the inherent inferiority of blacks by providing evidence that the reason for the conditions of black Americans were structural. History also was a means of proving the heroic efforts on the part of blacks, labor, and other ordinary people in challenging inequality. Moreover, history revealed lessons in the ways people struggled to eradicate inequality. Once people were introduced to the truth, it would act as a stimulus for action. Noting her experience teaching at Wadleigh High School in Harlem, an all-girls school, TU member Virginia L. Snitow wrote in an article published in the *Nation* that her students came from maladjusted homes and extreme poverty, lived in dilapidated housing, and many were from the South, where they had received an inadequate education. Despite their difficult conditions, Snitow argued that "it is not money we lack, but honest understanding, courage and the will to wipe out an old evil. So simple a thing as introducing discussions of Richard Wright's *Native Son*, of important figures in Negro history and culture, of the Negro newspaper" and the "People's Voice, produced a changed class."[30]

The TU used a number of methods to promote black history, ranging from the creation and distribution of pamphlets for teachers to use in the classroom to sponsoring events featuring scholars of African American history. As in the textbook campaign, the Harlem Committee took the lead in the Negro history campaign. The committee created and distributed to New York City schoolteachers literature on the accomplishments of African Americans. The committee's efforts in disseminating information on black history reflected its belief that if teachers had the information they would incorporate it in their teaching. The material included bibliographies of books on black history and on blacks in art, literature, science, and labor. In addition, the *New York Teacher* published articles on prominent black figures.[31]

By the early 1950s, the TU and its Harlem Committee were issuing kits with materials offering an alternative view of the past and the role played by blacks. One area of focus was the American Reconstruction era. Greatly influenced by W. E. B. Du Bois's 1935 work, *Black Reconstruction*, the Harlem Committee's pamphlet on Reconstruction framed it as one of the most crucial periods in America history, a time of promise for race relations in the South and for American democracy. However, Reconstruction failed to achieve true democracy, and instead, poverty and prejudice triumphed in the South.[32]

The pamphlet listed what it labeled as distortions and truths of Reconstruction. One distortion promulgated by historians, the committee asserted, was that the South should have been left to resolve its own situation after the war, with the Reconstruction Act of 1867 portrayed as a vindictive measure the political purpose of which was to keep the Republican Party in power. The committee refuted this view by arguing that the "southern ruling class" attempted to restore white supremacy and subjugate blacks. The establishment of the black codes (laws passed by former confederate state governments to deny African Americans full citizenship), violence waged against blacks, and southern state legislatures' rejection of the Fourteenth Amendment all proved the South's attempt to reestablish white rule. Other distortions noted in the pamphlet included the uncritically positive portrayal of Andrew Johnson, accusations that congress members Thaddeus Stevens and Charles Sumner's actions to limit racism in the South were motivated by revenge, and assertions that Reconstruction governments were corrupted and dominated by "Carpetbaggers," "scalawags," and ignorant blacks. One of the most notorious distortions by historians was the argument that the Ku Klux Klan was created only in response to the excesses of blacks.[33] The committee provided teachers with a large body of information gathered from Du Bois's *Black Reconstruction*, John Hope Franklin's *From Slavery to Freedom*, E. Franklin Frazier's *Negro in the United States*, and Carter G. Woodson's *The Negro in Our History*, all providing as a corrective ample evidence of black agency, the work of the Freedmen's Bureau, and the accomplishments of Reconstruction state governments.[34]

The Harlem Committee used the same approach in its kit on "The Negro in the American Revolution," dispelling the myth that blacks played no role in the nation's fight for independence. It noted that five thousand blacks participated in the revolution, motivated by the promise of liberty and equality. Black soldiers fought alongside whites and distinguished themselves in some of the key battles of the war, including Bunker Hill. Blacks also presented a number of petitions to colonial legislatures requesting their freedom and, in Massachusetts, suing for their freedom. "Negro Slavery in the United States" was the focus of another of the committee's study guides. Relying on Herbert Aptheker's *Negro Slave Revolts in the United States, 1526–1860*, Joseph C. Carroll's *Slave Insurrections in the United States, 1800–1865*, Shirley Graham's *There Was Once a Slave,* and other works on slavery, the committee addressed the myths of docile slaves satisfied with their plight and a benevolent slave system. Familiar with the recent shift in the literature from emphasizing the "benevolence" of the institution to acknowledging the victimization of blacks by slavery, the Harlem Committee's guide depicted the system as one of "moral and cultural degradation." Slaves lived under conditions that robbed them of their culture and destroyed their families. They were subjected to corporal punishment, forced to work long grueling hours, and provided with minimum food and clothing. But the guide on slavery also went beyond victimization to focus on slave resistance, including slave revolts.[35]

Negro History Week, dedicated to the study of black history, was first established by historian Carter G. Woodson in 1926 and held in the second week of February. The union headlined black history each February starting in 1951 by issuing a special supplement in *New York Teacher News*. Supplements prepared by the TU's Anti-Discrimination Committee appeared in the paper the week of Lincoln's birthday and included excerpts from works by African American poets, novelists, historians, and social scientists as well as book reviews and a section titled "What's Your Quotient?" Other material for teachers and parents concerning children's books on African Americans were also made available. The members of the Anti-Discrimination Committee believed black history was being neglected in the classroom because teachers just did not have enough material. By providing the supplements, they tried to convince their colleagues that teaching black history was a sure way to counter bigoted textbooks used in the public schools.

In one supplement issue, Lucille Spence argued in "The Struggle for Integration" that "our struggle has been not to get separate courses or to have one Negro History Week, but to get the placing of the history and contributions of the Negro in every level of social studies, literature and science wherever it naturally comes." The union, Spence asserted, was "keeping with the struggle" of the NAACP's fight to eradicate school segregation. Spence called for writing Negro history into courses in order to "engender pride for the Negro child and appreciation for the white child." Thus the union emphasized the psychological merits of an integrated society for both black and white children.

The "Negroes of the Year" column in the supplement provided synopses of the lives of prominent African Americans such as Mary Church Terrell, Thurgood Marshall, and Judge Louis Flagg Jr., the first black elected to a judgeship in Brooklyn.[36] The supplement also had a photo of the members of the NAACP's Defense Fund who were handling Brown v. Board of Education before the Supreme Court, addressing what Spence declared to be the most pertinent civil rights issues facing the nation. The 1957 supplement, for instance, focused on civil rights in the South and contained a section called "Unsung Heroes in [the] Current Struggle," which included a photo of Martin Luther King Jr. and a quotation from a December 3, 1956, address he gave at the First Annual Institute on Non-Violence and Social Change. There was also a salute to the Little Rock Nine, nine black high school students who integrated the all white high school in Little Rock, Arkansas, and a piece on the bravery of the men and women in the forefront of the movement such as Daisy Bates, president of the Little Rock, Arkansas branch of the NAACP and advisor to the Little Rock Nine, Roy Wilkins, executive secretary of the NAACP, Thurgood Marshall, legal counsel to the NAACP who argued the Brown case before the Supreme Court, and A. Philip Randolph, labor and civil rights leader.[37]

Although the material in the supplement on Negro history was geared for social studies classes, some of the pieces could also be used in other disciplines, especially science classes, for example, the extensive "Scientists and Scholars Demolish the Myth of Negro Inferiority." In another supplement there appeared a lengthy article on the African American physician Charles Drew, an expert on blood transfusion. In the same issue a column titled "Great Negro Scientists" outlined the accomplishments of Benjamin Banneker and George Washington Carver, among others.[38]

One of the most significant aspects of the supplement was that it offered an alternative view of the black experience, countering popular racist notions. For example, the nine-page study guide "The Negro in New York, 1625–1865" contained material about blacks from the Colonial period to the Civil War, describing the repressive features of slavery under the British but also highlighting black resistance by including information on the 1712 slave revolt. The role of heroic whites in the black freedom struggle was also an important theme in TU guides. For instance, when examining the Draft Riots of 1863, the union publication noted that the "homes of anti-slavery white people" as well as blacks were destroyed. In the article "Historic Places," the TU noted that John Brown's home had been opened to the public and a memorial statute for the famous abolitionist erected. Although the union constructed the history of the militant abolitionist movement as an interracial one, it placed greater emphasis on the agency of blacks. All four of the abolitionists discussed in a piece titled "Abolitionist Movement" were black. The fact that two of the four abolitionists, Sojourner Truth and Harriet Tubman, were women gave some indication of the union's effort to address the issue of gender as well. A separate article, "Abolition and Women's Rights," focused on black and white women in the antislavery movement and how their efforts led to the women's rights movement.

The union's efforts won praise from civil rights leaders and activists, civic organizations, and parents. Vivian Kuch, secretary of the Far Rockaway branch of the NAACP, asked the TU to send a copy of its materials on Negro history to Minnie Caldwell, chair of the Education Committee, because the civil rights organization wished to use it in its community. D. McDonald, secretary of the Southern Christian Leadership Conference, thanked Lederman for the article "Negroes of the Year–1962," which featured Martin Luther King, Jr., and he told the union president that King, who was out of the country, would learn of the thoughtful gesture. Author Dorothy Sterling expressed her gratitude to the TU for the supplement and for the "discerning" review of her book. The union had to turn down one person's request for numerous copies of the Negro history week supplement because the supply had been almost depleted. In 1963 the union notified people who in the past had requested large quantities that they should place their orders by mail and would be charged close to fifteen dollars for one thousand copies.[39]

The Negro history supplement was a pioneering venture because it offered teachers materials on the most recent trends in American historiography, challenging an older literature that distorted the images of blacks. Students were provided with a better understanding of the impact on the nation of slavery and Jim Crow. They were also provided with a clearer portrait of the struggle to make the United States a democratic nation. The promotion of black history and culture not only made teachers and children cognizant of the legacy of people of African origins in the United States and elsewhere but also of the social, economic, and political conditions of many Americans in their own time.

INCREASING THE NUMBER OF BLACK TEACHERS

Outside of the school integration campaign in the 1950s, no other civil rights measure created as much controversy as the effort to persuade the

Board of Education to increase the number of black teachers in the system. By the late 1940s the Teachers Union was working to expose a problem: a lack of black teachers in the system and the deliberate concentration of the few black teachers in schools in predominantly black areas. It pushed what would later be called affirmative action, making the workplace more racially inclusive.

More than four years before the United States Supreme Court's 1954 Brown v. Board of Education decision and five years before Kenneth Clark's accusation (detailed below) that the New York City Board of Education was maintaining segregated and unequal schools, the Teachers Union was systematically addressing segregation among the teaching staff. In 1949 the union's Committee Against Discrimination distributed its first survey on the racial makeup of school faculties to union members. The survey asked for the name of the respondent's school, total number of teachers, the number of substitutes, the number of blacks who had a regular license, and the number who had a substitute license. While the survey was an admittedly imprecise tool, the Board of Education kept no records on the racial composition of its teaching staff, so the union's effort was the first systematic attempt to gain insight into hiring patterns. Lederman issued a letter on October 24, 1949, announcing publication of the "brief" on the employment of blacks in the school system and the discriminatory treatment of black applicants for teaching licenses by the Board of Examiners.[40]

The survey examined twenty schools in Harlem, the Lower East Side, Bedford-Stuyvesant, and the South Bronx. It reported that in 1948-49 the number of black teachers in those schools had decreased from 96 to 90 while, at the same time, the number of teachers overall had gone from 1,073 to 1,107. Even the number of black teachers with substitute licenses had decreased from 44 to 23.[41]

The union maintained that one reason for the decrease was the board's revocation of the licenses of qualified teachers with years of service in the system. Because of the wartime need for teachers, a number of people who were able to pass an oral English examination had been issued emergency licenses. Many of these teachers were black and were given satisfactory ratings for their job performance. They worked in mostly poor black areas and were allowed to continue their services right after the war. But in January 1949 the board decided to lay off teachers, citing budgetary concerns. The first to be fired were those with emergency licenses. The Teachers Union,

along with parents and school administrators, protested the announced firings, forcing school officials to delay their action and allowing the teachers to work until June 1949. However, shortly after that year's school term
ended the licenses were canceled.[42]

The TU called on the board to issue a regular substitute license to teachers with the emergency licenses who had received satisfactory ratings. This
was one way of increasing the number of blacks in the school system. However, because it did not want to confine blacks to secondary status, the TU
asked that black teachers with emergency licenses be provided opportunities to qualify for regular appointments. The teachers who had lost their
emergency licenses faced several hurdles, including the board's delay in offering exams for regular licenses and its failure to grade the exams of those
who had taken them. The Teachers Union demanded that the board end its
discrimination against qualified black teachers by validating the canceled
licenses. The union's plan identified a group already functioning satisfactorily in the system and pressured the board to recognize the importance of a
racially diverse professional staff.[43]

The Committee Against Discrimination's survey became the union's
major instrument in determining the racial makeup of the teaching staff
of New York City, and it offered evidence of the dearth of black teachers.
Although the small number of black faculty was not proof of a deliberate policy of discrimination, it demonstrated that the New York Board of
Education was doing nothing to address the imbalance. A broader survey
in 1951 —conducted by Mildred Flacks, a teacher at P.S. 35, Brooklyn, and
secretary of the Bedford-Stuyvesant and Williamsburg Schools Council,
Dorothy Rand, a teacher at P.S. 170 and member of the Harlem Committee,
and Arthur Newman, a teacher at Samuel Gompers High School and chair
of Better Schools of the South-East Bronx—appraised one-third of the city's
35,000 teachers. There were only 257 blacks among the 10,200 surveyed,
and only 150 of them had regular appointments; 82 were substitutes. The
others were clerks and laboratory assistants. The TU commented that in a
city where there were more than 750,000 blacks, making up 10 percent of
the population, blacks made up just 2.5 percent of the teaching staff. Fifty-
seven of the 76 academic and vocational schools included in the survey had
a combined teaching faculty of 7,385. However, there were only 76 black
staff members, or 0.1 percent, in those 57 schools: 19 of the 76 were substitutes, 12 were clerks, and 2 were laboratory assistants, leaving a grand total

of 43 blacks as regular appointed teachers. More alarming is the fact that 28 of the 57 high schools had no black faculty as of September 1951.[44]

A comprehensive survey, the union conjectured, would probably show that the percentage of black teachers was lower than 2.5 percent, since the 1951 survey returns were from schools known to have black teachers. The survey also revealed that there were only 175 black teachers in a combined faculty of 2,756 in the 54 elementary/junior high schools examined. Only 107 of the 175 had regular appointments, while 63 were substitutes, 4 were clerks, and 1 was a substitute clerk. To make matters worse, 92 percent of black teachers in the elementary and junior high schools surveyed were teaching in the predominantly black communities of Harlem, Bedford-Stuyvesant, and South-East Bronx, which suggested that the board segregated its faculty.[45]

The union argued that, even if the student body were predominantly white, black, or mixed, "the absence of Negro teachers on the faculty undermines the concept of democracy and equality that our schools should offer the children, not merely by precept, but more especially by practice." The dearth of black teachers in the system, the union maintained, had a devastating impact on both white and black children. The board, it charged, had a "conscious policy of assigning Negro teachers to schools" in predominantly black areas. While it claimed that its survey revealed a "consistent pattern of discrimination" against blacks, the union acknowledged that the lack of black teachers could also be caused by "basic social and economic factors." Nonetheless, the school system was guilty of not addressing the horrible conditions for blacks in the schools. Instead of providing the special services so urgently needed by students in predominantly black schools, the board did nothing: "Thus, at the very outset, the Negro children of New York City, forced by poverty and Jim-Crow housing restrictions to live in ghetto slums, are condemned to physical, social and cultural deprivations. Because of these by-products of their political and economic second-class citizenship, the city owes our Negro youngsters an abundance of the services and training our schools can supply. The sad fact is, however, that schools in these depressed areas are most deficient in the very facilities required for such compensation."[46]

The solution was to provide Harlem and other black communities with "better schools, smaller classes, an extensive remedial program, more recreation centers and playgrounds, and expanded health, nutrition and guidance services." The union's mixture of remedies addressed what it saw as cultural deprivations and systemic racism. It called on the board to take affirmative steps to increase the number of black teachers by encouraging black students to prepare for teaching careers and inviting black college students and those in teacher training institutions throughout the nation to apply for positions in New York City. The Board of Examiners should implement new procedures to assure the employment of black teachers rather than creating measures that would eliminate them from the system.[47]

The Teachers Union argued not only that the exclusion of black teachers hindered democracy but also that the inclusion of blacks would help foster a color-blind society. The "experience of being instructed by a Negro teacher and having all the normal teacher-pupil relationships and other forms of contact with Negro teachers in a school would be extremely valuable in achieving an important aim of our educational system—the inculcation of respect for the worth and dignity of all people, regardless of race, color or creed." In a resolution adopted by its membership in January 1951, the TU called for a committee to recommend measures to increase the number of black teachers. The board should initiate a system of assigning black teachers to city schools to "strengthen the concept of democracy and equality that schools should offer children, both Negro and white, not merely by precept, but more especially by practice."[48]

The 1951 survey drew the public's attention. In late February 1952 William P. Viall, an associate in the teacher certification program of the state education department, sent Lederman a letter telling him that he was in "real sympathy with the purpose in attempting to place more Negroes" in the New York schools. Noting that a commission was being formed to administer a recruitment plan, he asked if the TU could send a copy of its survey to the new commissioner of education. State Commissioner of Education Lewis A. Wilson said that he read with a "great deal of interest" the TU's letter on recruiting black teachers in the public schools and offered to send the TU more detailed information in regard to the Board of Regents' proposed program on teacher recruitment and training. Lederman also received letters from many individuals expressing their support for the union's recommendation to establish a special committee to consider ways of increasing the number of black teachers in the school system. Despite the Timone Resolution, the union had become the major player in the fight to increase the number of black teachers. Congressman Adam

Clayton Powell Jr. declared that the union's findings were "astounding," and he "heartily agreed that this situation should be corrected as quickly as possible."[49] Thus one of the nation's leading civil rights and political figures publicly supported the union's efforts.

Clearly embarrassed and offended by the TU's efforts, board officials responded to the union's accusations. Expressing his irritation with the union, Jacob Greenberg, associate superintendent, defended the board's hiring record by invoking a color-blind nondiscriminatory argument: "We do not know how many Negroes we have in our public school system when we make appointments. We have no knowledge of the race, color, or religion of the candidates." Contending that candidates were appointed from the eligibility list furnished by the Board of Examiners, Greenberg cited his and former Board of Education president James Marshall's earlier action trying to convince a "number of Negro teachers" to prepare for "higher licenses" in the system. As a counterattack, Greenberg charged that, if the union had proof of discrimination in appointment of teachers but failed to present it, it was "guilty of racial discrimination. Anyone who charges discrimination where none exists is equally guilty of racial discrimination."[50]

In addition to taking surveys, the union reached out to professional, labor, civic, and community organizations for support of its campaign. For example, when the union heard that the state was forming a special committee to address the teacher shortage in New York, Lederman sent a letter to William Hagerty, president of Teachers College of the State University of New York in New Paltz, expressing interest in the plan. Although the committee's purpose was to address the teacher shortage problem, the union leader pointed out that the state could take advantage of the problem as a way to confront the issue of the lack of black teachers. Lederman told Hagerty that there were plenty of qualified black teachers who, when faced with obstacles in obtaining employment, left the state for positions elsewhere. There were many black potential candidates who could enter the teacher training program, and other qualified black teachers who could be attracted from outside New York. The newly formed committee could solve the teacher shortage and increase the number of black teachers in the state. Thus the union did not limit itself to pointing its finger at the Board of Education but attempted to use any venue at its disposal to work for the hiring of black teachers.[51]

Proof of the union's dedication to that effort can be seen in the longevity of the campaign. In the late winter of 1953, three and a half years after its first preliminary survey, Bernard Kesselman, chair of the Anti-Discrimination Committee, wrote to Herbert L. Wright, youth secretary of the NAACP, telling him that he had read a February *Amsterdam News* article reporting that the youth division of the civil rights organization had renewed its campaign to increase the number of black professors at colleges and universities. Kesselman asserted that the TU had long been concerned with the small proportion of black faculty, a "serious shortcoming in the democratic education of the children," citing the 1951 study and several conferences with leading figures in the State Department of Education. Kesselman charged that the New York City Board of Education still refused to acknowledge the seriousness of the problem. The problem was even worse in the colleges, and Kesselman offered the union's cooperation in the campaign the youth division was undertaking.[52]

A TU strategy used to increase the number of black teachers was to offer assistance to blacks attempting to find jobs as New York City schoolteachers. In early spring 1953 the Teachers Union established a counseling service for black prospective teachers as a component of its campaign. Union members who were experienced teachers were willing to offer their services to help support black applicants attempting to secure teaching licenses. Specifically, the union promised to help black applicants prepare for the written tests. It would also provide speech diagnosis, since a major argument used by the Board of Examiners for rejecting black applicants was their poor performance on the oral examination. It also promised to help them meet eligibility requirements, assist them in appealing unfavorable ratings, and help place them in vacancies.[53]

While the psychological impact of the black teacher shortage was noted by the Teachers Union, before the Brown decision its primary argument for addressing the shortage was cast in political terms. It focused on the distribution of black faculty, accusing the board of placing black teachers in predominantly black areas. In the fall of 1953 Lederman called to Jansen's attention an October 4 forum on racial discrimination in the schools organized by the Flushing branch of the NAACP. All participants, educators and lay people, agreed that black teachers should be distributed more evenly throughout the city's schools rather than segregated in schools whose student bodies were predominantly black. Participants also said that white students needed to have experience with black teachers "as a means of breaking down" bias and promoting interracial mutuality, a democratic value. The unfair distribution of black teachers, Lederman insisted, denied children "a most effective, easy and natural opportunity to experience democracy in action in the very important area of race relations, since having Negro teachers would undoubtedly be an important factor in the realization of a basic goal of education—the inculcation of respect for people of all races and colors."[54]

The union's dedication to increasing the number of black teachers in the school system was again made clear when, in April 1955, it released the results of its second large survey of black employment in the schools. The situation was no better than it had been four years earlier. Larger than the 1951 survey, this one involving 245 schools with 14,130 regularly appointed teachers and 2,416 substitutes. There were only 312 regularly appointed and 232 substitute black teachers among the over 16,000 teachers included in the survey. The percentage of regularly appointed black teachers was 1.9 percent. The survey revealed that 29 of the 63 academic and vocational high schools in the survey had no black teachers. The situation was also dismal in elementary and junior high schools; 89 of the 182 schools surveyed reported having no black teachers. The numbers were disgraceful in a city with close to 1 million black residents. Nor had the geographical distribution of black teachers improved by 1955: 87 percent of black teachers in the system were still located in schools in predominantly black areas.[55]

The Supreme Court's 1954 decision in the Brown case reinforced the Teachers Union argument that hiring black teachers was a democratic issue of interracial mutuality. In its June 1955 program to increase the number of black teachers, the union asserted that the "present teacher employment situation in New York City constitutes an injustice not only to Negroes but also to the white children of the city, since they are largely deprived of the valuable experience in practical democracy of having a Negro teacher. Too often the sole experience these children have with Negroes is to see them as domestic workers and in other similar positions. Television, radio and movies help perpetuate the stereotype Negro." Hence a diverse teaching staff was considered key to overcoming this undemocratic practice. Realizing that integration of the student body might lead to the firing of black teachers who were employed in a segregated school system, the union suggested that the board launch a recruitment drive to attract those black teachers to the New York system. The union once again called on the board to place advertisements in teacher publications, emphasizing that the school agency was eager to hire new teachers regardless of race, color, or creed. To increase the chance that the ads reached black readers, the union suggested that the *Journal of Negro History*, *Negro History Bulletin*, and the *Crisis*, as well as other black publications, carry them. The board should also send representatives to historically black colleges and universities as well as initiate a teacher training program encouraging students in the New York City public schools to seek a career in education.[56]

The TU was also concerned to address the problem of racist tracking of black students into vocational high schools. To make a change in this old pattern, the TU said the board should create a program that would help direct black youth to select academic careers, thus raising the "educational level" of black students so they could compensate for "cultural, economic, and social deprivation." The union's program emphasized that the lack of black teachers was due in part to social deficits and the poverty of black culture, but blame also fell on institutional racism. The union called for a study of the practices of the Board of Examiners, which played a major role in excluding blacks from the system. How did its policies serve to eliminate qualified black candidates? The Board of Examiners' "restrictive standards" in speech, the union said, barred many black applicants "who have displayed in practice excellent teaching ability." The union also hammered away at the board for concentrating black teachers in ghetto schools.[57]

While the TU's campaign was far-reaching and innovative, the 1951 and 1955 surveys completely ignored Latino teachers. Although the number of Latino students was increasing, especially through migration from Puerto Rico, the union failed to mention them. One reason for this neglect was that blacks far outnumbered Latinos in the city, but there was also an element of tradition involved. Like the Communist Party, union members had focused on black oppression for decades because blacks faced the worst form of endemic racism and class exploitation in America. The long history of slavery, Jim Crow, ghettoization, and institutional racism had placed people of African origins in a special category of oppressed, working-class people.

That oversight aside, the union truly demonstrated not only resolve but also genuine creativity in its efforts. In a September 1955 letter to Charles Silver, Lederman cited an article in the August 20 *Amsterdam News* reporting that eighty-six black teachers had lost their jobs in Oklahoma since desegregation began, and he suggested that the board take advantage of the situation by recruiting those teachers. Lederman noted the obstacles to hiring out of state, such as travel for examinations and relocation expenses. However, many teachers in the New York system had at one time faced these same problems. An announcement sent to the Oklahoma Association of Negro Teachers asking members to apply to the New York school system, would help the board to address racial imbalance as well as rebuke the "unconscionable racists who have misused the U.S. Supreme Court decision against segregated schools to cause teachers to lose their positions." Board authorities could thus contribute toward the eradication of the "most shameful blot on our American democratic traditions." Doubting Silver would respond, the union president sent a copy of the letter to the Oklahoma Association of Negro Teachers, inviting the association to send him suggestions for any other action the TU could take to assist it in helping the fired teachers.

The Teachers Union had brought to the attention of school officials a problem few had bothered to recognize: the disregard that states forced to integrate had for black teachers. The American Civil Liberties Union reported, in its December 24, 1956, weekly bulletin, that hundreds of black teachers from Oklahoma, Missouri, Kentucky, Maryland, and Delaware had been fired during the past year as a result of the integration of the public schools. Although most were placed in other positions, over 300 of the black teachers who lost their jobs in Oklahoma, about one-sixth of the 1,697 black teachers in that state, remained unemployed. These Oklahoma teachers were fired, in part, because the state closed 112 black schools due to desegregation. Only a handful of black teachers were able to find positions in integrated schools. According to the ACLU, Missouri had 125 black educators teaching in integrated schools. In Kentucky that number was 115, in Maryland and Delaware just 100. The vast majority of black teachers were in segregated schools.[58]

Comparing the textbook campaign to the push to hire black teachers, there is no doubt that providing evidence of racist and biased images was easier than demonstrating that the board practiced racial discrimination in its hiring. However, the TU's surveys made the city aware of the existing disparity in the professional staff in a city with a significant black population. Its campaign to help create a more integrated workforce distinguished the

TU from other teacher unions, and for many in the civil rights community, the union's broad focus made it a valued ally.

SHIFTING THE FOCUS

Before the Supreme Court decided Brown v. Board of Education, the TU's principal civil rights push dealt with textbooks, black history, and black teacher employment. However, it would be a mistake to assume that it did not also pay attention to student body segregation in the city. Three weeks before the Brown decision, the union issued its program for integration, which was divided into several areas: building, staffing, integration and zoning, pupil achievement, and high schools. Each section spelled out the major existing problems and suggested remedies. The union called for an emergency program on construction and renovation of schools in black neighborhoods, where the oldest, most overcrowded and dilapidated buildings in the city could be found. The schools in these neighborhoods should have play space, school libraries, and science rooms. Besides the renovating of segregated schools, the TU advocated acquiring sites in "fringe areas" where black and whites resided, making it easier to assign children to those schools. Revising zoning practices would also quicken the pace of school integration. School officials should work with New York City's housing and planning bodies to end residential segregation, which was "an important factor in causing school segregation." The union was not the first organization to draw attention to the horrible conditions in the schools of New York City's black communities. The Harlem Committee in the 1930s and the Schools Council of Bedford-Stuyvesant and Williamsburg, formed in 1943 and consisting of members of the Teachers Union, parents, and civic leaders, both advocated full-day instruction, replacement of old dilapidated structures with new buildings, hot lunches for students, and health and welfare facilities.[59]

The union noted that 70 percent of New York City's elementary schools were segregated, having either 90 percent or more black and Latino or 90 percent or more "continental white" student bodies. The TU advised the board to look at studies made by the New York University Research Center on fringe area districts and be flexible about district lines, not simply adopting the ones created by holders of real estate. A manual of suggestions for its administrators and teachers could provide guidance on the best ways of integrating schools and classrooms. The union's boldest suggestion was for the board to "mandate that there be no all-white or all-Negro classes in schools with mixed populations."[60]

Integration did not just mean that black and white students should occupy the same school building. The union's program insisted the board's manual direct administrators to assure that black children in integrated schools would not be victims of discrimination when it came to selecting monitors, messengers, guards, actors in plays, and other positions. Hall and classroom pictures should include black as well as white heroes, social studies bulletins should be racially inclusive, schools should have meaningful Negro history week programs, and black and Puerto Rican speakers should be part of assembly programs. Thus every aspect of the schools and learning should be racially integrated. The union called for a study of the relationship between segregation and the practice of grouping pupils according to IQ or ability within a school and in individual classrooms. High school district lines should be drawn for the purpose of fostering integration, and black children should not be channeled to vocational schools.

It is evident in the TU's pre-Brown language that it was not accusing the board of carrying out a program to segregate children by race. This was also true immediately after the Brown decision, which, in a press release, the TU called a "history-making landmark, not only in education but in American democracy." The eradication of the separate but equal doctrine created the means for the elimination of segregation, which had done "irreparable damage not only to the education of children, but also to the fabric of our entire society." According to the union, segregation existed in New York City and in the school system not because of law but because of custom. Once again it urged the school superintendent and the board to take special measures to remove racist textbooks from its approved list of books, to hire more black teachers, and to end segregation of the few black teachers in the system.[61]

The May 29 edition of *New York Teacher News* reiterated the need to eliminate racist textbooks from the approved list and sought a solution to the problem of the near exclusion of regularly appointed black teachers, which denied children the democratic experience of having a Negro as a teacher. However, it also called for the elimination of "Jim Crow practices in housing," which led to segregated schools, pointing its finger to problems beyond the control of the board. In fact, the *New York Teacher News* did not accuse the board of having a policy of racially segregating the student body, nor did it question the neighborhood school concept.[62]

Civil rights activists and scholars, however, were not afraid to point their finger directly at the board's policies. In April 1954, just before the Supreme Court decision, the Intergroup Committee of New York Public Schools, consisting of twenty-six civic, labor, and religious groups, charged that the board subjected black children to an inferior education in segregated schools in Harlem and elsewhere. A month later Dr. Kenneth Clark, speaking before the National Urban League, said that black children attending schools in predominantly black communities received an inferior education, and he blamed institutional racism. Segregation, Clark maintained, not only resulted in an inferior education but also reinforced a sense of inferiority in black children. Segregation deprived black and Latino children of access to academic and other specialized high schools. It was the board, according to Clark, that deprived black and Puerto Rican children of the "ability to compete successfully with others." Such criticism eventually led the school agency to ask the Public Education Association to investigate the allegation of Jim Crow practices in the school system.[63] The subsequent study's disturbing finding was that forty-two New York schools were racially segregated (i.e., had a student body that was 90 percent or more black and Puerto Rican).

Activists began to challenge the Board of Education, using direct action tactics. One of the earliest protests, right after Brown, was at Yorkville Vocational High School Annex, located at York Avenue and 78 Street. Close to 95 percent of its student body was black and Puerto Rican, and parents demanded that the board take action to integrate the student body. The board defended itself by arguing that segregation was caused by discriminatory housing patterns and there was nothing it could do to alleviate the situation. It was the board's practice to evoke the neighborhood school concept and defend the notion that children should go to schools close to home, but in the Yorkville case, the students were coming from outside the neighborhood to attend.[64]

The Teachers Union took up the cause of the parents. In a June 11 letter to Jansen, Lederman wrote that at the end of their school day at Yorkville the black and Latino children made a mass exodus to their respective neighborhoods. "For all practical purposes, the effect of this situation is to create a school which is as effectively segregated as one which is so by virtue of a Jim Crow law." Lederman's use of the phrase Jim Crow law marked a difference from his May 24 news release where the segregation of children was not mentioned. His letter also varied from the earlier *Teacher News* article, which blamed housing patterns rather than the board's deliberate policy for segregation of the student body. Once parents and civil rights activists took action to integrate the schools, the union shifted to a more militant tone. The TU now joined the activists accusing the school system of purposely segregating children. Lederman stressed that it was imperative Jansen not allow segregation to continue and adopt measures to remedy the situation before September. The union was on its way to becoming a leading advocate for student integration.

Some students actually elected to go to Yorkville because of its nursing program. However, when students first arrived at the school, they were given a placement examination, and based on the results, some were assigned to the annex, where they received no pre-nursing courses. At the annex students' education was "terminated" after receiving only three rather than the full four years of course work. Although these students supposedly "graduated," the annex did not issue them a high school diploma. Among the courses they were required to take at the annex were home nursing and homemaking. Students were not provided classes in music, art, or mathematics. Some students were also compelled to take courses they had previously taken and passed. There was no remedial program for students who were classified as "retarded in their educational achievement."[65]

Lederman raised the point that, while it bragged about building new schools, the board allowed substandard conditions to continue at Yorkville and other vocational schools where the student body was predominantly black and Latino. Yorkville, he stressed, was even worse than other schools in the black and Latino communities: narrow corridors created a potential disaster in the case of fire, there was only one lavatory and one water fountain in the two-story building, and the school did not have a lunchroom, gymnasium, or lockers. The school library, a "small room containing three book cases," was opened only on Thursdays. Students accessed the library only with their English class, and only one class at a time could occupy the small room. The physical conditions, Lederman declared, were clearly "scandalous" and comparable to "Jim Crow schools in the South." Ridiculing the board's claim that New York City "demonstrated that we can have good schools without segregating Negro and white children," the TU president argued that black children attending the city's public schools were not provided equal education.[66]

Jansen's response only confirmed, for many, his racial insensitivity. The superintendent refused even to entertain the idea that the school system was treating people of color unfairly. Lederman informed the *Amsterdam News* in June that the superintendent had attempted to whitewash school conditions in Harlem by making the "ludicrous" statement that there was a "better teaching staff in Harlem than elsewhere in the city." Such a statement, Lederman claimed, flew in the face of reality, given that 25 percent of the teachers in the junior high schools of that area were substitutes, the highest percentage in the city. To add to the problem, the board had a policy of assigning newly appointed teachers to Harlem. In 1953 over two hundred teachers, most of them assigned to Harlem, failed to show up at their schools because of intolerable school conditions, demonstrating the discriminatory way school officials treated the predominantly black community.[67]

Adding insult to injury, Jansen made the ridiculous claim that the board did "not provide Harlem with segregation," attributing the problem to "natural segregation." Blasting Jansen, the TU president declared that anyone who believed people chose to live in slum dwellings was ignorant or suffered from "stupidity that is almost incredible." Jansen claimed that the board had "discriminated in favor of Negro boys and girls" by allowing them to attend any high school in the city, a choice not offered to other students. But there was not a single academic high school in the community and only one vocational high school (Wadleigh), which was for girls and already scheduled to close. Lederman asked a fundamental question: why were so many black children attending vocational high schools and so few enrolled in academic high schools?[68]

In addition to addressing the Yorkville crisis, the TU would go on to support the Rev. Milton Galamison and the school integration movement in New York City. Galamison, pastor of the Siloam Presbyterian Church in Brooklyn and president of the grassroots organization Parents Workshop for Equality in New York City Schools, led boycotts and demonstrations in an attempt to force the Board of Education to come up with a timetable and plan to integrate the school system. Galamison accepted the TU's invitation to speak at its annual education conference in April 1960, and that October he paid tribute to Rose Russell, Abraham Lederman, and Lucille Spence at an event honoring the three for their struggle to improve education in New York City. Despite the subversive label placed on the Teachers Union, Galamison praised it for its militant leadership on behalf of all children and for its support of the movement.[69]

Scholar Lauri Johnson writes that the Timone Resolution had a chilling impact on the Teachers Union: "Although the Teachers Union would continue to publish their Black History supplement and advocate for school integration until the union disbanded in the early 1960s, the Timone Resolution marked the beginning of a protracted and costly battle by union activists to defend their livelihoods and their sense of direction as an organization. Without official status as a union, they were often refused even the right to hold meetings with teachers in schools."[70] Although Johnson's assertion is correct, as far as it goes, this is not the complete story. The Teachers Union became a potent force for civil rights, especially by the early 1950s. Despite the fact that it was purged from both the AFL and, later, the CIO, the TU won recognition from labor, civil rights, civic and parent organizations as a strong voice for social justice.

The TU became one of the strongest advocates in the city for eliminating biased textbooks, hiring more black teachers, and promoting black history in the public schools. It joined with parents and civil rights groups in helping bring to the public's attention the racial disparities in the schools and the discriminatory practices and policies of the Board of Education. The union helped forge a united front in fighting for the elimination of racist depictions of blacks in the textbooks that countless children used on a daily basis in the classrooms of the New York City public school system. The union claimed that the racist images in textbooks, the absence of any mention of blacks' roles in shaping the nation, and the dearth of black professionals in the classroom were all civil rights issues because they reinforced children's misperceptions that people of color were inferior to whites. Addressing these same issues would eventually be important objectives of the black equality struggle in the 1960s. In fact, many civil rights activists fighting for school integration would adopt an important element of the TU's legacy, its method of surveying the number of black teachers in the school system—a meaningful tribute to the union's efforts.

Throughout its history the vast majority of members of the New York City Teachers Union were women. Although much has been written about the Teachers Union and race, there is little information about the role women played in the union. Ruth J. Markowitz's *My Daughter the Teacher: Jewish Teachers in the New York City Schools* is the most comprehensive work embracing that subject to date. Markowitz explains why women joined the TU, the percentage of women in the leadership, and the activities of a number of individual women in the TU, including Alice Citron and Celia Zitron. Lauri Johnson's article "A Generation of Women Activists: African American Female Educators in Harlem, 1930–1950" looks at the activities of black educators, including Lucille Spence, one of the founders of the TU's Harlem Committee. In another piece, Johnson highlights the role women in the TU played in shaping intercultural education and the work of Mildred Flacks in the Bedford-Stuyvesant community. Historian Marjorie Murphy also writes about prominent women in the TU, including Bella Dodd, Rose Russell, Celia Zitron, and Alice Citron. She notes Citron's involvement in the Harlem Committee and how that organization built strong ties with parents. However most of her focus on the Teachers Union is on TU women and the red scare. Historian Alice Kessler Harris claims that instead of women vying for leadership positions in the TU, they "opted to support the communist leaders" of the union, "believing that radical ideas harbored the best hope for opening up the union movement, as well as for social change."[1] Despite these contributions by Markowitz, Johnson, Murphy, and Harris, there is still a dearth of information on how women helped shape the Teachers Union.

This chapter takes a closer look at how women helped mold the TU into a social protest union. Without question, the two most prominent TU leaders were Bella Dodd and Rose Russell. Although they never served as its presidents, because of their extraordinary leadership skills Dodd and Russell were recognized by the rank and file, political figures, labor, and the public as the union's most dominant figures. They, not the male presidents, were the major spokespersons for the Teachers Union. Dodd and Russell helped forge ties with politicians, labor, parents, and civic organizations. In addition to profiling individual women leaders, this chapter examines the way in which women collectively carved out leadership positions through the numerous TU committees. TU leadership rested not just with elected officers but also in the hands of committee chairs, and women on TU committees who helped determine the issues that the union would address and the strategies it would adopt to achieve its objectives. By means of committees, women focused on community work, creating an alternative path to leadership.

BELLA DODD

Bella Dodd, more than any other TU leader, helped structure the union into a social protest organization. Through her leadership, the union developed strong ties with labor leaders, state and city political figures, and civic leaders. These ties were used to wage effective battles to assure that children received a decent education, eliminate racial and gender discrimination, and improve working conditions for teachers. Under Dodd's direction as its chairperson, the Legislative and Political Action Committee became the union's most important committee. Before the TU split in 1935, the Political Action Committee was called the Committee on Legislative and Teachers Interests and was led by Abraham Lefkowitz. Under his leadership, the committee recommended to the executive board that it endorse bills favorable to teachers and students and oppose bills the committee deemed harmful to schools. One way the union took an active part in influencing whether a bill became law was to lobby in Albany. Union members were encouraged to send letters to state legislators and the governor, asking them either to support or oppose specific bills. At the February 15, 1930, executive board meeting committee members proposed that the union send letters of endorsement to the state assembly and senate's committees on education for a bill to provide psychologists in the bureau of attendance. In March the committee also recommended that the union endorse the

Downing-Moffat Bill concerning the "permanency of the present salary schedule," the "Graded Salary Bill," which would provide a uniform salary for principals, the "Love Bill" preventing religious discrimination," and a host of other bills pending before the legislature.[2]

After the schism, Bella Dodd took over the leadership of the newly re-named Legislative and Political Action Committee. The change of name reflected the committee's new emphasis on a militant approach. The committee continued to press for the passage of bills that would improve working conditions for teachers and worked to defeat legislation that threatened academic freedom, job security, and state cuts to education. In March 1939 Dodd received the support of the executive board for a bill in the state legislature abolishing the category of substitutes. Dodd asserted that part of her success as the legislative representative of the TU was because she had developed ties with state lawmakers and had made "allies among lobbyists, the legislators, and the press correspondents."[3]

Under Dodd's leadership, the committee broadened its approach from just lobbying the state legislature to enacting "political action" strategies to pressure lawmakers, for example, mass demonstrations and rallies, sending large delegations to "meet" with lawmakers in Albany, sending a weekly list of directives to schools, and establishing union committees to "interview" state legislators on particular bills with which lawmakers were familiar.[4] In late October 1938, for example, Dodd announced to the executive board that a delegation had been organized to go to City Hall on November 3 to protest decreasing state funding for education. In late February 1939 she persuaded the executive board to adopt a motion calling for the preparation of a mass delegation to Albany to protest state cuts to education.[5]

The union's militant approach was evident in its fight on behalf of those who were reduced to doing substitute teaching. Dodd claimed that she pressured the Board of Education to "fulfill its moral obligation to thousands of substitute teachers who had been in the school during the depression as per-diem employees. They taught a full program on a par with regularly appointed teachers in all things except that they did not receive an annual wage, had no vacation pay, and were docked for every day ill or absent." Dodd claimed that she attracted thousands of nonunion teachers to the campaign.[6] On April 26, 1937, she led a delegation of one thousand substitute teachers from New York City to Albany calling for passage of the Steingut-Fischel Bill granting substitutes with at least three years of consec-

Figure 11.1 Teachers Union members protesting in Albany against state budget cuts to education, February 12, 1940. Bella Dodd at microphone holding petitions, President Charles Hendley is left of Dodd. United Federation of Teachers, part 1, folder 512.

utive service a regular license.[7] In the winter of 1938 the TU sent out a petition written by Dodd and members of the Legislative Committee calling on Mayor LaGuardia to stop the Board of Education's "wave of retrenchments," which would result in overcrowded classrooms. Dodd claimed that the cuts would lead to "maladjustment and delinquency" among children.[8]

Over two thousand teachers attended a "protest mass meeting" at Textile High School, Manhattan, in January 1939, demanding that Governor Lehman call a special session of the state legislature to restore $5,300,000 cut from education funds. Dodd knew that such mass rallies, not just individual lobbying, would draw media attention, and to win public support, she consistently argued that children were the major victims of budget cuts. Dodd claimed that the governor received 150,000 telegrams from teachers and parents protesting the cuts and asking him to call a special session, and she claimed that he would soon receive another 150,000.[9] In June 1939 Dodd presented to the

State Assembly Finance Committee a petition with several thousand names protesting the $5,300,000 cut in state aid to education. In addition, she led a delegation of 1,500 teachers for a "protest meeting."[10] Continuing the protracted fight, in October 1939 she called for one million signatures on a petition to the governor and state legislature protesting the cuts.[11]

Public demonstrations were also a way of showing solidarity with labor, parents, and civil rights groups as well as publicly opposing actions and policies the union deemed would harm the education of children. In order to build a united front to prevent federal and state aid cuts, Dodd recommended the executive board invite a number of labor leaders, including George Meany, president of the New York State Federation of Labor to its March 17, 1939, membership meeting.[12] That same year Dodd also helped organize a committee of substitute teachers to talk with city council members and noted that a "[d]elegation will be called if deemed advisable."[13]

Dodd also became a voice against racial and gender discrimination. The *New York Times* reported on March 15, 1939, that Dodd, along with the American Jewish Committee, the American Jewish Congress, B'nai Brith, the Jewish Labor Committee, and the Jewish War Veterans, lobbied in support of a number of antidiscriminatory bills in the state legislature, including one that prohibited public utilities from refusing employment to anyone based on race, color, or creed and one that outlawed discrimination in renting or leasing of residences. Speaking in favor of the antidiscriminatory legislation at a hearing in the senate chamber, Dodd emphasized that racial discrimination was a reality in the New York City school system.[14]

One of the most important steps taken on behalf of women by Dodd and the Legislative Committee was their campaign to end discrimination against teachers who became pregnant. Although the Board of Education had fired pregnant women in the early part of the twentieth century, a New York state court of appeals in 1913 supported a teacher who had been dismissed because of the board's policy, forcing the school agency to reinstate her.[15] Despite the court's ruling, the board continued to discriminate against women. Women who had resigned because of the board's policy of banning married women were not allowed to have their jobs back because the school agency claimed it never forced them to quit. In particular, women who became pregnant were dismissed by the board.[16]

By 1913 women had begun to organize to fight the board's discriminatory policy and for equal pay and the rights of married women. Teachers and feminist groups used a variety of tactics, including litigation, press conferences, and meetings with city officials to press their case. One of the issues women teachers also championed was maternity leave, a crucial issue because women lost ground in achieving salary equity when they decided to take time off from work to give birth and care for their infants. Paid maternity leave would assure that women who left the workplace to raise children would not be punished economically of fall behind in earned salary, thus benefiting both the teachers and their families. Under Dodd's urging, the executive board approved a motion calling for a minimum maternity leave of eighteen months with an option to extend it an additional term or year "at the discretion of the mother."[17] Dodd also persuaded the executive board to approve a motion urging the Board of Education to grant a sabbatical payment to a teacher who would be eligible for a sabbatical during part of her maternity leave. In addition, the motion called for giving the teacher the option to take the sabbatical after her maternity leave. This option assured women the same opportunity as their male counterparts to take advantage of a sabbatical to improve job skills, gain more knowledge of their field by taking courses, receive an advanced degree, or otherwise seek professional enrichment.[18]

Dodd joined the larger fight to end discrimination in employment against married women. In June 1939 she made a motion to the executive board calling for the creation of a "committee to campaign against any abrogation of the rights of married women who are teachers." It was adopted.[19] In 1941 she proposed a bill to the state legislature that would create nursery schools. The objective of this "mild" proposal, according to Dodd, was to create jobs for teachers and to "aid working women with small children."[20] Dodd's fight against race and gender discrimination helped to shape the TU into an organization whose interests extended beyond the classroom. Dodd's efforts helped place the union in the broader campaign for social justice.

ROSE RUSSELL

By the middle of the 1940s the most prominent figure in the union was Rose Russell. Russell was born in New York City in 1900. She graduated cum laude and Phi Beta Kappa from the University of Michigan and taught high

Figure 11.2 Rose Russell, author Norman Mailer, and Dr. Harlan Shapley, December 18, 1948. United Federation of Teachers, part 1, folder 519.

school for seventeen years before becoming legislative representative for the TU in 1945. Although, unlike Dodd, she did not have a law degree, Russell nonetheless became the most visible union leader defending the rights of teachers.[21]

Russell became the face of the TU. She was featured in the *New York Teacher News* on a consistent basis, speaking out on issues that had an impact on the union. For example, one front-page headline noted that "Mrs. Russell Pleads for Support of $500 [Raise] Before the City Council." Russell, according to the paper, was "the only teacher representative present" at a City Council Finance Committee meeting where she argued for the adoption of a cost of living bonus bill for city workers and a $500 raise across the board. The November 3, 1945, *New York Teacher News* reported that Russell "Scores Regents Probe," condemning a call for an investigation by the Board of Regents of subversives in the schools. The lead story of the January 26, 1946, *New York Teacher News* had the headline: "Russell Calls Board Budget Inadequate on Vital Needs." Speaking before a Board of Education hearing on its budget, Russell called for salary increases for teachers, the hiring of additional teachers to address the shortage, and a continuation of a $350 bonus to help teachers fight the rising cost of living.[22] On a number of occasions, a photo of Russell appeared alongside an article featuring her activities. On March 20, 1948, a photo of Russell appeared in conjunction with an article about the Teachers Union criticizing the state legislature and Governor Dewey for advocating bills that would deny teachers membership in any totalitarian group, effectively creating a "little Dies Committee" (an early name for HUAC) and a loyalty oath for teachers.[23]

Why was Russell the only woman to receive so much attention? Bella Dodd contended that Russell was handpicked by the Communist Party to be her successor and she (Dodd) helped "establish" the new legislative representative's leadership. "I tried to pass on to her what I had learned over the years. I introduced her to the public officials with whom I had worked. She did not have to face the hostility I met when first I went to Albany. . . . I was in Albany frequently as the representative to the Communist Party and was able to spend much time with Rose."[24] Dodd may indeed have opened doors for Russell, but it was Russell's talent as a leader that accounts for her success and the attention she garnered. Russell was charismatic, a quick thinker and fierce debater. She expressed the views of the TU better than anyone else, and her ability to debate issues with her adversaries was unsurpassed by those in the union's leadership. It was because the union leaders acknowledged these skills (whether overtly or just in practice) that they so often allowed Russell, rather than the male presidents, to speak for the union.

During the years of the purges, Russell was always at the frontline challenging Board of Education officials, and she publicly defended the union against the board's campaign. In October 1948 Russell represented the TU at the American Freedom Conference, where she addressed the witch hunts in the schools. She was also the TU leader who represented the union in the mass media. In October 1948 Russell was a guest on the Raymond Walsh Radio Program where she argued that the union's interest in the welfare of children made it a "thorn in the side of the people who do not want to spend money to provide" a decent education.[25] Appearing on *Night Beat*, a one-hour late-night program featuring celebrities and other newsmakers, Russell made the case for Communists teaching in the classroom. Claiming that there was a "secret police system" operated by the New York City Board of Education, she criticized Moskoff for arguing that anyone who is a member of the Communist Party should not be allowed to teach. It seemed "odd" to her, Russell said, "that Mr. Moskoff . . . should set himself up in telling you that, as one who proclaims what ideology a person should be allowed to have." Moskoff, Russell argued, would have to admit, because he was present at some of the trials, that "their records, their character, their influence on children, their patriotism, their loyalty to our country as demonstrated by their words, their whole record" was flawless. According to Russell, "everyone testified that there was no blemish on the records."[26]

It was not Abe Lederman, the president of the TU, but Russell who was selected for its most important public debate. In March 1958 the legislative representative faced Assistant Corporation Council Saul Moskoff on *Night Beat*. The debate was a great opportunity for the union to present its case to the public. Russell was direct and persuasive, stressing that no "teacher should be disqualified for his opinions or beliefs or his political associations. . . . And this goes for Communists as well as for people of any other faiths or beliefs." She argued that performance in the classroom and not one's personal or political beliefs should determine whether one was qualified to teach. She even compared the treatment of Communists in New York City to the treatment of black teachers in the South, noting that in several southern states black teachers were fired because of their membership in the NAACP. "When a political test, a test of opinions were applied there was no end to the harm to teachers, children and the school system."

Russell's best moment came when Moskoff defended his attempt to get teachers to inform on their colleagues, arguing that informing was proof that such teachers "recognized the errors of the past." They are, he said, "asked to reveal the facts." This was the "best reason," Russell retorted, "for not having a witch-hunt of this sort, because you cannot start hunting Communists without having a spy-system and you don't go after just Communists, you go after suspected Communists, you go after people who are engaged in any kind of progressive activity, that somebody calls 'Communist,' and this has been proved in life to such an extent that there's no question about it any longer." None of the people "who turned informer," Russell argued, volunteered to do so, but rather was " squeezed." Moskoff did not deny Russell's accusation, but said he thought he should refrain from that particular discussion. Knowing she had the upper hand, Russell shot back: "It's in the public record."[27]

One sign of Russell's status as a prominent leader in the TU was the recognition she received from those outside the union. James Egert Allen, president of the New York Conference of the NAACP, praised Russell, Samuel Wallach, president of the TU, Eugene Jackson, chairman of the union's salary committee, and the TU's program for raising the awareness of Americans of the role of education. "To Mrs. Russell and Messrs. Wallach and Jackson the citizens of New York are grateful because of the unselfish service they have rendered. . . . Never in the history of the nation has the story of education reached the public in such a dramatic way."[28] Stanley M. Issacs, a Manhattan councilman, praised Russell, Wallach, and Jackson for working to secure raises for teachers and for the "proper treatment of those responsible for the care of our children."[29] Although Louis Hollander, president of the New York State Council of the CIO, and Harold J. Garno, secretary-treasurer of that organization, wrote that they deemed it a "privilege to join with officers and members" of the TU to honor the work of Russell, Wallach, and Jackson, their letter especially noted Russell's efforts. "We would like to call particular attention to the excellent work of Rose V. Russell in Albany and to her untiring efforts on behalf of the members of Local 555 and all the teachers in New York State."[30]

Even when union members were being forced out of their jobs and the union was not allowed to hold meetings in schools or permitted to represent teachers before any board official, Rose Russell nonetheless managed to help the TU receive recognition. She did this by forging relationships with political figures and labor and civic leaders and by helping to make the union an important player in the fight for civil rights, adequate funding for public schools, and decent pay and improved working conditions for teachers. No TU official was more outspoken in defense of academic freedom than Rose Russell during the union's darkest days. One newspaper noted that she and the TU were "inseparable." Under her "stewardship," which covered the McCarthy period, she did not yield

an inch in the hostile setting. . . . Russell led the fight against the Feinberg Law which legalized the witch-hunt in New York's schools, and against the

deprivation of teachers' rights in red-baiting hearings and political investigations. She successfully led the fight against a New York City Board of Education resolution making refusal to become an informer grounds for dismissal
of a teacher. This saga of the defense of academic freedom will one day be
recognized and honored as a great chapter in U.S. history.[31]

TU WOMEN AND COMMITTEES

The TU made a point of publicizing its campaign for racial equality. However, it was less vocal when it came to gender equality. In fact, it seemed that
the union was less committed to assuring fairer representation of women
on its executive board after 1935 than it was before the schism. Fourteen
of the twenty-three executive board members attending the April 18, 1931,
meeting were women. By May 1931 seven of the thirteen people elected to
the executive board were women. Eighteen of the twenty-eight board members at the September 16, 1931, meeting were women.[32] Seventeen of the
twenty-five executive board members in March 1933 were women. Moreover, women headed some key committees under the Linville-Lefkowitz
leadership including the Membership Committee (Florence Gitlin), Elections Committee (Clara Naftolowitz), and Experimental Education (Laura
Branson). Women also held top leadership positions. In May 1931 Bertha
Hayes defeated David Wittes for second vice president, and Johanna Lindof
was elected third vice president. Five of the nine delegates to the AFT in
1931 were women.[33]

After the schism in 1935, women were no longer the majority on the executive board. Of the twenty-nine members at the executive board meeting
on January 8, 1937, only ten were women. Ten of the twenty-four members
attending the December 12, 1937, board meeting were women. Twelve of
the twenty-nine board members at the September 11, 1939, meeting were
women. It would not be until the 1940s that women once again made up
the majority of executive board members. Women were also absent from
the top positions in the union. Three women were top officers in 1937:
Rose Riegger became vice president representing the elementary schools,
Bella Dodd served as the legislative representative, and Layle Lane was the
recording secretary. However, no woman ever served as president.[34] In 1941
only two of the seven top officers were women.[35] Even its rival, the New

York Teachers Guild, selected a woman to head the organization, starting in 1940. The declining number of women on the executive board is puzzling because women dominated union membership. The October 1940 record listed 6,034 members, of which 4,035 were women.[36]

Despite the evidence of these numbers, it would be a mistake to conclude that women were being marginalized after the schism. Women managed to move into positions of power where they were able to determine the issues the union would support and the methods the TU would adopt to accomplish its objectives. Women helped assure that the TU would remain an organization dedicated to children's well-being, academic freedom, civil rights, and women's rights. They helped create alliances with parents, labor, and civil rights groups with the goal of assuring that all children receive the best education possible. Women took the lead in the fight for sufficient funding of schools, the construction of new school buildings, the reduction of class size, the elimination of racially biased textbooks, and academic freedom. Women, like their male colleagues, worked to improve the working conditions of teachers, but they also became vociferous advocates of social movement unionism.

While Dodd and Russell were the most prominent TU leaders, women who were not in the public eye also played a crucial role in guiding the union. In particular, women involved in a number of permanent and working committees helped shape the direction of the TU. One of the important permanent committees was the Academic Freedom Committee. Academic freedom had been an important issue to teachers; specifically, teachers fought against loyalty oaths, which they viewed as an attack on academic freedom. In 1919 a joint committee of the New York State Legislature, popularly known as the Lusk Committee to Investigate Seditious Activities, launched an investigation of individuals and organizations suspected of advocating overthrow of the United States government. The Lusk Committee obtained information on numerous groups and individuals by confiscating materials found during raids on offices of organizations, infiltrating meetings, and arresting thousands. In its report in 1920 the committee recommended that educating citizens in traditional economic, political, and social values was crucial for American democracy. To assure the loyalty of public school teachers, it called for "re-educating" teachers. Before an individual could be allowed in the classroom, he or she would have to receive a certificate recognizing that he or she was of good character and was loyal to the state and nation. Any teacher refusing to seek such certification could be fired. The TU launched a campaign against passage of the Lusk Committee's recommendations, sending a letter to the governor arguing that the recommendations were antithetical to decent education and a clear danger to freedom of speech and thought. Although the state legislature passed the recommendations in 1920, Governor Alfred Smith, a Democrat, vetoed them. When Republican Nathan Miller was elected in 1921 he signed into law bills containing the Lusk Committee recommendations. Two years later, Smith regained the governorship and repealed the laws.[37]

In May 1931 the TU's executive board approved a resolution, to be presented at the AFT's national convention, calling on the national to oppose the "policy of the Daughters of the American Revolution of campaigning in the several states for the enactment of legislation that will impose upon public school teachers the wholly unnecessary obligation to take the oath of allegiance to the United States." The TU claimed teachers were not obligated to take such an oath, since it was customary that only federal employees take an oath, and schoolteachers were not employed by the federal government. The "spirit of loyalty cannot be developed by legislation," and such an oath in the field of education hinders freedom. "For teachers freedom is a necessary condition to thinking, as thinking is a condition necessary to progress." Americans could not hope to persuade gifted young men and women to "enter the profession of teaching in the face of the risk of having their thinking subjected to the censorship of reactionaries or ignorant federal officials."[38]

As part of its effort to assure academic freedom, the TU defended teachers who were dismissed because they failed to teach "'instinctive' respect for Government bodies," and it challenged political repression as early as World War I by calling for freedom of speech.[39] After 1933 the union organized an Academic Freedom Committee and appointed Joseph Jablonower to head it. Under Jablonower the committee adopted a resolution arguing that the "defense of academic freedom is one of the most important functions of the Teachers Union" and a campaign by the union was the best defense to assure such freedom. The committee endorsed the policy of assuming the costs of teachers' legal defense by organizing a fund and engaging "individually with cases as they arise."[40] The committee also created a pamphlet in June 1934, *You May Be Next*, that noted numerous breaches of academic freedom, including the cases of Isidore Begun and Williana Burroughs, both of whom had been fired for criticizing the Board of Education at a dismissal hearing of another TU member.[41] The committee also supported Alice Citron, who received an unsatisfactory rating, thus denying her a permanent license, after she attended a meeting of the Harlem Parents' Association. The board issued a report accusing Citron of not defending it when a Harlem pastor publicly criticized it at the meeting. Responding to protests by the Academic Freedom Committee and the Harlem community, the board granted Citron her permanent license the following year.[42]

After the schism, the Academic Freedom Committee, headed by Celia Zitron, resumed the fight for academic freedom by introducing a number of resolutions for consideration at the American Federation of Teachers convention in the summer of 1938. Among these were resolutions assuring that teachers be permitted to exercise their constitutional right of free speech; opposing discrimination against teachers due to their race, color, creed, "or political opinion"; granting teachers the right to join a teacher organization of their choice; and calling for the repeal of loyalty oaths.[43] In 1939 Zitron asked the executive board of the TU to support the a resolution presented to the Board of Education's Law Committee by Alberto Bonaschi, the board's member from the Bronx. The Bonaschi Resolution would allow New York City public school teachers to join any organization of their choice as well as giving them the right to hold meetings in the schools.[44] The resolution would give teachers the right to join the TU without fear of retaliation from the Board of Education. Zitron also introduced a motion that called on the TU to notify school representatives to press for the Bonaschi Resolution and to communicate with other teacher groups asking them to work for its passage.[45] Zitron asked for and received permission from the executive board for the Academic Freedom Committee to plan a meeting to be held in early 1940 to address "teachers' rights in a time of crisis." Despite the outbreak of World War II, Zitron and the committee wanted to ensure that academic freedom would not become a casualty of war.[46]

Under Zitron's leadership the Academic Freedom Committee continued its efforts against laws requiring loyalty oaths; specifically, calling for the repeal of the law mandating the Ives Loyalty Oath. Passed by the state legislature in 1934, the law required all teachers to sign a pledge of allegiance to the Constitutions of the United States and New York State.[47] The union also opposed cutting off funding to State Senator John McNaboe's committee investigating Nazism in New York.[48] The committee called for procedural rights for all teachers at all hearings, and even opposed an oath intended for students graduating from high schools. Like the Legislative Committee, the Academic Freedom Committee pushed for social equality.

Zitron observed that the Linville-Lefkowitz leadership (pre-1935) had not supported many of the teachers whose academic freedom was violated. However, under her leadership, the committee had "challenged with a remarkable degree of success every case of interference with teachers' rights to criticize school authorities and of discrimination against Union membership by principles." Zitron and the committee also addressed discrimination in the schools, calling for repeal of a section of the education law that it claimed made it possible to practice "discrimination against Negro children."[49]

One of the most celebrated TU committees was the Harlem Teachers Committee, first headed by Lucille Spence. Born in Prosperity, South Carolina, in 1899, Spence graduated from Wadleigh High School in 1919. She was among the few black women who attended Hunter College, where she graduated cum laude in 1923. After receiving her master's degree from Columbia University's Teachers College in 1926, Spence began her teaching career at Wadleigh High School as a biology teacher. Testifying before the Senate Internal Security Sub-Committee in 1952, Spence denied that she had ever joined the Communist Party; and, indeed, there is no evidence that she joined. Despite her denial, the Federal Bureau of Investigation launched an "investigation," noting it had evidence that Spence was in the Party. Manning Johnson, of the Cafeteria Employees Local and a former member of the Communist Party, claimed before the Rapp-Coudert Committee that he first met Spence in 1935 at a Communist Party meeting in New York City. The bureau noted, moreover, that she sent a letter to Governor Thomas E. Dewey requesting a pardon for Morris U. Schappes, a professor at City College and member of the Communist Party who was convicted of giving false testimony before the Rapp-Coudert Committee and sentenced to serve eighteen months in state prison. However, the letter to Dewey and other allegations, including that Spense attended a meeting of the Council of African Affairs and served as a delegate to the National Negro Labor Council Conference, were based on circumstantial evidence. In fact, John Lautner, the former "National functionary of the Communist Party" who identified Abraham Lederman and Rose Russell as members of the Communist Party, said he had no knowledge of Spence's membership.

Figure 11.3 W. E. B. Du Bois receiving the Teachers Union annual award (1952). Abraham Lederman and Rose Russell are on his left. Lucile Spence is on his right. United Federation of Teachers, part 1, folder 524.

Eventually the FBI placed Spence's case in "closed status" because the agency could not substantiate her party membership.[50]

Despite claims that the TU was a Communist front, Spence joined the union and in 1935 helped organize the Harlem Committee, the activities of which are detailed in Chapter 10. As author Patrick J. Finn argues, Spence "would prove a key leader" in the promotion of intercultural education, "advocating the professional development of teachers around issues of race, and community organizing for school reform" that helped distinguished the TU from other teacher organizations.[51]

One way the Harlem Teachers Committee fostered strong teacher-community relations was to help teachers gain greater knowledge of the children they taught, emphasizing the value of studying black history and culture. Under Spence's leadership, the committee created a number of in-service courses for teachers including "The Contribution of the Negro People to American Civilization," "Problems in Intercultural Education," "African Background," "The Negro in Early American History," "The Negro in the Reconstruction Period," "The Negro in Literature, Art and Music," "The Negro in Science and Industry," "The Negro in Education," "The Negro Worker and

Trade Unionism," and "The Negro in the Twentieth Century."[52] The goal of these in-service courses was to furnish teachers with a better understanding of the social, economic, and political conditions of African Americans. By informing teachers of the African American experience, they would also be in a better position to incorporate black history into their lessons. The courses were usually held at the Teachers Union Institute, an educational center for teachers created by the union in 1938.[53] The committee also urged Local 5 to request that a course in African American history taught by Max Yergan, the first African American professor hired by City College of New York, be made available to teachers; who, it was hoped, would take advantage of the opportunity and incorporate what they learned into their classes.[54]

The formation of the Permanent Committee for Better Schools in Harlem illustrates the lengths to which Spence and members of the Harlem committee went to foster strong ties with the community. In response to the 1935 Harlem Riot, in March 1936 the Harlem committee joined community groups in sponsoring a meeting at St. Martin's Episcopal Church of hundreds of delegates, representing over seventy labor unions and civic and religious organizations. The delegates organized the Permanent Committee for Better Schools in Harlem to address the deplorable conditions in neighborhood schools. The Rev. John W. Robinson, pastor of the Christ Community Church, was selected as president of the Permanent Committee. He spoke forcefully against school conditions, arguing that schools in Harlem were intentionally segregated and that high school students received a watered-down education ensuring their continued low socioeconomic status. The committee pointed out that there were at least four hundred school textbooks portraying blacks as slaves and/or as idle and indolent. The fact that Lucille Spence was selected as the secretary of the Permanent Committee pointed to her reputation in the community.[55]

The Permanent Committee for Better Schools in Harlem helped lead a protest urging the removal of Gustuv Schoenchen, the principal of P.S. 5. On October 21, 1936, Robert Shelton escorted his cousin to her first grade class at P.S. 5. The historical record is not clear about the sequence of events, but Shelton claimed to the police that he was beaten on the head with a stick by Principal Schoenchen. Two physicians examined Shelton and wrote in an affidavit, "there were contusions of the left forearm about the wrist and postero-laterally about three inches below the left elbow." Shelton also had contusions on his left shoulder and "traumatic injury to the muscles involving the area between the sixth and eight ribs inclusive about the angles." There were also injuries on his scalp, "one and a quarter inches long in left frontal region." Schoenchen had a reputation of being hostile and insulting to parents who attempted to talk with him about their children's problems. As a result of Shelton's injuries and complaints from parents, the TU passed a resolution calling on the board to "investigate thoroughly the charges against Mr. Schoenchen," and urging that "he be discharged from his principalship."[56]

In the wake of the Schoenchen affair, the Permanent Committee helped organize a "mock trial" of the Board of Education, which took place at Abyssinian Baptist Church in January 1937. Some of the nation's most prominent black leaders played a major role in the mock trial, including the Rev. Adam Clayton Powell Jr., pastor of Abyssinian, who served as "judge." Charles Hamilton Houston, dean of Howard University Law School, Frank Crosswairth, chair of the Negro Labor Committee, Lester Granger, organizer of the Los Angles branch of the National Urban League (and later the executive director of the NUL), and United States congressman Vito Marcantonio all served on the jury. It was estimated that two thousand people attended the trial and listened to speaker after speaker charge the Board of Education with discriminating against and neglecting children in Harlem schools.[57] The committee accused the board of deliberately placing black and Latino children into overcrowded and dilapidated school buildings, tracking children into underresourced classes, racially segregating black and Latino high school students and denying them adequate recreational.[58] Although the Board of Education continued to claim that Schoenchen was innocent of the charges, the event demonstrated that the Teachers Union, through its Harlem Committee alliance with parents and the Harlem community, empowered the community in addressing their concerns with the school agency.

Alice Citron was another outspoken member of the Permanent Committee for Better Schools in Harlem and of the Harlem Committee. Citron was a strong advocate of teaching black history in the schools, joined the campaign to eliminate biased textbooks and called for the construction of new schools to relieve overcrowding. She consistently argued that the solution to urban blight was providing proper funding to schools and communities. In one case Citron challenged media portrayals of Harlem as a haven for out-of-control young "thugs" who should be controlled by using police power. Responding to what the *New York Times* reported was a "recent outbreak of crime in Harlem," Citron expressed her shock that Harlem was classified as a "crime center" and that hundreds of additional police should be placed in the community as a means of solving the problem of juvenile delinquency and other social ills. In an editorial the *Times* asserted that gangs of boys between 8 and 18 launched careers in "lawbreaking by petty thefts from storekeepers" to "murder."[59] Following the killing of a white teen by three black youths, the paper pronounced Harlem to be in the grips of a crime wave. "We need more police protection in areas where such crimes occur. We may be appalled at the youth of the criminals, but they must be run down and placed where their viciousness will no longer endanger the public."[60] In November Commissioner Valentine ordered 250 additional police officers for Harlem to combat the "outbreaks of crime" in the area.[61]

Critical of the police commissioner's decision to solve juvenile delinquency by adding more cops in Harlem, on November 12, 1941 Citron wrote to the *Times* that she had witnessed increasing rates of unemployment there, "the most wretched of housing conditions," and "thousands of mothers of our Negro children" being forced to work for wretched wages to supplement the family income. Thus it was no surprise that the children of Harlem were not well behaved. However, Citron insisted that her "intimate contact with the people of Harlem" proved to her "how deep and strong are the aspirations of Negro mothers and fathers for their children. How many untold sacrifices have I seen made by mothers who are forced to scrub floors" so that their children "may rise above their present economic degradation."[62]

Citron argued that Harlem's needs included a wider slum-clearing project, thousands of jobs for its young people, and the enforcement of FDR's executive order ending discrimination in the defense industry and vocational training for skilled trades such as aviation, auto mechanics, and civil service. She also called for the building of recreation centers as a way of preventing young people from looking to the streets for entertainment and for an all-inclusive health program that included a dental chair and full-time doctor and nurse in each Harlem school. Citron also emphasized the need for changes in school curricula by calling for a "full program of Negro history and culture." Such a program was needed so black and other children would "become aware the great part Negro people have played in the building and progress of our country." Citron's proposed history curriculum would, she said, instill pride in children, helping to overcome feelings of inferiority and resulting in better behaved children.[63]

The model of teacher-community relationship fostered by Spence and Citron in Harlem was also evident in Bedford-Stuyvesant, Brooklyn's largest black community, where Mildred Flacks was one of the most ardent advocates of forging close ties between community and teacher. The youngest of five children, Flacks grew up in an Orthodox Jewish home on the Lower East Side. She graduated from Columbia University's Teachers College, married at the age of twenty-one, and became a permanent substitute teacher at P.S. 35 in Bedford-Stuyvesant, where she taught first and second grade. Although they never spoke publicly about it, Mildred and her husband David were members of the Communist Party. They were also both members of the Teachers Union and were active in union politics. After years of working as a permanent substitute teacher, Flacks received a regular appointment in 1936. She decided to stay at P.S. 35, despite the fact that the school was overcrowded and one of the oldest school buildings in the area. One reason she decided to stay was because of the large contingent of Communist teachers in the area. Along with their efforts to recruit teachers for the party, these teachers also worked to improve conditions in the school, actions that Flacks found appealing.[64]

Flacks was inspired by the work of Citron and other teachers in Harlem. Richard Flacks notes that his mother "couldn't imagine being a teacher of these children without being concerned about the environment in which they were living." But her concern was not rooted just in a Communist worldview. Jewish tradition also played a key role. She grew up in a home where Jewish communal tradition was stressed. This tradition meant looking out for those in the community and a concern for the less fortunate. Sociologist Jonathan Rider contends that the "Jewish political culture contained a vigorous strain of universalism." Stephen M. Cohen and Charles Liebman argue that it is too simplistic to attribute the Jewish left to religious tradition. Instead, they contend, it was the result of factors that included "socialization by parents and friends," a "historical memory of a collective struggle against discrimination," and the perception that politically conservative forces were more anti-Semitic than their liberal counterparts. Peter Hass maintains that the reason Jews leaned more leftward had to do not with the "Jewish religious and halachic tradition" but with what they saw through the decades as self-interest. Whatever the source of a Jewish left-of-center tradition, Flacks as well as others who embraced this tradition had a deep concern for the plight of the less fortunate.[65]

Armed with Jewish communal traditions and influenced by colleagues in Harlem who had created the Harlem Teachers Committee and were instrumental in forming the Permanent Committee, Flacks decided to dedicate herself to improving conditions in Bedford-Stuyvesant and worked to help create the Bedford-Stuyvesant Neighborhood Council. Made up of seventy-seven affiliated block organizations and a number of social agencies, the Bedford-Stuyvesant Neighborhood Council worked to improve "community health, education, sanitation, recreation and human relations." Flacks served as the group's vice president.[66]

To create greater collaboration between teachers and parents, in 1943 a number of PTAs organized the Bedford-Stuyvesant and Williamsburg Schools Council. The executive board of the council was made up of parents from twenty PTAs, and its officers consisted of parents and teachers. The president of the council was Ada B. Jackson, longtime community activist and city council candidate for the American Labor Party. Flacks served as membership secretary of this council. The goals of the Schools Council were to ensure that schools in the areas were staffed with regular licensed teachers for every classroom instead of day-to-day substitutes and that students received a full day of instruction instead of the shortened day that many in Bedford-Stuyvesant received. Members also fought to end discriminatory zoning and for the construction of new schools and the provision of textbooks, hot lunches, health facilities, and additional guidance counselors.[67]

In her position as vice president of the Bedford-Stuyvesant Neighborhood Council and secretary of the Bedford-Stuyvesant and Williamsburg Schools Council Flacks helped define to the public the role a teacher could play in a community; a teacher's responsibilities included the physical and psychological well-being of the communities she served, and as a community member she was obligated to work jointly with parents on the community's behalf. The neighborhood council worked to improve community health, education sanitation, recreation, and human relations.[68]

Flacks saw schools as people institutions, therefore the community should be empowered to see that schools provide children the best possible education and social services. Her image conflicted with that of those who saw schools as institutions operated by teachers, administrators, and others of the professional class. In line with her view that schools were people institutions, Flacks believed that teachers had to be strong allies of the communities they served. A teacher's day did not end when children went home. Teachers should work with parents, activists, and leaders to improve schools. The Bedford-Stuyvesant and Williamsburg Schools Council and the Bedford-Stuyvesant Neighborhood Council were vehicles to accomplish that end. Testifying at Flacks' Board of Education hearing in October 1952, Samuel Levenson, assistant superintendent of Districts 32, 33, and 34, Brooklyn, acknowledged that she was active in the community. He said he was aware that she was a member of the Bedford-Stuyvesant Neighborhood Council. "I think she joined in with the block associations in the Bedford-Stuyvesant community and was active with the people in the block associations." He also testified that Flacks attempted to improve the conditions at P.S. 35, noting that the school building was dilapidated. "We all joined in that movement and we finally persuaded Miss [Mary] Dillon who was the President of the Board of Education at the time, and the members of the Board of Education, and the Building Department to give a new building for [PS] 35, and that was given." When asked by Flacks's attorney, if she was interested and played an active role in getting better schools in Bedford Stuyvesant, he replied, "The answer is yes."[69] Levenson also acknowledged that, of the fourteen hundred teachers under his supervision, he had selected Flacks to serve on the Board of Human Relations, a group he organized to create amity between the school and community, because "I thought that she was doing a very nice job."[70]

Mildred Flacks's work with Brooklyn parents helped create an organizational structure that would play a pivotal role in the New York City school integration struggle of the 1950s and 1960s. Many of the parent associations involved in the Bedford-Stuyvesant and Williamsburg Schools Council would also work with Milton A. Galamison in the NAACP Parent Workshop, later the Parents' Workshop for Equality in New York City Public Schools, for school integration. Thus Flacks must be given credit for helping to nurture parents in their fight to improve the education of their children.

Women also led the child welfare, library, social, and parents committees, groups that were important in helping to define the TU's social movement unionism. The Child Welfare Committee became very active after the split in 1935. Headed by Blanche Haber, the committee concentrated on providing health services for children in school and in their communities.

It sent representatives to the Board of Estimate's health budget hearings to present the TU's own health care program. The committee lobbied the union to support the Wagner Health Program, which would subsidize states so they could "make more adequate provision for public health prevention and control of disease, maternal and child health services, construction and maintenance of needed hospitals and health centers, care for the sick, disability insurance and training of personnel."[71] The Library Committee, headed by Elizabeth French, focused on improving working conditions, increasing salaries, and reducing the work load of librarians. The committee also pushed to increase library staff, provide adequate funding for school libraries, end censorship of books and magazines, and encourage a "more progressive tone" in books selected for libraries. French and her committee also advocated a stronger relationship between librarians and teachers, and making the public aware of the plight of libraries and librarians.[72]

The Social Committee, lead by Augusta Karlin, helped build bonds among TU members as well as raise money by organizing a number of events, including dances, theater parties, weekend excursions, and cabarets.[73] Rose Olson's Unemployment Committee led a campaign to save the jobs of teachers in training by urging collaboration with other teacher organizations protesting the board's proposed ban on employing substitutes for "absences of less then five days."[74] A big objective of the Parents Committee, led by Blanche Steinberg, was to form a strong working relationship with parents. A December 1937 conference between Local 5 and the United Parents Association created a joint program of the two organizations. The TU agreed to "seek the cooperation of [the] Parents Association in its district activities." When local parent organizations came to the TU for assistance, the union would direct the parents to "their logical organization, the United Parents Association." The TU agreed to urge its allies, such as the American Labor Party, and its own members who were parents to join parents associations.[75]

In December 2008 the *New York Teacher* reported that fifteen hundred "concerned demonstrators" rallied in Albany demanding Governor David Patterson "leave schools, colleges, hospitals and other essential services off the chopping block."[76] Holding demonstrations in front of the state capitol to protest budget cuts in education and other services is a strategy that points to the legacy of the New York City Teachers Union. It was the TU that first used mass rallies to place pressure on elected officials to provide adequate funding for education and other vital services. Women in the TU helped forge ties with parents, labor, and civic groups to swell attendance at such rallies and increase the pressure.

Bella Dodd and Rose Russell were the most prominent TU figures working with both state and city political figures, and the two women must be viewed as having held the most powerful position outside the presidency. Serving as the union's legislative representative they helped direct its legislative agenda, lobbying, negotiating, and collaborating with state legislators, the mayor, and other officials. However, Lucille Spence, Mildred Flacks, and the other women who decided to work at the community level were also important leaders, and the TU's reputation as a strong ally of the black and Latino communities was due, in large part, to their work. Belinda Robnett has argued that, while women were absent from formal leadership in social protest movements, many became what she calls bridge leaders, those who "kept their pulse on the community. The goal of bridge leaders was to gain trust, to bridge the masses to the movement and to act in accord with their constituents' desires."[77] They functioned in the "movement's or organization's free spaces, thus, making connections that cannot be made by formal leaders." Free space is a "niche that is not directed by formal leaders or those in their inner circle. It is an unclaimed space that is nevertheless central to the development of the movement."[78] Although Dodd and Russell were able to move into formal leadership positions, others such as Spence, Citron, Zitron, and Flacks cultivated leadership by building strong alliance with community. They intertwined the concerns of teachers with those of parents, labor, and civil rights groups, attempting to reach common objectives. Women leaders in the TU were able to present the union as more than a group of professionals trying to gain better wages, improve working conditions, and extend benefits. They helped lead the TU in its efforts to improve education for all children and achieve social equality.

12 / THE TRIUMPH OF THE UNITED FEDERATION OF TEACHERS AND THE DEFEAT OF SOCIAL UNIONISM

The formation of the United Federation of Teachers in 1960 helped move teacher unionism in a new direction. The UFT's militancy led to dramatic improvements in teacher salaries and working conditions, catapulting it into a leadership position unmatched by other teacher organizations. In fact, in return for its willingness to confront the Board of Education, the UFT would become the sole collective bargaining agent for forty thousand New York City public school teachers, sealing the fate of the Teachers Union.

THE FORMATION OF THE UNITED FEDERATION OF TEACHERS

Although the TU had long supported collective bargaining, it was the Teachers Guild that was able to succeed in winning this right for New York City teachers. The delegate assembly voted in 1956 to make collective bargaining the guild's primary objective.[1] In 1958 Mayor Robert Wagner issued an executive order allowing collective bargaining and voluntary dues checkoff for city employees, the latter authorizing employers to withhold union dues from members' paychecks. The order helped make New York one of the most labor-friendly cities in the United States. Although the New York City Board of Education was not bound by the mayor's executive order, Wagner's move gave teachers hope. The major obstacle to collective bargaining for teachers was the large number of teacher organizations. The High School Teachers Association, for example, advocated a differential salary scale for secondary school teachers, giving them higher salaries than teachers in elementary schools. The numerous groups organized by the National Education Association, such as the Elementary Teachers Association, opposed trade unionism for teachers and instead advocated that they be recognized as professionals. The guild saw the many teacher groups that had their own specific objectives as an obstacle to effective bargaining.[2]

Without the knowledge of the leadership, young militants in the guild, including Albert Shanker, David Selden, and George Altimore (all of these would become important leaders in the UFT), began negotiating with officials of the High School Teachers Association soon after its successful evening high school teachers strike in 1959. The HSTA maintained its support for a salary differential for secondary school teachers, in contrast the guild supported a single salary across divisions. Sam Hochberg and Roger Parente, members of the HSTA's executive board, realized that unity with the guild's position would strengthen the teacher union movement. Without informing the rest of the HSTA leadership, Hochberg, Parente and the young militants in the guild settled their differences over the single-pay position by agreeing that teachers with more years of teaching and academic preparation would receive higher salaries. The HSTA leadership, upset over the secret negotiation, rejected any proposed merger with the guild and accused Hochberg and Parente of violating HSTA's policy of rejecting incremental salary increases.[3]

Despite the HSTA's objection, Hochberg and Parente, along with another HSTA member, John Baily, formed a merger support group, the Committee for Action Through Unity (CATU). The guild again attempted to negotiate a merger with HSTA and failed; leaders of the Teachers Guild then offered to negotiate with the CATU, which had gained support among high school teachers. The guild and the CATU worked out a scheme that included the distribution of power.[4] On March 16, 1960, the guild's delegate assembly voted 295 to 12 in favor of merging with the CATU, creating the United Federation of Teachers. Just before the merger, the guild claimed it had 6,000 members. Although only 100 high school teachers formed the CATU when it was created, by the time of the merger it declared that it had grown to 1,000 members, with the support of 2,400 secondary school teachers. The UFT claimed, without presenting evidence, that it had the support of one quarter of New York City's 40,000 public school teachers. Charles Cogen, who was president of the guild, became president of the UFT.[5]

To maintain, and even increase, its support, the UFT had to deliver. One issue would win the UFT support and put the final nail in the coffin of the TU: the new union would need to become the sole collective bargaining agent for teachers. The militant wing in the UFT decided to pressure the Board of Education.[6] In late March 1960 over 1,500 UFT members voted in favor of a resolution calling for a strike if the city did not agree to the union's demands, which included collective bargaining, voluntary dues checkoff, duty-free lunch period for elementary school teachers, and a base pay schedule ranging from $5,000 to $10,000 in ten steps. President Charles Cogen reflected the militant tone of the new union when he contended that it would give the mayor and the Board of Education time to settle but would persevere until it achieved a "favorable conclusion." Jules Kolodny, a member of the UFT's negotiating team, accused Superintendent John Theobald of brushing off the union's demands when he said that educating children was not a matter of collective bargaining.[7]

The militancy of the UFT helped define the new teacher unionism. Standing up for fair salaries, improved working conditions, and assured job security were all major concerns of the Teachers Union, but the TU linked these issues to such broader political objectives as fighting racism and improving community relations. The UFT focused on major concerns specific to rank and file teachers, such as poor pay. The success of the UFT was due, in large part, to a group of dedicated young members who were first active in the guild. David Selden, one of the young activists, served as executive secretary of the guild and was an important organizer. To assure that teachers were aware of the guild, Selden sent flyers to schools. He also helped design a "school by school" approach to organizing. Guild members in a school, no matter how few, would see themselves as a little union; they would elect a chairperson, hold weekly meetings, come up with a program to improve conditions, represent teachers at grievance hearings, and hold discussions for union and nonunion members, even allowing nonmembers to vote on union policy. Guild members became faculty leaders, helping to raise the profile of the union among teachers. Leaders also developed a Big Guild, Little Guild approach: after careful study of the issues that most concerned teachers, the union would submit a report to the executive board. Selden argued that the union should portray itself as a "bargaining agent." It should "do things which would gain teacher support. It should also avoid actions which would alienate any group of teachers. . . . The Guild should emphasize the bread-and-butter issues of salaries, fringe benefits and working conditions. Once the union had become the bargaining agent, it could more safely turn its attention to broader issues." According to Selden, this strategy would attract teachers to the guild and help it become their collective bargaining agent. Thus, from its start, the UFT, and its guild precursors, cultivated a militant image of unionists fighting to improve salaries and working conditions for teachers.[8]

The UFT wasted little time in flexing its muscle. When Mayor Wagner proposed a city budget that included a cut in the annual school budget, the UFT responded, "The day has passed when the budgetary masterminds can hand out prefabricated salary gimmicks and expect teachers to accept them." The union announced that it had established a strategy committee to make plans for a work stoppage, demonstrating to teachers and the public that it was prepared to live up to its militant rhetoric. In an attempt to compete publicly with its new rival, the Teachers Union demanded that Wagner add $35 million to the school allotment, with $10 million provided for raises. But the TU had become almost irrelevant. It was the UFT that was in a position to call for a work action that could threaten the normal functioning of the system.

The Board of Education recognized the UFT as a formidable foe. On April 10 Theobald publicly responded to Cogen's threat, warning that he would not tolerate a teachers' strike and would enforce the Condon-Wadlin Act, passed in 1947 and calling for firing any state employee who went on strike. The UFT's willingness to stand up to a management threat promoted an image of the union as bold and determined to improve the plight of the city teachers. The union and superintendent played out their differences in the press, both trying to use the media to their advantage. The UFT told the board that the school allotment in the proposed executive budget was "inadequate." Theobald attempted to portray himself as a person who supported teacher raises but would not tolerate any job action. It had all the elements of a classic struggle between labor and management, however, the UFT leadership shrewdly did not present it that way to the public. Cogen characterized the union's effort as a crusade for justice, painting its members as brave warriors determined to stand up to intimidation. He told the press he was appalled that Theobald would attempt to coerce teachers by threatening to use the Condon-Wadlin Act: "We cannot allow any threat by the Superintendent to deter us from our just demands and from any action that may be necessary to attain them." By characterizing the fight between the UFT and the board not as a struggle over wages but one for "just demands," the union's rhetoric evoked a David and Goliath scenario. The union used this narrative to draw more teachers into its camp, and the UFT's growing attractiveness only weakened the TU.[9]

The UFT won a major victory when Theobald and Charles Silver, president of the board, announced that they would request additional money in the 1960–61 budget for teacher salary increases. The superintendent also agreed to meet with UFT leaders, although he claimed he would not negotiate with them. While Theobald denied that his action had anything to do with the UFT's call for a work stoppage, his announcement was a sign to the public and, more important, to city teachers that the board was responding to the new union's militant position.[10]

The UFT had the upper hand. Cogen continued to threaten a teachers' strike, even after a two-hour meeting with Theobald. After the meeting Cogen told the press the union would go ahead with its plans for a work stoppage because the superintendent had failed to make assurances about the union's concerns. In response to Theobald's threat to use the Condon-Wadlin Act, Cogen said: "you can't solve the teacher shortage by firing 10,000 teachers. Instead of talking about threats or reprisals, the Superintendent should sit down and negotiate with us until an agreement is reached."[11]

The UFT also filed a petition in the Manhattan Supreme Court claiming that overcrowding at several schools was so severe it would endanger the lives of teachers and students in the event of a fire. Overcrowding had been an ongoing issue for the Teachers Union, parents, and community leaders, but the UFT was able to take advantage of media attention to press the matter, gaining additional support among teachers, parents, and community groups. Theobald responded by accusing the union of a publicity stunt and asking it for specifics. He said he was glad the union had gone to court "because now they will have to prove their charges." Esther Klugherz, parent of a student in one of the overcrowded schools, joined Benjamin Muzin of the UFT to present a petition that listed fifty-seven overcrowded schools, in some of which children were "compelled to sit in aisles;" in addition, lunchrooms had a limited number of exits.[12]

On April 27, the UFT's four-hundred-member delegate assembly voted to strike on May 17 if there was no "substantial progress" made in improving pay and working conditions. Cogen argued that the walkout would bring attention to the "shameful neglect of our schools." He blamed school officials for allowing education "to deteriorate," citing overcrowding, the dearth of qualified teachers in junior high schools, the inability to attract new teachers due to low salaries and poor working conditions, and the large number of unfilled specialist positions.[13] This language suggested the union was fighting for education reform and not just to improve teachers' working conditions.

Although the UFT garnered a great deal of publicity by threatening a strike, not all of it was favorable. A *New York Times* editorial noted that the Condon-Wadlin Act, was the law. The UFT could call it "unconstitutional" if it wished, but "wishing it so does not make it so. Only a court of law can do that, and it hasn't happened." The paper scolded the new union, arguing that teachers "set a bad example to youth when they threaten to break the law" and damaged their standing with the public.[14] The UFT was taking a risk. If it failed to get enough teachers to walk out and the strike fizzled, the board would see it as ineffective and, worse, it would lose all credibility among teachers. Why would the leaders of the young union try such a risky maneuver as provoking enforcement of the Condon-Wadlin Act? UFT leaders had assessed the current crisis and concluded that they would be victorious. There was a severe teacher shortage in the city, and the school system could not afford to lose ten thousand teachers, making up one-third of the staff. In addition, Cogen had been assured by the union's attorney that the act was unconstitutional. Attempting to win the propaganda campaign, the union responded to the *New York Times* in a May 6 letter in which Cogen and Hochberg asserted that the act was unconstitutional and they would challenge it in court. They also maintained that the provision to discharge public employees for going on strike had never been used because it was not enforceable on "realistic and moral grounds." It would be impossible to fire ten thousand teachers in the midst of a teacher shortage. Firing even a smaller number was not feasible because "you are dead wrong and the public knows it." Was it moral for the board to crowd students into already overcrowded classes to be taught by overworked teachers? Was it moral to deny children "necessary guidance and remedial learning services?" Was it moral to deprive teachers of a duty free lunch period? In their litany of accusations, UFT leaders also hammered at the embarrassingly low teacher salaries and the board's refusal to negotiate with the union. Expressing confidence that the union had the city's labor movement of one million members and their families on its side, Cogen and Hochberg claimed the support of "hundreds of thousands of organized parents for whose children we are fighting and the civic organizations that have expressed disgust with the educational budget. . . . If you are really interested in avoiding a strike we suggest that you take a different tack. Your pressure is being exerted in the wrong direction. We suggest you try the superintendent of schools and the Mayor."[15] The UFT emphasized that it represented the rights of students, not just its members.

Some teacher groups attacked the UFT. The HSTA and the Teachers Union were both wary of the new union. Several National Education Association (NEA) affiliates formed the Joint Committee of Teachers Organization in an attempt to deny the UFT sole collective bargaining status. In his biography of Albert Shanker, president of the UFT from 1964 to 1984 and of the American Federation of Teachers from 1974 to 1997, Richard Kahlenberg claims that the "Communist-dominated Teachers' Union, in particular put out flyers saying the strike was not legitimate, and their members crossed the picket lines." However, the Teachers Union's response was more nuanced than Kahlenberg presents it. When the UFT asked the Teachers Union for strike support, TU executive board member Paul Becker sent a letter seeking clarification on a number of points. Would the UFT defend striking TU members who were singled out by the Board of Education? With a history of investigation and purges, TU executive board members feared the school agency would use the strike as grounds for dismissal. What role, if any, would the TU play in negotiations? The Teachers Union never received a response from the UFT.[16] The executive board of the TU decided not to take a position on the strike; instead it urged its members not to cross the picket line if "a majority or sizable minority of the faculty engages in the stoppage." The TU faced a dilemma: if it supported the strike initiated by the UFT, it would acknowledge the new union as the teachers' representative, undermining its own independence and identity; if it took a position against the job action, it would be accused of representing management and not siding with teachers.[17] Trying to carve out a place for itself in the conflict, the TU offered its own plan for teachers, including a $300 raise across the board for all school personnel.

The TU's support was not critical to the UFT, and the leaders of the new union were not willing to make any concessions to or compromise with its old rival. Theobald's proposal of a new salary plan was strong evidence that board officials perceived the UFT as a formidable force. The superintendent's proposal would grant teachers annual increases of from $200 to $400. The

UFT called for $400 at the starting salary and $600 in the top bracket, with other salary adjustments raising the maximum pay to $10,000—$900 above Theobald's plan.[18] Wagner agreed to sit down with union representatives, but Cogen continued to threaten that the schools would close if the parties failed to reach an agreement. City officials were under pressure, with the possibility of thousands of teachers striking, creating unsafe conditions in the schools. Theobald responded to Cogen by telling the press, "I wouldn't think of it."[19]

Worried about his chances of reelection, Mayor Wagner averted a UFT strike in May by promising a collective bargaining election that would commit the city to contract negotiations with the representatives of one union. The promised package included voluntary dues checkoff and five days of annual sick leave. Teachers would receive $16,500,00 in salary and increases in pension payments. While the salary increase was offered earlier and had been rejected by the union, the collective bargaining election meant the UFT would become the only body recognized to hold contract negotiations for public school teachers. Cogen recommended that the executive board and delegates accept the offer. The UFT was on the verge of making history.[20]

Both the executive board and the delegate assembly voted in favor of the agreement. Theobald and Silver announced the vote, calling off the threatened strike and also saying they would recommend holding a collective bargaining election to the Board of Education at its May 26 meeting.[21] Wagner's support of collective bargaining was not surprising; city employees were key to his attempts to build a liberal coalition in New York City. His announced support helped redefine teacher unionism in New York City and began a process that would eventually stamp teacher unions throughout the country in the UFT mold. The brand of teacher unionism advocated by the TU, social unionism linking community concerns, would be pushed aside to focus on improved working conditions, increased salaries, and benefits. With the UFT as the collective bargaining agency, issues that were critical to black and Hispanic communities—such as the practice of assigning the least experienced teachers to their schools and segregating the student body—would be marginalized. Just as important, black and Latino communities would lose a strong ally that, since 1935, had fostered ties between teachers and those communities.

THE STRIKE

It seemed that the UFT had hammered out an agreement with the mayor. Theobald and Board of Education President Charles Silver, however, had mentioned that they would "recommend" to the Board of Education a collective bargaining election. The board had referred the matter to the corporation counsel to rule if collective bargaining for teachers was legal. Theobald raised additional concern about the board's position when he told Bronx community school board members he was not certain that the board could provide sick leave for substitutes. The board's stalling tactics and apparent broken promises infuriated the UFT, and by September it responded by calling for a strike. It seemed inevitable that the UFT would be selected as the sole collective bargaining agent for teachers, but its rivals were not going to go down without a fight. The Joint Committee of Teachers Organization opposed collective bargaining on the grounds that teachers were professionals, not trade unionists, and it refused to support the UFT's call for a strike. Both the HSTA, which changed its name to Secondary School Teachers Association to include junior high school teachers and the TU supported collective bargaining, but they wanted an equal opportunity to present their positions to teachers. The SSTA filed a lawsuit in the state supreme court challenging the constitutionality of the Condon-Wadlin Act. Theobald said he would welcome an interpretation of the act's legality, but the UFT dismissed the suit as a "completely phony attempt to substitute legal hocus-pocus for effective action." The UFT called for teachers to challenge the law by walking out, rather than relying on the courts. Cogen and the leadership saw such militancy as a way to persuade the city and the superintendent of schools to come to the bargaining table. Influenced by the civil rights movement, which challenged unjust laws by using nonviolent civil disobedience, the UFT depicted its struggle as a moral crusade on behalf of teachers.[22]

When, after several months, the Board of Education still had not called for a collective bargaining election, Cogen threatened to take "appropriate action." Theobald countered that the proposals for collective bargaining and dues checkoff were before the board's Law Committee. Nevertheless, the delegate assembly voted to strike on November 7,[23] prompting the *New York Times to* lambaste the union for threatening the city and calling the proposed job action lawless. Some labor leaders attacked the UFT, including

AFL-CIO president George Meany, who questioned how much support the union had among the city's forty thousand teachers.[24]

Despite the attacks, in late October 1960 over 90 percent of the delegates and over thirty-five hundred UFT members voted for the proposed November 7 strike. Soon after the strike vote the union set up thirteen picket lines throughout the city in order to get "the public accustomed to the appearance of the real thing." To maintain their legitimacy, union leaders knew they would have to act. They accused the board of breaking its promises regarding collective bargaining, sick pay for substitute teachers, a duty-free lunch period of fifty minutes, voluntary dues deduction, and equal salary steps.[25] Theobald insisted that the process was moving along, but again threatened to invoke the Condon-Wadlin Act "if I want to keep my self respect and be a law-abiding citizen." The superintendent acknowledged he had been informed by Corporation Counsel John H. Tenney that a limited form of collective bargaining was allowed, but that there could be no strike as part of such an agreement. In addition, the board, as a public agency, could not deny other unions the right to be heard. Still, since 1950, the board had been invoking the Timone Resolution, which prohibited it from recognizing the Teachers Union.[26]

The TU knew that it was finished if the UFT won the sole right to bargain collectively for teachers. The Teachers Union took issue with the UFT's estimate of ten thousand members. Rose Russell questioned how the UFT could claim sole bargaining rights when, based on per capita payments to the AFT, the new union actually represented approximately four thousand teachers, one-tenth of the teachers in the system. Knowing it had no chance of winning a collective bargaining election, the TU pushed for a joint council of major teacher organizations as a bargaining agency, a strategy that would restore its rights to represent teachers before the board.[27]

By the end of October a teachers' strike seemed inevitable and tempers flared. Cogen, alleging that Theobald allowed him only two hours off to tape an interview for the WCBS radio program "Let's Find Out," accused the superintendent of interfering with "due process of the freedom of speech and free access to the media of communication." Theobald shot back that it was "high time that Mr. Cogen learned that he is not a part-time teacher," indicating Cogen could have taped the program at another time. In any case, he was not going to cooperate with someone who was urging teachers to break the law.[28]

The UFT's strike threat was designed to demonstrate to teachers that it was the only teacher organization in the city that could win substantial gains and garner enough support to become the collective bargaining agency. The superintendent declared that the proposed union action was a "shameful reach on the part of a few for organizational power and self aggrandizement," and he urged teachers not to sacrifice the welfare of children and their own status as professionals.[29] The SSTA also characterized the proposed job action as an effort by a "small group to grab power and control the destiny of all teachers." The TU harbored similar fears, but would not publicly express them. Instead, it accused the UFT of exaggerating its numbers.[30]

The board did not want a strike, but could not afford to appear easily intimidated. To present itself as acting in good faith, in late October it approved funds for employing 760 lunchroom aides to help provide elementary school teachers a duty-free lunch period. But in the eyes of the UFT, the board's action fell far short of it's the union's demands. Determined to test its power, the union created "honor picket lines" at over seventy-five schools. Theobald announced his own preparations for the strike, including plans to assign 600 non teachers to lunchroom duty in 191 special services and 380 non special services schools in attempt to prevent disturbances in those schools.[31]

In late October the SSTA stepped up its criticism of the UFT. In a joint statement, the New York Teachers Association, the Bronx Boro-wide Teachers Association, the Staten Island Teachers Association, the Brooklyn Teachers Association, the Teachers Alliance of New York City, the Elementary School Teachers Association, and the NEA Council announced their opposition, calling the job action a "needless, illegal strike" that would harm only children. The seven groups feared a public backlash if a work stoppage was called and maintained that the legitimate goals of the UFT could be achieved without striking. "A strike by one minority teacher group," Max Weiss of the New York Council of the NEA asserted, "could cause resentment against all teachers on the part of parents of school children. The result of such a strike would be the weakening of teacher status at a time when we should all work together to achieve our goals in as effective and professional manner."[32] Responses to the proposed strike indicated an ideological divide. The NEA and other associations rejected a strike because they saw themselves as professionals, not workers, and refused any association with the labor movement. This created a dilemma for the Teachers Union. On the one hand, the TU had championed trade unionism for teachers, so it could not join with the other teacher organizations and push professionalism. On the other hand, by siding with the UFT it would relinquish leadership to its rival and assure its own demise.

The TU called for the SSTA and the UFT to join a demonstration against the board's recent ban on strike meetings in the schools, hoping to convince teachers of its leadership role. However, the fact that it called for other organizations to participate reinforced the perception that the TU did not have the strength to act on its own. The SSTA's narrow focus on secondary school teachers, its criticism of the strike and stress on legal solutions, ruled it out as a viable alternative to the UFT. Still, the United Federation of Teachers was taking a tremendous gamble that teachers would see it as the only organization willing to take extraordinary action on their behalf. If the strategy failed, it would weaken the union before the board and teachers and undermine teacher unionism in the city. Teachers would be reluctant to join, and the board could refuse with impunity to negotiate with any teacher union.

As the strike deadline neared, criticism of the UFT grew. A week before the strike, Silver announced that he would not consider the issues of collective bargaining and dues checkoff until November 17, at a meeting of all the teacher organizations. The TU had given board officials ammunition in its public campaign against the UFT, and Silver repeated the TU's charge, voiced on WCBS radio, that the new union likely had four thousand, not ten thousand members. Cogen, for his part, continued trying to win support from the public by arguing that the board had broken its promises.[33]

The UFT now faced an avalanche of criticism. The *New York Times*, which had run two editorials opposing the job action, again attacked the UFT, praising other teacher groups for criticizing the "illegal strike" and calling the UFT membership a "small minority" within the profession. Insisting that the vast majority of teachers considered a strike "unprofessional," the *Times* credited Theobald and the Board of Education "with moving with reasonable speed to correct the inequities and injustices, and are cognizant of the fact that economic remedies lie largely with the Board of Estimate." Mayor Wagner threw his support to Theobald, saying that no negotiation could take place with a "gun pointed at your head" and that he would support invoking the Condon-Wadlin Act. Also publicly opposed to the UFT's actions were parent organizations such as the Policy Consultation Committee, consisting of the City-Wide High School Parents Council, the Metropolitan District of the State Congress Parents, the Teachers Staten Island Federation of Parent Teacher Associations, the Queensboro Federation of Parents Clubs, and the Brooklyn Federation of Parent Teachers Association. Although it did not directly assert its support for Theobald, the United Parents Association expressed deep concern about the UFT's threat.[34]

Just days before the strike, the TU clarified its position. Distinguishing itself from other teacher organizations that refused to identify with trade unionism, the TU insisted that it was ready to support a strike in what it called "accepted trade union policy and practice." The Teachers Union criticized both Theobald's threat to use the Condon-Wadlin Act and his policy of not allowing teachers to hold in-school meetings to discuss the strike. (Theobald claimed school accommodations should not be used to encourage a strike.) The TU also characterized the UFT's actions as "incredible": since no specific salary demand was being made, every means short of a strike should be used to resolve the dispute. Although it was still using the language of trade unionism, the TU had finally joined others in opposing the November 7 strike.[35]

On November 2 Theobald and Silver shifted their position, agreeing to meet with the UFT in hopes of preventing the job action.[36] Before the strike, the UFT was seen as the clear winner in the contest between it and the board. By refusing to back down, it had convinced board officials to negotiate. Theobald and Silver's willingness to sit down with the UFT undercut the TU, which had been attempting to paint itself as the only teacher organization that remained true to trade union principles. The UFT's threat to use the strongest weapon available to a trade union was forcing management's hand, and New York City public school teachers could see the tactic was having an impact.

The November 3 meeting between board officials and the UFT was described by the *New York Times* as "unproductive."[37] In a last-minute effort to prevent a strike, the board set April 1, 1961, as a tentative date for the collective bargaining election. It stood firm on dues checkoff, maintaining it would not grant this privilege to any organization threatening to strike. Theobald threatened to invoke not only the Condon-Wadlin Act but also the board bylaw on "conduct unbecoming a teacher."[38] The board's threats went unheeded. On November 7, 1960, the first teachers' strike in New York

City history began. The *New York Times* reported that thousands of teachers stayed out of schools, many forming picket lines. The board reacted by suspending 4,600 teachers charged with conduct unbecoming a teacher. They would be allowed to return to work, pending disposition of the charge. If found guilty, the teachers could be fired or stripped of tenure rights for five years and denied salary increases. Theobald refuted Cogen's assertion that 15,000 teachers were on strike, claiming it was "pure nonsense" and that the UFT president was "either misinformed or lying." The strike's impact was uneven. Junior high schools and academic high schools, where the UFT was strongest, were most affected by the action. The board admitted that 30 of the 126 junior high schools reported having more than half their teachers out and 56 had one-fifth not reporting to work. Only 23 junior high schools reported having enough staff to function normally. Of the 19 vocational schools, 9 reported having above normal teacher absences, 10 of the 591 elementary schools reported one-third to one-half of the faculty absent. Three academic high schools reported that more than half their teachers were out; 28 high schools noted more than one-fifth were absent. The remaining 25 reported normal absenteeism.[39]

The New York City Police Department reported 267 schools had been picketed by a total of 2,000 teachers, although Cogen claimed there were 7,500 teachers demonstrating. A number of teachers who picketed identified themselves not as UFT members but as members of other teacher organizations with their own leadership. In some high schools students showed their support for striking teachers. For example, at the Bronx High School of Science, 800 of the 2,800 students refused to cross the picket line. Cogen claimed that one-third of the 2,500 students at Stuyvesant High School refused to attend classes. In some schools classes were canceled, students met in the auditorium because there were not enough teachers, and/or numerous substitutes were hired to cover classes.[40]

Having become the most dominant teacher organization in the city, the UFT called off the strike on November 8, claiming the board had offered not to take action against the teachers. Moreover, the UFT claimed that Mayor Wagner promised a collective bargaining election. In addition, the head of the city trade council was putting pressure on the union because the strike was jeopardizing Wagner's reelection. David Dubinsky, head of the International Ladies Garment Workers Union, organizer of the New York Liberal Party, and vice president of the AFL-CIO, offered to mediate.

But the decision to end the work stoppage was not without internal opposition. Although a majority at the delegate assembly voted to end the strike, a vocal minority accused the leadership of selling out. Dozens of members walked out of the meeting because no concessions had been made by the Board of Education. However, Silver's announcement that he would not punish strikers if they returned to work could be seen as a victory. While board officials estimated only five thousand teachers were on strike, they also admitted the strike had caused significant disruptions and concerned parents might keep their children at home if it continued. Board officials realized there were just too many teachers to punish: disciplinary action might lead to greater support for the UFT.[41]

The *New York Times* continued to criticize the UFT, arguing that the strike was a "setback" for the union's "headstrong action." However, the new union had proved it was powerful enough to disrupt the school system, a particularly important factor as the collective bargaining election drew nearer. The Teachers Union, in an unrealistic attempt to save itself, asked for a meeting with the UFT, the SSTA, and the Elementary Teachers Association. Given its mission to become the sole collective bargaining agent for teachers, the UFT saw no reason to meet with the TU or any organization it was competing with in the election.[42] The TU persisted, calling for a "common plan of action" against the board, claiming "thousands of teachers are ready to take militant action on their problems" and that the school system could be "crippled and hundreds of schools could be closed." The call was ill timed. The UFT had already taken action without the TU's support, and Wagner had already named a mediation committee, recommended by AFL-CIO president George Meany, consisting of David Dubinsky, Jacob Potofsky, president of the Amalgamated Clothing Workers of America, another vice president of the AFL-CIO, and Harry Van Arsdale Jr., president of the City Central Labor Council. Cogen expressed confidence in the committee, declaring his belief that it would recognize the union's just demands.[43]

The Teachers Union adopted its own proposals at the December 9, 1960, membership meeting, calling for a basic salary of from $6,000 to $12,000 in ten equal annual increments. It also recommended "experience increments" of $500 for each five years of teaching, starting after the twentieth year and continuing until the thirty-fifth year.[44]

In early January 1961 the mayor's three-person committee submitted its report, prepared with the help of the special counsel to the AFL-CIO, Arthur

J. Goldberg. Noting the special position of teachers as a professional class facing all the problems of employees, the report recommended allowing a vote on collective bargaining, along with other items favorable to the UFT. It urged the board to implement equal pay across the divisions, create a salary schedule from $5,000 to $10,000, and provide sick leave for permanent substitutes and duty-free lunch periods for all teachers. It also urged the city to seriously consider dues checkoff.[45]

The board appointed a Commission of Inquiry on Collective Bargaining to find out by polling teachers how many were in favor of collective bargaining. After a number of hearings with representatives of twenty-eight teacher organizations, the commission could not reach any conclusion and urged the board to hold an election. The board ignored that recommendation. Instead, it argued that any agreement reached under collective bargaining could be terminated by the school agency, demonstrating an obstinacy that could force another confrontation. In the summer of 1961, when the school agency found itself in a scandal involving contracts for repairs, Wagner saw an opening. He convinced the state legislature to terminate the sitting board and give the mayor the authority to appoint a new one. The new board ordered a collective bargaining election in late December 1961.[46]

The Teachers Union did not oppose the election, but it objected to the timing, accusing the labor department of "rushing the election while teachers were still scheduling meetings to hear speakers from each organization." Fighting a rear guard action, the TU claimed to teachers that "schools reported that TU speakers invariably made the best impression" in CB meetings;" then, facing reality, it adopted a resolution asserting that "if the TU wins the election we will invite the other two organizations to have representatives on the negotiating committee." This was a desperate attempt to persuade the UFT to provide the TU a space at the table and to assure its own members their union could play a significant role.[47] At its October membership meeting, the TU adopted a resolution calling on members to increase their efforts to "bring union material and literature into the schools, take the initiative in calling for meetings at which representatives of the three major organizations would speak, and increase efforts to get new members into the union."[48]

On December 16, 1961 the United Federation of Teachers became the sole collective bargaining agent for New York City public school teachers, receiving 20,045 of the 33,119 votes cast. The Teachers Bargaining Organization, which came in second, got 9,770, fewer than half the votes the UFT received. The TBO, created with the support of the NEA, was made up of the Elementary School Teachers Association, the Secondary School Teachers Association, and the NYC chapter of the National Education Association. The TU registered an embarrassing 2,575 votes, placing it a distant third. In its prime the TU claimed to be a force of 6,000, making it the then largest teacher organization in the city. By the time of the collective bargaining election the TU had between 800 and 1,000 members.[49] The UFT had managed to receive the support of close to 50 percent of all teachers. Harry Starfield, vice president of the TU, complained the election had been "unfairly administered," a "rushed job" that gave the union little opportunity to present its case; Rose Russell pointed to irregularities.[50]

The TU's complaints had validity. The UFT's success was, in large part, due to the fact that the Teachers Union had been banned from operating in the New York City schools for over a decade. It had been in the forefront of the civil rights struggle in the city, fighting for funding equity, the hiring of black teachers, the elimination of racist and biased textbooks, acknowledgement of black history, and school integration. But, without a presence in the schools, the TU did not seem to be a viable collective bargaining agent. By 1960 many of the city's teachers had been hired after the TU was banned, and they were unfamiliar with its past militancy; even more teachers knew the TU as a proscribed union whose members had been forced out because of the union's Communist ties. Many teachers were now less interested in the type of issues the TU had come to be identified with since 1950, especially as it remade itself into an organization that pushed a social justice agenda. The TU had, in fact, always been interested in issues that directly affected teachers—even during its darkest days, in the 1950s, it championed higher salaries, reducing class size, and increasing pension benefits—but those objectives were often overshadowed by its strong emphasis on social justice.

The UFT, in contrast, became a militant force mostly by focusing on improved working conditions and economic viability. Its agenda reflected the concerns of a vast number of teachers, and it had demonstrated that it was willing to take action on their behalf. Although the UFT had an interest in improving conditions for poor children, that was not its primary goal. In fact, the UFT eventually fell silent on that subject, retreating from its earlier criticism of the board's policies it saw as hurting black and Latino communities. The strike was about teachers' interests. After the UFT's dramatic win, teachers flocked to that union, surrendering in the end on the TU.

After the UFT's victory the TU leadership still did not immediately consider disbanding the union. But at that point, was the Teachers Union just going through the motions, still pretending to be a viable teacher advocacy organization? To be sure, it was finding it hard to function. It did not have enough members to reach every teacher in the city; there was no assurance that its literature would be placed in the mailboxes. It maintained a roster of between eight hundred and one thousand members, but only a handful was willing to serve on committees, distribute literature in the schools, and carry on day-to-day functions of the TU. The union's full-time paid staff members were making next to nothing in salary. More important, there was no need for teachers to join the TU when they were already members of the UFT. Attendance at TU meetings was so low that membership and executive board meetings were combined.[1] The TU was on life support. On September 16, 1963, the union held a special executive board meeting to discuss the future of the organization. Should it disband and its members join the UFT, or should it continue? Those calling for disbandment argued they could be more effective working within the UFT; those opposed contended that the union was continuing to play a role in raising the consciousness of teachers on issues that impacted them directly. As outsiders, TU members could not serve as delegates, run for union office, or have any real impact on UFT policy; yet only as a separate entity could the TU provide a voice for those who opposed the UFT's unionism. During the special executive board meeting, the proposal that the Teachers Union disband was forwarded to a committee consisting of Paul Becker, Dave Weiner, Anne Matlin, Fred Rosenberg, Albert Ludwig, and Lawrence Lane.[2]

At its September 26 meeting the executive board decided to postpone any mention of the issue of decision in New York Teacher News. One probable explanation for this is that such an announcement would result in a flurry of rumors from the TU's enemies; the leadership did not want to alert the public to the discussion prematurely. However, a discussion on dissolution was placed on the board's October 3 meeting and a letter would be sent to the membership after the October 3 notifying them that the leadership has raised the issue of disbanding the union.[3]

Also on October 3, members received the news that Abraham Lederman, a man who had dedicated his life to building the TU and defending the rights of teachers, had died of a long illness. Executive board members approved a motion authorizing the staff of *Teacher News* to draw up an obituary for the former president, which would appear in print in December. But the crucial item on their agenda that day was the future of the TU. In a vote of eighteen to two with two abstentions, the executive board called for the dissolution of the TU. But, in a show of democracy, it appointed a committee to present a minority report that would be sent to union members.[4]

The draft resolution to dissolve the TU recognized the union's work but argued that since the Timone Resolution it had labored under "severe handicaps." Extraordinary leaders and a huge number of members, the resolution declared, had been lost. The creators of the resolution attempted to construct the union's history, contending that the union had had seven thousand members in 1950, but, while it continued to have achievements, since 1950 the thousands of new teachers entering the system had never heard of the Teachers Union. The results of more than a decade of being banned from operating in the schools made the union's disastrous defeat in the collective bargaining election in 1961 a foregone conclusion. The Timone Resolution had not been lifted until 1962, "a year after the unfair conditions in which" the collective bargaining "election was held." The TU was powerless when it came to playing a direct role in collective bargaining. After a long discussion at the executive board level, it was determined that the best way for TU members to continue struggling for better schools was to join the "other union." The dissolution of the TU, the executive board acknowledged, would make it more difficult to fight bigotry, discrimination, and segregation, and defend academic freedom and civil liberties. The TU would disband as an independent union on December 31, 1963, and its members join the United Federation of Teachers, where they would "loyally and actively participate in the formation and support of policies, programs and actions best suited to create a school system in New York City educationally and democratically second to none."[5]

In the minority statement the opposition argued that the objectives of the TU would not be carried out by any other organization in the near future. How could the union, in "good conscience," disband when the school system was beset with several critical problems? Attacking the "realists" who argued that the TU could not operate as a "bona fide union," they countered that the union could still play a positive role, improving economic and working conditions through analysis of the educational budget and other issues. The Teachers Union had organized trips to Albany as part of an intensive lobbying campaign and maintained a legislative representative in the state capital. Its many publications, including *Teacher News*, were important sources of information, turning the spotlight on vital issues such as the dropout rate, bias in textbooks, the myth of IQ tests, and the need for Negro History Week publications. By asserting "There is no need for a closed shop in our schools today," the opposition was in part arguing for dual unionism. Those opposed to dissolution contended that centralized negotiating ignored the uniqueness of each particular school, and it was naive to assume the UFT would protect all teachers. The minority statement argued that the union continued to face challenges such as McCarthyism. Still, disbanding seemed inevitable.[6]

As TU members contemplated the fate of their organization, they also gathered to say goodbye to Abraham Lederman. The October 12 edition of *Teacher News* pointed to the TU's close relationship with New York City's civil rights groups, labor organizations, and parents. A statement by the Urban League of Greater New York praised Lederman as "prominent" in the integration effort, and the Parents Workshop for Equality in New York City Schools acknowledged the "loss of a great friend in the integration movement." Albert J. Fitzgerald, president of the United Electrical Radio and Machine Workers of America, cited Lederman's "devotion to honest, militant trade unionism, an inspiration not only to the members of the teaching profession but to all of us who have fought to protect the welfare of the people of the city and country." The staff of P.S. 64, Manhattan, sent a statement expressing regret at Lederman's passing, calling him "fearless and [a] tireless leader in the fight for the welfare of all students and teachers."[7] Lederman's death was symbolic of the union's fate.

The final resolution on dissolution was adopted at the January 9, 1964, executive board meeting and would be presented at the January 17 membership meeting. It read, "Pursuant to the decision of the Membership, the

Executive Board decides and determines: That the Teachers Union of New York be dissolved effective upon the adjournment of its next membership meeting to be held on January 17, 1964." Following the recommendations of the advisory committee, the union created a three-person committee to act as trustees after dissolution to liquidate the assets and settle the affairs of the union, including paying outstanding debts, such as accounts payable, salaries, and severance pay to staff and officers. A pension would also be paid to Rose Russell by the purchase of an annuity, and the union would establish a trust fund, up to a $1,000, to the Lederman Memorial Fund for payment of legal fees in the pending cases brought by the union. Arrangements would be made for preserving the records of the TU.[8]

Whereas Lederman's death marked the end of the union, the tribute to Rose Russell held on January 4, 1964, was a celebration of its legacy. Among the two thousand people who attended the event at the Grand Ballroom of the Waldorf-Astoria were teachers, parents, government officials, clergy, civil rights leaders, and school administrators. Speakers included Dr. Mark McCosky, chair of the New York State Youth Commission, Cleveland Robinson, member of the NYC Commission of Human Rights and vice president and secretary-treasurer of District 65, and the Rev. Milton Galamison, pastor of Siloam Presbyterian Church and leader of the school integration campaign. Galamison praised Russell for her "prophetic" role in the struggle to improve schools for children, saying she had "brought so much light to a school system lumbering and lost in a consuming darkness." In poignant words he contended, "just as there could not be Florence Nightingale . . . without the Crimean War . . . no Dr. Salk without polio . . . there could be no Rose Russell without the school system: deaf to the cries of those whose need it fails, resisting change in a changing world and suffering a sickness unto death. There is no major problem in the system on which this union has not taken an articulate and unmistakable position."[9]

The tribute demonstrated that the TU still had its admirers. Greetings were sent by sixty people, including Dr. Linus Pauling, chemist and Nobel Prize winner, who wished he could be there to see Russell's "sweet face," and poet Langston Hughes, who called Russell a "wonderful lady" who was "helping to make some-day a wonderful world." Coretta Scott King wanted to add her name to the "thousands of others who congratulate you for the fine and dedicated service that you have rendered over the years to the teachers of New York and to the whole field of educa-

Figure 13.1 W. E. B. Du Bois at the podium addressing the annual TU conference (1952). United Federation of Teachers, part 1, folder 524.

tion." State Commissioner of Education James Allen apologized for not being able to attend the much-deserved tribute, and Abraham D. Beame, New York City's comptroller, praised Russell for her work for the Teachers Union as well as public education.[10]

As expected, on January 17, 1964, the membership voted in favor of disbanding the Teachers Union. An article in the final edition of *New York Teacher News*, published on January 18, 1964, blamed the union's demise on the witch hunts of the 1950s, asking when those who conducted that campaign would atone for purging excellent teachers. The UFT had "failed to rise to the occasion." While the TU indirectly blamed the UFT for its demise, the editorial board did not want to end on a sour note. The article recounted the TU's struggle for academic freedom, citing an impressive roster of past recipients of the Teachers Union annual award, including Eleanor Roosevelt (1939), Franz Boaz (1940), Sidney Hillman (1945), Albert Einstein (1950), and W. E. B. Du Bois (1952). A piece titled "Equal Opportunity and Dignity for All Children: Long Before May 4, 1954" traced the union's long campaign for racial equality, reaching back to cite a November 1941 article in *Teacher News* that had made a case for improving schools in poor areas of New York because better schools help "breed happy, wholesome children." The Teachers Union had waged a fight for equal opportunity long before the words school boycott and integration made headlines.[11]

The TU's unwillingness to take a more independent path from the Communist Party and its public adoption of Communist Party positions confirmed, in the eyes of both its challengers and the general public, that it was a Communist front. The TU's cozy relationship with the Party masked its good work on behalf of children, parents, and teachers, particularly at the height of anti-Communist hysteria in the late 1940s through the 1950s. The opponents of the union effectively manipulated public opinion of the union's relationship with the Party and were thus able to weaken and eventually destroy it.

No matter how unwise was the TU's decision not to take an independent path and instead support the Party line at all times, that was not the reason for its downfall. Even after the 1935 schism and accusations that the TU was a Communist front, the union managed to attract thousands of members. Rather, the campaign launched by Jansen, the Board of Education, and a host of anti-Communist forces was responsible for the TU's end. I argue in this study that, no matter how close the TU was to the Communist Party, the Board of Education never proved that any TU member who was purged from the system was involved in attempting to indoctrinate students or found to be incompetent in the classroom. The teachers forced out of the school system were victims of a Board of Education and an anti-Communist coalition that cared little about academic freedom, civil liberties, fair play, or justice. The board, Jansen, and others involved in the purge were motivated by ideological concerns in their zeal to rid the system of Communists.

In 1987 TU member Mildred Flacks, a key figure in the Bedford-Stuyvesant-Williamsburg Council for Better Schools, criticized the United Federation of Teachers' 1968 strike against community control of the city' public schools. She asserted that she herself could never have taken part in that strike: "I could have never done that to the children."[12] Her reason for not supporting a labor strike seemed strange, given her political views. After all, she was both a member of the American Communist Party and an ardent trade unionist. However, a closer examination of Flacks's statement reveals that her view of unionism went beyond providing benefits and higher wages for teachers. The Teachers Union's objective—building a radical movement for social change—connected its concerns to working-class black and Latino communities. TU members were seen as partnering with parents for change. The TU helped established a culture of teacher-community unparalleled in the city's history. But then cold war hysteria made the TU a target. From 1949 until the late 1950s over eleven hundred TU members were grilled by the superintendent or his representatives about their political beliefs and associations, and hundreds of TU members were fired, or forced to resign or retire. The investigations and purges and the Timone Resolution led to a mass exodus of the membership and the union's eventual demise. An important model was lost: a community-teacher coalition working to improve schools by ending segregation and race-based discrepancy in funding, providing black and Latino children with experienced teachers, hiring more black and Latino teachers, and directly linking the union's welfare to the communities that it served.

Public education in the United States faces many challenges. The push for privatization of schools and services and state and local government cuts in school budgets have made it more difficult for public school systems to operate successfully. There has also been a nation-wide push to replace public schools with charter schools, and even though charter schools are public institutions, they are operated by private interests and the faculty is usually made up of nonunion teachers. Charter schools have been used as a union-busting tool. Since Mayor Michael Bloomberg gained control of the New York City Public school system in 2002, he and the Department of Education (formerly the Board of Education) have closed ninety-one schools, replacing them with smaller schools and charter schools. Bloomberg has also advocated changing New York State law so that more charter schools can be built in the city.[13]

An important lesson learned from the Teachers Union is that teachers cannot stand isolated in the fight to save public education. The TU's advocacy of teacher-parent cooperation is now being adopted by the United Federation of Teachers as a tactic to help stop the closing of public schools. In 2001 the UFT teamed up with Association of Community Organizations for Reform Now (ACORN) to stop Edison Learning Incorporated, a private corporation that receives contracts from municipalities to run their public schools, from running some of New York City's pubic schools. Starting under the leadership of UFT president Randi Weingarten, the union had worked to build stronger ties with parents. Each UFT borough office had a parent outreach staff person. The UFT joined with the Coalition for Educational Justice (CEJ), a parent-led organization fighting to end inequities in the public school system, and the Working Families Party to challenge the mayor's attempt to shut down public schools. In April 2007 the UFT and the CEJ met with Bloomberg and convinced him to include representatives from the union and parent group at Department of Education meetings discussing reorganization of the school system. The Department of Education also agreed to create a formal consultative process that would allow the UFT and parents to have input on school funding and other policy decisions.[14]

Not only has the UFT starting working with parent organizations, it has reached out to the civil rights community in New York to oppose the closing of schools. In early 2010, the UFT, the NAACP, and the Alliance for Quality Education, a New York State community-based group consisting of 230 organizations of parents, children advocates, teachers, clergy, and others, filed suit and halted Mayor Bloomberg and Chancellor of Schools Joel Klein from closing nineteen public schools, most of them in black and Latino areas. On March 26 Judge Joan B. Lobis of the State Supreme Court in Manhattan ruled that the Department of Education had violated a number of state laws governing mayoral control of the public schools, including a law mandating that details be provided on the impact closings would have on children and on other schools in the communities.[15] Despite efforts by the UFT, it still had not spelled out a clear plan to organize teachers, parents, and community groups to confront the wholesale attacks on public education.

The TU's support of a totalitarian regime that was responsible for the deaths of millions would leave a negative mark on its history. However, its history also consisted of a form of unionism that surpassed the model of seeking higher wages and improving working conditions for its members while remaining alienated from the communities where they taught. Rather, the TU created a form of unionism that worked to advance equality in schools and in the larger society. The union's vision embraced the possibility of creating a city and nation where all vestiges of social and economic injustice could be eliminated through a wider struggle, one that involved teachers, parents, and the communities they served.

NOTES

INTRODUCTION

1. These works include Philip Taft, *United They Teach: The Story of the United Federation of Teachers* (Los Angeles: Nash, 1974); William Edward Eaton, *The American Federation of Teachers, 1916–1961* (Carbondale: Southern Illinois University Press, 1975); Robert W. Iversen, *The Communists and the Schools: How the Communists Tried to Infiltrate the Schools and How the Schools Fought Back* (New York: Harcourt, Brace, 1959); and Bella Dodd, *School of Darkness* (New York: Kennedy, 1954).

2. These works include David Caute, *The Great Fear: The Anti-Communist Purge Under Truman and Eisenhower* (New York: Simon and Schuster, 1978); David Alison, *Searchlight: An Exposé of New York City Schools* (New York: Teachers Center, 1951); Celia Lewis Zitron, *The New York City Teachers Union, 1916–1964* (New York: Humanities, 1968).

3. National Coalition of Education Activists, "Social Justice Unionism: A Call to Education Activists" *Rethinking Schools* 9, no. 1 (Fall 1994).

4. Jerald Podair, *The Strike That Changed New York: Blacks, Whites, and the Ocean Hill-Brownsville Crisis* (New Haven: Yale University Press, 2002); Steve Golin, *The Newark Teachers Strikes: Hopes on the Line* (New Brunswick: Rutgers University Press, 2002); Ron Whitehorne, "The Philadelphia Federation of Teachers and the Black Community, a Troubled History," paper given at the Organization of American Historians, March 28, 2008, New York City.

5. Richard D. Kahlenberg, *Tough Liberal: Albert Shanker and the Battles Over Schools, Unions, Race, and Democracy* (New York: Columbia University Press, 2007), pp. 67–71.

6. Vincent J. Cannato, *The Ungovernable City: John Lindsay and His Struggle to Save New York* (New York: Basic Books, 2001), p. 281.

7. Ibid., pp. 283–88.

1. THE WAR WITHIN

1. Robert W. Iversen, *The Communists and the Schools: How the Communists Tried to Infiltrate the Schools and How the Schools Fought Back* (New York: Harcourt, Brace, 1959), p. 17.

2. Ibid., p. 20; William Edward Eaton, *The American Federation of Teachers, 1916–1961* (Carbondale: Southern Illinois University Press, 1975), pp. 89–99; testimony of Benjamin Mandel before the State of New York investigation into the educational system (Rapp-Coudert Committee hearings), January 18, 1941, pp. 22., Manuscript and Special Collections, New York State Library, Albany.

3. Philip Taft, *United They Teach: The Story of the United Federation of Teachers* (Los Angeles: Nash, 1974), p. 28.

4. Testimony of Henry R. Linville, Teachers' Union of the City of New York Records, box 25, folder 7, Kheel Center for Labor-Management Documentation and Archives, Cornell University Library.

5. Testimony of Ben Davidson before the State of New York investigation into the educational system (Rapp-Coudert Committee hearings), November 28, 1940, pp. 24–26; see Henry R. Linville, "A Study of Communist Tactics in a Trade Union," typescript (1936), 6, AFT Local 2 Papers (Accession 5279), box 2, folder 15, Teachers' Union of the City of New York Records.

6. Albert Fried, *Communism in America: A History in Documents* (New York: Columbia University Press, 1997), pp. 24–25.

7. Iversen, *The Communists and the Schools*, pp. 23–29.

8. Testimony of Benjamin Mandel, p. 5.

9. Testimony of Isidore Begun before the State of New York investigation into the educational system (Rapp-Coudert Committee hearings), October 28, 1941, pp. 5–6; Teachers Union executive board minutes, September 26, 1932, box 49, folder 9; Iversen, *The Communists and the Schools*, pp. 36–37.

10. Testimony of Isidore Begun, October 28, 1941, pp. 5–10

11. Testimony of Isidore Begun. The following were early members of the Rank and File who were public school teachers and asked by Begun if they were CP members: Williana Burroughs, Alice Citron, John Kenneth Ackely, David Goldway, William Olsen, Philip Horowitz, Meyer Case, Julius Metz, Frank Gross of Seward Park, Hyman Coppleman of Boys High School, Abraham Levin of P.S. 64, Max Diamond of Clinton H.S., Rapp-Courdert hearings; Begun would be fired because of his political activity. By 1939 he ran for a city council seat on the Communist Party ticket. For Begun, see Celia Lewis Zitron, *The New York City Teachers Union*, pp. 179–180; Iversen, *The Communists and the Schools*, pp. 42–46, 99–100. Steve Leberstein, "Morris Schappes: An Activist Life," *Clarion*, November 11, 2004, p. 11.

12. Testimony of Benjamin Mandel, p. 5; Ruth Jacknow Markowitz, *My Daughter, the Teacher: Jewish Teachers in the New York City Schools* (New Brunswick, NJ: Rutgers University Press, 1993), pp. 164–65.

13. Obituary of Alice Citron, *New York Times*, January 23, 1988; copy of Citron obituary, January 30, 1988, property of David Weiner; testimony of Benjamin Mandel.

14. Board of Education files, box 19, folder 5.

15. Celia Lewis Zitron, *The New York City Teachers Union, 1916–1964* (New York: Humanities, 1968), p. 15; Marjorie Murphy, *Blackboard Unions: The AFT and the NEA, 1900–1980* (Ithaca: Cornell University Press, 1990), pp. 152–153; Andrew Feffer, "The Presence of Democracy: Deweyan Exceptionalism and Communist Teachers in the 1930s," *Journal of the History of Ideas* 6, no. 1 (January 2005): 83.

16. Feffer, "The Presence of Democracy," p. 83; testimony of Ben Davidson, pp. 9–10.

17. Fried, *Communism in America*, pp. 93, 110.

18. Mark Solomon, *The Cry Was Unity: Communists and African Americans, 1917–1936* (Jackson: University Press of Mississippi, 1998), pp. 95–103.

19. Robert F. Pecorella, "Coping with Crises: The Politics of Urban Retrenchment," *Polity* 17, no. 2 (Winter 1984): 305–5.

20. Rank and File meeting, January 26, 1934, box 74, folder 2.

21. Ibid.

22. TU executive board minutes, February 3, November 3, 1934, box 49, folder 13. For Benjamin Davidson, see TU executive board minutes, September 16, 1932, box 49, folder 9.

23. TU executive board minutes, February 3, 1930, February 15, 1930, box 49, folder 6; April 9, 1932, box 49, folder 9; February 4, 1933, box 49, folder 12; February 3, 1934, box 49, folder 13.

24. "On Building the Union," Rank and File statement, May 2, 1934, box 74, folder 2.

25. Ibid.

26. Bella Dodd, *School of Darkness* (New York: Kennedy, 1954), chapter 6.

27. Ibid.

28. Testimony of Ben Davidson, pp. 30–31.

29. Fried, *Communism in America*, pp. 98–99; Mathew Worley, *In Search of Revolution: International Communist Parties in the Third Period* (New York: I. B. Tauris, 2004), pp. 9–11; Frank Warren, *Liberals and Communism: The Red Decade Revisited* (New York: Columbia University Press, 1993), p. 101.

30. TU executive board minutes, February 3, 1934, box 49, folder 17.

31. Program of the Rank and File for Immediate Action (no date), box 74, folder 2; Rank and File, "The Need for Unity of Issues Confronting Teachers," December 7, 1934, Meeting, box 74, folder 2.

32. Executive Board Minority Report Against Expulsions, box 74, folder 4a; Iversen, *The Communists and the Schools*, p. 37.

33. Executive Board Minority Report Against Expulsions, box 74, folder 4a; Taft, *United They Teach*, pp. 30–31.

34. Ibid.

35. The other committee members were Esther Gross, Max Kline, and Raphael Philipson. Special Report of the Joint Committee, October 27, 1932; Report of the Special Grievance Committee of the Teachers Union, April 29, 1933, box 74, folder 4a; Taft, *United They Teach*, p. 32.

36. Report of the Special Grievance Committee of the Teachers Union.

37. Ibid.

38. Ibid.

39. Executive Board Minority Report Against Expulsions, box 74, folder 4a.

40. Ibid.

41. Ibid.

42. Iversen, *The Communists and the Schools*, pp. 37–47.

43. Ibid.

44. Ibid., pp. 47–48.

45. Ibid., pp. 49–50.

46. Resolution for investigation of factional activities within the Teachers Union, adopted by the Executive Board, May 28, 1935.

47. Ibid. Members of the UCSU consisted of Louis J. Rosenthal, who was chair of the group, Meyer Case, secretary, A. J. Brooks, Majorie Cohen, Ben Davidson, Eve Davison, Bernice Everett, Louis Fein, Joseph Gallant, Morris J. Heller, Abe Lederman, Clara Rieber, May Shandalow, Rebecca Shapiro, Louis Shuker, Mollie Sobel, Erling Thollsen, Edith Vanderwoude, and David Wittes.

48. AFT Charter Revocation 1935, box 25, folder 7.

49. Transcript from hearing, Saturday June 7, 1935, box 25, folder 7, Teachers Union of the City of New York Records.

50. Ibid.

51. Ibid.

52. "The Case for Local Five," *Cleveland Teacher* 1, no. 11 (September 1935): 1–2, box 25, folder 7.

53. Ibid.

54. Ibid.

55. Ibid.

2. COMMUNIST FRONT?

1. Philip Taft, *United They Teach: The Story of the United Federation of Teachers* (Los Angeles: Nash, 1974), pp. 48–49.

2. Sidney C. Gould, "A History of the New York City Teachers Union and Why It Died," *Educational Forum* 29, no. 2 (January 1965): 207–15.

3. Taft, *United They Teach*, p. 44; William Edward Eaton, *The American Federation of Teachers, 1916–1961* (Carbondale: Southern Illinois University Press, 1975), p. 107.

4. Celia Lewis Zitron, *The New York City Teachers Union, 1916–1964* (New York: Humanities, 1968), p. 32; Lauri Johnson, "'Making Democracy Real, Teach': Teacher Union and Community Activism to Promote Diversity in the New York City Public Schools, 1935–1950," *Urban Education* 37, no. 5 (November 2002): 566–87.

5. Frazer M. Ottanelli, *The Communist Party of the United States from the Depression to World War II* (New Brunswick, NJ: Rutgers University Press, 1991), p. 50.

6. Harold Selig Roberts, *Roberts's Dictionary of Industrial Relations*, 4th ed. (Washington, D.C: Bureau of National Affairs, 1986) p. 518; Ottanelli, *The Communist Party*, p. 50.

7. Ottanelli, *The Communist Party*, pp. 51–55.

8. Ibid., p. 68.

9. Albert Fried, *Communism in America: A History in Documents* (New York: Columbia University Press, 1997), p. 228.

10. Ibid., p. 248.

11. Ibid., pp. 97–98, 232.

12. James G. Ryan, *Earl Browder: The Failure of American Communism* (Tuscaloosa: University of Alabama Press, 1997), pp. 72–80.

13. Teachers Union Rank and File meeting, December 7, 1934, box 74, folder 2; Mary Jo Buhle, Paul Buhle, and Dan Georgakas, *Encyclopedia of the American Left* (Urbana: University of Illinois Press, 1990), pp. 25–26; "Introduction to the American League for Peace and Democracy Records, 1933–1939," www.swarthmore.edu/library/peace/cdga.a—L/aplpd.htm—10k.

14. TU executive board minutes, May 28, 1935; United Committee to Save the Union, The Teachers' Union Gets Down to Work: A Busy Year Ahead for Us, 1935, box 74, folder 3.

15. Unity of teachers into the Teachers Union of the AFT, 1935, box, 74, folder 3.

16. TU executive board minutes, June 25, 1937, January 8, 1938, January 22, 1938, box 50, folder 1.

17. "The Independent" (n.d.), Hendley Papers, Tamiment Library, NYU.

18. Ibid. TU executive board minutes, June 25, 1937, October 29, 1938, box 50, folder 1; TU executive board minutes, January 27, 1939, box 50, folder 1; *New York Teacher*, June 1938; Buhle, Buhle, and Georgakas, *Encyclopedia of the American Left*, pp. 2–4.

19. "Building the Union," box 74, folder 3.

20. Ibid.

21. Ibid.; TU executive board minutes, June 4, 1937, box 50, folder 1; The Activity Program of Local 5 (n.d.), Hendley Papers, Tamiment Library, NYU.

22. TU executive board minutes, October 1, 1938, box 50, folder 1; Zitron, *The New York City Teachers Union*, pp. 78–79.

23. The Activity Program of Local 5; TU executive board meeting minutes, January 8, 1937; "Report of Committee on Resolutions to Be Presented to the Convention of the American Federation of Teachers," August 1938, box 25, folder 8.

24. "Report of Committee on Resolutions to be Presented to the Convention of the American Federation of Teachers,"August 1938.

25. TU executive board meeting minutes, May 21, 1937.

26. Ibid.

27. Ibid.

28. TU executive board meeting minutes, November 19, 1938; the Activity Program of Local 5.

29. TU executive board meeting minutes, January 8, 1937.

30. The Teachers Union Legislative Report (n.d), Hendley Papers, Tamiment Library, NYU.

31. Taft, *United They Teach*, pp. 44–47.

32. Ibid., p. 43; Judith Stepan-Norris and Maurice Zeitlin, *Left Out: Reds and America's Industrial Unions* (New York: Cambridge University Press, 2003), pp. 54–62.

33. Stepan-Norris and Zeitlin, *Left Out*, pp. 66–67.

34. Program Committee, September 2, 1935, box 74, folder 2.

35. Ibid.

36. Ibid.

37. TU executive board meeting minutes, September 30, 1935.

38. Statement of United Progressives, Teachers Union Election, 1936, box 74, folder 3.

39. Progressive Group Bulletin, November 1936, box 74, folder 3.

40. United Progressives, "The Program on Current Basic Union Problems (n.d.), Hendley Papers, Tamiment Library, NYU.

41. "Rank and File Meeting, Thursday, April 30, 1936," April 25, 1936, Hendley Papers, Tamiment Library, NYU.

42. Hendley to members, September 22, 1936, Hendley Papers, Tamiment Library, NYU.

43. Executive board minutes, June 4, 1937.

44. "Vote the Program That Built the Union: Vote the Majority Slate" (n.d), Hendley Papers, Tamiment Library, NYU.

45. Progressive Group Bulletin, December 1937, Hendley Papers, Tamiment Library, NYU.

46. Ibid.

47. Ibid., "Progressive Group Bulletin," January 7, 1938, Hendley Papers, Tamiment Library, NYU; "Vote the Program That Built the Union"; "The Independent," January 7, 1938, Hendley Papers, Tamiment Library, NYU.

48. Robert W. Iversen, *The Communists and the Schools: How the Communists Tried to Infiltrate the Schools and How the Schools Fought Back* (New York: Harcourt, Brace, 1959), pp. 99–100.

49. John Earl Haynes and Harvey Klehr's books include *The American Communist Movement: Storming Heaven Itself* (Woodbridge: Twayne, 1992); *The Secret World of American Communism* (New Haven: Yale University Press, 1996); *In Denial: Historians, Communism and Espionage* (San Francisco: Encounter, 2005); *Early Cold War Spies: The*

Espionage Trials That Shaped American Politics (New York: Cambridge University Press, 2006); *The Rise and Fall of the KGB in American* (New Haven: Yale University Press, 2009).

50. Haynes and Klehr, *In Denial,* pp. 2–8, 32–35.

51. Ibid., pp. 227–28.

52. Harvey Klehr, John Earl Haynes, and Fridrikh Igorevich Firsov, *The Secret World of American Communism* (New Haven: Yale University Press, 1995), pp. 14–15, 20–27, 81–82, 222–24, 232–49, 309–21.

53. John Earl Haynes and Harvey Klehr, *Venona: Decoding Soviet Espionage in America* (New Haven: Yale University Press, 1999), pp. 279, 372.

54. Ibid., pp. 279–80.

55. "New Yorkers Tied to Trotsky Killer," *New York Times,* December 5, 1950.

56. Klehr, Haynes, and Firsov, *The Secret World of American Communism,* pp. 199–202.

57. Committee on Un-American Activities, House of Representatives, July 26, August 30, October 18, 1950.

58. Ellen Schrecker, "History in Red—and White and Blue," *Radical History Review* 93 (Fall 2005): 159–69.

59. TU executive board minutes, January 8, 1937, May 21, 1937, June 4, 1937, October 14, 1937, November 19, 1938, January 14, 1939, box 50, folder 1; "Vote the Program That Build the Union"; Teachers Union Membership List, 1940, Rapp-Coudert Files, State Library of New York, Albany, New York.

3. THE FIGHT OVER REVOCATION

1. *New York Times,* August 22, 1939, p. 1.

2. Maurice Isserman, *Which Side Were You On? The American Communist Party During the Second World War* (Urbana: University of Illinois Press, 1993), pp. 32–33; James Kirby Martin, Steven Mints, Linda O. McMurry, and James H. Jones, *America and Its Peoples,* vol. 2: *From 1865* (New York: Pearson Longman, 2003), p. 701.

3. Isserman, *Which Side Were You On?* pp. 39–40.

4. William Edward Eaton, *The American Federation of Teachers, 1916–1961* (Carbondale: Southern Illinois University Press, 1975), pp.105–8.

5. Ibid. pp. 108–10; Paul William Preisler Papers, 1858–1972, www.umsl.edu/~whmc/guides/whm0235.htm.

6. In the Matter of the Investigation Into the Educational System of the State of New York Pursuant to Joint Resolution of the Senate and Assembly, adopted March 29, 1940, Simon Beagle testimony, Hearing, March 18, 1941; Philip Locker's Testimony, Hearing, March 20, 1941; Maurice Isserman, *Which Side Were You On?* p. 64.

7. Robert W. Iversen, *The Communists and the Schools: How the Communists Tried to Infiltrate the Schools and How the Schools Fought Back* (New York: Harcourt, Brace, 1959), pp. 115–116.

8. William Edward Eaton, *The American Federation of Teachers, 1916–1961* (Carbondale: Southern Illinois University Press, 1975), pp. 112–113.

9. Allen Rostron, "Inside the ACLU: Activism and Anti-Communism in the Late 1960s," *New England Law Review* 33–32 (Winter 1999): 430–31.

10. Statement of the Independent Group, May 1940, box 74, folder 4.

11. Ibid.

12. Ibid.

13. Eaton, *The American Federation of Teachers,* pp. 111–15.

14. "Two Teachers Union Face a Showdown," *New York Times,* September 22, 1940.

15. Ibid.

16. *New York Times,* September 23, 1940, p. 1.

17. Teachers Union, "Threat of Dual Unionism in the American Federation of Teachers," October 10, 1940, box 74, folder 4.

18. Ibid.

19. Isserman, *Which Side Were You On?* p. 42–43.

20. Teachers Union, "Threat of Dual Unionism."

21. Ibid.

22. Ibid.

23. AFT Executive Council Minutes, December 31, 1940, pp. 84–90; Statement of Local 5 on Proposed Revocation of Its Charter, box 25, folder 7A; Counts to Hendley, February 2, 1941, box 74, folder 4; Eaton, *The American Federation of Teachers,* pp. 115, 224, n. 123.

24. Ibid., pp. 115–16.

25. Statement of Local 5 on Proposed Revocation of Its Charter, 1941, box 25, folder 7A.

26. Ibid.

27. Ibid.

28. *American Teacher,* April 1941, p. 2; Eaton, *The American Federation of Teachers,* p. 117.

29. Eaton, *The American Federation of Teachers,* pp. 118–19.

30. Draft of a United and Effective AFT by Locals 5, 192, and 537, March 17, 1941, box 74, folder 4.

31. Ibid.

32. Robert Zieger and Gilbert J. Gall, *American Workers, American Unions* (Baltimore: Johns Hopkins University Press, 2002), pp. 114–15.

33. Draft of a United and Effective AFT.

34. Marjorie Murphy, *Blackboard Unions: The AFT and the NEA, 1900–1980* (Ithaca: Cornell University Press, 1990), pp. 170–71.

35. Martha Biondi, *Stand Up and Fight: The Struggle for Civil Rights in Postwar New York City* (Cambridge: Harvard University Press, 2003), pp. 28–29.

36. Draft of Constitution–Teachers Union, Local 555, United Public Workers of America, CIO, September 19, 1943, box 70, folder 7; Celia Lewis Zitron, *The New York City Teachers Union, 1916–1964* (New York: Humanities, 1968), pp. 38–42.

4. TO BE A GOOD AMERICAN

1. Martha Biondi, *Stand Up and Fight: The Struggle for Civil Rights in Postwar New York City* (Cambridge: Harvard University Press, 2003), pp. 243–244; Joshua Freeman, *Working Class New York* (New York: Free Press, 2000), pp. 72–74; *New York Teacher News,* October 9, 1943.

2. Freeman, *Working Class New York,* p. 73; *New York Teacher News,* October 9, 16, 1943.

3. 1940 New York City Teachers Membership List, Rapp-Coudert Files, State Library of New York, Albany, New York.

4. Leonard Dinnerstein, *Anti-Semitism in America* (New York: Oxford University Press, 1994), pp. 128–29; Ruth Jacknow Markowitz, *My Daughter, the Teacher: Jewish Teachers in the New York City Schools* (New Brunswick, NJ: Rutgers University Press, 1993), p. 163.

5. Dinnerstein, *Anti-Semitism in America,* pp. 129–31.

6. Robin D.G. Kelley, *Hammer and Hoe: Alabama Communists During the Great Depression* (Chapel Hill: University of North Carolina Press, 1990), pp. 13, 15, 17, 42–43; Mark Solomon, *The Cry Was Unity: Communists and African Americans, 1917–1936* (Jackson: University Press of Mississippi, 1998), p. 70; Daniel Perlstein, *Justice, Justice: School Politics and the Eclipse of Liberalism* (New York: Lang, 2004), p. 58.

7. Michael Denning, *The Cultural Front* (London: Verso, 1997), pp. 4–9.

8. Clarence Taylor, *Knocking at Our Own Door: Milton A. Galamison and the Struggle to Integrate New York City Schools* (New York: Columbia University Press, 1997), p. 62.

9. Doxey Wilkerson, "Caste in Education," *New York Teacher* 3, no. 6 (March 1938): 12–13.

10. Ibid.

11. Ibid.

12. *New York Teacher News,* October 2, 1943.

13. *New York Teacher News,* October 9, 1943.

14. *New York Teacher News,* October 2, 1943.

15. "Road to Victory," *New York Teacher News,* November 13, 20, 1944.

16. Ibid.

17. *New York Teacher News,* January 8, 1944.

18. "Road to Victory," *New York Teacher News,* November 13, 1943.

19. *New York Teacher News,* February 26, 1944.

20. *New York Teacher News,* January 22, 1944.

21. Ibid. "No Diploma for Anti-Semites," *New York Teacher News,* February 26, 1944.

22. Robert Michael Harris, "Teachers and Blacks: The New York City Teachers Union and the Negro, 1916–1964," M.A. thesis, Brooklyn College, 1971, p. 70; *New York Teacher News,* June 30, 1945; . Robert Michael Harris, "Teachers and Blacks: The New York City Teachers Union and the Negro, 1916-1964," M.A. thesis, Brooklyn

College, 1971, p. 70; TU, Pamphlet Schools to Victory, 1942, Hendley Papers, Tamiment Library, NYU.

23. *New York Teacher News,* January 22, 1944.

24. Teachers' Union, "Policy for the Teachers Union, 1941–1942," Hendley Papers, Tamiment Library, NYU.

25. Ibid.

26. "Teachers' Part in Victory for Democracy" (n.d.), Hendley Papers, Tamiment Library, NYU; "Education and National Defense" (n.d), Hendley Papers, Tamiment Library, NYU.

27. Seventh Annual Educational Conference, "Education for Victory in 1943," Hendley Papers, Tamiment Library, NYU.

28. Ibid.

29. *New York Teacher News,* January 15, 1944.

30. *New York Teacher News,* November 20, 1943.

31. *New York Teacher News,* November 6, 1943.

32. *New York Teacher News,* January 8, 1944, January 29, 1944.

33. Ibid., January 29, 1944.

34. Markowitz, *My Daughter, the Teacher,* p. 2.

35. Sheldon Spear, "The United States and the Persecution of the Jews in Germany, 1933–1939," *Jewish Social Studies* 30, no. 4 (October 1968): 215–42; "Immediate American Responses to the Nazi Book Burnings," *United States Holocaust Memorial Museum Encyclopedia,* 2009: http:www.ushmm.org//wlc/en/index.php?moduleid-=10005143.

36. Peter M. Carroll, *The Odyssey of the Abraham Lincoln Brigade: Americans in the Spanish Civil War* (Stanford: Stanford University Press, 1994), pp. 2, 14–18; Fraser Otanelli, "American Jews in the Spanish Civil War," in Stephen Norwood and Eunice C. Pollack, eds., *Encyclopedia of American Jewish History* (Santa Barbara: ABC-Clio: 2008), pp. 328–29.

37. *New York Teacher News,* June 1938; "Road to Victory," *New York Teacher News,* February 26, 1944.

38. Rachel Davis DuBois, *All This and Something More: Pioneering in Intercultural Education, An Autobiography* (Bryn Mawr: Dorrance, 1984), pp. 3–18.

39. Ibid.. pp. 30–34.

40. Ibid., 47–88; Barbara Diane Savage, *Broadcasting Freedom: Radio, War, and the Politics of Race, 1938–1948* (Chapel Hill: University of North Carolina Press, 1999), pp. 24–25.

41. *New York Teacher* 3, no. 9 (June 1938): 23.

42. Mary Milstein and Jenny L. Mayer, "Schools for Tolerance II," *New York Teacher News,* January 1939, pp. 10–11.

43. Ibid.

44. Ibid.

45. Harris, "Teachers and Blacks," pp. 71–76; Zitron, *The New York City Teachers Union,* pp. 94–96.

46. *New York Teacher News,* April 8, 1944.

47. *New York Teacher News,* June 30, 1945.

48. *New York Teacher News,* September 15, 1945.

49. *New York Teacher News,* April 1, 1944.

50. Harris, "Teachers and Blacks," p. 75.

51. Margaret M. Caffrey, *Ruth Benedict: Stranger in This Land* (Austin: University of Texas Press, 1984), pp. 282–84.

52. Ibid., pp. 284–86; Judith Schachter Modell, *Ruth Benedict: Patterns of Life* (Philadelphia: University of Pennsylvania, 1983), pp. 247–48.

53. Program, of the Annual Award of the Teachers Union, April 20, 1940, Hendley Papers; Harris, "Teachers and Blacks," p. 71.

54. *New York Teacher News,* November 20, 1943.

55. "Road to Victory," *New York Teacher News,* January 15, 1944.

56. Ute Gacs, Aisha Khan, Jerrie McIntyre, and Ruth Weinberg, *Women Anthropologists: A Biographical Dictionary* (New York: Greenwood, 1988), p. 376.

57. Ruth Benedict and Gene Weltfish, "The Races of Mankind," in Ruth Benedict, *Race: Science, and Politics* (New York: Viking, 1945), pp. 169–71.

58. Ibid., pp. 177–86.

59. Ibid., pp. 187–88.

60. Harris, "Teachers and Blacks," p. 73; *New York Teacher News,* December 18, 1943.

61. *New York Teacher News,* June 1938.

62. "Road to Peace," *New York Teacher News,* February 16, 1946.

63. Ibid.

5. THE OPENING SALVO

1. Some works are Madeleine Kalb, *Congo Cables: The Cold War in Africa from Eisenhower to Kennedy* (New York: Macmillan, 1982); Thomas Borstelmann, *The Cold War and the Color Line: American Race Relations in the Global Arena* (Cambridge: Harvard University Press, 2003); Odd Arne Westad, *The Global Cold War: Third World Interventions and the Making of Our Times* (New York: Cambridge University Press, 2007); Richard J. Aldrich, Gary D. Rawnsley, and Ming-Yeh T. Rawnsley, *The Clandestine Cold War in Asia, 1945–65* (New York: Routledge, 2000), and Michael Grow, *U.S. Presidents and Latin American Interventions: Pursuing Regime Change in the Cold War* (Lawrence: University Press of Kansas, 2008).

2. Abraham Lederman, testifying before the Taft-Hartley Committee in 1948, claimed that the union had fifty-six hundred members.

3. Teachers Union flyer, "The Case of Mr. Louis Jaffe," January 1, 1949, Hendley Papers, Tamiment Library, NYU; brief submitted by Louis Jaffe to Assistant Superintendent Moskowitz, June 17, 1948, Hendley Papers, Tamiment Library, NYU.

4. Brief submitted by Louis Jaffe to Assistant Superintendent Moskowitz of the High School Division, June 12, 1948; documents no. 1, Observation Report Made

by Mr. Glassman of Mr. Jaffe's Lesson on the Veto Power, March 23, 1948, Hendley Papers, Tamiment Library, NYU.

5. Ibid.

6. Documents no. 2, Observation Report Made by Mr. Glassman of Mr. Jaffe's Lesson on the Atomic Bomb, March 24, 1948, Hendley Papers, unprocessed collection, Tamiment Library, NYU. The Baruch Plan called for the exchange among nations of scientific information for peaceful purposes, limiting atomic energy to only peaceful means, destroying atomic weapons meant for mass destruction, as well as using inspections and other ways to safeguard against violations. Bernard Baruch, "The Baruch Plan" (presented to the United Nations Atomic Energy Commission, June 14, 1946), www.streitcouncil.org/content/pdf_and_doc/the20Baruch%20plan.pdf. The Gromyko Plan called for an international convention to ban atomic weapons and for an international agreement that would punish violators. The plan also called for the creation of a United Nations committee to investigate ways nations could exchange scientific data in the nuclear field and another UN committee to work on ways to ensure that nations would not violate the agreement. Moreover, the Gromyko Plan called for the destruction of all atomic weapons within three months after a nation signed it. See Harralambos Athanasopulos, *Nuclear Disarmament in International Law* (Jefferson, NC: McFarland, 2000), pp. 11–12.

7. Brief Submitted by Jaffe to Assistant Superintendent Moskowitz, June 17, 1948, Hendley Papers, Tamiment Library, NYU.

8. Ibid.

9. Document no. 4, Mr. Jaffe's Formal Objections to Mr. Glassman's Observation Reports, May 19, 1948, Hendley Papers, Tamiment Library, NYU.

10. Document no. 6, Mr. Glassman Requests the Notebook of Mr. Jaffe's Classes, May 20, 1948, Hendley Papers, Tamiment Library, NYU.

11. Document no. 7, Mr. Glassman Files Answer Defending his Observation Reports and Makes Further Accusations Against Mr. Jaffe, May 24, 1947. (Although the date was listed 1947, it was 1948.)

12. Document no. 8, Mr. Jaffe's Reply to Mr. Glassman's Letter on May 24, 1948, Hendley Papers, Tamiment Library, NYU.

13. Ibid.

14. Document no. 9, Dr. Lefkowitz's reply to Mr. Jaffe's Letter on May 24, 1948, Hendley Papers, Tamiment Library, NYU.

15. Document no. 19, Mr. Glassman's Letter to Mr. Jaffe, Accusing Him of Conducting a Whispering Campaign, June 11, 1948, Hendley Papers, Tamiment Library, NYU; "The Mundt-Nixon Bill," Karl Mundt Archives, Dakota State University, Karl Munt Library, 2004.

16. Ibid.

17. Document no. 11, Mr. Jaffe's Reply to Dr. Lefkowitz's Letter of June 9," June 16, 1948, Hendley Papers, Tamiment Library, NYU.

18. Document no. 12, Dr. Lefkowitz Reply to Mr. Jaffe's Letter of June 16, June 17, 1948, Hendley Papers, Tamiment Library, NYU.

19. Brief Submitted by Mr. Louis Jaffe to Assistant Superintendent Moskowitz of the High School Division, June 17, 1948; document no. 13, Mr. Jaffe's Reply to Lefkowitz's Letter of June 18, 1948, Hendley Papers, Tamiment Library, NYU.

20. Document no. 14, Mr. Jaffe's Addition to His June 17, 1948, Brief Submitted to Assistant Moscowitz, June 28, 1948, Hendley Papers, Tamiment Library, NYU.

21. Ibid.

22. Document no. 15, Mr. Jaffe's Letter to Dr. Jansen Urging That Action on His Transfer Be Deferred Pending a Formal Hearing, June 28, 1948, Hendley Papers, Tamiment Library, NYU.

23. Brief Submitted by the Teachers' Union in Behalf of Mr. Louis Jaffe, Teachers of Social Studies at Samuel J. Tilden High School, June 28, 1948, Hendley Papers, Tamiment Library, NYU.

24. Document no. 16, Petition Signed by Approximately Half of the Faculty of Mr. Jaffe's School, protesting his transfer, June 29, 1948, Hendley Papers, Tamiment Library, NYU.

25. Document no. 17, Jansen's Reply to the Brief Submitted by the Teachers Union on June 28, 1948, July 9, 1948, Hendley Papers, Tamiment Library, NYU.

26. Document no. 18, The Teachers Union's Reply to Dr. Jansen's Letter of July 9, August 25, 1948; document no. 19, Mr. Jaffe's Reply to Dr. Jansen's Letter of July 9, August 25, 1948, Hendley Papers, Tamiment Library, NYU.

27. Documents no. 20, Copy of Letter of Recommendation Written by Glassman on February 5, 1948, Hendley Papers, Tamiment Library, NYU; *New York Times*, October 13, 1948.

28. Abraham Lefkowitz, "My Last Will and Testament on the Teachers' Union and the Jaffe Case," October 11, 1948, Hendley Papers, Tamiment Library, NYU.

29. Ibid.

30. Ibid.

31. Rose Russell, "Open Letter to Dr. William Jansen," October 11, 1948, box 10, folder 2.

32. *New York Times*, October 14, 1948.

33. Teachers' Union, "The Case of Mr. Louis Jaffe: A Threat to Security, Tenure and Academic Freedom of All Teachers," January 14, 1948, Hendley Papers, Tamiment Library, NYU.

34. Ibid.

35. Ibid.

36. Statement on the forthcoming Hartley Committee investigation presented by Mrs. Rose Russell, legislative representative, adopted at the membership meeting of the Teachers Union, September 17, 1948, box 10, folder 3.

37. Ibid.

38. TU Press Release, September 18, 1948, box 10, folder 3; Hearings Before a Special Subcommittee of the Committee on Education and Labor, House of Representatives, Eightieth Congress, Second Session Pursuant to H. Res. 11, September 27–30, October 1 and 19, 1948.

39. Hearings Before a Special Subcommittee of the Committee on Education and Labor, House of Representatives, Eightieth Congress, Second Session, Pursuant to H. Res. 11, September 27–30, October 1 and 19, 1948.

40. Ibid.

41. Ibid.

42. Ibid.

43. Bella Dodd's testimony before the Taft-Hartley Subcommittee, 1948.

44. Abraham Lederman's testimony before the Subcommittee of the House Committee on Education and Labor.

45. Ibid.

46. Ibid.

47. Ibid.

48. Ibid.

49. Rose Russell's Testimony before the Subcommittee of the House Committee on Education and Labor.

50. Ibid.

51. Ibid.

52. Ibid.

53. Ibid.

54. Ibid.

55. *New York Times*, September 29, 1948.

56. Ibid.

57. *New York Times*, October 2, 1948.

58. Ibid.

59. Ibid.

60. TU leaflet, "Support the Teacher Who Is Defending the Bill of Rights;" Russell Letter, October 8 1948, box 10, folder 3.

61. *New York Times*, December 25, 1948.

62. Ibid.

63. Rose Russell, "To All Members of the Board of Education and the Superintendent of Schools," December 24, 1948 (a copy of Gutride's letter to Jansen was included in her letter to board members), box 11, folder 11.

64. *New York Times*, December 25, 1948.

65. Russell, "To All Members of the Board of Education."

66. *New York Times,* December 25, 1948.

67. Russell to O'Dwyer, December 27, 1948; press release, December 27, 1949, box 11, folder 7.

68. Russell and Lederman's press release, December 28, 1948; Russell to friend, December 30, 1948, box 11, folder 7.

69. Lederman and Russell, "A New Year's Message to the Superintendent of Schools and Members of the Board of Education," December 31, 1948, box 11, folder 7.

6. THE FIRST WAVE OF SUSPENSIONS AND DISMISSALS

1. *New York Sun*, December 27, 1948; *New York Times*, December 28, 1948.
2. Lederman to Jansen, January 8, 1949, box 11, folder 7.
3. *New York Teacher News*, March 12, 1949, March 19, 1949.
4. *New York Teacher News*, March 19, 1949.
5. *New York Times*, April 3, 1949; David Caute, *The Great Fear: The Anti-Communist Purge Under Truman and Eisenhower* (New York: Simon and Schuster, 1978), p. 342; Marjorie Heins, "A Pall of Orthodoxy: The Painful Persistence of Loyalty Oaths," *Dissent* (Summer 2009): 67–68.
6. *New York Times*, May 18, 1949.
7. Text of Jansen Order on Teacher-Loyalty Reports, *New York Times*, September 13, 1949.
8. In March 1952 the Supreme Court found in Adler v. Board of Education that section 3022 of the state education law, added by the Feinberg Law, found no unconstitutional infirmity, Adler v. Board of Education, 342 US 485 (1952). It would not be until January 1967 in Keyishian v. Board of Regents that the Supreme Court ruled that Feinberg was unconstitutional, Keyishian v. Board of Regents (no. 105) 514 U.S. 673.
9. *New York Times*, May 3, 1949.
10. Ibid.
11. Ibid.
12. Schneiderman to Jansen, January 3, 1950, box 16, folder 2.
13. Schneiderman to Greenberg, March 7, 1950, box 16, folder 2.
14. Ibid.
15. Russell to Jansen, March 9, 1950, box 16, folder 2.
16. TU Press Release, March 9, 1950, box 16, folder 2.
17. P.S. 3 Teachers' Interest Committee to Moss, March 16, 1950, box 16, folder 2.
18. Ibid.
19. Edwin Smith to editor of the *New York Times*, March 17, 1950.
20. Simonson to Jansen, March 3, 1950, Teachers College; Simonson to Jansen, March 11, 1950., box 16, folder 2.
21. Russell's letter to "Friend," March 18, 1950, box 16, folder 2.
22. Russell's letter to "Friend," March 24, 1950, box 16, folder 2.
23. Edwin Smith to the editor of the *New York Times*, March 24, 1950, box 16, folder 2.
24. Cammer to Jansen, April 22, 1950, box 16, folder 2.
25. Material for Questioning of Seven Teachers, Monday, April 24, 1950, New York City Board of Education Archives, Special Collections, Teachers College, Columbia University, #750300, box 19, folder 5.
26. *New York Times*, April 25, 1950; Jansen to the Board of Education, May 3, 1950, Charles Bensely Papers, New York City Board of Education Archives, Teachers College,

Columbia University, box 4, folder 63; *New York Times*, May 4, 1950; Rose Russell, "Statement Requesting Rejection of Charges and Reinstatement of Eight Teachers, for Presentation at Board of Education Meeting," May 9, 1950.

27. Jansen to the Board of Education, May 3, 1950, Charles Bensley Papers, New York City Board of Education Archives, Teachers College, Columbia University, box 4, folder 63; *New York Times*, May 4, 1950, May 9, 1950; Rose Russell, "Statement Requesting Rejection of Charges and Reinstatement of Eight Teachers, for Presentation at Board of Education Meeting," May 9, 1950, folder 17, box 11.

28. *New York Times*, May 5, 1950

29. Ibid.

30. *New York Times*, May 5, 1950.

31. TU Leaflet, "Actions That Your Organization Should Take on the Suspensions," Hendley Papers, Tamiment Library, NYU.

32. Edel to Moss, May 7, 1950, box 17, folder 11; Celia Lewis Zitron, *The New York City Teachers Union, 1916–1964* (New York: Humanities, 1968), p. 230.

33. Chair of the Legislative Committee of the Parent Teacher Association JHS 115, Manhattan, box 21, folder 10; Corresponding Secretary of the PTA of P.S. 86, Copper to the Board of Education, Parent Teachers Association of P.S. 150, Brooklyn, box 21, folder 10.

34. Shapiro to Jansen, May 26, 1950; Dranow letter to colleagues, June 12, 1950, box 21, folder 10.

35. Excerpts from letters sent by individuals and organizations in foreign countries to Mr. Maximilian Moss protesting suspension of eight teachers, box 19, folder 2.

36. Other letters included the New South Wales Teacher Federation, which argued that public school teachers had a right to job security and promotion solely on the grounds of service and personal capacity, regardless of their political beliefs and affiliation. One of the most critical letters came from V. Romunny, general secretary of the Madras State Elementary School Teachers Federation: "It is a pity that authorities in the United States which claims at the top of its voice and propagates throughout the educational system in India through its Embassy and consulates about the infallibility of American democracy, about the protection of civil liberties and individual rights and above all the American way of life, has begun their persecution against the teaching profession, whose only fault is that they courageously decided to uphold their freedom of conscience by refusing to answer their political believes and affiliations." Ibid.

37. TU, *What Kind of Teachers for Your Child: The Facts Behind the Suspension of Eight Excellent Teachers*, May 5, 1950.

38. Ibid.

39. TU leaflets, "No Racial, Religious, Political Tests for Teachers," May 1950; "Your Children Have Lost Eight of Their Best Teachers," May 1950, Hendley Papers, Tamiment Library, NYU.

40. TU, *Teachers on Trial*, October 1950, Hendley Papers, Tamiment Library, NYU.

41. J. Edgar Hoover's testimony before the House Committee on Un-American Activities, Hearings on H.R. 1884 and H.R. 2122, Eightieth Congress, First Session, March 26, 1947, in Ellen Schrecker, *The Age of McCarthysim: A Brief History with Documents* (Boston: St. Martin's, 1994), p. 119.

42. John McGrath, "Matter of Dismissal of Teachers Based on Their Membership in the Communist Party," New York City Board of Education Archives, Teachers College, Columbia University, box 27, folder 3; Schrecker, *The Age of McCarthyism*, pp. 41–44.

43. McGrath, "Matter of Dismissal of Teachers."

44. Ibid.

45. *New York Times*, May 29, 1950; Special Meeting of the Board of Education, June 12, 1950, Teachers College, Columbia University.

46. Opening Statement by Hon. John P. McGrath, Corporation Counsel of the City of New York at the Departmental Trial of David L. Friedman, September 18, 1950, box 18.

47. Ellen Schrecker, *No Ivory Tower: McCarthyism and the Universities* (New York: Oxford University Press, 1986), pp. 94–103.

48. Raymond Allen, "Communists Should Not Teach in American Colleges," *Educational Forum* 13, no. 4, May 1949.

49. Danny Postel, "Sidney Hook, an Intellectual Street Fighter," in *Chronicles of Higher Education*, November 8, 2002; Ronald Radosh, "Sidney Hook Was Right, Arthur Schlesinger Is Wrong," *New York Sun*, December 16, 2002.

50. Ibid.

51. Testimony of Sidney Hook before the Rapp-Coudert Committee, May 1941, Rapp-Coudert Files.

52. Sidney Hook, "Should Communists Be Permitted to Teach?" *New York Times*, February 27, 1949.

53. Ibid.

54. McGrath, "Matter of Dismissal of Teachers."

55. Ibid.

56. Ibid.

57. Ibid.

58. TU pamphlet, *The Test of a Teacher: Professional Excellence or Political Conformity?* (n.d); "In the Matter of Charges Referred by William Jansen, Superintendent of Schools, Against David L. Friedman, a Teacher of P.S. 64," Manhattan trial memorandum in support of charges, box 18; *Tablet,* August 24, 1947.

59. "In the Matter of Charges Referred by William Jansen."

60. Ibid.

61. Ibid.

62. TU, *The Test of a Teacher.*

63. Statement by Mrs. Rose Russell. The statement is included in TU, *The Test of a Teacher,* pp. 5–27.

64. Ibid.

65. Ibid.

66. Ibid.

67. "In the Matter of Charges Referred by William Jansen."

68. Ibid.

69. Ibid.

70. Ibid.

71. Ibid.

72. Ibid.

73. TU, *What Kind of Teachers for Your Child.*

74. TU, *Teachers Fight for Freedom: Eight New York City Teachers on Trial* (1950), pp. 18–26.

75. "In the Matter of the Trial of the Charges Proferred by Dr. William Jansen, Superintendent of Schools, Against Mrs. Celia L. Zitron"; "In the Matter of the Trial of the Charges Preferred by Dr. William Jansen, Superintendent of Schools, Against Louis Jaffe; "In the Matter of the Trial of the Charges Preferred by Dr. William Jansen, Superintendent of Schools, Against Mr. Abraham Lederman"; "In the Matter of the Trial of the Charges Preferred by Dr. William Jansen, Superintendent of Schools, Against Miss Alice Citron"; "In the Matter of the Trial of the Charges Preferred by Dr. William Jansen, Superintendent of Schools, Against Mr. Abraham Feingold"; In the Matter of the Trial of the Charges, Preferred by Dr. William Jansen, Superintendent of Schools, Against Isadore Rubin"; "In the Matter of the Trial of the Charges Preferred by Dr. William Jansen, Superintendent of Schools, Against Mark Freidlander; TU," *Teachers Fight for Freedom*, pp. 7–8, Zitron, *New York City Teachers Union*, p. 236.

7. BANNING SUBVERSIVES

1. "Records of the Eight Suspended Teachers," subject files, box 17, folder 8.

2. Memo, Moskoft to Jansen, April 1, 1955, box 17, folder 7.

3. *New York Times*, March 8, 1946; Celia Lewis Zitron, *The New York City Teachers Union, 1916–1964* (New York: Humanities, 1968), p. 201.

4. *New York Times*, March 15, 1946; a copy of the leaflet is in David Alison, *An Expose of New York City Schools* (New York: Teachers Center Press, 1951), p. 27.

5. *New York Times*, March 19, March 21, 1946.

6. *New York Times*, April 9, 1946.

7. *New York Times*, June 23, 28, 1945.

8. *New York Times*, July 25, 26, 1945.

9. *New York Times*, January 3, 1946

10. *New York Times*, December 19, 31, 1945.

11. *New York Times*, October 13, 1942.

12. *New York Times*, June 17, 1946.

13. *New York Times*, October 13, 1946.

14. *New York Times*, February 20, 27, 1947.

15. *New York Times*, October 14, 21, 1947.

16. *New York Times*, October 23, 24, 1947.

17. *New York Times*, October 24, 1947.

18. Ibid.

19. Ibid.

20. *New York Times*, October 29, 1947; December 14, 1946.

21. Ibid.

22. *New York Times*, November 3, 1947.

23. *New York Times*, January 21, 1949.

24. Sergey Mamay, "Theories of Social Movements and Their Current Development in Soviet Society," http://lucy.ukc.ac.uk/casacpub/russian/mamay.html.

25. Robert H. Zieger, *The CIO, 1935–1955* (Chapel Hill: University of North Carolina Press, 1995), pp. 253–61.

26. Ibid., pp. 271–90.

27. Iushewutz to O'Dwyer, March 1, 1950, Special Collections, Milbank Library, Teachers College, Columbia University; *New York Times*, March 11, 1950.

28. Hillard to staff, March 9, 1950; *World-Telegram and Sun*, March 10, 1950.

29. Joint Resolution on Teachers Union–UPW, Local 555, March 10, 1950, Special Collections, Milbank Library, Teachers College, Columbia University.

30. Joint Committee Against Communism's Press Release, "All Veteran Organizations Band Together to Demand Board of Education Withdraw Recognition of CIO-Ousted Teachers Union Are Joined by Civic Leaders," March 13, 1950, Special Collections, Milbank Library, Teachers College, Columbia University.

31. *New York Daily Mirror*, March 14, 1950.

32. Memorandum, Timone to All Members of the Board of Education, Superintendent of Schools, Associate Superintendent Greenberg, Law Secretary, March 14, 1950, Special Collections, Milbank Library, Teachers College, Columbia University.

33. Memorandum, Timone to All Board of Education Members, Jansen, Dr. Greenberg, Law Secretary, March 15, 1950, Special Collections, Milbank Library, Teachers College, Columbia University.

34. Memorandum, Timone to All Members of the Board of Education, March 20, 1950, Special Collections, Milbank Library, Teachers College, Columbia University.

35. Russell to Frederick McLaughlin, April 12, 1950, box 29, folder 2.

36. Resolution on the Right of Teachers to Join Organizations of Their Own Choice, March 17, 1950, box 16, folder 2.

37. Lederman, Russell, Zitron, and Samuel Greenfield to colleague, March 22, 1950, box 22, folder 2.

38. Addresses Made at the Meeting of the Board of Education on April 6, 1950, in Re: Item no. 26, Banning Teachers Union, Bensely Papers, Special Collections, Milbank Library, Teachers College, Columbia University.

39. Ibid.; William A. Barry to Charles Bensley, Charles Bensley Papers, Special Collections, Milbank Library, Teachers College, Columbia University.

40. Addresses made at the meeting of the Board of Education on April 6, 1950, Special Collections, Milbank Library, Teachers College, Columbia University.

41. Ibid.

42. Ibid.

43. Ibid.

44. Ibid.

45. Ibid.

46. Ibid.; Julius Bernstein to Charles J. Bensley, April 5, 1950, box 29, folder 2; copies of resolutions and statements against the Timone Resolution already adopted by teachers and faculties, box 29, folder 2.

47. Addresses Made at the Meeting of the Board of Education, April 6, 1950, in Re: Item # 26, Banning Teachers Union, in Charles Bensley Papers, Special Collections, Milbank Memorial Library, Teachers College, Columbia University.

48. Ibid.

49. Ibid.

50. Addresses Made at the Meeting of the Board of Education on April 6, 1950, in Re: Item # 26, Banning Teachers Union, Charles Bensley Papers, Special Collections, Milbank Library, Teachers College, Columbia University.

51. Speakers against the resolution included Arthur Garfield Hays of the ACLU, who said that the resolution was a "denial of the right of workers to negotiate through representatives of their own choosing," Frederick McLaughlin of the Public Education Association, Rabbi May Felshin of the Radio Synagogue, Rabbi Jonah Caplan, ministers, a state assemblyman, and a city council member. Lederman, Russell, Lewis, and Greenfield to union member, April 12, 1950, box 29, folder 2; *Tablet*, April 7, 1950,

52. Addresses made at the meeting of the Board of Education, on April 6, 1950, Special Collections, Milbank Library, Teachers College, Columbia University.

53. Ibid.

54. Ibid.

55. Statement by Rose Russell, legislative representative, on the Timone Resolution, April 6, 1950, box 29, folder 2.

56. Ibid.

57. Ibid.

58. Ibid.

59. Ibid.

60. Julius Bernstein to Charles J. Bensley, April 5, 1950; Resolution, P.S. 116, Brooklyn to Bensley, April 19, 1950, box 29, folder 2; Shirely Weinraub to Bensley, April 25, 1950, E. Roathman, April 25, 1950, box 29, folder 2; Julius Lemansky to Bensley, May 1, 1950, Special Collections, Milbank Memorial Library, Teachers College, Columbia University; Yetta Hoffman to Bensley, May 9, 1950, Special Collections, Milbank Library, Teachers College, Columbia University; Eugene Jackson to Moss, May 10, 1950; Faculty Association of P.S 184, May 30; Lionel Burrow to Bensley, May 30, 1950; Rebecca Solinger to Bensley, May 31, 1950; Julius Lemansky to Bensley, May 1; Teachers Council of P.S. 61 to Sir, May 31, 1950, Special Collections, Milbank Memorial Library; Teachers College, Columbia University; Teachers Interest Committee of P.S. 106 to Bensley (n.d.); Natanial Em to Bensley, May 22, 1950; Yetta

Hoffman to Bensley, May 9, 1950, Special Collections, Milbank Library, Teachers College, Columbia University.

61. *New York World-Telegram and Sun,* April 16, 1950.

62. Alexander Hamilton Vocational High School to Moss, May 4, 1950; Jessie Bolton to Bensley, May 6, 1950; Myra G. Fleming to Bensley, May 18, 1950, Charles Bensley Papers, Special Collections, Teachers College, Columbia University.

63. Lederman to Delegates, April 28, 1950, box 29, folder 2; Margaret Demarist to Bensely, May 26, 1950; Francis D. Vougcut to Bensley, May 26, 1950; Lillian Deinall to Bensley, May 26, 1950, Bensley Papers, Special Collections, Teachers College, Columbia University.

64. Memo to Bensley from Moss, on Postcards from April 29 to May 23, Urging Defeat of The Timone Resolution, (n.d.), Special Collections, Teachers College, Columbia University.

65. Resolution Adopted by the Board of Education at Meeting Held on June 1, 1950, no. 750300, box 10, folder 10, Special Collections; Dissenting Statement by Charles Bensley in Voting Against the Timone Resolution, June 1, 1950, box 29, folder 1; *New York Times,* June 2, 1950.

66. Lederman to delegates, June 3, 1950, box 29, folder 2.

67. Lederman and Russell to friend, June 8, 1950, box 29, folder 2.

8. ANTI-SEMITISM

1. Subject Files Related to Hearings, box 17, folder 7, Teachers College, Columbia University.

2. David Alison, *Searchlight: An Expose of New York City Schools* (New York: Teachers Center Press, 1951), p. 280.

3. New York City Teachers Union Papers, box 21, folder 5.

4. New York City Teachers Union Papers, box 21, folder 5, box 15, folder 5.

5. "Rotten Kike," letter, box 21, folder 5; Dear Fellow Rabbi, box 15, folder 5.

6. "Damn Them," New York City Teachers Union Papers, box 21, folder 5.

7. In another letter emphasizing the disloyalty of Jews, a letter writer called the suspended teachers a "bunch of lousy troublesome Jews" and asked "why the hell don't you go to Russia?" Even Jewish refugees to the United States were "constantly bitching about something." The writer added: "and if they don't get it they yell, Hate, Bigot, Anti-Semite etc." Jews were "crying persecution," but, despite the fact that they obtained decent jobs, attempted to "betray us" by delivering the country into the hands of the Soviet Union; they "ruin" the minds of American children by touting the "glories of Russia. [I] would hang everyone of you." "Why do so many Jews go for Communism?" one hate writer queried Mildred Grossman in 1952, after her suspension was made public. "Joe [Stalin] doesn't like Jews anymore than Adolph [Hitler] did. And if Communism is so nice why don't you Jews flock into Russia instead of wanting to live in America?" New York City Teachers Union papers, box 15, folder 5.

8. Letter to Minnie [Minna] Finkelstein (n.d); Letter to Mildred Grossman (n.d.), box 15, folder 5.

9. Ann Knight, American mother, box 21, folder 5.

10. Ibid.

11. The American Jewish Committee Thirty-Fifth Annual Report (1942), p. 5. www.ajcarchives.org/AJC—DATA/1942_1943_9_AJCAnnualreport.pdf.

12. Press release, March 9, 1950, box 16, folder 2.

13. Flyer for March 16 hearing, box 16, folder 2.

14. Russell to Dr. Richard B. Kennan, March 20, 1950; Russell to Virginia Kinnaird, March 20, 1950; Russell to James A. Cullen, March 21, 1950; Russell to Philip Wardner, March 21, 1950; Russell to Nathaniel Kaplan, March 20, 1950, box 16, folder 2.

15. Author's interview with Ann Filardo, New York, March 7, 2007.

16. Edel to Moss, May 7, 1950, box 17, folder 11.

17. B. Z. Goldberg, "Questions to the Suspended Teachers," *Day*, May 24, 1950.

18. *What Kind of Teachers for Your Child: The Facts Behind the Suspension of 8 Excellent Teachers,* May 1950.

19. Ibid.

20. Parents to Jansen, May, 1950, box 21, folder 10.

21. Lederman to colleagues, March 22, 1950, box 16, folder 2.

22. *New York Times,* May 5, 1950.

23. Ibid.

24. Lester J. Waldman to Russell, May 5, 1950, box 17, folder 11.

25. Russell to Waldman, May 19, 1950, box 17, folder 11.

26. Jansen to Russell, May 10, 1950, box 17, folder 11.

27. Waldman to Russell, June 5, 1950, box 17, folder 11.

28. Russell to Benjamin G. Browdy, June 3, 1950, box 17, folder 11.

29. Ibid.

30. Browdy to Russell, June 14, 1950, box 17, folder 11.

31. Jewish Teacher Association letter to H. Katzen, March 3, 1952, box 1, folder 5.

32. Alexander Eiseman to Abraham Lederman, June 14, 1950, box 19, folder 3.

33. Ibid.

34. Ibid.

35. Ibid.

36. Leonard Dinnerstein, *Anti-Semitism in America* (New York: Oxford University Press, 1994), pp. 150–51.

37. Jonathan Sarna, *American Judaism: A History* (New Haven: Yale University Press, 2004), pp. 276–78.

38. American Jewish League Against Communism, *Newsletter*, 1951, box 12, folder 4; Ellen Schrecker, *Many Are the Crimes: McCarthyism in America* (Boston: Little, Brown, 1998), p. 44; American Jewish Committee, *American Jewish Year Book* (New York: Stratford, 1952).

39. American League Against Communism, *Newsletter*, 1951.

40. Ibid.

41. "Whenever an anti-Communist action is taken the Reds call it anti-Semitic or anti-Negro or both. Against the propaganda is that any campaign against Communists is directed against Jews. Do you realize how essentially anti-Semitic in effect such propaganda is?" "Teachers Union Give Support to Red Charge," *Tablet*, April 4, 1950.

42. Gerald Smith was the presidential candidate for the America First Party. After World War II Smith created the Christian Nationalist Party.

43. TU Press Release, "Comment by Mrs. Rose Russell, Legislative Representative in Behalf of Teachers Union, Replying to the Vilification by Ex-Rabbi Schultz and His Collaborators," March 13, 1950, box 16, folder 2.

44. Sylvia Sternberg, June 6, 1950, box 17, folder 11.

45. Russell to Sternberg, June 7, 1950, box 17, folder 11.

46. Ervin Wagner to Maximilian Moss, April 4, 1950, box 16, folder 2.

47. Matt Vincent to Rose Russell, April 7, 1950, box 16, folder 2.

48. *Tablet*, April 4, 1950.

49. *Tablet*, January 29, 1950.

50. "Teachers Union Meets Set-Back in Perjury Case," *Tablet*, March 25, 1950.

51. *Leonard Dinnerstein, Anti-Semitism in America*, p. 12.

52. "Father Charles E. Coughlin, the Radio Priest," *Detroit News; Rearview Mirror,* July 23, 1995, apps/history/index.php?.id=43.

53. "From the Desk of the Managing Editor," *Tablet*, February 25, 1950.

54. *Tablet*, March 18, 1950.

55. "Ten Jewish Groups Oppose a Loan," *Tablet*, October 10, 1950.

56. Ibid.

57. "From the Desk of the Managing Editor," *Tablet*, August 19, 1950.

58. Ibid., September 2, 1950.

59. Ibid., October 7, 1950.

60. Ibid., March 18, 1950.

61. "Teachers Union Give Support to Red Charge," *Tablet*, April 1, 1950.

62. Ibid.

63. "Teachers Openly Adhered to Red Polices," *Tablet*, June 17, 1950.

64. "Accused Teacher Refuses Change for Free Speech," *Tablet*, October 14, 1950.

65. Gary Gerstle, *American Crucible: Race and Nation in the Twentieth Century* (Princeton: Princeton University Press, 2001), pp. 4–7, 246–47; Barbara Ransby, *Ella Baker and the Black Freedom Movement: A Radical Democratic Vision* (Chapel Hill: University of North Carolina Press, 2003), p. 159.

66. Godfrey Hodgson, *America in Our Time* (New York: Vintage, 1976), pp. 72–90.

9. UNDERCOVER AGENTS, INFORMERS, AND COOPERATING WITNESSES

1. Dune and Blauvelt to Moskoff, April 22, 1957, box 17, folder 7.

2. Ibid., unsigned letter, 1957, box 17, folder 7.

3. Ibid.

4. Memo, Dunne and Blauvelt to Moskoff, April 22, 1957, subject files, box 1, folder 13.

5. Material for Questioning of Seven Teachers, April 24, 1950, subject files, box 19, folder 5.

6. Ibid.

7. Ibid.

8. James Lardner and Thomas Reppetto, *NYPD: A City and Is Police* (New York: Holt, 2000), p. 189; Jansen to O'Brian, May 1, 1950, subject files, box 17, folder 7; Material for Questioning Seven Teachers, April 24, 1950, box 19, folder 5.

9. Jansen to O'Brian, May 1, 1950, subject files, box 17, folder 7.

10. Dunne to Moskoff, August 28, 1951; Jansen to Monaghan, January 25, 1952; Jansen to Monaghan, April 23, 1952; Letter from Lieutenant Crane to Jansen, March 5, 1952, subject files, box 17, folder 7.

11. Monaghan to Jansen, May 6, 1952, subject files box 17, folder 7.

12. Dunne to Moskoff, July 7, 1952, box 17, folder 7.

13. Moskoff to Managhan, November 17, 1953, subject files, box 17, folder 7.

14. Moskoff to Adams, February 2, 1955, subject files, box 17, folder 7; Memo from Commanding Officer, BOSSI to Chief of Detectives, December 20, 1957, subject files, box 1, folder 13.

15. Moskoff to Loures, December 24, 1953, subject files, box 17, folder 7.

16. Ibid.; Moskoff to Jansen, October 7, 1957, box 17, folder 7.

17. Report, Operator 51, November 2, 1945; Memo, Report of Operator 51 # 164, March 31, 1953; Memo, April 11, 1953, box 1, folder 13.

18. Schneiderman, Sylvia, Summary of Information from Confidential Source "C," box 6, folder 2.

19. Moskoff to Managhan, November 17, 1953, box 17, folder 7. Memo from Saul Moskoff to Jansen, Re: Detective Mildred V. Blauvelt, October 7, 1957, subject files, box 1, folder 13.

20. Anoyomous memorandum to Moskoff, November 12, 1954, subject files, box 17, folder 7.

21. Memorandum, Jansen to Moskoff, April 4, 1955, subject files, box 17, folder 7.

22. List of 284 teachers, Moskoff to Crane, May 24, 1956, subject files, box 17, folder 7.

23. Moskoff to Timone, September 15, 1953, subject files, box 19, folder 3.

24. Moskoff to Levenson, May 1, 1956, subject files, box 17, folder 7.

25. Moskoff to McGarvey, December 24, 1952, Moskoff to McGarvey, April 5, 1954, subject files, box 18, folder 8.

26. Moskoff to Updike, January 28, 1955; Moskoff to McGarvey, February 2, 1955, McGarvey to Moskoff, February 4, 1955, subject files, box 18, folder 8.

27. Moskoff to Richard, July 16, 1955, subject files, box 18, folder 8.

28. Moskoff to Jansen, March 16, 1956, subject files, box 17, folder 4.

29. Jansen to Russell, March 10, 1950, subject files, box 19, folder 5; Report, Benjamin Mandel, Research Director, House Committee on Un-American Activities, subject files, box 20, folder 13; Benjamin Mandel, subject files, box 20, folder 2.

30. Blauvelt to Appel, Many 12, 1959; Moskoff to Jansen, March 16, 1956, subject files, box 17, folder 4.

31. Shaughnessy to Moskoff, February 10, 1954, subject files, box 4, folder 10.

32. Jansen to Moskoff, January 30, 1953.

33. Ibid.

34. Benjamin Mandel, box 20, folder 2.

35. Confidental memo, S. C. Lucey to Jansen, April 1950, Subject: Interview with Louis Bundenz, box 12, folder 12b.

36. list of informers, property of author; "Lucille Spence," December 5, 1951, subject files, box 13, folder 4, subject files, box 12, folder 8a, 1953.

37. Lucey to Gilman, April 17, 1950, subject files, box 23, folder 6; Lucy to Gilman, June 20, 1950; unsigned letter to Gilman, June 27, 1951; Castaldi to Gilman, subject files, box 32, folder 6.

38. "Dear Sir," Letter, March 1, 1951, subject files, box 23, folder 5.

39. Conference with Henry Appel and Harvey S. Hirsch of New Utrecht High School, September 23, 1952, subject files, box 1, folder 7.

40. Memorandum to Moskoff and Dunn (n.d), box 1, folder 7.

41. Summary of Evidence Secured Against Individuals Now in the Educational System," box 20, folder 1.

42. Ibid; Anonymous Letters to Jansen, subject files, box 20, folder 1. McGraff to Moskoff, February 20, 1952, box 11, folder 1; anonymous letter, November 17, 1959, box 11, folder 12.

43. Ibid.

44. Bella Dodd, *School of Darkness* (New York: Kennedy, 1954). The book is online at http://ca.geocities.com/yarmulkageo/dodd~0.1.html (accessed November 30, 2004); Robert W. Iversen, *The Communists and the Schools: How the Communists Tried to Infiltrate the Schools and How the Schools Fought Back* (New York: Harcourt, Brace, 1959), p. 314.

45. Dodd, *School of Darkness,* chapter 3.

46. Ibid, chapters 3 and 4; Testimony of Bella Dodd before the Subcommittee to Investigate the Administration of the Internal Security Act and Other Internal Security Laws, United States Senate Committee on the Judiciary.

47. Dodd, *School of Darkness,* chapter 6.

48. Ibid.; chapter 7; Testimony of Bella Dodd before the Subcommittee to Investigate the Administration of the Internal Security Act and Other Intrnal Security Laws, United States Senate Committee on the Judiciary.

49. Dodd, *School of Darkness,* chapter 8.

50. Ibid., chapters 8–11; Testimony of Bella Dodd before the Subcommittee to Investigate the Administration of the Internal Security Act and Other Internal Security Laws, United States Senate Committee on the Judiciary.

51. Ibid., chapters 11–12.

52. Ibid, chapter, 13; Jacques Duclos, "On the Dissolution of the Communist Party of the United States," in William Z. Foster et al., *Marxism-Leninism vs. Revisionism* (New York: New Century, 1946), pp. 21–35.

53. Ibid, chapters 13–14; author's interview with Annette Rubinstein, March 20, 2005, New York City.

54. Ibid, chapter 15.

55. Ibid, chapter 16.

56. Testimony of Bella Dodd before the Sub-Committee to Investigate the Administration of the Internal Security Act and Other Internal Security Laws.

57 Ibid.

58. Author's Interview with Dorothy Bloch, May 8, 2001; obituary for Dorothy Bloch, *New York Times,* January 15, 2005.

59. Memo to Scannel, Dorothy Funn, February 3, 1949, Board of Education subject files, box 14, folder 6; Clarence Taylor, *Knocking at Our Own Door: Milton A. Galamison and the Struggle to Integrate New York City Schools* (New York: Columbia University Press, 1997), pp. 61–62.

60. Memo to Scannel, Dorothy Funn, September 7, 1950, subject files, box 14, folder 6.

61. Ibid.

62. Ibid.

63. Dorothy Funn's Testimony Before the Committee on Un-American Activities House of Representatives, Eighty-Third Congress, First Session, May 4, 1953.

64. Funn to Jansen, May 23, 1949, box 14, folder 6.

65. Funn to Jansen, June 3, 1949, subject files, box 14, folder 6.

66. Funn to Jansen, January 11, 1950, subject files, box 14, folder 6

67. Confidential memorandum, Lucey to Jansen, May 31, 1950; Jansen to Funn, May 31, 1950, subject files, box 14, folder 6.

68. Memorandum, Scannel to Cataldi, re: Dorothy Kelso Funn, September 7, 1950; memo to Scannel, Dorothy Funn Subject files, box 14, folder 6.

69. Memorandum of Minutes of Interview with Mrs. Dorothy Funn, August 24, 1950, subject files, box 14, folder 6.

70. Funn to Jansen, January 4, 1950.

71. Jansen's Statement Re: Dorothy Funn, June 20, 1950, subject files, box 14, folder 6.

72. Dorothy Funn's Testimony before the Committee on Un-American Activities House of Representatives, Eighty-Third Congress, First Session, May 4, 1953.

73. Funn's Testimony before the Committee on Un-American Activities House of Representatives, May 5, 1953.

74. Author's interview with Mildred Flacks, May 23, 1987, Santa Barbara; author's interview with Annette Rubinstein, March 20, 2005; author's interview with Dorothy Bloch, May 8, 2001; Funn's Testimony before the Committee on Un-American Activities House of Representatives, May 5, 1953.

75. Memorandum, Moskoff to Jansen, October 20, 1953, subject files, box 14, folder 6.

76. Ibid.

10. CRUSADING FOR CIVIL RIGHTS

1. Phyllis Murray, "Black History Is Part of American History," a letter to the editor, *New York Teacher News,* February 1, 2007, p. 9.

2. John Badger, "Different Perspectives on the Civil Rights Movement," in *History Now.*

3. Russell to Hamilton, July 1, 1963, box 45.

4. W. E. B. Du Bois, *Black Reconstruction in America, 1860–1880* (New York: Touchstone, 1995), pp. 711–24; Carter G. Woodson, *The Mis-Education of the Negro* (Chicago: African-American Images, 2000), pp. 21–22; Celia Lewis Zitron, *The New York City Teachers Union, 1916–1964* (New York: Humanities, 1968), p. 101.

5. Jonathan Zimmerman, "Browning the American Textbook: History, Psychology, and the Origins of Modern Multculturalism in History," *Education Quarterly* 44, no. 1 (Spring 2004).

6. TU Pamphlet, *The Children's Textbooks,* April 15, 1948.

7. Teachers' Union, *Bias and Prejudice in Textbooks in Use in New York City Schools, An Indictment, 1950.*

8. Ibid.

9. Ibid.

10. Ibid.

11. Ibid.

12. Ibid.

13. Ibid.; Robert Michael Harris, "Teachers and Blacks: The New York City Teachers Union and the Negro, 1916–1964," M.A. thesis, Brooklyn College, 1971, pp. 108–9; Advertisement of "Bias and Prejudice," (n.d.), box 2, folder 5.

14. Lederman to Jansen, April 19, 1950, box 44, folder 3.

15. Lederman to Clauson, August 3, 1950, box 44, folder 3; Open Statement to Board of Education, October 10, 1950, box 2, folder 5.

16. TU, "Guide for Research in Bias in Books," January 17, 1951, box 44, folder 3.

17. Diane Ravitch, *The Great School Wars: New York City, 1805–1973* (New York: Basic Books, 1974), p. 252.

18. Jackson to Jansen, January 30, 1950, box 2, folder 5.

19. Pezzati to Board of Education, April 5, 1951, box 2, folder 5; Straus to Jansen, April 19, 1951, box 2, folder 5.

20. Press release, April 3, 1951.

21. TU, "A Biased Textbook," May 8, 1951, box 44, folder 3.

22. Lederman to Sir, June 1, 1951, box 2, folder 5.

23. Harris, "Teachers and Blacks," p. 109.

24. Lederman to Dear Sirs and Brothers, January 16, 1952, box 2, folder 4.

25. Lederman to Jansen, January 17, 1952, box 2, folder 4.

26. Gordon to Dear Sir, January 30, 1952; Teich to Jansen, February 6, 1952; Geis to Hawley, February 13, 1953, box 2, folder 6.

27. Huggard to Teich, February 20, 1952, box 2, folder 6.

28. Teich to Huggard, February 29, 1952, box 2, folder 6.

29. Woodson, *The Mis-Education of the Negro,* p. 192; Sean Gonsalves, "Why Black History Month?" *ZNet,* February 17, 2002.

30. Virginia L. Snitow, "I Teach Negro Girls," *New Republic,* November 10, 1942, pp. 603–5.

31. Zitron, *The New York City Teachers Union,* p. 94.

32. Harlem Committee, *Reconstruction,* January 12, 1951, box 44, folder 8.

33. Ibid.

34. Ibid.

35. Harlem Committee, *The Negro in the American Revolution,* May 1951, box 44, folder 8; Harlem Committee, *Negro Slavery in the United States, 1800–1865: A Study for Teachers,* box 44, folder 11.

36. Reprint of Negro History Week supplement in *New York Teacher News,* January 16, 1954 (first published in 1951); box 44, folder 18.

37. Reprint of Negro History Week, January 25, 1957, box 44, folder 18.

38. Ibid.

39. Kuch to Teachers Union, December 23, 1957, box 44, folder 17; anonymous note (n.d); McDonald to Lederman, February 19, 1963; Sterling to Lederman, February 11, 1963; Lederman to Frasier, January 21, 1963, box 44, folder 20.

40. Committee Against Discrimination, Survey, (n.d), box 45, folder 4; Lederman to Friend, October 24, 1949, box 45, folder 4.

41. "The Teachers Union Charges That There Is Discrimination Against Negro Teachers in the New York City Schools," box 45, folder 5.

42. Ibid.

43. Ibid.

44. TU press release, October 8, 1951, box 45, folder 4.

45. Ibid.

46. Ibid.

47. Ibid.

48. Resolution on the Employment of Negro Teachers in the Schools of New York City, January 16, 1951, box 45, folder 5.

49. Viall to Lederman, February 13, 1952; Lederman to Dear Friend, March 18, 1952, box 45, folder 4.

50. Greenberg Letter, February 25, 1952, box 45, folder 4.

51. Lederman to Hagerty, April 22, 1952, box 45, folder 4.

52. Kessleman to Wright, March 12, 1953, box 45, folder 4.

53. TU Press Release, March 31, 1954, box 45, folder 4.

54. Lederman to Jansen, October 19, 1953, box 45, folder 4.

55. "A Survey on the Employment of Negro Teachers in New York City Conducted by the Teachers Union, 1955," box 55, folder 6.

56. "Program to Increase Number of Negro Teachers Employed in New York City Schools in Order to Correct the Situation Revealed by Survey Conducted by Teachers Union," June 14, 1955, box 5, folder 5.

57. Ibid.

58. American Civil Liberties Union Weekly Bulletin no. 1882, December 24, 1956, box 45, folder 6; Lederman to Silver, September 14, 1955; Lederman to the Oklahoma Association of Negro Teachers, September 14, 1955, box 45, folder 5.

59. Teachers Union's Program for Integration of Schools, box 45, folder 6; Clarence Taylor, *Knocking at Our Own Door: Milton A. Galamison and the Struggle to Integrate New York City Schools* (New York: Columbia University Press, 1997), p. 62.

60. Ibid.

61. TU press release, May 24, 1954, box 44, folder 11.

62. *New York Teacher News,* May 29, 1954.

63. *New York Times,* April 25, 1954; Taylor, *Knocking at Our Own Door,* pp. 53–54.

64. Lederman to Jansen, June 11, 1954, box 45, folder 10; Taylor, *Knocking at Our Own Door,* p. 57.

65. Lederman to Jansen, June 11, 1954, box 45, folder 10.

66. Ibid.

67. Ibid.

68. Lederman to the *Amsterdam News,* June 14, 1954, box 45, folder 10.

69. Ibid.; Taylor, *Knocking at Our Own Door,* p. 92.

70. Lauri Johnson, "'Making Democracy Real, Teach': Teacher Union and Community Activism to Promote Diversity in the New York City Public Schools, 1935–1950," *Urban Education* 37, no. 5 (November 2002): 584.

11. WOMEN AND THE TEACHERS UNION

1. Ruth Jacknow Markowitz, *My Daughter the Teacher: Jewish Teachers in the New York City Schools* (New Brunswick, NJ: Rutgers University Press, 1930), pp. 151–17; Lauri Johnson, "A Generation of Women Activists: African American Female Educators in Harlem, 1930–1950," *Journal of African American History* 89, no. 3 (2004); Lauri Johnson, "'Making Democracy Real, Teach': Teacher Union and Community Activism to Promote Diversity in the New York City Public Schools, 1935–1950," *Urban Education* 37, no. 5 (November 2002): 566–87; Marjorie Murphy, *Blackboard Unions: The AFT and the NEA, 1900–1980* (Ithaca: Cornell University Press, 1990), pp. 157, 187.

2. Minutes of the executive board meetings, February 15, March 8, 1930, box 49, folder 6.

3. Bella Dodd, *School of Darkness* (New York: Kennedy, 1954), chapters 11 and 12.

4. Minutes of executive board meeting, October 29, 1938, January 27, 1939, box 50, folder 1.

5. Minutes of executive board meeting, February 25, 1939, box 50, folder 1.

6. Dodd, *School of Darkness,* chapter 9.

7. *New York Times,* April 27, 1937.

8. *New York Times,* February 20, 1938.

9. Ibid., January 18, 1939, box 50, folder 1.

10. Ibid., June 8, 1939, box 50, folder 1.

11. Minutes of the Executive Board, October 19, folder 1.

12. Minutes of the executive board meeting, March 11, 1939, box 50, folder 1.

13. Minutes of the executive board meeting, May 2, 1939, September 11, 1939, box 50, folder 1.

14. The Esquirol bill prohibited public utilities from refusing employment to anyone based on race, color, or creed. The second, the Garcia-Rivera bill, outlawed denying anyone relief based on race, color, or creed. The third, the Holly bill, would void state contracts with companies found guilty of practicing racial discrimination. The Goldberg bill outlawed discrimination in renting or leasing of residences. The bills were defeated in the Assembly Judiciary Committee. *New York Times,* March 15, 1939.

15. Richard J. Altenbaugh, ed., *The Teacher's Voice: A Social History of Teaching in Twentieth Century America* (New York: Routledge, 1992), pp. 50–54.

16. Ibid., pp. 56–57.

17. Patricia A. Carter, *"Everybody's Paid But the Teachers": The Teaching Profession and the Women's Movement* (New York: Teachers College Press, 2004), pp. 116–24.

18. Ibid. Minutes of the executive board meeting, January 22, 1938, box 50, folder 1.

19. Minutes of executive board meeting, June 17, 1939, box 50, folder 1.

20. Dodd, *School of Darkness,* chapter 10.

21. *New York Times,* January 4, 1965; *National Guardian,* January 9, 1965; program, tribute to Rose Russell for twenty years of inspired leadership, January 4, 1964, property of Ann Filardo.

22. *New York Teacher News,* October 6, 1945, November 3, 1945, January 26, 1946.

23. Ibid., March 20, 1948.

24. Dodd, *School of Darkness*, chapter 12.

25. *New York Teacher News,* October 16, 1948.

26. Mike Wallace interview with Rose Russell on *Night Beat,* May 15, 1950, transcript.

27. Ibid.

28. James Eget Allen to Ella Ratner, May 14, 1947, box 10, folder 5.

29. Stanley M. Issacs to Gentlemen, May 13, 1947, box 10, folder 5.

30. Louis Hollander and Harold J. Garno to Ella Ratner, May 19, 1947, box 10, folder 5.

31. *National Guardian,* January 9, 1965; minutes of the executive board meeting, January 4, 1930, April 18, 1931, September 16, 1932, box 49, folder 8.

32. Minutes of the executive board meeting, April 18, 1931, minutes of the executive board meeting, May 15, 1931, box 49, folder 8; minutes of the executive board meeting, September 16, 1932, box 49, folder 9.

33. Minutes of the executive board meeting, September 16, 1932, box 49, folder 9.

34. Minutes of the executive board meeting, June 4, 1937, box 50, folder 1.

35. Mabel Hawkins served as vice president and Bella Dodd was the legislative representative; Dale Zysman to James Marshall, September 17, 1941, Hendley Papers, Tamiment Library, NYU.

36. Minutes of the executive board meeting, January 8, 1937, December 12, 1937, September 11, 1939, box 50, folder 1; Rebecca Simonson served as president of the guild from 1940 to 1953, obituary of Rebecca Simonson, *New York Times*, June 30, 1982; New York Teachers' Union Membership List, Rapp-Coudert Files, State Library of New York, Albany, New York.

37. Todd J. Pfannestiel, *Rethinking the Red Scare: The Lusk Committee and New York's Crusade against Radicalism, 1919–1923* (New York: Routledge, 2003), pp. 100–5.

38. Minutes of the executive board meeting, May 15, 1931, box 49, folder 8.

39. Celia Lewis Zitron, *The New York City Teachers Union, 1916–1964* (New York: Humanities, 1968), p. 10.

40. Minutes of the executive board meeting, November 3, 1934, box 49, folder 13.

41. Zitron, *The New York City Teachers Union*, pp. 178–80.

42. Ibid.

43. Report of committee on resolutions to be presented to the convention of the American Federation of Teachers, August, 1938, box 25, folder 8.

44. *New York Times*, December 1, 1938.

45. New York Times, December 1, 1938; Minutes of the executive board meeting, June 17, 1939, box 50, folder 1.

46. Minutes of the executive board meeting, November 2, 1939, box 50, folder 1.

47. Minutes of the Rank and File meeting, December 7, 1934, box 74, folder 2; Harry M. Brackman, *Freedom of Speech: Words Are Not Deeds* (Westport, CT: Greenwood, 1994), p. 29; Zitron, *The New York City Teachers Union*, p. 188.

48. Martin E. Marty, *Modern American Religion*, vol. 2: *The Noise of Conflict* (Chicago: University of Chicago Press, 1997), p. 261.

49. Zitron, *The New York City Teachers Union*, p. 181.

50. Memorandum, to director, FBI from SAC, New York (100–115502), Subject: Lucille Spence, December 23, 1953, property of Alan Snitow.

51. Patrick F. Finn, "Teacher Education with an Attitude: Completing the Revolution," in Patrick Finn and Mary E. Finn, eds., *Teacher Education with an Attitude: Preparing Teachers to Educate Working-Class Students in Their Collective Self Interest* (Albany: State University Press of New York, 2007), p. 222.

52. Minutes of the executive board meeting, December 18, 1937, box 50, folder 11.

53. Harris, "Teachers and Blacks," pp.51–52.

54. Minutes of the executive board, June 4, 1937, box 50, folder 1.

55. Janet L. Abu-Lughod, *Race, Space, and Riots in Chicago, New York, and Los Angles* (New York: Oxford University Press, 2007), p. 156; Lauri Johnson, "A Generation of Women Activists: Female Educators in Harlem, 1930–1950, *Journal of African American History* 89 (2004): 226–27.

56. "Step-Children of New York," *New York Teacher* 2, no 1, (February 1937): 9–10; Mark Naison, *Communists in Harlem During the Depression* (Urbana: University of Illinois Press, 1983), p. 215.

57. Ibid.

58. Ibid.

59. "Crime Outbreak in Harlem Spurs Drive by Police," *New York Times,* November 7, 1941, p. 1.

60. "Tragedy in Harlem," *New York Times,* November 8, 1941, p. 18.

61. "250 More Police in Harlem to Stamp Out Crime Wave," *New York Times,* November 8, 1941, p. 1.

62. Citron, letter to the editor of the *New York Times,* November 12, 1941.

63. Ibid.

64. Mildred Flacks interview, April 14, 1991.

65. Sophie Louise Ullman, interview with Richard Flacks, June 2, 1997; Jonathan Rieder, *Canarsie: The Jews and Italiians of Brooklyn Against Liberalism* (Cambridge: Harvard University Press, 1985), pp. 48–49; Peter Haas, "The Future of Jewish Liberalism," 2004, http://www.vanderbilt.edu/jewishstudies/Hass%20talk.htm; Steven M. Cohen and Charles S. Liebman, "American Jewish Liberalism: Unraveling the Strands," *Public Opinion Quarterly* 61, no. 3 (1997): 405–30.

66. Sophie Louise Ullman interview with Mildred Flacks, April 14, 1991; Board of Education of the City of New York, "In the Matter of Charges Preferred by William Jansen, Superintendent of Schools, Against Mildred Flacks," October 1, 1952, box 52, folder 2; David Flacks, interview with Sophie-Louise Almond, June 2, 1997.

67. Clarence Taylor, *Knocking at Our Own Door: Milton A. Galamison and the Struggle to Integrate New York City Schools* (New York: Columbia University Press, 1997), p. 62.

68. "In the Matter of Charges Preferred by William Jansen, Superintendent of Schools, Against Mildred Flacks," October 1, 1952, box 52, folder 2.

69. Ibid.

70. Ibid.

71. Minutes of the executive board meeting, November 19, 1938, box 50, folder 1; Steven Jonas, *An Introduction to the U.S. Health Care System* (New York: Springer, 2003), p. 175.

72. Minutes of the executive board meeting, October 29, 1938, box 50, folder 1.

73. Minutes of the executive board meeting, June 17, 1939, box 50, folder 1.

74. Ibid.

75. Minutes of the executive board meeting, December 18, 1937, box 50, folder 1.

76. *New York Teacher*, December 11, 2008, pp. 3, 5.

77. Belinda Robnett, *How Long? How Long? African-American Women in the Struggle for Civil Rights* (New York: Oxford University Press, 1997), pp. 26–28.

78. Ibid.

12. THE TRIUMPH OF THE UNITED FEDERATION OF TEACHERS

1. David Selden, *The Teacher Rebellion* (Washington, DC: Howard University Press, 1985), pp. 20–21.

2. Ibid., pp. 32–33.

3. Ibid.

4. *New York Times*, February 23, 1960; Selden, *The Teacher Rebellion,* pp. 34–39.

5. *New York Times*, March 16, 1960.

6. Jack Schierenbeck, "Class Struggles: The UFT's Story," part 5, February 16, 1996, http://www.uft.org/about/history/uft_story5print.html.

7. *New York Times*, March 26, 1960.

8. Selden, *The Teacher Rebellion*, pp. 19–20.

9. *New York Times*, April 11, 1960.

10. *New York Times*, April 12, 1960.

11. *New York Times*, April 14, 15, 1960.

12. *New York Times*, April 16, 1960.

13. *New York Times*, April 28, 1960,

14. *New York Times*, April 29, 1960.

15. Charles Cogan and Samuel Hochberg, letter to the editor, *New York Times*, May 6, 1960.

16. *New York Times*, May 8, 10, 1960; Richard D. Kahlenberg, *Tough Liberal: Albert Shanker and the Battles Over Schools, Unions, Race, and Democracy* (New York: Columbia University Press, 2007), p. 47.

17. Author's interview with Paul Becker, New York, January 28, 2008; New York Times, May 10, 1960.

18. *New York Times*, May 11, 1960.

19. *New York Times*, May 15, 1960.

20. *New York Times*, May 16, 1960.

21. *New York Times*, May 17, 1960.

22. Selden, *The Teacher Rebellion*, pp. 43–44; *New York Times*, May 17, 1960.

23. *New York Times*, October 3, 6, 1960.

24. *New York Times*, October 18, 1960; Selden, *The Teacher Rebellion*, pp. 46–47.

25. *New York Times*, October 20, 1960.

26. Taft, *United They Teach*, p. 108; *New York Times*, October 21, 1960.

27. *New York Times*, October 22, 1960.

28. *New York Times*, October 25, 1960.

29. *New York Times*, October 25, 1960.

30. *New York Times*, October 26, 27, 1960.

31. *New York Times*, October 27, 1960.

32. *New York Times*, October 30, 1960.

33. *New York Times*, October 31, 1960.

34. *New York Times*, November 1, 1960.

35. *New York Times*, November 2, 1960.

36. *New York Times*, November 3, 1960.

37. *New York Times*, November 4, 1960.

38. *New York Times*, November 5, 1960.

39. *New York Times*, November 8, 1960.

40. Ibid.

41. *New York Times*, November 9, 1960; Selden, *The Teacher Rebellion*, p. 48, Schierenbeck, "Class Struggle: The UFT Story," part 6, www.uft.org/abouthistory/uft_story6/.

42. *New York Times*, November 10, 1960.

43. *New York Times*, November 13, 1960. For Wagner's Mediation Committee see the *New York Times*, November 10, 1960, and Taft, *United We Teach*, pp. 109–10.

44. Minutes of TU membership meeting, December 9, 1960, box 70, folder 7.

45. Taft, *United We Teach*, pp. 110–11.

46. Ibid., pp. 113–15.

47. Minutes of the TU membership meetings, December 8, 1961, box 70, folder 7.

48. Minutes of the TU membership meeting, September 15, 1961, October 20, 1961, box 70, folder 7.

49. Author's interview with Paul Becker, January 28, 2008.

50. *New York Times*, December 17, 1961.

CONCLUSION

1. Author's interview with Zephariah Bauman, New York, May 2, 2001; author's interview with Paul Becker, New York, January 8, 2008; author's interview with David Weiner, New York, April 25, 2001; meeting of joint membership and executive board meeting, June 8, 1962, box 70, folder 7.

2. Minutes of a special executive board meeting, September 16, 1963, box 50, folder 2.

3. Minutes of the executive board meeting, September 26, 1963, box 50, folder 2; minutes of the special executive board meeting, October 3, 1963, box 50, folder 2.

4. Minutes of the executive board meeting, October 3, 1963, box 50, folder 2; *New York Times* obituary, October 4, 1963.

5. Resolution approved at the Teachers Union executive board meeting in favor of dissolution, October 3, 1963, box 50, folder 2.

6. Minority statement on dissolution, property of Anne Filardo.

7. *New York Teacher News*, October 12, 1963.

8. Minutes of the executive board meeting, box 70, folder 7.

9. Program, "The Teachers' Union Tribute to Rose Russell for Twenty Years of Inspired Leadership," January 4, 1964, property of Anne Filardo.

10. Ibid.

11. Minutes of the Teachers Union membership meeting, January 17, 1964; box 70, folder 7; *New York Teacher News*, January 18, 1964.

12. Author's interview with Mildred Flacks, Santa Barbara, May 23, 1987

13. *New York Times*, March 26, 2010.

14. Deidre McFadyen, "Coalition Reaches Agreement with City on Planned Reorganization," *New York Teacher*, April 26, 2007, wwwluft.org/news/teacher/top/agreement.

15. Stephen Johnson, "Teachers, NAACP, Community Sue N.Y. Dept. of Education Over School Closing," *Amsterdam News*, February 8, 2010, www.theskanner.com/article/view/id/11352, March 8, 2010; *New York Times*, March 26, 2010.